Human-Computer Interaction Series

Editors-in-Chief
Desney Tan
Microsoft Research, USA

Jean Vanderdonckt
Université catholique de Louvain, Belgium

HCI is a multidisciplinary field focused on human aspects of the development of computer technology. As computer-based technology becomes increasingly pervasive – not just in developed countries, but worldwide – the need to take a human-centered approach in the design and development of this technology becomes ever more important. For roughly 30 years now, researchers and practitioners in computational and behavioral sciences have worked to identify theory and practice that influences the direction of these technologies, and this diverse work makes up the field of human-computer interaction. Broadly speaking it includes the study of what technology might be able to do for people and how people might interact with the technology. The HCI series publishes books that advance the science and technology of developing systems which are both effective and satisfying for people in a wide variety of contexts. Titles focus on theoretical perspectives (such as formal approaches drawn from a variety of behavioral sciences), practical approaches (such as the techniques for effectively integrating user needs in system development), and social issues (such as the determinants of utility, usability and acceptability).

Titles published within the Human-Computer Interaction Series are included in Thomson Reuters' Book Citation Index, The DBLP Computer Science Bibliography and The HCI Bibliography.

More information about this series at http://www.springer.com/series/6033

Tracy Hammond • Stephanie Valentine
Aaron Adler • Mark Payton
Editors

The Impact of Pen and Touch Technology on Education

Editors
Tracy Hammond
Texas A&M University,
  Sketch Recognition Lab, Department
  of Computer Science & Engineering
College Station
Texas
USA

Aaron Adler
Raytheon BBN Technologies
Cambridge
Massachusetts
USA

Stephanie Valentine
Texas A&M University,
  Sketch Recognition Lab, Department
  of Computer Science & Engineering
College Station
Texas
USA

Mark Payton
Dept. Information Technology
Whitfield School
St. Louis
Missouri
USA

ISSN 1571-5035
Human-Computer Interaction Series
ISBN 978-3-319-37232-7   ISBN 978-3-319-15594-4 (eBook)
DOI 10.1007/978-3-319-15594-4

Springer Cham Heidelberg New York Dordrecht London
© Springer International Publishing Switzerland 2015
Softcover reprint of the hardcover 1st edition 2015

Printed on acid-free paper

Springer International Publishing AG Switzerland is part of Springer Science+Business Media
(www.springer.com)

Introduction

We are in perhaps the most exciting and demanding era of education change. These changes include entirely new interfaces for expression and communication; pen and touch computing are among these new interfaces. This monograph features applications and research that are integral to realizing the promising and often extraordinary advances in technology and education. Applications of ink-based computing-such as those from current tablet and surface computing devices-have demonstrated compelling and often transformative advantages over traditional keyboard/mouse interfaces for promoting student learning and effective educational practice. These applications motivate a new landscape for such interfaces to alter the use of technology enabling effective collaboration and learning experiences.

In the four years since the last monograph, the presence of hand-held computing devices in education has significantly increased. Touch interfaces on Android and iPad tablets and phones have enabled them to join Windows-based Tablet PCs in the classroom and research lab. Microsoft is again focusing on digital ink across its product line, including their new Tablet PC hardware, and Windows has added touch as a primary interface method on tablets and other small devices.

The pedagogical benefits of sketching have been shown to be enormous. Students retain information better, students better internalize ideas, and students are better able to discuss their ideas with drawing. Many of the papers that follow reflect and demonstrate these benefits.

Purpose of the Monograph

This edited volume is inspired by the research presented at the Workshop on the Impact of Pen and Touch Technology (WIPTTE) over the last two years, a conference dedicated to providing and evaluating change. WIPTTE provides an excellent opportunity to present and share innovative applications and research. The conference is intended to leverage a shared passion for the potential educational use of pen and touch-based computing, such that educators and researchers alike may benefit from and contribute to new emerging interfaces.

The beauty of WIPTTE is in the multi-contextual diversity of the attendees. As opposed to standard conferences that focus on a single type of clientele, WIPTTE has a wide variety of participants who bring an array of different types of knowledge together. Past attendees hold a wide range of positions with academia and industry; from K-12 teachers and administrators to university deans; from sales directors to systems engineers. The participation list speaks well of the diverse group of individuals impacted by the WIPTTE conference. The papers included in this monograph include reflections from these various perspectives. WIPTTE 2014 had 150 attendees who had flown in from at least 8 different countries, highlighting the international impact the topic has.

This monograph represents selected papers from the 2013 and 2014 WIPTTE conferences which provide solid evaluation data and discuss new and existing applications of digital ink and touch and the proven impact they have on pedagogy across disciplines. At the same time, it reinforces the ongoing research interest in digital ink as a powerful tool for education with a promising future–six authors of a paper in this monograph are high school students themselves.

Combined papers from current and previous monographs have reported on studies involving many thousands of students and many hundreds of educators from Pre-K through higher education at institutions around the world and in a very broad spectrum of academic disciplines.

Monograph Organization

This book is organized into four sections. The first section presents a perspective by one of our *keynote speakers*. The second section presents *emerging technologies* for integrating pen and touch technologies in classrooms and early childhood development. Most of the technologies in this section were invented by the authors, and each paper identifies the success of these technologies in scientific deployments. The third section presents papers regarding *technologies in practice*. Papers in this section offer perspectives of classroom educators regarding the success of pen and touch technology integration in their own classrooms or schools. The final section contains papers that propose *works in progress*—systems that are not complete yet, but that hold great promise for pedagogical effectiveness.

WIPTTE Venue 2013

WIPTTE 2013 included a diverse set of enriching experiences including academic and practicum talks and tutorials, and hands-on workshops. WIPTTE 2013 was held at Pepperdine University in Los Angeles, California. In 2006 and 2007, the Princeton Review ranked Pepperdine first on the "Most Beautiful Campus" list, and highly on the "High Quality of Life" and "Dorms Like Palaces." The Peace Corps of America named Pepperdine University to be "One of the Top Producing Colleges and Universities." US News and World Report Ranked Pepperdine University as the 53rd best national university for undergraduate education. Pepperdine University's Dispute Resolution program in the School of Law is first in the nation. US News and World Report ranked The School of Law 54th across the nation's law schools and the Graziadio School of Business and Management at 82 compared against the nation's business schools. Forbes magazine ranked the Fully Employed MBA within the top 20 when examining return on investment.

WIPTTE Venue 2014

WIPTTE 2014 included a diverse set of enriching experiences including academic and practicum talks and tutorials, campus research tours, grant and networking breakout sessions, hands-on workshops, a high school contest, and social events, including a banquet at the local winery. WIPTTE 2014 took place March 12-15, 2014. WIPTTE 2014 was held in College Station, Texas on the Texas A&M University campus, *Home of the Fightin' Texas Aggies*. The Dwight Look College of Engineering is consistently ranked in the top ten by US News and World Report. Texas A&M boasts the following:

- 1st in Texas in student retention and graduation rates – overall and for minorities
- 1st in nation in "payback ratio"—what graduates earn compared to the cost of their college educations, Smart Money magazine
- 1st in Texas and 8th among public universities in New York Times survey of business leaders worldwide based on the top institutions from which they recruit, 2011
- 1st in Texas and 17th nationally as "best value" among public universities, Kiplinger, 2013
- 4th in nation among universities based on "contribution to the public good," Washington Monthly, 2014
- 2nd in the nation among public universities in "great schools, great prices," U.S. News & World Report, 2012
- 2nd in nation for preparing graduates for the workforce, The Wall Street Journal
- Top 10 in nation for return on investment, or what graduates earn in their careers compared to their college costs, PayScale
- Top 10 in nation among public schools in earnings of alumni with 10–20 years of experience, Forbes
- 2nd in nation in a survey of top U.S. corporations, nonprofits and government agencies, based on graduates recruiters prefer to hire, The Wall Street Journal
- 4th among U.S. public universities and 10th overall with an endowment of more than $5 billion
- 4th nationally among public universities in affordability combined with high quality education and high return on investment, AffordableCollegesOnline.org, 2013

Talks were held at the Mays Business School. The opening reception on Wednesday was held at the Benjamin Knox Gallery, a rebuilt historic College Station train depot that draws inspirations of Texas A&M University and the city's roots when the original location of the depot marked the main entrance to the campus in front of the University's Academic Building. The surprisingly large gallery facility is the National Art Gallery Headquarters of Benjamin Knox, American Artist and Texas Aggie Class of '90. Thursday night's dinner consisted of music by Possessed by Paul James, great food from the Village Cafe, and a poster session and gallery tour at SEAD Gallery. SEAD Gallery offers exhibits juried by Arts Council of the Brazos Valley, while promoting cultural and heritage assets unique to the community. The gallery is housed in the Federal Building in Historic Downtown Bryan, which also houses the Innovation Underground, both community and economic development projects by Advent GX. Over the years, the building, which was built in 1915, served as the community post office and also housed the IRS and FBI. Village Cafe is a restaurant and art stage dedicated to the community. They promote local farms and serve farm fresh eggs, locally roasted coffee beans and local produce. Each month boasts art from a different artist, and different musicians play each week. Possessed by Paul James is a one-man band (Konrad Wert) from south Austin, Texas. The music is composed of string instruments including banjo, guitar, and fiddle with written roots within folk, blues, and punk. The banquet was held at the Messina Hof Winery. Messina Hof Winery & Resort, a Texas vineyard established in 1977 by Paul and Merrill Bonarrigo, is rooted in the union of two family heritages. Winemaker Paul Bonarrigo's family dates back seven generations to Messina, Sicily. Merrill's family is from Hof, Germany. Breakfasts and lunches were provided on site with catering from a different local restaurant each meal. All meals and rides were provided to ensure intense collaboration amongst the participants.

Keynote Speakers 2013

WIPTTE 2013 had three keynote speakers: **Ken Hinkley**, Principal Researcher at Microsoft Research, **Andries van Dam**, Professor of Technology, Education, & Computer Science at Brown University, and **Ken Forbus**, Professor of Electrical Engineering and Computer Science at Northwestern University.

Ken Hinckley is a Principal Researcher at Microsoft Research in Redmond, WA. His research on sensors, mobile devices, pen computing, and pen + touch interaction has been widely covered in the press and tech blogs (MIT Technology Review, The Wall Street Journal, Gizmodo, Engadget, Slashdot, and many others). Ken holds a PhD in computer science from the University of Virginia where he studied spatial interaction with Randy Pausch, now famous as the late author of "The Last Lecture."

Ken's research seeks to augment the capabilities of technologies and user experiences to match human abilities, skills, desires, and expectations. His work has often involved exploration of novel input devices and modalities, unusual sensors and device form-factors, with a dash of panache and a well-lets-just-try-it-and-see-if-it-works sensibility about things. He has a firm belief that you can learn a great deal by observing the natural behaviors of users and an equally firm belief that users can't tell you how to design an outstanding user experience. Sometimes you just have to put together a few insights, build something new that nobody has ever thought of the need to have before, and unleash it on the world to see what happens.

Ken Hinkley's talk discussed "The Fractured Frontier of Reading, Writing, and E-Creation." For students, knowledge workers, and creative professionals alike, the vast tectonic shifts now taking place in the world of publishing, electronic books, device form-factors, and emerging modalities of natural interaction create tremendous opportunity to sunder new realms of innovation from the fabled Pangaea of reading. These fault-lines are visible everywhere, if only one knows where to look. The moment a serious seeker of knowledge cracks open a book—electronic or otherwise—the fissures in the traditional monolithic view of reading begin to propagate. Multiple books and papers and yellow sticky-notes tile the tabletop like a riotous mosaic of stationary. Highlights emblazon the text and notations crowd the margins. These dedicated knowledge-seekers markup articles, tear out pages, and fill notebooks with handwritten insights. And from this teeming jungle of information, they synthesize and create anew. Natural ways of interacting with texts-from simple and expressive multi-touch gestures to markup with electronic pens to sensing the subtle motions of devices and their context of use-together promise, with appropriate design, to transform our experience of reading-and thereby to transform our students and other knowledge-seekers into a newly empowered generation of creative professionals. The keynote flashed a few glimpses of this new world, this e-Creation, and demonstrated some concrete technologies and techniques that illuminate the way forward. It is a many-forked path fraught with design dilemmas and unknowns, but in Ken's view the experience of reading and interacting with electronic information has only yet begun its incredible transformation

Andries van Dam is the Thomas J. Watson Jr., University Professor of Technology and Education and Professor of Computer Science. He has been a member of Brown's faculty since 1965, is a founder of Brown's Computer Science Department, and was its first Chairman from 1979 to 1985. From 2002 to 2006 he was Brown's first Vice President for Research. His research includes work on computer graphics, hypermedia systems, post-WIMP user interfaces (including pen-centric computing), and educational software. Over the last four decades he has worked on systems for creating and reading electronic books with interactive illustrations for use in education and research.

He is the co-author of nearly a dozen books, including "Computer Graphics: Principles and Practice", with James D. Foley, Steven K. Feiner, and John F. Hughes (Addison-Wesley 1990). He received a B.S. degree (with Honors) in Engineering Sciences from Swarthmore College in 1960 and a Ph.D. in Electrical Engineering from the University of Pennsylvania in 1966. He is a Fellow of ACM, IEEE, the American Association for the Advancement of Science, and the American Academy of Arts & Sciences, and is a member of National Academy of Engineering. His awards include the ACM Steven A. Coons Award for Outstanding Creative Contributions to

Computer Graphics and the IEEE James H. Mulligan, Jr. Education Medal. He holds honorary doctorates from Swarthmore College and and Darmstadt Technical University.

Andy Van Dam's talk discussed "Pen and Touch Computing: From Research to Resource." The keynote furnished multiple demonstrations of scholarship-support research from the Pen and Touch Computing (PTC) Laboratory at Brown University. Effective digital scholarship tools can sharpen researchers' focus, augment their capabilities, extend their reach, and multiply their impact. Two such tools from Brown University are Touch Art Gallery (TAG) and the WorkTop hypermedia framework. TAG is a walk-up application for museum visitors and curators. In kiosk mode, visitors can explore arbitrarily large 2D artworks, e.g., smoothly zoom in from an overview of the famous Garibaldi Panorama, which is the length of a football field, down to the detail of individual brushstrokes, or see a guided tour in the style of Ken Burns documentaries with its visual vocabulary of slow pan-zoom, auxiliary materials, and soundtrack for narration. Authoring mode enables curators to create exhibits and tours without need for programming aid. WorkTop is an IDE (Integrated Development Environment) for scholars that provides an unbounded 2D workspace and the ability to annotate and to link and between different types of media in a consistent fashion. Research tools can, of course, extend to a wider audience. One such example is FluidMath, a commercial package for tablet computers to be used in high school or low-level college math courses that evolved from their earlier pen-computing research project, MathPad, started more than a decade ago. TAG represents another such transfer from interactive, gesture-based museum and library support research, while the WorkTop framework contains both research-support tools and publication-support tools. All these projects are pen- and touch-centric and to varying degrees use both handwriting and gesture recognition as integral parts of the user experience.

Ken Forbus is the Walter P. Murphy Professor of Electrical Engineering and Computer Science at Northwestern University, where he carries out research on qualitative reasoning; spatial reasoning, analogical reasoning and learning, and learning from natural language. In his keynote comments he addressed the CogSketch tools developed in research on spatial learning in K-12 science, technology, engineering and mathematics (STEM) education fields.

Ken Forbus' talk discussed "CogSketch: Using human-like sketch understanding to help students learn." Sketching is a powerful way for people to think through ideas and to communicate with others. Sketch-based educational software offers tremendous potential for improving spatial learning. This talk described work on CogSketch, which uses models of human visual, spatial, and analogical reasoning to provide a new platform for sketch-based educational software. Two kinds of educational software built on CogSketch were described. Sketch Worksheets help students learn concepts expressed spatially, such as geological faults and how the circulatory system works. The Design Coach helps engineering students become more comfortable with using sketching to communicate design ideas. CogSketch is publicly available, and efforts underway to make it customizable by teachers were discussed.

Keynote Speakers—2014

WIPTTE 2014 had three keynote speakers: Barbara Tversky, Professor of Psychology and Education, at Columbia University; Randall Davis Professor of Computer Science and Engineering, Massachusetts Institute of Technology; and Olya Veselova, Program Manager, OneNote, Microsoft.

Barbara Tversky is a Professor Emerita of Psychology at Stanford University and a Professor of Psychology and Education at Teachers College, Columbia University. Tversky specializes in cognitive psychology, and is a leading authority in the areas of visual-spatial reasoning and collaborative cognition. Tversky's additional research interests include language and communication, comprehension of events and narratives, and the mapping and modeling of cognitive processes. Tversky received a B.A. in Psychology from the University of Michigan in 1963 and a Ph.D. in Psychology from the University of Michigan in 1969. She has served on the faculty of Stanford University since 1977 and of Teachers College, Columbia University since 2005. Tversky has led an esteemed career as a research psychologist. She has published in leading academic journals prolifically for almost four decades. Many of her studies are among the most significant in both cognitive psychology and experimental psychology generally. Tversky was named a Fellow of the American Psychological Society in 1995, the Cognitive Science Society in 2002, and the Society of Experimental Psychology in 2004. In 1999, she received the Phi Beta Kappa Excellence in Teaching Award. Tversky is an active and well-regarded teacher of psychology courses at both the introductory and advanced level. In addition, Tversky has served on the editorial boards of multiple prominent academic journals, including Psychological Research (1976–1984), the Journal of Experimental Psychology: Learning, Memory and Cognition (1976–1982), the Journal of Experimental Psychology: General (1982–1988), Memory and Cognition (1989–2001), and Cognitive Psychology (1995–2002).

Barbara Tversky's talk was entitled: "Thinking with Hands". The content of thought can be regarded as internalized and intermixed perceptions of the world and the actions of thought as internalized and intermixed actions on the world. Reexternalizing the content of thought onto something perceptible and reexternalizing the actions of thinking as actions of the body can facilitate thinking. New technologies can do both. They can allow creation and revision of external representations and they can allow interaction with the hands and the body. This analysis is supported by several empirical studies. One shows that students learn more from creating visual explanations of STEM phenomena than from creating verbal ones. Another shows that conceptually congruent actions on an iPad promote arithmetic performance. A third shows that when reading spatial descriptions, students use their hands to create mental models.

In 1978, *Randall Davis* joined the faculty of the Electrical Engineering and Computer Science Department at MIT, where from 1979–1981 he held an Esther and Harold Edgerton Endowed Chair. He later served for 5 years as Associate Director of the Artificial Intelligence Laboratory. He is currently a Full Professor in the Department, and a Research Director of CSAIL, the Computer Science and Artificial Intelligence Laboratory that resulted from the merger of the AI Lab and the Lab for Computer Science. He and his research group are developing advanced tools that permit natural, sketch-based interaction with software, particularly for computer-aided design and design rationale capture. Dr. Davis has been one of the seminal contributors to the field of knowledge-based systems, publishing some 50 articles and playing a central role in the development of several systems. He serves on several editorial boards, including Artificial Intelligence, AI in Engineering, and the MIT series in AI, and was selected in 1984 as one of America's top 100 scientists under the age of 40 by Science Digest. In 1986, he received the AI Award from the Boston Computer Society for his contributions to the field. In 1990, he was named a Founding Fellow of the American Association for AI and in 1995 was elected to a two-year term as President of the Association. In 2003, he received MIT's Frank E. Perkins Award for graduate advising. From 1995-1998, he served on the Scientific Advisory Board of the U.S. Air Force.

Randall Davis' talk was about "Pen-Based Interaction in the Classroom and The Clinic." His talk described three projects centered around pen-based interaction. PhysInk is a system that makes it easy to demonstrate 2D behavior by sketching and directly manipulating objects on a physics-enabled stage. Unlike previous tools that simply capture the user's animation, PhysInk captures an understanding of the behavior in a timeline. This enables useful capabilities such as causality-aware editing and finding physically-correct equivalent behavior. PhysInk is envisioned as a physics teacher's sketchpad or a WYSIWYG tool for game designers. We have all had the experience of drawing data structures on a blackboard to illustrate the steps of an algorithm. The process is tedious and error-prone, and even when done right the result is still a collection of seashell-dust on slate. Seeking something better, they have begun developing CodeInk, a system that provides a direct manipulation language for explaining algorithms and an algorithm animation tool embodying that language. CodeInk allows instructors and/or students to describe algorithm behavior by directly manipulating objects on the drawing surface. Objects on the surface behave appropriately, i.e., as data structures, rather than simply as drawings. Finally, ClockSketch is the first member of a family of applications that may revolutionize neuropsychological testing by capturing both the test result and the behavior that produced it. By capturing data with unprecedented spatial and temporal resolution, they have discovered very subtle behaviors that offer clinically interesting clues to mental status. This offers the possibility of detecting diseases like Alzheimer's and other forms of dementia far earlier than currently possible.

Olya Veselova is a Senior Lead Program Manager on OneNote—Microsoft's primary note-taking and inking application delivered as part of the Microsoft Office suite. Olya has worked on note-taking, inking, sketching, and the tablet experience for over twelve years. She started out at the MIT AI Lab working with Randall Davis on sketch understanding and shape recognition, where she developed a system for perceptually based learning of shape descriptions. She carried her passion for tablets and ink into her work in the industry, when she joined the OneNote team and Microsoft. She has worked on OneNote for the past ten years, developing the design and experience for a large number of OneNote features, including touch and ink and optimizing OneNote for tablets. Olya is a passionate advocate for the potential of digital ink and natural expression in education, work, and personal life, and is continually promoting ink related investments in OneNote and other Microsoft initiatives.

Olya Veselova's talk discussed "Perspectives on Microsoft OneNote and Education." The talk covered interesting aspects of OneNote history, and particularly the highlights and challenges of productizing ink and tablet experiences in Microsoft applications with the goal of broad reach. It also covered the exciting uses of tablets and ink seen in education and beyond, and a perspective on the future potential of digital ink and corresponding developments at Microsoft.

High School Contest 2014

The High School Contest was inspired as part of the yearly high school contest organized by the Sketch Recognition Lab and the Department of Computer Science & Engineering at Texas A&M University. Eighteen high school and middle school students combined into four teams from three different schools: the North Houston Academy of Science and Mathematics, Young Women's College Preparatory Academy, and North Crawley High School. The students first watched and commented on Dr. Tversky's keynote. They were motivated through a presentation delivered by the contest organizer, Stephanie Valentine. Their goal: "Choose a topic commonly taught in elementary, middle, or high schools and design a 'gamified' tablet application. You should design your application such that it adequately teaches your chosen topic, makes explicit use of tablet touch & gesture functionality, and strategically attracts users for long-term use (over many months)." Their task was then to create a 7-minute presentation to pitch their game. The four ideas constructed were incredibly creative and unique. A regular attendee of the TAMU CSE high school contest remarked: "This is my favorite computer science contest I do with my students. I believe it does more to show students what computer science truly is than all the programming competitions do. I would like to bring more teams so I can expose more students to the terrific opportunity."

Festschrift 2014

Many of the presenters over the years have been students of Randall Davis. Dr. Davis has advised and inspired many students to change the world of pen and touch computing. Four of them (Kimberle Koile, Tracy Hammond, Aaron Adler, and Olya Veselova) presented at the 2014 Festschrift, describing the research he advised as well as his overarching impact.

Fig. 1 The students of Dr. Randall Davis: From left to right: Olya Veslova, Dr. Aaron Adler, Dr. Randall Davis, Dr. Kimberle Koile, and Dr. Tracy Hammond

Feedback

Participants from both WIPTTE 2013 and WIPTTE 2014 emphasized the value of the talks as well as the community.

Comments from 2013: "I enjoyed being surrounded by so many Tablet PC users! The keynotes were great!" "I loved the diversity in viewpoints, whether it is from a teacher in the field, researcher, or sponsor/vendor because of the varying selling points of what they do/know." "The conference provided new views on technology resources and a network of new contacts." "I thoroughly enjoyed the conference. The size of the groups, as well as the dinner and accommodations (being near the conference location and the number of people there), etc. were conducive to increasing interaction, networking, and exchange of ideas." "I really enjoyed the networking especially with people working in different strands. I have learned a lot and have much to learn." "Great conference overall. As a K-12 educator, I deliberately sought out the university research presence and arguably learned about more tools than I would have from a K-12 format only. I have a much clearer idea now about the Windows pen/touch environment as well as what some researchers are thinking about." "Great concentration of info for a very relevant area of education." "Overall as a whole, I believe the conference was very well organized and implemented." "Very well organized. Very professional and informative." "The entire process was excellent; *I really felt a sense of community*. And my only regret is not bringing more faculty with me."

Comments from 2014: "My experience at the 2014 WIPTTE conference was very informative of what the future holds for education. I learned about some many possibilities of helping students with STEM learning." "Dr. Tracy Hammond and her whole team truly made this conference a most memorable one." Out of the hundreds of conferences I have been to or have run in my long career, the WIPTTE Conference at Texas A&M was one that kept everyone connected—audience and participants alike—and with the ambiance of the Bryan/ College Station events, kept the flavor "of' true Texans"' in full spirit. A very fun-filled conference with great speakers from companies and universities nationwide!" "I enjoyed hearing the various speakers. I had no idea how extensive pen-and-touch is. It was very interesting to learn about how pen and touch technology can help people who are blind or other technological advances in the medical field. I also enjoyed the banquet. It was great to have the opportunity to converse with other attendees. I also liked that snacks were available between presentations." "Great speakers: I especially enjoyed the keynotes by Olya Veselova and Randall Davis. Great social activities and great local food. I enjoyed trying out the Perceptive Pixel. The high school game dev contest was also really fun." "I learned a lot from other attendees it was nice to have food brought in as so not to waste time for the learning sessions, or travel to find eating establishments. Having all sessions in same room facilities were excellent." "I greatly enjoyed the conference. The food was excellent and everything seemed well planned out. It was an awesome experience to be able to hear from experts in the Pen and Touch Technology field, all of which had great insight and knowledge which enhanced my understanding of the interaction between humans and computers." "Overall—very well organized conference with lots of interesting information. Specifically, my favorite things included: conference location, time schedule and structured session times, quality of food provided, accessibility of conference organizers during the conference, and conference happenings." "I loved that all the papers were close to my research. I found the event very friendly and the talks—in the main—informative. The rooms for the event were good. I liked the single track layout it always makes for a better event than parallel tracks. I LOVED the raffle at the end—that was great fun. . . . and the wine was great-the bonkers dinner the night before was just funny:-) The poster session might have been better with a few more posters but the venue was cool enough. I liked the shuttle service but felt it was a tough on the penguins. . . " "Where do I begin? The planning for the conference was great. The accommodations that were arranged at the Hilton and the transportation to the various events were very convenient. The food was excellent. I loved that we were able to sample local College Station restaurants. The evenings in downtown Bryan and at the winery were wonderful ways to connect with other participants and begin to process the mass amounts of information we were receiving in the daytime sessions. The topics and speakers were great. I especially loved the keynote speakers. Barbara Tversky's research was phenomenal in showing us that pen/touch technology is not only interesting, clever and fun but it also is a great asset to pedagogy. I was surprised by the wide range of applications for pen and touch technology. It was exciting to see the speakers addressing varying areas-education, health care, technology, social media, etc. I think everyone especially loved the catholic high school girls' presentation showing us how this technology is truly used from an end-user perspective." "Great topics, great foot and shuttle service." "I loved that they have local food and snacks all day. I also very much enjoyed the presentations of various software programs like OneNote and FluidMath" "Overall I think it was very well done. Good set of papers chosen for presentation, which is perhaps the most important thing about a conference. Logistics were handled beautifully; everything seems to have been thought out in advance and taken care of. Very impressive.

Good facilities." "The keynote speaker's talk gave many interesting and thoughtful ideas and projects; High school group showed diversity, which is great; Different area not only focusing on programming showed importance and impressive effect of the topic: touch/pen application in education! Banquet is awesome; Volunteers are good; Drivers are good." "I think the food was great, and the way the attendees were treated was very nice. I was only able to attend one talk, but that was pretty sweet as well." "The facilities were well suited to the venue. The high school contest was well organized and the topic was terrific. I enjoyed the variety of topics that were presented on Saturday since that is when I was there with my high school students. Lunch was excellent—a nice variety and it was delicious. Breakfast tacos when we arrived was especially nice for the high school students who had to put in a Full days" work "right after they arrived." "Speakers are always great. Networking great. Food variety and Texas flavor was awesome. Facility was convenient and easy to find." "Location and TAMU staff were exceptional. The Shuttle drivers were amazing—and key to making the conference work. Schedule worked well." "liked the venue and the way the food was handled at the conference. The hands on sessions were extremely beneficial to me. The length of the presentations was about right. I also enjoyed the presentation by the students from Baton Rouge's St. Joseph's Academy." "Great Venue, Food and Speakers. I particularly like the single track format." "I found all the speakers and their information engaging. I actually liked the flow of the conference—with posters at the wine and cheese, and single sessions for most of the day, and then hands-on format where participants had several choices." "I had a very positive experience at the conference. All the students were very helpful and friendly. I could see all of the energy and effort that went into hosting such a conference." "I was very pleased with the quality of this conference, the size and topics presented. I feel thankful for the experience and the opportunity to present example technologies being used in educational research and clinical practice. I benefited highly from participation and hope to attend this conference again next year! Thank you for the financial support to help me increase my professional development and learning as a current doctoral student!" "Looking forward to the next one :-)" "Can I hire out you guys the next time I have to run a conference? You really did an excellent job." "This was definitely one of the most interesting workshops that I have attended." "This conference was well worth my spring break time off. I look forward to attending next year."

Organizing Committees

The chairs for WIPTTE 2013 were Dr. Eric Hamilton (Pepperdine University) and Dr. Joe Tront (Virginia Tech). The organizing committee of WIPTTE 2013 included Dr. Victor Adamchik (Carnegie Mellon University), Dr. Christine Alvarado (University of California San Diego), Rob Baker (Cincinnati Country Day School), Dr. Elizabeth Cheung (Pierce College), Stephanie Connor (Wacom, Inc.), Dr. Jane Dong (California State, Los Angeles), Dr. Tracy Hammond (Texas A&M University), Mark Payton (Whitfield School), Dr. Joseph Tront (Virginia Tech), and Michael Vasey (DyKnow).

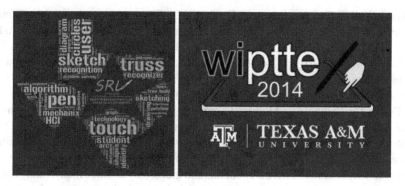

Fig. 2 *Front* and *back* of WIPTTE 2014 T-shirts

The chairs of WIPTTE 2014 were Dr. Tracy Hammond (Texas A&M University) and Mark Payton (Whitfield School). The paper chairs were Dr. Aaron Adler (Ratheon BBN Technologies) and Joel Backton (Choate Rosemary Hall), with assistance from Paul Taele (Texas A&M University). The poster chair was Dr. Jane Dong. The local chairs were Stephanie Valentine (Texas A&M University) and Dr. Teresa Leyk (Texas A&M University). Dr. Eric Hamilton (Pepperdine University) and Dr. Joe Tront (Virginia Tech) served as Ex-Officio members providing expertise at every step of the way. Sponsorship chairs were Stephanie Connor (Wacom) and Dr. Daniel Goldberg (Texas A&M University). The student volunteer organizer was Raniero Lara-Garduno (Texas A&M University). Taffie Behringer (Texas A&M University), Kathy Waskom (Texas A&M University), and Elena Rodriguez organized the logistics. Geoff Allison (Fujitsu), Michael Vasey (DyKnow), and Jeffrey Buchanan (Fujitsu) also served on the organizing committee. Dr. Tracy Hammond (Texas A&M University) designed and maintained the website. Folami Alamudun designed the t-shirt.

Acknowledgements

We also thank the contributing authors and presenters, reviewers, students and staff at Pepperdine University (2013) and Texas A&M University (2014) for the truly outstanding work that was done to produce, publish, present, and demonstrate at the conference, and in providing the behind-the-scenes work necessary to make it all possible.

The generous sponsorship of several corporations and organizations has been crucial to enabling WIPTTE to provide a high quality program at a very low cost to attendees. We would particularly like to thank our sponsors who have provided invaluable resources, both financial and in-kind. 2014 Platinum sponsors included: Texas Engineering Experiment Station, Texas A&M University Dwight Look College of Engineering, Department of Computer Science and Engineering, and the Sketch Recognition Lab. Specific thanks go to Dr. M. Katherine Banks, Dr. N.K. Anand,

Dr. Hank Walker, Dr. Nancy Amato, Dr. Dilma Da Silva, and members of the Sketch Recognition Lab, directed by Dr. Tracy Hammond. 2014 Gold sponsors include: Texas A&M University Dean of Faculties, with specific appreciation going to Dr. Michael Benedick. 2014 Silver level sponsors include Fujitsu and Wacom, with special thanks going to Stephanie Connor, Geoff Allison, and Jeffrey Buchanan. 2014 Bronze sponsors include: Esri, DyKnow, PDF Annotator, Microsoft, AggieStem, and The Center for Technology-Mediated Learning in Mathematics, with special thanks going to David DiBiase, Michael Vasey, Oliver Grahl, Dr. Jonathan Grudin, Olya Veselova, Jeff Han, and Dr. Sandra Nite. Sponsors of WIPTTE 2013 include Intel, Fujitsu, Wacom, Windows 8, KyKnow, TechSmith, and PDF Annotator.

The student volunteers were stupendous and graciously donated many, many hours of their time to ensure the participants enjoyed their time. Volunteers served as drivers at all hours of the day and night so that no participant needed to rent a car, worked the registration desk, facilitated technology, and helped organize the conference events. Thanks to TAMU student volunteers Ruiz Akpan, Folami Alamudun, Partha Baruah, Donald Beyette, Steven Bierwagen, Zach Brown, Sabyasachi Chakraborty, Chih-Yen Chang, Jenny Chen, Karrie Cheng, Gabriel Dzodom, Raniero Lara-Garduno, Ryan Gates, Shiqiang Guo, Mu-Fen Hsieh, Kira Jones, Hong-Hoe Kim, Jonathan Kocmoud, Jung In Koh, Andrew Koons, Jose Manriquez, Rafael Moreno, Larry Powell, Heriberto Rodriguez, Nick Melnyk, Prem Pokharel, Vijay Rajanna, Paul Taele, Grant Uland, Junqi Yang, Zhengliang Yin, and Aggie STEM volunteers Ali Bicer, Brittani Cain, Nick Lopez, and Cheryl Ann Peterson. Extra thanks to TAMU staff Taffie Behringher, Bekah Holle, Kathy Waskom, and Teresa Leyk. Pepperdine Volunteers include Kip Glazer, Hiroo Kato, Yueru Lu, Moses Okumu, Cheryl Peed, Joey Sabol, Bertha Roman, Paul Taele, and Ken Yeh.

WIPTTE would not be successful without our dedicated peer reviewers from 2013 and 2014: Victor Adamchik, Geoff Allison, Ruth Anderson, Rodolfo Azevedo, Joel Backon, Sam Bryfczynski, Carol Carruthers, Stephanie Connor, Ricky Cox, Jane Dong, Amelito Enriquez, Ed Evans, Bob Farrow, John Fons, Eric Hamilton, Patrick Haughian, Maki Hirotani, Ayden Kim, Gregory Klee, Peter Knoop, Herny Kraebber, Raniero Lara-Garduno, Teresa Leyk, Steven Lindell, Moses Okumu, Manoj Prasad, Carla Romney, Stacey Roshan, Christelle Scharff, Walter Schilling, Mei-Yau Shih, Carol Smith, Paul Taele, Joe Tront, Michele Villinski, and Connie White.

Conclusion

WIPTTE 2013 and 2014 brought together diverse audiences of researchers, educators, and students from varying backgrounds. The major characteristic that unified these groups is an ongoing commitment to discovering ways to leverage digital ink and touch interfaces to support teaching and learning. The sharing of experiences and best practices during the workshops continues to provide the bases for a new community of tablets-in-education researchers, practitioners and thought leaders. To participate in this community and find out more, visit http://www.wiptte.org.

Many other people contributed a great deal of time and energy to make these conferences successful. Thank you to all of the participants and other supporters.

Finally, we thank you, the reader, for your ongoing interest in trying to make education better through the intelligent application of digital ink and touch.

Your editors,
Tracy, Mark, Aaron, & Stephanie

Contents

Contributors

Victor Adamchik Carnegie Mellon University, Pittsburgh, PA, USA

Christine Alvarado Harvey Mudd College, Claremont, CA, USA

University of California at San Diego, San Diego, CA, USA

Cal Armstrong Appleby College, Oakville, ON, Canada

Rodolfo Azevedo Institute of Computing, State University of Campinas (UNICAMP), Campinas, Brasil

Mark Babatunde South Fayette High School, McDonald, USA

Ellen Breazel Department of Mathematical Sciences, Clemson University, Clemson, SC, USA

Sam Bryfczynski Clemson University, Clemson, SC, USA

Ricardo Caceffo Institute of Computing, State University of Campinas (UNICAMP), Campinas, Brasil

Carol Carruthers Seneca College of Applied Arts and Technology, Toronto, ON, Canada

Maria Chang Qualitative Reasoning Group, Northwestern University, Evanston, USA

Sharon Lynn Chu TAMU Embodied Interaction Lab (TEILab), Departments of Visualization & Architecture, Texas A&M University, College Station, TX, USA

Sam Cohen South Fayette High School, McDonald, USA

Thomas J. Colling Rancocas Valley Regional High School, Mt. Holly, NJ, USA

Melanie M. Cooper Clemson University, Clemson, SC, USA

John Cristy Bradley Department of Electrical & Computer Engineering, Virginia Polytechnic Institute and State University, Blacksburg, VA, USA

Martha E. Crosby Department of Information and Computer Sciences, University of Hawaii at Manoa, Honolulu, HI, USA

J. V. Gutierrez Cuba Universidad de las Américas at Puebla, Cholula, Puebla, Mexico

John Desjardins Bioengineering Department, Clemson University, Clemson, SC, USA

Wade Fagen Computer Science Department, University of Illinois, Champaign, IL, USA

Yi-Nan Fan Texas A&M University, College Station, TX, USA

Christopher Findeisen Department of Computer Science & Engineering, Texas A&M University, College Station, TX, USA

Kenneth D. Forbus Qualitative Reasoning Group, Northwestern University, Evanston, IL, USA

Tracy Q. Gardner Colorado School of Mines, Golden, CO, USA

Alicia Gonzalez Santa Monica High School, Santa Monica, CA, USA

Gus Greivel Colorado School of Mines, Golden, CO, USA

Nathaniel P. Grove University of North Carolina at Wilmington, Wilmington, NC, USA

Jan P. Hammond Department of Eduational Administration, State University of NewYork at New Paltz, New Paltz, NY, USA

Tracy Hammond Sketch Recognition Lab, Department of Computer Science & Engineering, Dwight Look College of Engineering, Texas A&M University, College Station, TX, USA

Page Heller HopesCreek, College Station, TX, USA

Sarah Hertzler South Fayette High School, McDonald, PA, USA

Josiah Hester Clemson University, Clemson, USA

Uta Hinrichs SACHI Research Group, School of Computer Science, University of St. Andrews, Saint Andrews, Scotland, UK

Matthew Horton University of Central Lancashire, Preston, UK

Sam Kamin Computer Science Department, University of Illinois, Champaign, IL, USA

Hiroo Kato Pepperdine University, Malibu, CA, USA

Andy Kearney Harvey Mudd College, Claremont, CA, USA

Alexa Keizur Harvey Mudd College, Claremont, CA, USA

Ben Kenawell South Fayette High School, McDonald, PA, USA

Taufiquar Khan Department of Mathematical Sciences, Clemson University, Clemson, SC, USA

Hong-hoe Kim Sketch Recognition Lab, Department of Computer Science & Engineering, Texas A&M University, College Station, TX, USA

Wendi Klaiber Oaks Christian High School, Westlake Village, CA, USA

Michael Klymkowsky University of Colorado, Boulder, CO, USA

Kimberle Koile MIT Center for Educational Computing Initiatives, Cambridge, MA, USA

Radhir Kothuri South Fayette High School, McDonald, PA, USA

Frank V. Kowalski Colorado School of Mines, Golden, CO, USA

Susan E. Kowalski Colorado School of Mines, Golden, CO, USA

Red Rocks Community College, Lakewood, CA, USA

Katherine Krueger-Hirt Marymount School of New York, New York, NY, USA

Raniero Lara-Garduno Sketch Recognition Lab, Department of Computer Science & Engineering, Texas A&M University, College Station, TX, USA

Jui-Teng Li Texas A&M University, College Station, TX, USA

Jeffrey Liew Department of Educational Psychology, College of Education and Human Development, Texas A&M University, College Station, TX, USA

Julie Linsey Georgia Institute of Technology, Atlanta, GA, USA

Jason Llorin Appleby College, Oakville, ON, Canada

Calvin Loncaric Harvey Mudd College, Claremont, CA, USA

Anne-Marie Mann SACHI Research Group, School of Computer Science, University of St. Andrews, St. Andrews, Scotland, UK

Eric J. Marcos Lincoln Middle School, Santa Monica, CA, USA

Elisa Beth McNeill Department of Health and Kinesiology, Texas A&M University, College Station, TX, USA

Enrique Palou Universidad de las Américas at Puebla, Chalula, Puebla, Mexico

Roy Pargas School of Computer Science, Clemson University, Clemson, SC, USA

Miranda Parker Harvey Mudd College, Claremont, CA, USA

Jessica Peck Harvey Mudd College, Claremont, CA, USA

Francis Quek TAMU Embodied Interaction Laboratory (TEILab), Texas A&M University, College Station, TX, USA

Aaron Quigley SACHI Research Group, School of Computer Science, University of St. Andrews, St. Andrews, Scotland, UK

Jose Israel Ramirez Gamez Spring Valley High School, Las Vegas, NV, USA

Dwayne Raymond Department of Philosophy, College of Liberal Arts, Texas A&M University, College Station, TX, US

Janet C. Read University of Central Lancashire, Preston, UK

Marilyn Reba Department of Mathematical Sciences, Clemson University, Clemson, CA, USA

Heloisa Vieira da Rocha Institute of Computing, State University of Campinas (UNICAMP), Campinas, Brasil

Carla A. Romney Boston University, Boston, MA, USA

Stacey Roshan Bullis School, Potomac, MD, USA

Andee Rubin TERC, Cambridge, MA, USA

Todd Ruskell Colorado School of Mines, Golden, CO, USA

Walter Schilling Milwaukee School of Engineering, Milwaukee, WI, USA

Kiley Sobel Harvey Mudd College, Claremont, CA, USA

Judy Storeygard TERC, Cambridge, MA, USA

Leigh Szucs Department of Health and Kinesiology, Texas A&M University, College Station, TX, USA

Paul Taele Sketch Recognition Lab, Department of Computer Science & Engineering, Texas A&M University, College Station, TX, USA

Fiona Tay Pivotal Labs, San Francisco, CA, USA

Joseph G. Tront Bradley Department of Electrical & Computer Engineering, Virginia Polytechnical Institute and State University, Blacksburg, VA, USA

Barbara Tversky Columbia Teachers College, New York City, NY, USA

Stanford University, Stanford, CA, USA

Jeffrey Usher Qualitative Reasoning Group, Northwestern University, Evanston, IL, USA

Stephanie Valentine Sketch Recognition Lab, Department of Computer Science & Engineering, Texas A&M University, College Station, TX, USA

Irina Viktorova Department of Mathematical Sciences, Clemson University, Clemson, CA, USA

Bert Wachsmuth Mathematics and Computer Science, Seton Hall University, South Orange, NJ, USA

Eric A. Walters Marymount School of New York, New York, NY, USA

Jon Wetzel Northwestern University, Evanston, IL, USA

Nicholas Wilke South Fayette High School, McDonald, PA, USA

Kelly Wilson Department of Health and Kinesiology, Texas A&M University, College Station, TX, USA

About the Editors

Aaron Adler is a Scientist at Ratheon BBN Technologies in Cambridge, Massachusetts. Dr. Adler has worked on variety of projects for DARPA and AFRL involving security, machine learning, robotics, artificial intelligence, and synthetic biology. Dr. Adler has a particular interest in creating intelligent user interfaces by automatically handling complexities to enable intuitive interfaces for users. He received his Ph.D. in Computer Science from MIT where he also received his M.Eng. in Computer Science and Engineering and S.B. in Computer Science. His Ph.D. thesis centered on constructing multimodal interactive dialogues: combining speech recognition and sketch recognition for user input and generating speech and sketching for multimodal computer output. The system helps the user describe simple mechanical (Rube-Goldberg-like) devices by asking probing questions.

Tracy Hammond Director of the Sketch Recognition Lab and Associate Professor in the Department of Computer Science and Engineering at Texas A&M University, Dr. Hammond is an international leader in sketch recognition and human-computer interaction research. Dr. Hammond's publications on the subjects are widely cited and have well over fourteen hundred citations, with Dr. Hammond having an h-index of 18, an h10-index of 27, and four papers with over 100 citations each. Her sketch recognition research has been funded by NSF, DARPA, Google, and many others, totaling over 3.6 million dollars in peer reviewed funding. She holds a PhD in Computer Science and FTO (Finance Technology Option) from MIT, and four degrees from Columbia University: an M.S in Anthropology, an M.S. in Computer Science, a B.A. in Mathematics, and a B.S. in Applied Mathematics. Prior to joining the TAMU CSE faculty

Dr. Hammond taught for five years at Columbia University and was a telecom analyst for four years at Goldman Sachs. Dr Hammond is the 2011–2012 recipient of the Charles H. Barclay, Jr. '45 Faculty Fellow Award. The Barclay Award is given to professors and associate professors who have been nominated for their overall contributions to the Engineering Program through classroom instruction, scholarly activities, and professional service.

Mark Payton is the Director of Technology and Library Services for Whitfield School, an independent 6–12 school in St. Louis, MO. He is in his seventeenth year as an IT Director in independent schools, having been at schools in Vermont and Madaba, Jordan previously. He started his IT career working in the ski industry at Killington and as IT Director for Burton Snowboards. Between the industry and academic stints, he was a software developer. Self-taught as a programmer and IT person, his training is in early childhood education with a BA from the University of Kansas. He has taught subjects as varied as Introductory Programming and Christian Theology, and to students of every grade between Pre-K and the undergraduate university level. He has been interested in pen-based computing since the days of the GRiDpad and Windows for Pen Computing and has been a member of the WIPTTE steering committee since the conference's inception.

Stephanie Valentine is a PhD student in the Department of Computer Science & Engineering at Texas A&M University. A Nebraska native, Valentine graduated Salutatorian of her class with a BA in Computer Science with a minor in Electronic Publishing from Saint Mary's University of Minnesota. Valentine is an NSF Graduate Fellow, winner of the Susan M. Arseven' 75 Make-A-Difference Award, and Vice President of the CSE Departmental graduate student association. Valentine's research focuses around understanding how children communicate in online social networks and empowering children to have safe, healthy, and expressive digital friendships. Valentine is also the founding president of Wired Youth, Inc., a 501(c)3 non-profit organization that works to educate the community about safe social networking for children as an active prevention strategy for cyberbullying, online predation, and other cyberthreats.

Chapter 1
Keynote Address: Tools for Thinking

Barbara Tversky

Abstract The content of thought can be regarded as internalized and intermixed perceptions of the world and the actions of thought as internalized and intermixed actions on the world. Reexternalizing the content of thought onto something perceptible and reexternalizing the actions of thinking as actions of the body can facilitate thinking. New technologies can do both. They can allow creation and revision of external representations and they can allow interaction with the hands and the body. This analysis will be supported by several empirical studies. One will show that students learn more from creating visual explanations of STEM phenomena than from creating verbal ones. Another will show that conceptually congruent actions on an iPad promote arithmetic performance. A third will show that when reading spatial descriptions, students use their hands to create mental models.

Thought in the Air: Gesture A sight no longer odd on urban sidewalks: people walking alone, talking into the air. What is also no longer odd is that most of them are gesturing. Their listeners cannot see their gestures, nor are the speakers looking at them. When people sit on their hands when they talk, they become less fluent [14]. Gesturing doesn't just help people talk, it helps them think, and it does so by structuring the thought into spatial-motor models. In one experiment, participants read descriptions of complex spatial environments, small towns, large gyms, museums for later testing. As they read, they gestured [8]. Line-like gestures represented the network of paths and point-like gestures represented the locations of landmarks. When they gestured, as they read or when they answered questions, they remembered better. In another experiment, participants read and solved spatial problems; for problems with a large number of components, most gestured [20]. When their gestures represented the problem structure correctly, they were more likely to solve it correctly, and when their gestures represented the problem incorrectly, they more likely to solve it incorrectly. Other research has shown similar phenomena: using the body to represent thought helps thinking (e.g., [4, 12]).

B. Tversky (✉)
Columbia Teachers College, New York City, NY, USA
e-mail: bt2152@columbia.edu

Stanford University, Stanford, CA, USA

© Springer International Publishing Switzerland 2015
T. Hammond et al. (eds.), *The Impact of Pen and Touch Technology on Education*,
Human-Computer Interaction Series, DOI 10.1007/978-3-319-15594-4_1

Appropriate representative gestures not only affect the thought of those who make them, they also affect the thought of those who view them (e.g., [4, 6, 12]). In one set of experiments, viewed gestures changed people's conceptions of temporal processes, from linear to cyclical or from sequential to simultaneous [7]. In another, action gestures accompanying an explanation of the workings of an engine enhanced people's understanding of the actions of the system even though the relevant information was entirely in the verbal script [9].

Touch and gesture interfaces incorporate these embodied expressions of thought into the ever-expanding digital world. Gestures that are congruent with thought can enable fluent and natural interactions and have been shown to augment thinking and performance. One example from our lab illustrates the benefits of congruent gestures. Addition is a discrete one-to-one task, and performance on addition tasks in low SES elementary school students was improved by gestures that were discrete and one-to-one with number of things to be added, more than gestures that were discrete but corresponded to the number of columns of things to be added. Similarly, number line estimation is a continuous task, and mapping the task to a continuous gesture enabled better performance than mapping the task to a discrete gesture [16].

Explaining the effects of gesture on those who make them and those who view them goes beyond this brief paper, but one line of explanation can be summarized this way: thinking is at least in part internalized action (e.g., [2, 13]) so that reexternalizing thought in the form of representative gestures (e.g., [18, 20]) augments thought. As will be seen, using the same actions to put thought on a page can have extra benefits.

Thought on the Page: Sketch and Diagram Although gestures can have significant consequence on thought, they are fleeting and disappear. A simple way to preserve them is to put them on a page, that is, to make a sketch or diagram. Conveniently, the hand does both, so the transformation from the air to the page is direct. Both gesture and sketch use actions or marks in space and place in space to express and communicate thought. Putting thought on a page off-loads limited memory and information processing, increasing both. Putting thought on a page makes thought public for self and others. Putting thought on a page fosters contemplation, inference, revision, and discovery, both by individuals and by groups (e.g., [17]). Because the mapping of thought to space and elements or actions in it is more direct than the mapping of thought to words, there are many (but by no means all) situations, especially educational situations, in which sketches and diagrams (like gestures) surpass words in facilitating communication, inference, and creativity (e.g., [10, 11, 17]).

Diagrams are helpful for teaching, and creating diagrams turns out to be helpful for learning, in spite of the fact that most examinations require students to produce words. In one set of experiments, junior high students first learned a STEM concept, either how a bicycle pump works or how chemical bonding happens [1]. Their mental rotation ability was also assessed; this is a common measure of spatial ability that correlates with performance in a wide range of tasks, including achievements in science and engineering courses.

For the case of chemical bonding, their knowledge was tested immediately after learning. Then, in both cases, the students were randomly divided into two groups:

students in one group crafted a standard verbal explanation of the bicycle pump or chemical bonding; students the other group crafted a visual explanation. Afterwards, they were tested on their knowledge of the structure and function of the bicycle pump or chemical bonding. In the case of the bicycle pump, low spatial students performed more poorly than high spatial students after producing a verbal explanation; this finding is common. However, producing a visual explanation brought low spatial students up to the level of high spatial students. Producing a visual explanation had no effect on the performance of high spatial students, perhaps because the task was too easy. The findings for the case of chemical bonding, a harder set of concepts, were more dramatic. Recall that their knowledge was tested soon after learning, then they produced verbal or visual explanations, and their knowledge was retested. The first surprising finding was that students improved on the second test as a consequence of producing explanations, with no additional teaching or study. The second surprising finding was that those who produced visual explanations improved far more than those who produced verbal explanations. Both high and low spatials gained from creating visual explanations, and high spatials performed better than low spatials after creating either type of explanation.

Why is producing visual explanations so effective? As noted earlier, the mapping from elements and relations in the world to elements and relations on the page is more direct than the mapping to words. More than that, visual explanations provide a test for *completeness*—are all the necessary parts there? They also provide a test for *coherence*—do the parts interrelate properly?

In the cases of learning and teaching, and in everyday cases like instructions to put something together or to get from A to B, clear direct diagrams that show structure and action work best (e.g., [22]). However, there are other cases in which ambiguity is most productive. Designers and artists make and revise sketches as in integral part of developing their ideas (e.g., [3, 5, 15, 19, 21]). The very ambiguity of their sketches allows them to see new configurations and relations, that is, to make new discoveries in their own sketches. Experienced designers are better at making new discoveries, especially more abstract ones, than inexperienced designers. Certain cognitive skills promote new discoveries, notably, a conceptual skill, finding remote associations, and a perceptual skill, finding small figures embedded in larger complex ones [21].

As sensory deprivation studies showed half a century ago, a mind without a body and the world can't think straight. The findings reviewed above, and many, many others like them, illustrate how dependent human thought is on the body and the world, some of the ways that the mind expands beyond the ears and uses the body and the world in order to think. These findings come at a fortunate time, when designers and engineers are increasingly able to build interfaces that can interpret human gestures and can provide sketches, diagrams, and tangible and digital worlds that enhance thought.

References

1. Bobek, E., & Tversky, B. (2014). *Creating visual explanations improves learning*. Proceedings of the 36th Annual Conference of the Cognitive Science Society. Austin, TX: Cognitive Science Society.
2. Bruner, J. S. (1966). On cognitive growth. In J. S. Bruner, R. R. Olver, & P. M. Greenfield (Eds.), *Studies in cognitive growth* (pp. 1–29). Oxford University Press: England.
3. Goel, V. (1995). *Sketches of thought*. Cambridge: MIT Press.
4. Goldin-Meadow, S. (2003). *Hearing gesture: How our hands help us think*. Cambridge: Belnap Press.
5. Goldschmidt, G. (1994). On visual design thinking: The vis kids of architecture. *Design Studies, 15*(2), 158–174. (Wiley).
6. Hosetter, A. B., & Alibali, M. W. (2008). Visible embodiment: Gestures as simulated action. *Psychonomic Bulletin and Review, 15,* 495–514.
7. Jamalian, A., & Tversky, B. (2012). *Gestures alter thinking about time*. In N. Miyake, D. Peebles, & R. P. Cooper (Eds.), Proceedings of the 34th Annual Conference of the Cognitive Science Society, pp. 551–557. Austin TX: Cognitive Science Society.
8. Jamalian, A., Giardino, V., & Tversky, B. (2013). *Gestures for thinking*. In M. Knauff, M. Pauen, N. Sabaenz, & I. Wachsmuth (Eds.), Proceedings of the 35th Annual Conference of the Cognitive Science Society. Austin, TX: Cognitive Science Society.
9. Kang, S., Tversky, B., & Black, J. B. (2012). *From hands to minds: How gestures promote action understanding*. In N. Miyake, D. Peebles, & R. P. Cooper (Eds.), Proceedings of the 34th Annual Conference of the Cognitive Science Society, pp. 551–557. Austin TX: Cognitive Science Society.
10. Larkin, J. H., & Simon, H. A. (1987). Why a diagram is (sometimes) worth ten thousand words. *Cognitive Science, 11,* 65–99.
11. Mayer, R. E. (2001). *Multimedia learning*. Cambridge: Cambridge University Press.
12. McNeill, D. (1992). *Hand and mind: What gestures reveal about thought*. Chicago: University of Chicago Press.
13. Piaget, J. (1954). *The construction of reality in the child* (trans: M. Cook). New York: Basic Books.
14. Rauscher, F. B., Krauss, R. M., & Chen, Y. (1996). Gesture, speech and lexical access: The role of lexical movements in speech production. *Psychological Science, 7,* 226–231.
15. Schon, D. A. (1983). *The reflective practitioner*. New York: Harper Collins.
16. Segal, A., Tversky, B., & Black, J. B. (2014). Conceptually congruent actions can promote thought. Journal of Research in Memory and Applied Cognition. dx.doi.org/10.1016/j.jarmac.2014.06.004.
17. Tversky, B. (2011). Visualizations of thought. *Topics in Cognitive Science, 3,* 499–535. doi:10.1111/j.1756-8765.2010.01113.x.
18. Tversky, B. (2014, in press). The cognitive design of tools of thought. *Review of Philosophy and Psychology*. Special issue on diagrammatic reasoning.
19. Tversky, B., & Chou, J. Y. (2010). Creativity: Depth and breadth. In Y. Nagai (Ed.), *Design creativity*. Dordrecht: Springer.
20. Tversky, B., & Kessell, A. M. (In press). Thinking in action. *Topics in Cognitive Science*.
21. Tversky, B., & Suwa, M. (2009). Thinking with sketches. In A. B. Markman & K. L. Wood (Eds), *Tools for innovation* (pp. 75–84). Oxford: Oxford University Press.
22. Tversky, B., Agrawala, M., Heiser, J., Lee, P. U., Hanrahan, P., Phan, D., Stolte, C., & Daniele, M.-P. (2007). In G. Allen (Ed.), *Spatial cognition: From research to cognitive technology*. Mahwah: Erlbaum.

Part I
Emerging Technologies—Handwriting

Chapter 2
Digital Pen Technology's Suitability to Support Handwriting Learning

Anne-Marie Mann, Uta Hinrichs, and Aaron Quigley

Abstract While digital technology is entering today's classrooms and learning environments, handwriting remains primarily taught using regular pencil and paper. In our research we explore the potential of digital writing tools to augment the handwriting process while preserving its cognitive benefits. In particular, we are interested in (1) how the characteristics of digital writing tools influence children's handwriting experience and quality, compared to regular pencil and paper and (2) what kind of feedback may be beneficial to digitally augment the handwriting process and how this can be integrated into handwriting technology. Here we describe findings of a study we conducted at a primary school to investigate how existing digital pens (iPad and stylus, WACOM tablet, and Livescribe pen) affect children's handwriting quality and the handwriting experience. As part of this, we discuss our methodology for evaluating handwriting quality, an inherently subjective activity. Furthermore, we outline the potential design space that digital writing tools open up when it comes to augmenting the handwriting process to facilitate learning.

2.1 Problem Statement and Context

Learning how to write is considered an essential skill that forms the foundation of education. The early years of education are therefore dominated by learning how to hold a pencil and how to form letters and words. As technology has developed, so too have expectations toward the skill sets children need to acquire over the years. For example, mastering technology such as PCs and, more recently, direct-touch tablets, has gained importance. However, the introduction of digital technology into the classroom means that there is now a divide in both time and opinion between traditional teaching practises, such as handwriting, and modern approaches that exploit digital technology such as touch-typing. Research has shown there are educational benefits in learning how to write using traditional methods [2, 11, 14]. Likewise, technology can be used to facilitate classroom activities [4, 30] and, potentially, the

A.-M. Mann (✉) · U. Hinrichs · A. Quigley
SACHI Research Group, School of Computer Science, University of St. Andrews, St. Andrews, Scotland
e-mail: am998@st-andrews.ac.uk

© Springer International Publishing Switzerland 2015   7
T. Hammond et al. (eds.), *The Impact of Pen and Touch Technology on Education*,
Human-Computer Interaction Series, DOI 10.1007/978-3-319-15594-4_2

process of learning to hand-write. As we move towards classrooms and teaching activities that involve digital tools, it is possible that, in the near future, young children will learn how to write using digital pen and paper, or tablet devices.

Our writing tools, analog or digital, greatly influence our writing experience and handwriting quality and, potentially, the context where we make use of them. If we think of digital handwriting technology in the classroom and how it should be designed, it is necessary to carefully consider (1) how this kind of technology will affect children's handwriting experience and (2) how it can potentially enhance the handwriting (learning) process. In this work we focus in particular on the first question. We conducted an in-situ study where we assess three existing digital handwriting tools (a WACOM tablet, an iPad, and a Livescribe pen) and how these affected children's writing experience and handwriting quality.

In the following sections we provide the context for our research including a description of our research questions. This is followed by an outline of our study including the methods used to assess handwriting quality and to evaluate different writing devices, whilst tackling the challenges of working with children as study participants. We present an overview of our study findings and discuss their implications with regards to future work in the area of augmenting the handwriting process using digital pen technology.

2.1.1 Research Context

Our research draws from previous work in education and psychology on the cognitive benefits of handwriting. In the field of HCI, research has introduced various approaches to pen technology to support handwriting processes in general as well as in classroom scenarios.

Educational & Cognitive Benefits of Handwriting Some argue that teaching practices need to adapt to reflect the prevalent technological advances to which today's children are exposed [3]. Yet, studies have shown that tools such as keyboards, cannot replicate the inherent cognitive and educational benefits that handwriting provides [2, 11, 14].

The most effective teaching methods, when introducing young children to the alphabet and letter sounds, incorporate both visual and haptic cues [2, 15]. Moving a pencil to form letter shapes leaves unique imprints in motor memory, which is why learning how to write by hand is more effective [12, 10]. In contrast, the haptic feedback from keyboard typing does not differ from letter to letter. On a higher level, the skill of handwriting has been shown to benefit literacy skills, specifically letter recognition [10], phonological associations and orthographic rules (grammar and spelling) [9, 14], as well as compositional skills and expression [19].

This positive influence of handwriting on cognitive and educational development, alongside the popularity of low-cost pen and paper, has motivated research into the development of digital writing tools. Such writing tools aim to complement these benefits with the additional functionalities that we so value in our digital writing tools.

Digital Handwriting Tools Research into pen and paper computing aims at combining the conventions of handwriting with the benefits of digital technology: such as the editing, sharing and processing of written information [29]. Successful applications of digital handwriting technology can be found in the context of design [27, 28], ideation [8], or education [4]. In classroom situations, the use of automatic handwriting recognition can translate handwritten information into typed text [21, 22, 24].

Digital pen technology can augment the handwriting process in different ways. Pens have been augmented to provide haptic feedback, resulting in improved letter recognition and phonological awareness in children [1, 17] and better handwriting fluency in adults when learning Japanese [6]. Beyond the pen itself, we see the integration of calculus functionality through digitally augmented pen and paper [30]. Other advances use pens to apply annotations on paper and also to navigate and control projected digital information [27, 28]. Similarly, digital projection on paper has been introduced to the classroom to better understand and support learning processes when teaching geometry [4].

Previous studies that have explored the differences of interacting with digital materials vs. pen and paper have shown that people continue to prefer paper [16, 18]. Other research has explored the potential of digital writing tools and handwriting recognition software as possible text entry devices in classroom scenarios [20, 22, 23]. However, we still lack studies exploring how today's digital pens (both display-based and paper-based) impact children's handwriting experience and quality.

We aim to close this gap by studying how existing digital pen technology compares to regular pencil and paper when it comes to handwriting experience and quality. Our findings inform the design of future digital writing tools and how to support the handwriting learning process for both children and adults.

2.1.2   Research Questions

The goal of our research is to explore the potential of digital pens as writing tools in classrooms, and to derive a list of considerations that will guide the process of designing and developing such digital writing devices. This implies the following two research questions:

Q1. How do Digital Pens Affect the Writing Experience? The handwriting tool has an effect on our general handwriting experience and, as such, the context in which we will consider using it. Writing with chalk on a blackboard feels different from writing with a pencil on paper. Writing with a fountain pen feels different to writing with a ballpoint pen. The interactions between writing implement and media dates back to the use of blunt reeds on clay tablets to create cuneiform. All these tools also affect the character and quality of our handwriting. In order for digital handwriting tools to become considered for classroom or other learning environments, it is important to explore how their characteristics, which differ from analog writing devices, will

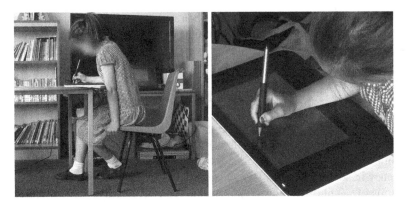

Fig. 2.1 Video cameras captured children's writing and posture

influence the handwriting experience. As a first step in our research, we explored how using digital pens affects children's writing experience and handwriting qualities.

As part of this, we recorded how the characteristics of the digital technology (e.g., size, weight, thickness, and feel of the pen on the digital surface) affect the handwriting process (e.g., body and hand posture during the writing process and handwriting result) (Fig. 2.1).

Conducting studies with children as participants can be a challenge in itself. Children express and explain experiences in unique ways that require further careful probing and interpretation. For example, they may express their immediate reaction to a writing tool but often find it challenging to explain what factors influence this experience. Furthermore, the unfamiliarity of the study situation coupled with interaction with the experimenter (a stranger) may influence how they express their opinion during interviews.

As assessment of handwriting can be subjective, we combined different approaches of eliciting feedback on handwriting quality from both the children themselves and two independent teachers. We also applied this process to characterise features that influence handwriting quality.

Q2. How can Pen Technology Support the Writing Process? Accomplished writers can use a pen or pencil as an extension of their mind to write words and sentences with a level of automaticity that requires little thought as to the physical process involved. For young children, learning this skill takes time and involves training that can be arduous. Consider a young child as they begin to write. They pick up their classroom pencil, having decided what they want to write, they adjust their sitting position and pencil grip and then start to form letters and words on the paper. During this process children are concentrating on what they want to say whilst also considering spelling, letter formation, spacing, sizing, location on the page and overall appearance. Traditionally it is the role of teachers to help children learn and progress to proficient writers by offering guidance, feedback and encouragement to their pupils. However, most classrooms have one teacher to many pupils so perhaps a digital pen could provide a level of support to each child in the absence of a teacher. The introduction of digital writing tools provides obvious additional functionalities, such as digital record keeping and analysis, which may be beneficial to writers. Beyond this, digital pen technology can potentially support the handwriting process itself. For instance, digital pens can provide direct feedback and instructions to the writer to help improve their handwriting style and skills. As part of our research, we consider if future digital writing devices can be more like teachers: providing guidance, feedback and encouragement, in order to assist children as they learn to write.

2.2   Method Employed

To address our first research question (Q1) we conducted a study with school children at a local primary school over the course of 1 week. The goal of this study was to assess the potential of existing digital pen technology to be used for writing exercises in the classroom. We were interested in (1) how existing digital writing tools are experienced by children and (2) how the different characteristics of these tools influence children's handwriting quality. During the study we asked children to complete short writing exercises using four different (digital) pen technologies and to describe, rate and compare their experiences and handwriting quality. We used a mixed methods approach combining both quantitative and qualitative methods to gain in-depth insights into the handwriting experience with the different tools from different perspectives. In the following subsections, we briefly describe the technologies explored, the study setup, and our data analysis.

2.2.1   Study Setup

We recruited 13 children from the same class (aged 9–10 years, 5 boys and 8 girls). Over the course of 4 days, each child completed 4 writing exercises (each with a different writing device). Each exercise was followed by a brief interview where we asked children to describe their experience with the writing tool. During the final interview we asked children to compare their experience with all 4 writing devices.

Digital Writing Tools Studied We asked the children to write using an iPad 2[1] and stylus, a Wacom Cintiq[2] and a Livescribe Digital Pen[3], as well as a common school pencil (see Fig. 2.2). Each of the digital pens used in the study was carefully chosen

---

[1] http://store.apple.com/us/buy-ipad/ipad2.

[2] http://www.wacom.eu/_bib_ user/dealer/bro_ c12_ en.pdf.

[3] http://www.livescribe.com/en-us/smartpen/echo/.

Fig. 2.2 Digital pen technologies used in study

to cover a range of characteristics that digital pen technology can offer: the iPad is becoming increasingly common in school environments [13, 26], and, in combination with a stylus, may become a legitimate writing surface in the future. In our study we used a popular iPad stylus (Adonit Jot Pro[4]). The writing application of our choice was SVG notes[5], which can replicate the line spacing comparable to notepads used in classrooms.

The WACOM Cintiq tablet is a high-end graphics tablet, specifically developed and commonly used by artists and designers for complex drawings and detailed pen work and, as such, should be suitable for handwriting tasks. The tablet features a built-in display (monitor). The Livescribe Digital Pen is a high-street adaptation of Anoto technology[6]. This digital pen resembles a normal ballpoint pen, but it is capable of "reading" ink from special patterned sheets of paper. Our final condition, using a common pencil and paper, formed the baseline of our study.

Each day children close-copied a different brief paragraph, which was carefully chosen considering the age and expertise of children, using the different writing tools. To eliminate ordering effects we counterbalanced the order in which children used each writing tool.

2.2.2 Data Collection

We collected each of the handwriting samples that children created during the study for comparison and analysis (see Fig. 2.3). In addition, each child was video and audio recorded during the writing exercise and the interviews.

During the interviews we encouraged children to describe their experiences with the writing tools in an open-ended way. In addition, we asked them to rate their handwriting samples (on a scale of 1–5), and to provide up to three words that would characterise their writing experience with each writing condition best. Children also indicated their preference of (a) each device versus a standard pencil (after every study session) and (b) which of the conditions they most preferred or disliked overall (at the very end of the study). Asking the children to report their opinions using various approaches allowed us to record meaningful experiences from each child.

---

[4] http://adonit.net/jot/pro/.
[5] https://itunes.apple.com/us/app/svg-notes/id569602013?mt=8.
[6] http://www.anoto.com/lng/en/pageTag/page:home/.

Fig. 2.3 Particpant 7's Handwriting samples from (**a**) Pencil on Paper, (**b**) Livescribe pen on Anoto paper, (**c**) Stylus on WACOM Cintiq and (**d**) Stylus on iPad

2.2.3   Data Analysis

For our data analysis we transcribed all interviews with the children. Based on these transcripts we iteratively coded and categorised children's statements according to themes such as physical characteristics of the writing devices, overall experience with the device, as well as positive and negative aspects of the devices that children identified.

We also analysed the ratings that children provided for each writing device and how they compared for each child individually and across all participants. In addition, we asked two independent teachers from different schools to assess and rate children's handwriting samples. These assessments were conducted blind to condition.

The recordings of the two video cameras provided insights into children's overall writing posture, writing grip and arm posture. Additionally, these recordings were analysed to deduce total writing time of each participant during the study (see Fig. 2.1).

We provide an overview of the results in the following section; we are in the process of conducting a more detailed analysis of our study.

2.3   Results

Our results provide rich insights into the suitability of currently available digital writing devices for children. Our final interviews with children where we asked them to compare the different writing devices they had tried across the week, indicated that, overall, the Livescribe pen was the most popular among the writing devices. Eight out of 13 children chose it as their favourite device (including two children who selected it as a joint favourite with the WACOM). In comparison, the WACOM received five votes as favourite (again, including the two children who selected it as a joint favourite with the Livescribe pen). The iPad and the pencil received only one nomination each as best overall device.

Additionally, day-to-day comparisons of the digital writing devices with a regular pencil indicated that the Livescribe was preferred over a pencil by nine of the 13 children. Likewise, nine children also preferred the WACOM to the pencil; only five children stated that they would prefer to use an iPad rather than a classroom pencil. A close analysis of the interviews with children and of the handwriting samples that were produced sheds light into the reasons for these preferences.

2.3.1 Children's Writing Experience

During the interviews, children were asked to express their thoughts about each writing device regarding their writing experiences, special characteristics, or benefits and drawbacks that the tools introduce. These comments capture children's differing opinions and writing experiences for each of the digital writing tools.

When talking about the regular pencil, children remarked "*it was easy and accurate*" [p1]. Whereas for the iPad condition children often commented that it was "*hard*", "*difficult*" or "*tricky*" to write with. Paradoxically, some still thought it made for a "good" writing experience. Children had a positive writing experience with the WACOM but felt that its display surface felt "*smooth*" and "*slippy*" which caused difficulties when controlling the pen on it. In contrast, most children praised the Livescribe as "*easy to control*"; this is not surprising considering that it closely resembles regular pen and paper.

When we collated all of the words children provided to characterise their writing experience, some interesting themes emerged. For the baseline condition of pencil and paper, children most often used the terms "*normal*" (five children), then "*comfortable*" (4) and also "*easy*" (3) to describe their writing experience. For the iPad condition, children used words such as "*cool*" (four children), "*fun*" (4) and "*different*" (4). Similarly, the WACOM was described first as "*cool*" (four children), "*easy*" (4) and also "*fun*" (3) to write with. Finally, the Livescribe pen was described as "*easy*" (seven children) followed by "*fun*" (3) and then "*big*" (2).

These descriptive words reflect children's attitude and perception of technology. For example, all digital writing tools were frequently described as "*fun*" or "*cool*". Interestingly, whilst the Livescribe pen was described as "*cool*" by some children, the most prevalent adjectives comment on its usability and physicality. Our analysis of all the descriptive words shows that children often commented on the physicality of this writing device (using words such as "*slippy*", "*light*", "*smooth*", or "*circular*"). Of all the pens in the study, the Livescribe pen was the thickest and heaviest (see Fig. 2.2, right). This may account for children's focus on its physical features.

2.3.2 Changes in Handwriting Quality

For the analysis of handwriting quality, we not only took into account children's self-assessment across all study days, we also collated the ratings of two independent teachers from two different schools. Both teachers have particular focus and expertise on handwriting education for primary school children. In the following, we describe how children's handwriting quality differed across devices from both the children's and teachers' viewpoints.

Children's Assessment of Handwriting Quality All children's writing samples (see Fig. 2.3) were rated by the children themselves on a Likert scale from 1 to 5 (where 1 is the worst and 5 is the best handwriting) immediately after they completed them. We analysed whether children believed their handwriting quality improved with certain devices, decreased or stayed the same in comparison to the baseline condition (Pencil & Paper) and to the handwriting quality they normally produce in the classroom.

For the pencil condition seven children identified their handwriting quality as the same as their normal level, but five children felt that their handwriting was of a lesser quality. This perhaps is a pointer to how the study situation impacted on either children's self-confidence or their ability to write to their full potential. When we look at the results when writing with the iPad, all children except one felt that their handwriting quality decreased. In the WACOM condition, five children felt the quality matched their normal performance, but six children felt it had a negative impact on their handwriting. When using the Livescribe pen, responses ranged from no change in handwriting quality (4 children), improved handwriting (5), and decreased quality (4). Based on this, the Livescribe pen fairs well as a writing tool, since it does not seem to impact handwriting quality as negatively as the other digital tools.

Interestingly, these results show that there is a similarity between handwriting quality ratings and the overall device preference described earlier. However, there is not a direct correlation between each child's overall preference and changes to handwriting quality. This suggests that handwriting quality is likely to be a contributory factor, but not the only consideration when children decide what they find desirable in a writing tool.

Teacher's Assessment of Handwriting Quality We passed copies of the children's handwriting samples to two teachers and asked them to provide a score for overall handwriting quality. In addition we asked the teachers to rate different contributory aspects to handwriting standards that we extracted from previous literature [5, 7, 25] (see Fig. 2.4). We compared teacher's handwriting quality ratings of children's handwriting samples created with pencil and paper, with those created with the digital pen tools. Teacher 1 indicated that the iPad decreased the quality of the handwriting in all cases, while Teacher 2 indicated a decrease in 10 participants. Both teachers indicated that handwriting quality was decreased when children wrote with the WACOM (Teacher 1: 10 children and Teacher 2: 12 children).

Similar to the children's ratings, Teacher 1 found a range of changes to handwriting ratings using the Livescribe (5 improved scores, 4 decreased scores and 4 scores with no change). However, Teacher 2 was more negative, rating the handwriting in 9 samples the same score as with a pencil and the remaining 4 as of less quality than the pencil samples.

This preliminary analysis of teacher's scores largely supports the children's scores and opinions. We are currently conducting a more in-depth analysis looking at the differences in teachers' and children's scores.

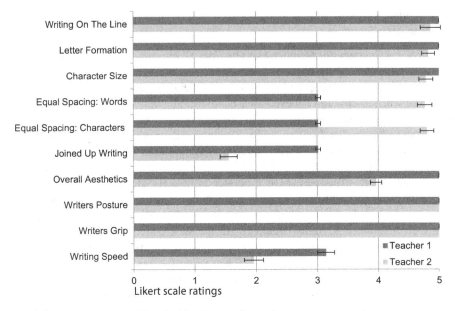

Fig. 2.4 Rated importance of handwriting features by teachers

2.3.3 Important Handwriting Features

Figure 2.4 shows the categories of handwriting features and their importance as rated by the teachers. It becomes clear that that both teachers agree that writing on the line, correct letter formation and character sizing are the most important aesthetic aspects of children's handwriting. In contrast, teachers' opinions slightly differ on the remaining factors: word and character spacing and joined up writing. This emphasises the highly subjective nature of handwriting assessment.

Physical contributory factors such as writer's posture and grip were both rated as highly important. While teachers' rating on the importance of writing speed differed, both scored this factor as of low importance compared to their other scores.

The information gathered from the teachers regarding important handwriting features will prove useful when considering the future steps of our work which includes an exploration of how to utilise digital pen technology to provide feedback on the handwriting process.

Effect of Devices on Physical Aspects of Writing We analysed the video data regarding children's writing posture and writing speed. Our initial observations indicate that children's posture changes when using a writing tool that includes a screen, i.e. the WACOM and iPad. When using a pencil, children used their non-dominant hand to support their writing process with this hand leaning on the paper, holding it in place. However, in the conditions including a digital screen, they constrained their non-dominant hand to not touch the display. Furthermore, children modified the posture of their dominant (writing) hand, keeping it above the display to avoid direct touch. It is likely that children avoided bringing their hands close to the display to avoid interference with the writing: the iPad screen reacts to all touches which, at times, caused some interruptions of the writing exercise. Although this is not an issue with the WACOM tablet, children may have transferred their experience with the iPad. Another factor that may have contributed to this behaviour is some children's concern with mishandling the display, which may have influenced them to modify their posture. We can assume that the change of posture is a contributory factor in the decreased handwriting quality with the WACOM and especially with the iPad (as visible in the samples shown in Fig. 2.3).

These results show that the different characteristics of the digital writing tools we evaluated, indeed, have an influence on children's handwriting experience and quality. The Livescribe pen seems to influence handwriting quality the least negatively and children found it easy to use because it reminded them of writing with a regular pencil on paper. We will therefore include it into our future research steps regarding how to augment the handwriting process. While the WACOM tablet led to slightly more negative results when it comes to handwriting quality, we will also include it in our further research, because its display offers a range of opportunities to provide visual feedback. We outline our future research directions in the following section.

2.4 Future Work

The discussion of our future work focuses on the question of how digital pen technology can support the handwriting process (Q2, see Sect. 2.2). This involves design considerations concerning (1) what features to provide feedback on, (2) when to provide the feedback, and (3) what kind of feedback to provide.

2.4.1 Features to Provide Feedback On

When teachers look at a child's writing, they can holistically assess the sample and identify where a student needs to improve. For digital pens to mimic this process, they need to be able to identify specific features of handwriting (as listed in Fig. 2.4). It may be that some features of handwriting will benefit from feedback more than others: for example, a writer being reminded how to form the letter "b" correctly, may prevent further "b" and "d" transpositions. However, pushing writers to increase their writing speed may result in a degradation of overall quality and legibility (though an increase in speed is desirable once a level of handwriting proficiency is achieved).

Similarly, some features of handwriting are easier to master than others [1]. For example, the ability to "write on the line" is easier to achieve than consistent character size and style. This has to do with children's physical development where fine-grained motor control refines over time—building a motor memory of how to form letters, making handwriting a consistent, easy process which is near-automatic and requires little cognitive effort.

Our next research steps therefore will explore which handwriting features would benefit the most from intervention through digital pen technology.

2.4.2 Guidance, Feedback or Encouragement

Teachers can provide guidance, feedback and encouragement in the handwriting process in different ways and at different stages. They can stand above a child as they write a paragraph, providing guidance in-situ. They can also provide feedback when writing is completed, when the pupil brings over a completed exercise to their desk. Even more removed from the situation, they can provide feedback on the pupil's handwriting when grading schoolwork at home.

In each of these examples the temporal aspect plays an important role for both the teacher's and the child's experience. In order to translate this role to the scope of a digital writing device, it needs to be considered *when* a child would receive guidance, feedback or encouragement about their handwriting. As in the example above, we propose that there are different options that can be considered here: during (termed as guidance), shortly after, or long time after writing (both termed as feedback). The timing and nature of assessment may prove instrumental in its level of efficiency.

Additionally, the potential scope for the nature of encouragement means that feedback may be at its most effective in different forms: it can be positive or negative, brief or detailed.

Direct Feedback In-Situ In-situ feedback is provided during the writing process. For example, it may be helpful to remind children to hold the pencil in a certain way or to sit correctly while they are in the process of writing, enabling the child to adjust immediately. Similarly, it is difficult for a teacher to comment on a child's posture when assessing a piece of written work. Furthermore, guidance provided immediately before a child writes may inspire a child to do well i.e. providing outlines for children to trace or emphasising the line on which the child should write. This would contrast greatly from instantaneous feedback that may highlight when the child should have or did write on the line, just as they complete a word, sentence or paragraph.

Reminders & Comments Some advice on the handwriting process and quality may be more appropriate after the child has finished a paragraph or the entire exercise. Reminders and comments provided less immediately during the writing process but still in-situ focus on aspects such as character formation or size. Here, an overview of the produced handwritten text where certain features are highlighted could be provided: *"Look at this page . . . can you see that the 'a' looks like 'u'? Try to write the 'a' correctly by closing the circle.".* This kind of feedback may be more detailed and encourage the child to focus on particular aspects in the next writing exercise.

When considering the temporal aspect to guidance and feedback, it may be that a layered approach is effective, i.e., providing the same feedback at different points in time, or providing feedback only when it is most likely to be effective. We will conduct studies to explore this further. Another important consideration is the nature of the guidance and feedback provided, which we discuss next.

Nature of Encouragement: Positive or Negative There are negative and positive approaches to providing encouragement, and both may prove to be effective. Consider for example that, children may benefit from private encouragement that highlights only the positive features of their work, which will make them feel good about their work: we shall term this as positive encouragement. However, negative encouragement, where attention is drawn to aspects of their handwriting that requires improvement, forces the child to reflect on mistakes. Teachers in class may use a mixture of negative or positive approaches to encourage their pupils. However, children may not feel engaged with a digital pen and will not respond to the pen's guidance in the same way they would with a teacher. Regression to the mean will naturally be observed in quality of the learners performance, so careful consideration as to the nature of the private or public encouragement and feedback is required. Further studies should seek to evaluate whether positive, negative or a mix of both would be the most suitable approach for encouragement in a digital handwriting aid.

2.4.3 Feedback Type

Another important aspect to consider is how to provide feedback. Consider the role of our teacher in the analogy described earlier, feedback could be provided verbally (such as *"well-done, try to . . . "*) or visually (through textual/ pictorial annotations). Furthermore, past handwriting samples can be kept in order to compare a child's progress over time. Digital pen technology could provide similar feedback using different approaches.

Audio Feedback Audio feedback, including phrases or sounds, can easily be provided with the addition of (external or integrated) speakers (as is the case with the mainstream LeapFrog LeapReader[7]). An advantage of audio feedback is that it does not interfere visually with handwriting, however, use in the classroom may be impractical and distracting to other children unless headphones are used.

Visual Feedback Digital pen technology that includes a display (e.g., the WACOM Cintiq) makes it possible to provide visual guidance and feedback alongside or integrated into the handwriting in textual or abstract form (shapes or colours). With other digital pen technology, such as the Livescribe pen, that utilises paper instead of a digital display, it is possible to use projection to augment the writing surface. Visual feedback can be provided directly in-situ or later on as part of a broader analysis. Access to a writer's past writing samples, will allow for comparison and monitoring of progress—as a teacher might. Furthermore, this kind of technology may be of

---

[7] http://www.leapfrog.com/en_gb/landingpages/leapreader.html.

interest for teachers as well as an additional tool to assess the handwriting skills of children and to provide better guidance for particular areas for improvement.

Haptic Feedback Another approach that digital pen technology can provide feedback on the handwriting process is through haptic cues. As discussed earlier, haptic feedback can be beneficial when learning to write [6, 7, 17]. Introducing haptic feedback to students in order to improve their handwriting, therefore, shows promise. Further types of feedback such as thermal or guided nib control can also be considered.

Intensity of Feedback: Subtle or Disruptive Cues A further consideration is the degree of subtlety of the provided feedback. For example, the feedback could be so subtle that it can easily be ignored, or more obvious, creating an urge to react upon it immediately. Some types of feedback may be more disruptive by nature (e.g., audio feedback), while others allow for larger ranges of subtlety. The intensity of feedback provided may change with timing and type of feedback.

Additionally, we have to consider that certain types of feedback may be detrimental to the writing process because they may add too much complexity to the activity itself, specifically when considering that children are our target group. It is therefore necessary to consider the spectrum of the feedback level that is provided to the user. This may mean that some feedback is so subtle it is barely perceptible by the writer. The level of perceptibility can continue up a scale to where it is disruptive to the person's work. In an extreme case (which may not be desirable), for instance, the ink will vanish if the child does not form a letter correctly, forcing them to write and rewrite the letter until they can produce it perfectly! Clearly, this type of guidance could be very frustrating if not controllable by the learner.

If a digital pen can provide meaningful feedback, guidance and encouragement to the user, then it stands to reason that, digital pens can potentially make the process of learning to write easier. However, considering the delivery of feedback in terms of form and intensity leaves a large scope for exploration. We are currently planning a series of future design explorations and studies where we will design prototypes and evaluate them in classroom environments. The challenge will be to assess when a certain design can be considered successful, since handwriting learning is a long-term process.

2.5   Conclusion

In this work we have explored the potential of existing digital pen technology for handwriting with children. We conducted a study, where we asked children to complete short writing exercises using different digital pen technologies. Our findings show that the different characteristics of different digital pen technologies influence handwriting quality and children's writing experience. We also show that children are willing to adopt digital pen technology and that it may be suitable for use to support the handwriting learning process. Based on these initial findings, we discuss the design space that digital pen technology opens up regarding augmenting the handwriting process in the classroom. In particular, we consider what, when, and how digital pen technology can integrate feedback on the handwriting process.

Acknowledgements We thank all our study participants and the teachers who helped us analyse our study data. We would also like to thank the primary school involved in our study for their generous support of our study. Last but not least we thank our colleagues of the SACHI group for their invaluable support and feedback on this work. This work is funded by EPSRC and SICSA.

References

1. Bara, F., & Gentaz, E. (2011). Haptics in teaching handwriting: The role of perceptual and visuo-motor skills. *Human Movement Science, 30*(4), 745–759.
2. Bara, F., Gentaz, E., Colé, P., & Sprenger-Charolles, L. (2004). The visuo-haptic and haptic exploration of letters increases the Kindergarten-children's understanding of the alphabetic principle. *Cognitive Development, 19*(3), 433–449.
3. Bavelier, D., Green, C. S., & Dye, M. W. G. (2010). Children, wired: For better and for worse. *Neuron, 67*(5), 692–701.
4. Bonnard, Q., Jermann, P., & Legge, A. (2012). Tangible paper interfaces: Interpreting pupils' manipulations. In *proceedings of ITS*, pp. 133–142.
5. Cornhill, H., & Case-Smith, J. (1996). Factors that relate to good and poor handwriting. *The American Journal of Occupational Therapy, 50*(9), 732–739.
6. Eid, M., Mansour, M., El Saddik, A. H., & Iglesias, R. (2007). A haptic multimedia handwriting learning system. In *proceedings of Emme*, pp. 103–108.
7. Falk, T. H., Tam, C., Schellnus, H., & Chau, T. (2011). On the development of a computer-based handwriting assessment tool to objectively quantify handwriting proficiency in children. *Computer Methods and Programs in Biomedicine, 104*(3), 102–111.
8. Geyer, F., Budzinski, J., & Reiterer, H. I. (2012). A hybrid workspace and interactive visualization for paper-based collaborative sketching sessions. In *proceedings of NordiCHI*, NordiCHI '12, ACM (New York, NY, USA, 2012), pp. 331–340.
9. Guan, C. Q., Liu, Y., Chan, D. H. L., Ye, F., & Perfetti, C. A. (2011). Writing strengthens orthography and alphabetic-coding strengthens phonology in learning to read Chinese. *Journal of Educational Psychology, 103*(3), 509–522.
10. Longcamp, M., & Boucard, C. (2006). Remembering the orientation of newly learned characters depends on the associated writing knowledge: A comparison between handwriting and typing. *Human Movement Science, 25*(4–5), 646–656.
11. Longcamp, M., Zerbato-Poudou, M.-T., & Velay, J.-L. (2005). The influence of writing practice on letter recognition in preschool children: A comparison between handwriting and typing. *Acta Psychologica, 119*(1), 67–79.
12. Longcamp, M., Boucard, C., Gilhodes, J.-C., Anton, J.-L., Roth, M., Nazarian, B., & Velay, J.-L. (2008). Learning through hand or typewriting influences visual recognition of new graphic shapes. *Journal of Cognitive Neuroscience, 20*(5), 802–815.
13. Los Angeles Unified School District. Common core technology project. http://cctp-lausd-ca.schoolloop.com/. Accessed 15 Dec 2013.
14. Mangen, A., & Velay, J. (2010). Digitizing literacy: Reflections on the haptics of writing. In M. H. Zadeh (Ed.), *Advances in Haptics*, ISBN: 978-953-307-093-3, InTech, DOI: 10.5772/8710. http://www.intechopen.com/books/advances-in-haptics/digitizing-literacy-reflections-on-the-haptics-of-writing.
15. Overvelde, A., & Hulstijn, W. (2011). Learning new movement patterns: A study on good and poor writers comparing learning conditions emphasizing spatial, timing or abstract characteristics. *Human Movement Science, 30*(4), 731–744.

16. Oviatt, S., Arthur, A., & Cohen, J. (2006). Quiet interfaces that help students think. In *Proceedings of UIST*, pp. 191–200.
17. Palluel-Germain, R. (2007). A visuo-haptic device Telemaque increases Kindergarten children's handwriting acquisition. In *Proceedings of EuroHaptics*, pp. 72–77.
18. Piper, A. M., & Hollan, J. D. (2009). Tabletop displays for small group study: Affordances of paper and digital materials. In *Proceedings of CHI*, pp. 1227–1236.
19. Puranik, C. S., & AlOtaiba, S. (2012). Examining the contribution of handwriting and spelling to written expression in Kindergarten children. *Reading and Writing, 25*(7), 1523–1546.
20. Read, J. C. (2007). Children using digital ink for writing. In *Pen-Based Learning Technologies, 2007*, IEEE, pp. 1–5.
21. Read, J. C., MacFarlane, S. J., & Casey, C. (2002, August). Endurability, engagement and expectations: Measuring children's fun. In *Interaction Design and Children* (Vol. 2, pp. 1–23). Eindhoven: Shaker Publishing.
22. Read, J., MacFarlane, S., & Casey, C. (2004). CobWeb—a handwriting recognition based writing environment for children. In *Proceedings of Writing'04*.
23. Read, J., Horton, M., & Mazzone, E. (2005). The design of digital tools for the primary writing classroom. In P. Kommers & G. Richards (Eds.), *Proceedings of the Conference on Educational Multimedia, Hypermedia and Telecommunications* (pp. 1029–1035). AACE (Montreal, Canada, June 2005).
24. Read, J. C., MacFarlane, S., & Horton, M. (2005). The usability of handwriting recognition for writing in the primary classroom. In S. Fincher, P. Markopoulos, D. Moore, & R. Ruddle (Eds.), *People and Computers XVIII—Design for Life* (pp. 135–150). London: Springer.
25. Rosenblum, S., Weiss, P., & Parush, S. (2003). Product and process evaluation of handwriting difficulties. *Educational Psychology Review, 15*(1), 41–81.
26. Smith, J. L. (2013). Meet your Child's New Teacher: the iPad. The Telegraph: http://www.telegraph.www.telegraph.co.uk/education/10230335/Meet-your-childs-new-teacher-the-iPad.html. 2013. Accessed Sept 2013.
27. Song, H., & Grossman, T. (2009). PenLight: Combining a mobile projector and a digital pen for dynamic visual overlay. In *Proc. of CHI*, pp. 143–152.
28. Song, H., Guimbretiere, F., Grossman, T., & Fitzmaurice, G. (2010). MouseLight : Bimanual interactions on digital paper using a pen and a spatially-aware mobile projector. In *Proc. of CHI*, pp. 2451–2460.
29. Steimle, J. (2012). *Survey of pen-and-paper computing*. In *Pen-and-Paper User Interfaces* (pp. 19–65). Heidelberg: Springer.
30. Wellner, P. (1993). Interacting with paper on the digitalDesk. *Communications of the ACM, 36*(7), 87–96.

Chapter 3
Studying Digital Ink Technologies with Children—Methods and Insights for the Research Community

Janet C. Read and Matthew Horton

Abstract Digital ink as a rich file format has shown promise as a text creation and text input modality. When used with children, who are emerging writers, studies have shown that the text can be recognized with a reasonable degree of accuracy but the possibilities for other uses of the ink, especially for diagnostic purposes has been understudied. This chapter sets out some of the possibilities for digital ink for writing with children and describes a study with children that sought insights from the children as to the possibilities of the media whilst also exploring the possibilities for a new method for the study of free writing text input with children. The chapter presents a set of research challenges for the digital ink community.

3.1 Introduction

Since its inception, digital ink has shown promise as an alternative text input method. The naturalness of pen-based input is often cited as a good reason for its development but this is often contested by those who consider that input at a keyboard is the new modality and is, in fact, replacing the use of pens and paper. The increased availability of tablet devices was considered to be a possible avenue for the promotion of digital ink interfaces—the proliferation of stylus-less tablets has partially depressed this possibility, although there are still good sales for some of the digital ink applications, especially amongst artists and designers. The application, therefore, of digital ink for writing, seems always to be thwarted. One factor that constantly mitigates against digital ink is the accuracy concerns when it is converted into ASCII text. There is always a recognition problem to be overcome, which either requires careful writing or individual training of the software.

Janet C. Read (✉) · M. Horton
University of Central Lancashire, PR1 2HE Preston, UK
e-mail: jcread@uclan.ac.uk

M. Horton
e-mail: mplhorton@uclan.ac.uk

© Springer International Publishing Switzerland 2015   23
T. Hammond et al. (eds.), *The Impact of Pen and Touch Technology on Education*,
Human-Computer Interaction Series, DOI 10.1007/978-3-319-15594-4_3

Rather than becoming a mainstream input method for writing, it is enticing to think what digital ink is good for. Instead of placing it in competition with the QWERTY keyboard, this paper seeks to determine 'what is it good for?'

The work described here is situated in the context of the UK education system which is organized in several key stages, each key stage aligning (approximately) to a Piagetian stage of development and with each child being assessed at the end of each key stage for progress in the agreed common curriculum.

In the curriculum for language and literacy, children in key stages 1 and 2, (ages 5–10) are expected to make specific improvements to their writing, both with regard to composition (story creation) and handwriting. Considerable time and effort is given to the development of writing skills in primary classrooms yet writing has constantly lagged behind reading with respect to the value of interventions and evidence of related improvements.

One difficulty for teachers in developing the children's writing is that all too often the product of the writing is all that can be evaluated. Thus, where a child may have had a great idea for his or her writing, in a storytelling sense, difficulties with the construction and transcription of that writing may lead to a much poorer narrative than the child first intended.

A second concern for teachers is in the instruction of writing where, typically, children go back to work they have already created and add language or rearrange plots. This process is also difficult to track. One solution that is commonly employed is for the children to edit their writing on a computer, typically using word processing software.

When children carry out composition activities (story writing) in the classroom, the general structure is as follows:

- The teacher provides some story ideas
- The teacher provides some key vocabulary
- The teacher highlights which elements of written grammar are being focused on
- The children write their stories
- The children read their stories out to the other children (typically only a few get to do this due to pressure of time)
- The teacher comments on each child's work in a way appropriate to the needs of the individual child.

Given the constraints of the classroom, in particular the shortage of technology and the need for a non-intrusive system, digital ink was considered as an option for a new technology product.

The chapter presents some background literature on the use of digital ink for writing interfaces with children and then presents a scoping study that sought to both answer the question of the 'value' of digital ink whilst also designing a protocol to later study this value.

3.2   Previous Work

Related work is presented in several sections that consider technologies for children's writing, the use of digital ink in this instance and then in relation to the methods used to research digital ink systems with children.

3.2.1   Technology Supporting Children's Writing

Children love to tell stories and they typically have highly imaginative ideas for their own stories. The stories that children create can be narrated orally, one to another, or may be committed to text; a process that generally involves the handwriting of a story using paper and pencil.

Interactive technology has been used to support children's storytelling in a number of ways. Some applications have been developed to assist in the creation of ideas and to encourage narrative; others are more concerned with the structuring of the story. For ideas creation, tangible props are often used, Rosebud [1] and SAGE [2] both used stuffed animals to encourage fantasy story creation whereas PageCraft [3] used a playmate with objects to encourage ideas. Several studies have explored the link between storytelling and programming, notable examples are the work on the Alice Storywriter [4] and the Ghostwriter [5] projects, both of these encourage structure and flow in storytelling by encouraging children to be authors in a world removed from writing narrative.

Less creative, but more structured products have been developed to improve the grammar and language of children's stories. These applications tend to use intelligent tutoring and story listening systems (often with embedded speech recognition) and offer adaptive behaviours to help the child create a 'better' story [6, 7].

One area that has not been well studied is the creation of tools to assist children in the recording of stories. Whilst audio can be used, many children are left having to input their stories to word processors with all the associated traumas, poor text input speed, errors, and shortage of technology.

3.2.2   Digital Ink and Children's Writing

Digital ink is a fully supported file type. It is created when a stylus writes on a supported surface. One variation uses a digital pen on special 'digital' notepaper. The pen has a small camera aligned with the standard ballpoint nib and while writing is created with the ballpoint pen in the usual way, the camera captures stroke information thus allowing a replica of the ink writing to be created which can later be displayed on a computer screen. The camera does not only capture the strokes, it also captures time information so the writing can be replayed showing the order in which each stroke or part stroke was created.

Digital ink supported by pen and paper has always appeared a good option for a classroom as the technology needed is cheap (a pen and paper costs less than 100

USD), non intrusive (the pens look like normal pens and the digital paper is simply held in a standard A5 notebook), and easy to use (the child uses the pen just like he or she would use any other pen) [8, 9].

The digital nature of digital ink allows it to be easily shared. Several studies have used this feature to effect in learning classrooms across many key stages. Additionally, the widespread introduction of whiteboard technology into classrooms has facilitated projection of work; recent technical digital ink sharing solutions include the innovations shown at www.steljes.com.

3.2.3 Difficulties with Digital Ink Interfaces

In the creation of digital ink writing, there have been several studies that have shown that, especially where the medium is paper and pen, children of all ages have little difficulty [8]. It is generally reported that the creation of digital ink with pen and paper is no more difficult than the creation of handwriting.

Problems arise with digital ink when the writing is later 'recognized' and turned into ASCII text. The way writing is created can have a profound impact on the chances of it being accurately recognized. In particular, where letters are formed in unorthodox ways (perhaps starting with the curve rather than the stick for example) recognition rates plummet. Previous work has shown a behaviour, common in children, that has a significant effect on recognition, which is the 'beautifying of text'. This beatification takes one of two common forms; the elongation of ascenders and descenders after the word is completed, and the embellishment of crossing strokes and dots [8].

Thus, where writing is created with the intention of later having it recognized, there is a requirement for the writing to be formed well. In the traditional classroom, children are encouraged to form their letters correctly and make the correct joins in their work, however the teacher cannot easily monitor the letter formation and so children quickly slip into bad habits (habits which, if writing is stored as digital ink, can be replayed and discovered).

When handwriting is used with recognition software, the user of the digital pen may write the correct letters but the system may produce an incorrect representation of their words [10]. These mistakes cannot easily be predicted, although inspection of the writing can often inform as to why a written word was presented back in a certain way. One difficulty arises when the recognition software refers to a dictionary for a 'close' word, at which point, the clues to the mis-recognition that could be gleaned from the character by character recognition can be lost.

Each of these 'behaviours' poses a problem for a recognition tool. Indeed, when this writing is pushed through an untrained recognizer, the resulting text can have several errors. Children seem to be tolerant of errors in recognition—Lalomia [11], suggested that adults needed recognition accuracy in the region of 97 %, but a later study by Read [12] hinted that children would accept lower rates than adults and a 90 % recognition rate might be enough.

3.2.4   *Evaluating Digital Ink*

The accuracy of text input technologies is typically evaluated in experimental studies where 'writers' are either required to copy phrases from a catalogue of phrases, or, from a single phrase [13], [14]. The rationale for this as a method is that it allows the inputted text to be evaluated against the intended text and thus errors can be isolated. When using a phrase set it is assumed that the phrases collectively represent a corpus of usual text. When a single phrase is used it is often chosen to include all the letters of an alphabet. In both cases the idea is that the work can be memorized so that when it is written the writer is not having to attend to the words as well as the text input (writing) task.

A phrase set for use with children in these sorts of evaluations was developed by Kano et al. [15] and was shown to be comparable to the adult version. With this evaluation protocol, accuracy (or error rate) scores are generated by comparing a string of presented text (input) (PT) with a string of transcribed text (output) (TT), [16, 17] and [18]. The two strings are aligned by applying a minimum string distance (MSD) algorithm which enables consistent and realistic results to be generated and each subsequent 'error' in the transcribed text is classified as an insertion (I), a deletion (D) or a substitution (S) [19].

These methods are great when the topic of interest is accuracy and the research is comparing systems. They are less useful for exploratory research where the aim is to see the potential within a non-perfect system. Methods that rely on copying text, as opposed to the composition of text, fail to deal with complex and made up spellings and fail to typically include proper nouns and words that are 'non-standard'.

When the writers of text are children, free composition is easy in digital ink studies but when the recognition process is activated it can be impossible, in some cases, to identify what the intended text was as in many cases the spelling can be quite random. An example is shown in Fig. 3.1 below, which shows the problem when children write freely.

Fig. 3.1 When children write what they like

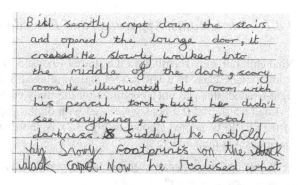

3.3   Extras

Given the difficulties with copied and composed text in terms of research tools, we propose a new method, referred to here as EXTRAS (Experimental protocol for Text entry Research that takes Account of Spellings). Simply, this method has children copying text that is interspersed with images of words and on encountering an image the child is expected to write the associated word.

There are three aspects to this protocol, the first is to locate appropriate text, the second is to identify words in that text that will provide spelling challenges to at least some of the children being evaluated, and the third is to find appropriate images that will be memorable for the children doing the writing.

As the intention is not to 'puzzle' the child, but simply to include words where the spelling cannot be copied, the method for using this protocol was that the passage would be looked at with the children before the text copy activity and the children would collectively 'guess' the images and have their guesses confirmed or corrected before writing began. Uncertainties which would be tested in the study were:

a. would the children be able to write easily with the mixture of images and text
b. would children remember the agreed versions of the images and
c. would the protocol have the desired effect (i.e. facilitate exploratory spellings)

3.4   Research Study

The study described here aimed to:

a. test out the 'EXTRAS' method for carrying out handwriting recognition/digital ink evaluations
b. seek inspiration for the future uses of digital ink for writing with children

3.4.1   Participants, Apparatus, and Procedure

Nine children were recruited to the study (4 boys, 5 Girls). The children were all from a single class in a UK school and were aged 8 and 9 years. They were all right-handed (this was not a condition for the study but was recorded).

Logitech digital I/O pens were used with digital paper. Each child had a copy of the text to be copied (shown in Fig. 3.2). A short survey of the following four questions was prepared.

1. If you had these pens in school, what do you think they would let you do that your own pens don't?
2. Can you imagine what < teacher name > would be able to do if (s)he had your pen with all your writing on it?
3. What else do you think you could do with these pens as well as writing?
4. How do you imagine these pens could help you with spelling and writing?

He found what he was looking for in his inside

It seemed to be a silver
lighter.

He flicked it open, held it up in the air, and clicked it.
The nearest street lamp went out with a little pop. He
clicked it again -- the next lamp flickered into
darkness.

12 times he clicked the Put-Outer, until the only

left on the whole street were two tiny

pinpricks in the distance, which were the 👀 of the
cat watching him.

If anyone looked out of their 🪟 now, even beady-
eyed Mrs Dursley, they wouldn't be able to see

anything that was happening down on the

.

Dumbledore slipped the Put-Outer back inside his
and set off down the street toward number four,
where he sat down on the wall next to the cat.

Fig. 3.2 The text the children copied

The children came to the study two at a time. The study was held in a small room next to the school office. The children had the procedure explained to them, were asked if they were right or left handed, and were then talked through the EXTRAS sheet with the writing on. Together the children identified the images (in a vaguely competitive way) and then, when all the images had been correctly 'labelled', the two children started to write, each copying off his/her own story. This took around 15 min. Once both children had finished, they were shown, together, how the writing could be taken from the pen to the computer and they had the technology explained to them in terms of there being a camera, the paper having little dots to help the camera 'know' what was written and the possibility for the pen to hold all their work were they to have these in the school.

The two children were then separated and each went to a different researcher who asked them the four questions from the short survey. The children answered free form and the researchers noted the answers. The children were then thanked and they returned to their classroom.

3.4.2   Results

All the children were able to complete the text entry (writing) task and had no difficulties. The writing from the children was analysed for spelling errors. These were counted in four ways (Table 3.1);

Table 3.1 Errors and mistakes in the copying activity

CHILD	EI	MI	EC	OW
G1R	1		2	1
G2R	2			1
G3R	1	1	2	3[a]
G4R	2	1	7	1[b]
G5R			1	
B1R	2	2	2	1
B2R	2		3	
B3R	2	1		1
B4R	1	1	1	2[c]

[a]Two of these three omissions were of phrases rather than words, although in each case the remaining words made sense.
[b]The missed word was one of the images.
[c]One of the missed words was one of the images.

a. errors in words that were presented as images (EI)
b. image written as another 'close' word (MI)
c. errors in words that could be copied (EC)
d. omitted word(s). (OW)

The answers from the children, to the four questions, were coded

1. *If you had these pens in school, what do you think they would let you do that your own pens don't?*

The answers here were mostly about the permanence of the pen (save it, can't lose it), portability (take it home) and the technology 'add-ons'—these included the possibility to have the work on the computer, as well as being able to have the pen 'talkback' to you in Spanish. One child remarked that the teacher would be able to see what you had been doing.

2. *Can you imagine what < teacher name > would be able to do if (s)he had your pen with all your writing on it?*

Most of the answers here were about the teacher being able to see the writing (visibility), the permanence was also mentioned here. One child suggested that the pen would make it 'harder' for the teacher—i.e. it would have all sorts of advantages for the child but be more 'boring' for the teacher. This child remarked that the teacher could be forced to watch a 'film' of the writing so it would be slow for them to read and mark the work.

3. *What else do you think you could do with these pens as well as writing?*

Only about half of the children could think of anything else the pens could do. The two answers given were the ability to do drawings and the notion of filming, with one child suggesting you could watch a film of the pen, and another that you could film things.

4. *How do you imagine these pens could help you with spelling and writing?*

Four children answered this question—each mentioned spelling. There was a suggestion that the pen could remember spellings, that you would be able to have the pen spell for you and that the pen somehow just made spelling easier.

3.5 Discussion

From the two studies, the writing and the survey, there are several insights. These are discussed here in two initial sections; one for each aspect. The closing section considers the EXTRAS method as an alternative protocol for studies of digital text input with children.

The writing activity revealed the problems with children copying text in so far as there were still a reasonable number of errors within the written text. Children did not copy all the spellings from the text they were given and also missed words.

Missed words indicate that children often read a chunk of the text and then attempt to write it (in a chunk), and are then either bad at remembering what was to be written, or do not return to the right location in the text to continue. Misspelt words indicate that, for many words, children are not copying them letterwise but are reading the word and then writing it from their own memory of the spelling. Common errors in this activity were missing the 'c' or 'k' in the words that required 'ck', adding extra 'l's in words like 'until', and using the wrong versions of 'where' and 'were'.

The survey revealed that children understood most of the functionalities of the pen and the digital ink. They had clearly 'latched on' to the notion of filming and the use of the camera and had highlighted that there would be possibilities associated with this component of the pen. Use of the pen and the ink for 'learning' was mainly considered from the point of view of spelling—children in the UK often struggle with spelling and at the age of these children (aged 9 and 10) they are learning more complex words that they cannot spell, which causes a major obstacle to the writing process. The novel idea that came from this study was of a rather 'naughty' pen that delivered in one way to the children and a different way to the adults. This was an interesting aspect that deserves further study.

The EXTRAS method was intended to allow a better examination of the aspects associated with copying and spelling. The intention with the design was to create a means by which the problems of copying and the problems of composition were reduced. Copying text is often needed in order to control the text inputted and in order to make comparisons across different input modalities but it lacks realism especially when the task has small phrases that children remember and then write. Adding the images into a lengthy piece of text allowed the investigation of spelling; it didn't allow free composition but is perhaps a half-way method. The children all failed to spell cigarette and this demonstrated that, to some extent, the method worked. The method was limited as only nouns could be shown with images.

The EXTRAS protocol showed some potential to understand the way different children approached the activity. Some children would have been very focussed on copying, others would have perhaps read a little and then written it without looking up. The mistakes made may indicate which of these two approaches were being taken.

Acknowledgments Thanks are noted to the children who participated in this study.

References

1. Glos, J. (1997). *Digital augmentation of keepsake objects: a place for interaction of memory, story, and self, MIT,* Cambridge: MIT.
2. Bers, M., & Cassell, J. (1998). Interactive storytelling systems for children: using technology to explore language and identity. *Journal of Interactive Learning Research, 9,* 183–215.
3. Budd, J., et al. (2007). *PageCraft: Learning in context: A tangible interactive storytelling platform to support early narrative development for young children. IDC2007.* Aalborg: ACM Press.

4. Kelleher, C., Pausch, R., & Kiesler, S. (2007). *Storytelling alice motivates middle school girls to learn computer programming. CHI 2007*. San Jose: ACM Press.
5. Robertson, J., & Good, J. (2005). Story creation in virtual game worlds. *Communications of the ACM, 48,* 61–65.
6. Tartaro, A. (2006). Storytelling with a virtual peer as an intervention for children with autism. *ACM SIGACCESS Accessibility and Computing archive, 84,* 41–44.
7. Halpin, H., Moore, J. D., & Robertson, J. (2004). *Towards automated story analysis using participatory design. SRMC'04*. New York: ACM Press.
8. Read, J. C., & Horton, M. (2004). *The usability of digital tools in the primary classroom. EdMedia2004*. Lugano: AACE.
9. Cattelan, R. G., et al. (2008). Inkteractors: interacting with digital ink. *Proceedings of the 2008 ACM symposium on applied computing*. ACM: Fortaleza, Ceara, Brazil. pp. 1246–1251.
10. Noyes, J. (2001). Talking and writing-how natural in human-machine interaction? *International Journal of Human-Computer Studies, 55*(4), 503–519.
11. LaLomia, M. J. (1994). *User acceptance of handwritten recognition accuracy: in companion proceedings of. CHI '94*. New York: ACM Press.
12. Read, J. C., MacFarlane, S. J., & Casey, C. (2003). *Good enough for what? Acceptance of handwriting recognition errors by child users. IDC 2003*. Preston: ACM Press.
13. MacKenzie, I. S., & Soukoreff, R. W. (2003). *Phrase sets for evaluating text entry techniques. CHI 2003*. Ft. Lauderdale: ACM Press.
14. Butts, L., & Cockburn, A. (2002). *An evaluation of mobile phone text input methods. AUIC2002*. Melbourne: Australian Computer Society.
15. Kano, A., Read, J.C., & Dix, A. (2006). Children's phrase set for text input method evaluations. 4th Nordic Conference on Human-Computer interaction. Oslo, Norway: ACM Press, New York, NY.
16. Frankish, C., Hull, R., & Morgan, P. (1995). *Recognition accuracy and user acceptance of pen interfaces. CHI'958*. Denver: ACM Press/Addison-Wesley Publishing Co.
17. MacKenzie, I. S., & Chang, L. (1999). A performance comparison of two handwriting recognizers. *Interacting with Computers, 11*(3), 283–297.
18. Tappert, C. C., Suen, C. Y., & Wakahara, T. (1990). The state of the art in on-line handwriting recognition. *IEEE Transactions on Pattern Analysis and Machine Intelligence, 12*(8), 787–808.
19. Soukoreff, R. W., & MacKenzie, I. S. (2003). *Metrics for text entry research: An evaluation of MSD and KSPC, and a new unified error metric. CHI2003*. Ft. Lauderdale: ACM Press.

Chapter 4
EasySketch: A Sketch-based Educational Interface to Support Children's Self-regulation and School Readiness

Hong-hoe Kim, Stephanie Valentine, Paul Taele, and Tracy Hammond

Abstract Fine motor skills and executive attentions play a critical role in determining children's self-regulation. Self-regulation contributes to children's school readiness. Fine motor skills and executive attentions can be taught through sketching and writing activities. The growing ubiquity of touch-enabled computing devices can enhance children's sketching ability via sketch-based playful educational applications. From the applications, children can draw sketches and potentially develop their fine motor skills. Unfortunately, those applications do not analyze the maturity of children's fine motor skills in order to help parents and teachers understand the strengths and weaknesses of a child's drawing ability. If an intelligent user interface can determine children's fine motor skills automatically, teachers and parents can assess children's fine motor skill ability and help children to improve via practicing drawings with touch-enabled devices or pencil and paper. The improvements can also extend to the children's self-regulation ability and thus their school readiness. In this paper, we present our sketch-based educational application EasySketch. The application teaches children how to draw digits and characters, classifies the sketcher's level of fine motor skill automatically, and returns feedback corresponding to that result.

H.-h. Kim (✉) · S. Valentine · P. Taele · T. Hammond
Sketch Recognition Lab, Department of Computer Science & Engineering, Texas A&M
University, College Station, TX, USA
e-mail: hhkim@cse.tamu.edu

S. Valentine
e-mail: valentine@cse.tamu.edu

P. Taele
e-mail: ptaele@cse.tamu.edu

T. Hammond
e-mail: hammond@tamu.edu

© Springer International Publishing Switzerland 2015

T. Hammond et al. (eds.), *The Impact of Pen and Touch Technology on Education*,
Human-Computer Interaction Series, DOI 10.1007/978-3-319-15594-4_4

4.1   Problem Statement and Context

Children need self-regulation skills to successfully participate in and learn from everyday school activities [14]. Fine motor control and executive attention skills (i.e., skills needed to complete tasks and goals even in the face of distractions or competing interests [2]) are important in developing children's self-regulation skills. Also, fine motor control and executive attention skills may be important for mastering basic skills required in the classroom such as drawing and writing [12]. Educational psychologists theorize that the maturity of fine motor control and executive attention predict adaptive skills, social communication skills, and study skills [13]. Researchers in the educational psychology field utilize various methods to assess children's fine motor control and executive attention skills. For example, Kochanska et al. developed and validated a battery of assessments for behavioral self-regulation [11, 16]. Several of the assessments focus on fine motor control, requiring children to trace geometric figures such as a star or a circle using a pencil as slowly as possible without going outside the designated lines of the figures. To complete such a task accurately, children must demonstrate fine motor inhibitory control and executive attention (i.e., pay attention and follow the instructions of not tracing outside the lines). From the link between behavioral self-regulation, positive developmental, and academic outcomes, improving children's fine motor skills may have positive influences on learning and academic outcomes. Therefore, assessing the maturity of children's fine motor skills to know their self-regulation skills may be beneficial for teachers and parents for their children's school readiness and academic success.

As touch-based devices become increasingly more commonplace, sketch-based applications have great potential that impact young children's development of fine motor and self-regulation skills. There exist many applications [1, 4] that provide learning materials to children, using such techniques as allowing children to draw shapes via touch—or pen—gestures. From these applications, children can learn from study materials and also develop their fine motor skills in fun ways. For example, the application "Create & Learn" by Fisher-Price (Fig. 4.1) runs on iPad and iPhone for preschoolers. The application shows a shape such as the letter "A", and asks children to draw the letter in upper and lowercase. Using this application, children can practice drawing the letter "A" and also can develop their fine motor skills. The application "Dexteria Jr." by BinaryLabs has a set of hand and finger exercises to develop fine motor skills and handwriting readiness (as shown in Figs. 4.2 and 4.3). As a result, these applications help preschoolers ready for kindergarten.

However, these applications do not provide feedback about the level of fine motor skills from children's sketches, rather they provide only binary feedback of their drawings' correctness (if they provide feedback at all) and hope that children can develop their fine motor skills while using the applications. As a result, because these applications cannot determine the level of fine motor skills automatically, teachers or parents should watch children's drawings and determine the children's fine motor skill abilities manually, which can be time-consuming and error-prone. This motivated us to build an application that determines the maturity of children's fine motor skills

Fig. 4.1 The "Create & Learn" app encourages preschoolers to develop their fine motor skills in a fun and exciting way by tracing shapes [4]

Fig. 4.2 An example of "Dexteria Jr." Children can develop fine motor skills by tracing in the shaded area [1]

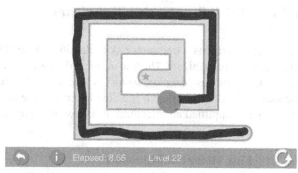

Fig. 4.3 An example of "Dexteria Jr." Children can develop fine motor skills by tracing a letter [1]

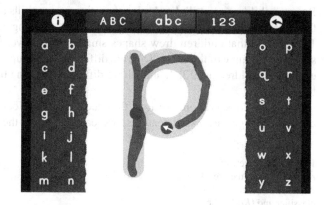

automatically. Teachers and parents can help children to develop their fine motor skills and regularly check the children's fine motor skill development progress using our application.

As a result of the existing limitations of sketch-based playful educational applications, we explore three key research questions in this paper. How can we determine the level of maturity of children's fine motor skills? How can we make this application interesting to children? How can we make feedback that encourages children to improve their drawing skills without frustration?

4.2   Method Employed

We implemented our sketch-based playful educational application EasySketch. The application teaches children how to draw digits and letters and determines children's fine motor skills as "*developmental*" (needs more developmental progress) or "*mature*" (reached reasonable developmental progress). Finally, the application shows the overall accuracy of their shape drawings (did the child draw the shape they were asked?). The following sections will summarize our sketch algorithms, the interface of our application, and a case scenario of our application in action.

4.2.1   Sketch Recognition Techniques

EasySketch contains a fine motor skill classifier (KimCHI) and a shape recognizer (the Valentine recognizer). The fine motor skill classifier determines the drawer's fine motor skill ability as "*developmental*" or "*mature*". The shape recognizer determines the shape of a drawer's sketch (i.e., the letter "A", the number "7", etc.). Figure 4.4 provides an simplified architectural overview of our approach.

4.2.1.1   Fine Motor Skill Classifier

Because children are still developing their fine motor skills and domain knowledge, their drawing behaviors are different from adults' drawing behaviors. Kim et al. [9, 10] reported that children drew shapes smaller and slower than adults. Figure 4.5 shows an example of the letter "D" from different age groups. As we can see from the examples, children ages 3, 4, and 7 have difficulty drawing both straight and curved lines.

From this observation, we hypothesized that if we focus on *how sketches are drawn* using gesture-based features, we can recognize the maturity of children's

Fig. 4.4 Overview of recognizer architecture: (*Left*) KimCHI: Fine motor skill classifier and (*Right*) the Valentine recognizer: Shape recognizer

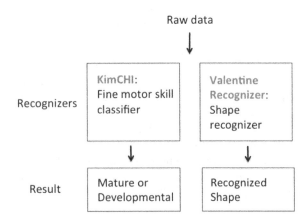

Fig. 4.5 An example of the letter "D" from each age group [10]

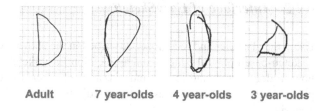

Adult   7 year-olds   4 year-olds   3 year-olds

fine motor skills. Therefore, we used gesture-based approaches which are popular in the field of sketch recognition (e.g. [18, 19]). These approaches include features such as the angles between important points in the sketch, and can determine shapes based on *how sketches are drawn*. More technical details regarding the recognition process can be found in [9, 10]. We began with all of the gesture-based features from [5, 8, 15, 18, 19], performed a dimensionality reduction step to find the most relevant features, and then built our fine motor skill classifier Kim Computer-Human Interaction (KimCHI).

4.2.1.2   Shape Recognizer

Though many sketch-based educational applications for children exist [17, 22], applications cannot recognize children's drawings well because the recognizers are trained on adults' drawings. To investigate this point, we utilized a template-based recognizer (the Valentine recognizer [20, 21]) with adult-drawn shapes as templates.

The Valentine recognizer takes as input two shapes—one template shape (whose shape definition is known) and one user shape (whose shape definition is unknown). The recognizer will output a value between 0 and 1 that reflects the confidence that the two shapes are similar. To calculate this confidence, the recognizer first scales and translates the shapes into a 40×40 bounding window to ensure both shapes are approximately the same size. Then, the recognizer resamples the points in both shapes so each is made up of 40 equidistant points [20, 21]. This resizing and resampling step is especially important, since we have found that adults tend to draw much faster than children, meaning adult sketches would contain fewer points.

After preprocessing, the recognizer considers each point in each shape (80 points total) and records the distance from that point to the closest point in the other shape. From these shortest-distances, we calculate three similarity metrics: the maximum of the distances (called the Hausdorff distance), the average of the distances (a modified Hausdorff distance), and the ratio of points with shortest distances less than 4 pixels over the total number of points (the Tanimoto coefficient). The recognizer normalizes the distances to a value between 0 and 1, and then the three measures are averaged to form the final similarity confidence value. If that confidence value is above our empirically defined threshold of 0.65, the two shapes are deemed similar [20, 21]. Thus, the user's shape could be defined by the template's shape definition. The recognizer labels the user shape with the shape definition of the template with the highest similarity confidence value.

4.2.2 Interface of EasySketch

Using the classifier and recognizer described in the above sections, we implemented a sketch-based playful educational application EasySketch, which teaches children how to draw digits and letters and classifies children's fine motor skills. The application includes sixteen basic shapes (digits 0–9 and letters A–F) as learning materials.

Since our target users are preschoolers, they are apt to lose focus using applications that do not interest them [6]. Druin further extends this stance by stating that children notice "*what is cool, how easy things are to learn, what things look like*" and "*how much multimedia there is in a product*" [3]. In order to address the problem of developing an application that interests children, we primarily considered [10]:

- **Ease of use.** Since the target users are children, the user interface should ideally be capable of being used independently after an initial guided practice with a parent or teacher.
- **Ease of following.** The application includes animated image files, which show how to draw digits and letters. We did not restrict children's interaction by these animated instructions, rather, we provided them in case the child does not know how to draw the shape.
- **Ease of reviewing.** Children can review their drawings by clicking the play button. The application then plays back the children's strokes so that they can compare them to the animated images containing the suggested visual structure.
- **Motivational.** Many children are motivated by using computer technology, especially through novel methods such as sketching. When intrinsically motivated, students can continue to draw and learn without being prompted by a teacher or parent.
- **Straightforward feedback.** Feedback provides the result of the analysis of the children's drawing abilities, with timely and informative feedback proving crucial to their motivation. Therefore, our application includes textual and audio feedback that are specifically catered to children. For example, if our classifier determines that a child's drawing is "*developmental*", then the application shows the text feedback "Yay! You are learning!" while simultaneously playing an audio cue corresponding to that result.

Figure 4.6 explains the interface of our application. The application includes five panels as follows:

- **Question Panel.** Prompts the child with the shape to draw.
- **Instruction Panel.** Displays an animated image of the sample shape and instructions on how to draw that shape.
- **Editing Panel.** Allows the child to edit their drawings, which includes five editing activities: erase, save, go to next question, replay, and check the answer.
- **Feedback Panel.** Displays the text feedback.
- **Sketch Panel.** Allows the child to draw sketches.

Fig. 4.6 EasySketch, a sketching interface for teaching children how to draw digits and letters and displaying their developmental progress [10]

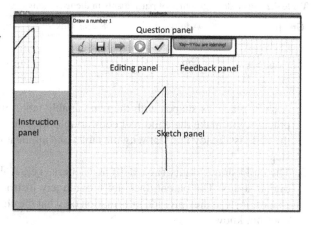

After the child finishes drawing sixteen shapes (i.e., 0–9 and A–F), EasySketch shows a total summary of the child's sketch recognition accuracy score and correctness of each of the sixteen shapes. From this information, parents and teachers can assess what particularly a child has difficulty with when drawing.

4.2.3 Case Scenario

According to Piaget, between infancy and adolescence children move through four stages of cognitive development (Table 4.1). Along with the cognitive development, Piaget also described that sensory and motor experiences are the basis for all intellectual functioning [7]. Therefore, we decided our target user groups to be preschoolers, those who are still developing their fine motor skills and preparing to go to kindergarten (i.e., typically age 5–6 in United States). Our target user group can also include children who are already attending kindergarten, but still have less fine motor skill ability than their peers.

Below, we describe a representative case scenario with our target users [10].

1. A child sits with a pen-capable tablet placed on a table while holding a digital stylus, and the parent sits next to the child.

Table 4.1 Piagets stage of cognitive development [23]

Stage	Age	Characteristic
Sensorimotor	0–2	Begin to make memory
Preoperational	2–7	Gradually develop language, Ability to think symbolically form
Concrete operational	7–11	Able to solve concrete problem in logical fashion
Formal operational	11–adult	Able to solve abstract problem in logical fashion

Table 4.2 Basic demographics of participants in the user study

Group	Adults	7–8 year-olds	3–4 year-olds	Overall
# of volunteers	4	12	8	24
# of sketches	320	227	178	725

2. A child practices shapes with the pen-capable tablet with a digital stylus. This practice will make the child feel comfortable with the device and application. If the child is already familiar with the tablet and application, the child can skip this step.
3. The child draws digits (i.e., 0–9) and letters (i.e., A–F) on the tablet with the digital stylus. The parent does not provide any instruction on how to draw the shapes, instead they provide information on what the child has to draw if the child does not know.
4. Whenever the child draws the shapes and clicks the checkmark button in the application, the application recognizes the child's fine motor skill from feedback provided by the fine motor skill classifier. The application returns output such as, "Yay! You are learning!" if the classifier determines the child's sketching skill as novice level. If the classifier determines the sketching skill as mature level, then the application returns output such as, "You are already a Master!".
5. Finally, the application displays how many times the child drew the shapes correctly for each drawn shape.

4.3 Results and Evaluation

We are planning to test the usability of our novel interface with children. Because we do not have user test data with children yet, we will present and discuss from the previous studies on how well our motor skill classifier and our shape recognizer worked [9, 10].

Our user study group includes 20 children and 4 adults, where the latter were graduate engineering students (Table 4.2). Since children's learning skills differ by their age as described in Table 4.1, we categorized the children into two different groups: preschoolers and grade schoolers. We also conducted the data collection on the adults separately from the children: the adults provided data in a research lab environment, and the children provided data in more familiar environments (e.g., home, church) while accompanied by their parents. In order to ensure that children produced natural sketches in our data collection, we requested that parents not assist their children during sketching.

For the data collection, we provided two different procedures to the participants. For the adult and grade schooler participants, we asked them to draw each digit (i.e., 0 through 9) and letter (i.e., A through F) exactly twice. For the preschoolers, we asked them to draw a reduced testing set of each digit (i.e., 0 through 9) and letter (i.e., A through D) only once. Each participant was allowed to draw each shape naturally, without restriction to stroke order. The participants were also were informed that they could stop drawing at any time, but everyone successfully completed their drawings. Since our data collection involved child participants, we limited the time duration for the children to up to forty-five minutes as suggested by Hanna et al. [6]. All participants were able to complete the data collection within twenty minutes using a Panasonic Toughbook and corresponding digital stylus.

Our hypothesis was that grade schoolers and adults will have better fine motor skill ability than preschoolers. So, we distinguished sketches of preschoolers and more mature sketchers (grade schoolers and adults). Our fine motor skill classifier could determine fine motor skill information with a precision of 0.909, recall of 0.909, and an f-measure of 0.904 with 10-fold cross-validation. The disparity between feature values of each class was statistically significant (p-value ≤ 0.001) for all features included in the recognizer. We also found that curvature-related sketch features can distinguish fine motor skills. From this result, we believe that children who have more mature fine motor skills will draw curves better than children who are still developing fine motor skills [9, 10].

Following that analysis, we ran a study to assess how well our application recognizes children's shape drawings. We compared adults', grade schoolers', and preschoolers' shape drawing recognition accuracy and found that our recognizer determined adults' and grade schoolers' drawings well with 90.0 and 83.75 % accuracy, where the accuracy as the ratio of the correctly recognized drawings of an age group to the total number of drawings of that age group, respectively, but worked poorly on preschoolers' drawings with 34.4 % accuracy (Fig. 4.7). To further understand what shapes they have difficulty drawing and check the correlation with those shapes and fine motor skills, we compared recognition accuracy of each shape. Figure 4.8 shows that both grade schoolers and preschoolers drew straight lines fairly well (e.g. digit "1" and "4"). However, they could not draw curved shapes well (e.g. digit "3" and "5"), which gives further evidence that curvy shape drawing ability will determine fine motor skill ability.

From these two sets of results, we found that grade schoolers drew shapes better than preschoolers and adults draw shapes better than both grade schoolers and preschoolers. Furthermore, both preschoolers and grade schoolers can draw straight lines better than curves, and preschoolers had significant difficulty with drawing curves. We hypothesize that the difference in the level of development of fine motor skill ability influences this result.

4.4   Future Work

Promising results from our emerging technology research work related to our initial intelligent interface that assesses the maturity of fine motor skills encourage us to continue working with children, those who are still developing their fine motor skills. We strongly desire for our interface to have a more child-friendly interface that has larger icons and a more straight-forward interface (Fig. 4.9). After enhancing our interface, we will test our interface with preschoolers and regularly check their fine

Fig. 4.7 The Valentine recognizer [20, 21] determined adults' and grade schoolers' shapes fairly well. However, the recognizer performed poorly on the preschoolers' shapes [10]

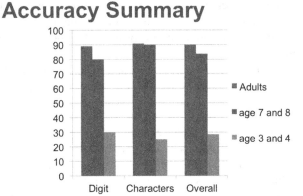

Fig. 4.8 Recognition accuracy between age groups for the full gesture set. *Circled areas* indicate shapes that yielded numerous recognition differences [10]

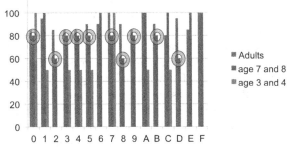

Fig. 4.9 We are planning to make our interface more child-friendly

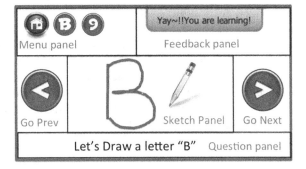

motor skill progress with our interface and determine whether it helps children to prepare for kindergarten.

Acknowledgements We thank all our study participants for their time and input. We thank Dr. Jeff Liew, Dr. Erin McTigue,and the members of the Sketch Recognition Lab for their insight. We thank NSF for funding in part through the REU program as well as inspiration from EEC 1129525 and EXP 1441331.

References

1. BinaryLabs. (2013). Dexteria jr.—Fine motor skill development for toddlers & preschoolers. https://itunes.apple.com/us/app/dexteria-jr.-fine-motor-skill/id624918435?mt=8. Accessed 23 Jan 2014.
2. Diamond, A. (2013). Executive functions. *Annual Review of Psychology, 64,* 135–168.
3. Druin, A., Bederson, B., Boltman, A., Miura, A., Knotts-Callahan, D., & Platt, M. (2008). Children as our technology design partners. *The Design of Children's Technology: How we design and why?*, Morgan Kaufmann Publishers Inc., San Francisco, pp. 51–72.
4. Fisher-Price. (2013). Create & learn. https://itunes.apple.com/us/app/create-learn/id5873982-01?mt=8. Accessed 23 Jan 2014.
5. Fonseca, M. J., Pimentel, C., & Jorge, J. A. (2002). Cali: An online scribble recognizer for calligraphic interfaces. *Sketch Understanding, Papers from the 2002 AAAI Spring Symposium,* pp. 51–58.
6. Hanna, L., Risden, K., & Alexander, K. (1997). Guidelines for usability testing with children. *Interactions, 4*(5), 9–14.
7. Henniger, M. (2010). The importance of motor skills. http://www.education.com/reference/article/importance-motor-skills. Accessed 23 Jan 2014.
8. Hse, H., & Newton, A. R. (2004). Sketched symbol recognition using zernike moments. *Proceedings of the pattern recognition, 17th International Conference on (ICPR'04) volume 1-volume 01*, ICPR '04, IEEE Computer Society, Washington, DC, USA, pp. 367–370.
9. Kim, H. (2012). Analysis of children's sketches to improve recognition accuracy in sketch-based applications. Thesis, Texas A&M University.
10. Kim, H., Taele, P., Valentine, S., McTigue, E., & Hammond, T. (2013). Kimchi: A sketch-based developmental skill classifier to enhance pen-driven educational interfaces for children. *Proceeding SBIM Í3 proceedings of the international symposium on sketch-based interfaces and modeling*, pp. 33–42.
11. Kochanska, G., Murray, K., & Coy, K. (2013). Inhibitory control as a contributor to conscience in childhood: From toddler to early school age. *Child Development, 68,* 263–277.
12. Liew, J., Chen, Q., & Hughes, J. (2010). Child effortful control, teacher–student relationships, and achievement in academically at-risk children: Additive and interactive effects. *Early Childhood Research Quarterly, 25,* 51–64.
13. Liew, J., Johnson, A., Smith, T., & Thoemmes, F. (2011). Parental expressivity, child physiological and behavioral regulation, and child adjustment: Testing a threepath mediation model. *Early Education & Development, 22* (4), 549–573.
14. Liew, J., Johnson, A., Smith, T., & Thoemmes, F. (2012). Effortful control, executive functions, and education: Bringing self-regulatory and social-emotional competencies to the table. *Child Development Perspectives, 6,* 105–111.
15. Long, A. C., Jr., Landay, J. A., Rowe, L. A., & Michiels, J. (2000). Visual similarity of pen gestures. *Proceedings of the SIGCHI conference on human factors in computing systems,* CHI '00, ACM, New York, NY , USA, pp. 360–367.
16. Murray, K., & Kochanska, G. (2002). Effortful control: Factor structure and relation to externalizing and internalizing behaviors. *Journal of Abnormal Child Psychology, 30,* 503–514.
17. Paulson, B., Eoff, B., Wolin, A., Johnston, J., & Hammond, T. (2008). Sketch-based educational games: Drawing kids away from traditional interfaces. *Proceedings of the 7th international conference on interaction design and children*, ACM, pp. 133–136.
18. Paulson, B., Rajan, P., Davalos, R., Osuna, R., & Hammond, T. (2008). What!?! no rubine features?: Using geometric-based features to produce normalized confidence values for sketch recognition. *VL/HCC workshop: Sketch tools for diagramming Herrsching am Ammersee,* pp. 56–63.
19. Rubine, D. (1991). Specifying gestures by example. *Proceeding of the 18th annual conference on Computer graphics and interactive techniques*, SIGGRAPH 91, pp. 329–337.

20. Valentine, S., Field, M., Smith, A., & Hammond, T. (2011). A shape comparison technique for use in sketch-based tutoring systems. *2011 intelligent user interfaces workshop on sketch recognition*.
21. Valentine, S., Vides, F., Lucchese, G., Turner, D., Kim, H., Li, W., Linsey, J., & Hammond, T. (2012). Mechanix: A sketch-based tutoring system for statics courses. *The twenty-fourth conference on innovative applications of artificial intelligence*.
22. Vides, F., Taele, P., Kim, H., Ho, J., & Hammond, T. (2012). Intelligent feedback for kids using sketch recognition. *ACM SIGCHI 2012 Conference on human factors in computing systems workshop on educational interfaces, software, and technology*. ACM.
23. Woolfolk, A. (2010). *Educational psychology: Modular Active Learning Edition, (11th Edition)* Prentice Hall.

Part II
Emerging Technologies—K-12 Learning Systems

Chapter 5
Machine Interpretation of Students' Hand-Drawn Mathematical Representations

Kimberle Koile and Andee Rubin

Abstract The *INK-12: Interactive Ink Inscriptions in K-12* project is investigating the use of a pen- based wireless classroom interaction system in upper elementary math and science classrooms. This chapter reports on the progress made on the machine interpretation of students' drawings created using that system in learning multiplication and division. The problem addressed is that of finding the balance between freehand drawing and structured drawing, e.g., with pre-defined machine-readable icons. The innovation reported is what we call a *stamp*, which enables students to draw an image, then duplicate the image to create a mathematical representation, e.g., four groups of six. The stamp contains a hand-drawn image, but also creates a structured vocabulary that a machine can interpret. The resulting interpretation can be used to sort and group student work in order to help teachers in identifying students who need assistance and in choosing pedagogically interesting examples for class discussion.

5.1 Problem Statement and Context

In the *INK-12: Interactive Ink Inscriptions in K-12* research project, we are continuing our investigation of the impact of a pen-based wireless classroom interaction system on teaching and learning in upper elementary mathematics and science [3]. *Pen-based* interaction enables students to create *inscriptions*, by which we mean handwritten marks, including text, drawings, and scribbles. Inscriptions have meaning and are especially important as visual representations in mathematics and science, where they play a key role in enabling students to articulate their understanding. In elementary math, these inscriptions are often in the form of drawings, which support student creativity and self-expression, engender ownership, and mediate between concrete and abstract [1, 5, 6]. (See [4] for further discussion).

K. Koile (✉)
MIT Center for Educational Computing Initiatives, Cambridge, MA, USA
e-mail: kkoile@mit.edu

A. Rubin
TERC, Cambridge, MA, USA
e-mail: andee_rubin@terc.edu

© Springer International Publishing Switzerland 2015
T. Hammond et al. (eds.), *The Impact of Pen and Touch Technology on Education*,
Human-Computer Interaction Series, DOI 10.1007/978-3-319-15594-4_5

Fig. 5.1 Student's multiplication problem

Wireless communication supports easy and prompt sharing of representations, visual and otherwise, enabling teachers and students to explore alternate problem-solving strategies and ideas. Using our tablet-PC-based technology, which we call Classroom Learning Partner (CLP), students work in an electronic notebook, wirelessly submitting "pages" of their work to the teacher. The teacher can view student work in real time, identifying students who may need help and conducting class discussion based on example work that she can share publicly with the class. This sharing of student work and the resulting conversations about multiple representations and problem-solving strategies are critical to student learning.

How, though, does a teacher choose pedagogically interesting examples for these conversations? And what happens when each student in a class of 25 decides to create several different representations, either to correct perceived mistakes or to suggest alternate strategies? The teacher gets a wealth of examples that could give her insight into her students' thinking, but as we have observed in classrooms, viewing and identifying pedagogically interesting work and gaining insight into what students know—or don't—can be challenging even with a small number of students. What if the student work, however, could be sorted into groups so that the teacher could easily see similarities and differences or responses that illustrate correct reasoning or common misconceptions? One of the goals of our research is to provide the teacher with this kind of information by developing technology that can collect, but also interpret, group, and sort student work. Machine interpretation of handwritten text is possible, but interpretation of freehand drawings is extremely difficult. How could a machine, for example, "understand" that the student work shown in Fig. 5.1 represents eight groups of three? One of the goals of our project is to investigate this question.

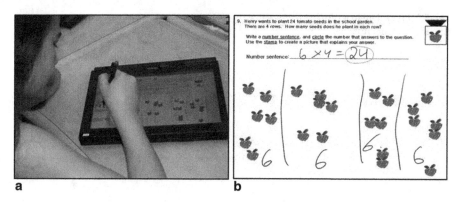

Fig. 5.2 **a** Student using stamps for division. **b** Problem shown at left: How many seeds per row?

5.2 Method Employed

The key idea behind machine interpretation of a drawing is to add enough structure to enable the interpretation, but not so much that a student cannot still draw creatively. In upper elementary mathematics, there are many kinds of computational problems in which students may find it helpful to draw multiple copies of an image, such as in Fig. 5.1. This observation led to the design and development of what we call a *stamp*, which enables students to draw then create identical images, much as a physical stamp does. The stamp creates a structured vocabulary, which a machine then can interpret.

Taking a design research approach [2], we prototyped new software features, trialed the features in classrooms, and used the results to inform redesign, then repeated the process. The classroom setup in the trials is as previously described [3]: Students and teacher each have a tablet computer, and a tablet is connected to a projector. At the start of a lesson, students log in and are automatically connected to a wireless peer-to-peer network. They load the lesson's electronic notebook, which the teacher has created using an authoring system we have implemented. Students work through the lesson—individually, in groups, or as a class—and wirelessly submit their responses, which appear on the teacher's machine and are stored on a local classroom server. The teacher views student work, circulating through the classroom identifying students who need help. She also conducts class discussion focused on student work examples that she has selected and sent wirelessly to the projector to be displayed anonymously.

The mathematics problems discussed in this paper focus on multiplication and division, a topic for which representations with multiple identical images, and hence stamps, are ideal. Shown in Fig. 5.2a, for example, is a student using a stamp to "draw" a representation for a division problem that asks her to explain how many seeds would be in each of four rows if she starts with 24 seeds; her work is shown in Fig. 5.2b.

Fig. 5.3 Popped up icons for
deleting, moving, resizing

Creating Representations   To provide the stamp functionality, we devised a way for
the pen to be used for three distinct functions: to draw an image, make copies of an
image, and operate on the stamp object itself—move, delete, and resize. We separated
the functionality in the following way: In the body of the stamp, the pen draws. The
handle—a black trapezoidal region that resembles a physical stamp handle—is used
for copying: Holding the pen down on the handle turns the region green to indicate
that it has been "grabbed." Then dragging with the pen down causes a copy of the
stamp to follow the path of the pen. Raising the pen in a final location places a copy
of the stamp's image, much as using a physical stamp produces a copy of an image.
Finally, operating on a stamp itself is achieved by means of hovering over a stamp's
handle to pop up operators, as shown in Fig. 5.3. On the copies of the stamp's image,
students can draw with the pen or hover to pop up operators; they also can delete
a copy by turning the pen over, using the button on the top of the pen as if using a
pencil eraser.

Interpreting Representations   In a mathematical representation containing multiple
identical images, the identity and grouping of the images is critical to understanding
the representation. We can see easily in Fig. 5.2b, for example, that the images are
organized into four groups of six and that each image represents one object, namely
a seed. In order for a machine to produce this interpretation, it too needs to know
how the images are grouped and what each image represents—both the syntax and
the semantics of the images.

Consider the examples in Fig. 5.4. In the example on the left, a machine can
identify that two different stamps were used and that the representation includes
two copies of one and four of the other. It cannot tell, however, that one stamp
represents two things (legs) and the other represents four. Similarly, in the example
on the right, the machine can identify four copies of one stamp and three copies of
a second one. In that example, we asked the students to write in a word for what
each stamp represented. The student whose work is shown also wrote the number
of things represented, which is the semantic information the machine needs in order
to interpret the representation correctly as "four groups of four and three groups
of eight," rather than simply "one group of four and one group of three." Note
that supplying a word for what a stamp represents is not sufficient for enabling the

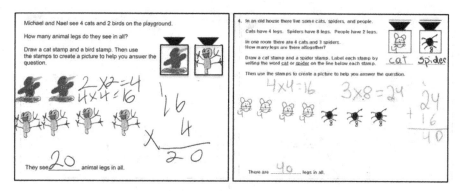

Fig. 5.4 Student multiplication problem representations that use multiple stamps

machine to infer the number of things represented by a stamp. The problem on the right in Fig. 5.4, for example, could be asking about a cat, rather than a cat's four legs. Rather than attempting to identify the stamp's drawing or using information supplied by a teacher, we will ask the student to supply information about what the stamp represents.

Grouping in the Fig. 5.4 examples above is achieved by having each stamp represent a group, e.g., a group of four legs. The examples in Figs. 5.2 and 5.5 illustrate alternate ways in which students have created groups. In each example, a student has drawn an image on a blank stamp and created a representation using copies of that image. In Fig. 5.5c, d the author supplied pre-made stamps—of a person and a box—to help students organize their thinking.

Figures 5.2a, 5.5a, and 5.5b illustrate students using ink to group their stamped images via discrete lines, contiguous lines, and discrete boxes, respectively. In order for the machine to identify the groups, and return an interpretation such as "four groups of six," it must recognize the regions delineated by the ink and the stamped images within those regions. Figure 5.5b also illustrates a benefit of using stamped images: The overlapping ink strokes do not cause a problem for machine interpretation since the strokes are stored in separate stamped images. Figure 5.5c illustrates another method for grouping, namely grouping by image proximity. This example also illustrates a potential problem with this sort of grouping by machine: We can see that the student intended seven groups of four. Some of the stamped images, however, are equally close and could be considered part of more than one group, e.g., the four pencils on the right side might be considered part of a group of five that also included one pencil just to their left. Finally, the example in Fig. 5.5d illustrates grouping with what we call "containers"—stamped images that serve to organize other stamped images. In this example, a student created a stamp for an orange, then used that stamp to fill in the boxes to represent five groups of six. As in previous examples, in order to produce this interpretation, the machine needs to be supplied information about what the stamp represents—a single object in these examples.

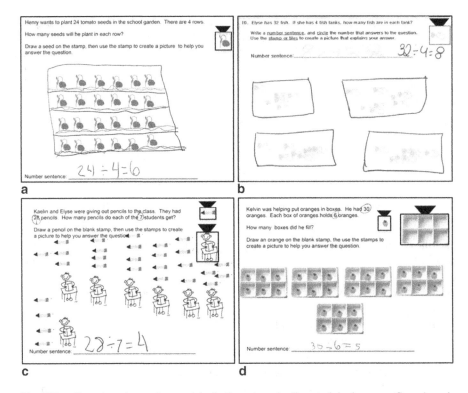

Fig. 5.5 **a** Grouping via contiguous ink. **b** Grouping via discrete ink shapes. **c** Grouping via proximity. **d** Grouping via containers

5.3 Results and Evaluation

5.3.1 Creating Representations

We have tested the stamp functionality so far in two schools, with three teachers, 75 fourth and fifth grade students, over the course of 16 classroom sessions and 68 math problems that employed stamps. A typical classroom session lasted from 50 to 90 min, and we usually worked in the same classroom for three to five days at a time. We experimented with several different stamp designs, e.g., with different locations and shapes of stamp handles and means of creating stamped images. In one classroom session, we asked students to compare the use of the pen and the use of touch for creating copies of a stamp. Most students preferred the pen—they could more accurately position the stamped images by placing the pen on the handle and dragging the pen: The pen did not obscure the stamp as their hand did when using a finger to place an image. In addition, they liked not having to change the grip on the pen, as they did when using a pen for drawing and a finger for dragging the stamp.

Our current stamp design has been used to good effect. Teachers reported that stamps helped students stay engaged and focused on mathematical thinking. They liked that the stamps enabled students to draw, but without getting distracted or perseverating over details of their drawings. Students' multiplication work using stamps has shown clear organization and use of strategies, e.g., repeated addition. One special education teacher noted that the stamps appeared to be just the right amount of structural scaffolding for her students: It was clear how the students were to start (draw on the stamps) and what they needed to do next (create several copies). Indeed, for some of her students, extended practice with stamps appeared to facilitate significant growth in their multiplicative thinking. (See the companion paper [4] for details of a learning study conducted with this teacher and her students.)

5.3.2   Interpreting Representations

Our interpretation routines are able to identify the location and number of particular stamps on a student work page. Given problems with multiple stamps, as in Fig. 5.4, and information about what the stamps represent, e.g., four legs, the routines also can return an interpretation such as "four groups of four and three groups of eight." We are currently testing Microsoft's shape recognizer to see if it can be used to recognize ink lines and shapes that students use to demarcate groups. We are implementing and testing our container routines. Preliminary results indicate that if a stamp has been explicitly tagged as a container by the author, then identifying stamped images that overlay it, and that therefore can be considered part of a group, is fairly straightforward. If each group is understood to contain only one kind of image, then our routines have been able to deduce when a stamp plays the role of a container: If a single stamped image, for example, is overlaid with five images created from a different stamp, the machine can interpret the images as a group of five, without including the deduced container in the group. If, however, groups can contain images that are not all identical, containers must be tagged; the machine cannot deduce the correct grouping, but will return one group that may erroneously include what should be considered a container. We will continue to test and refine our grouping routines using work from classroom trials last spring, as well as new work from upcoming trials.

5.4   Current and Future Work

We have recently started working with a group of 12 students in an after-school program. We noted during our first trip there that several of the students seemed to have trouble hovering over the stamp handle in order to access the stamp operators. We plan to experiment with an alternate design that has a distinct region for accessing stamp operators, leaving the handle for only copying. We will experiment, for example, with students popping up stamp operators by tapping on a bar at either the top or bottom of the main body of the stamp. This design may prove easier for new users.

As mentioned earlier, we are currently evaluating our interpretation routines on representations created by fourth and fifth grade students using stamps for multiplication and division problems. In addition, we are working on an interface for students to use when entering information about stamp semantics, e.g., how many things a stamp represents and whether the stamp serves as a container. The work involves both technical considerations, e.g., whether to use handwriting recognition routines; and curriculum development, e.g., determining the best way to ask students what their stamps represent. Some students, for example, may not understand the distinction between an object and its parts, e.g., one bicycle vs. two wheels; or may not be proficient with "part-whole" terminology.

We are working on clustering routines that will group student work based on interpretation of representations. We also are developing routines that will evaluate student work with respect to teacher-supplied representations. These clustering and evaluation routines will be integrated with the interface that supports viewing and sorting student work so that teachers, for example, can view all student work that exhibits a particular representational strategy.

Acknowledgments This research is funded by NSF DRK-12 collaborative awards DRL-1020152 (Koile), DRL-1019841 (Rubin); many thanks to program officers Michael Haney and Robert Gibbs for their support. The PIs gratefully acknowledge the contributions from the MIT CLP research group: Steve Diles, Claire DeRosa, Eryn Maynard, Jessie Mueller, Kelsey Von Tish; Lily Ko and Judy Storeygard at TERC; Katie Sawrey at Tufts; and David Reider at Education Design, Inc.

References

1. Carruthers, E., & Worthington, M. (2006). *Children's mathematics: Making marks, making meaning.* London: Sage Publications.
2. Design-Based Research Collective. (2003). Design-based research: An emerging paradigm for educational inquiry. *Educational Researcher, 32*(1), 5–8.
3. Koile, K., Reider, D., & Rubin, A. (2010). INK-12: a pen-based wireless classroom interaction system for K-12. In R. Reed & D. Berque (Eds.), *The impact of tablet pcs and pen-based technology on education: Evidence and outcomes.* West Lafayette: Purdue University Press.
4. Koile, K., & Rubin, A. (2013). *Machine interpretation of students' hand-drawn mathematical representations.* In Proceedings of WIPTTE.
5. Smith, S. P. (2003). Representation in school mathematics: Children's representations of problems. In J. Kilpatrick, W. G. Martin, & D. Schifter (Eds.), *A research companion to principles and standards for school mathematics* (pp. 263–274). Reston: National Council of Teachers of Mathematics.
6. Woleck, K. R. (2001). Listen to their pictures: An investigation of children's mathematical drawings. In A. Cuoco (Ed.), *The roles of representation in school mathematics* (pp. 215–227). Reston: National Council of Teachers of Mathematics.

Chapter 6
Supporting Special Needs Students in Drawing Mathematical Representations

Andee Rubin, Judy Storeygard, and Kimberle Koile

Abstract The *INK-12: Interactive Ink Inscriptions in K-12* project, a collaboration between MIT and TERC, has been investigating the use of a pen-based wireless classroom interaction system in upper elementary math and science classes for the past 4 years [3]. This chapter reports on a study that investigated the ways in which a pen-based drawing tool could support 4th and 5th grade special needs students in learning multiplicative reasoning. The drawing tool is what we call a *stamp*, which enables students to draw an image, then duplicate the image to create a mathematical representation, e.g., four groups of six. We worked with a class of eight special needs students for 10 classroom sessions of between 45 minutes and an hour, using a structured sequence of multiplication and division problems. We identified several specific ways in which stamps helped the students gain more proficiency with multiplicative reasoning and, based on pre- and post- assessments, saw evidence of their academic progress.

6.1 Problem Statement and Context

Asking elementary students to draw representations of mathematical situations is a common strategy for helping the students understand the meaning of basic operations. Teachers often suggest that students "draw a picture" to help them figure out what a problem is asking. Mathematics education researchers have studied children's drawings in response to math problems and see such drawings as an important bridge between the specific and concrete objects in the problems and the abstractions that underlie mathematical reasoning. Woleck [5], for example, notes that students often use drawings as mathematical manipulatives, similar to Unifix cubes or counters,

A. Rubin (✉) · J. Storeygard
TERC, Cambridge, MA, USA
e-mail: andee_rubin@terc.edu

J. Storeygard
e-mail: judy_storeygard@terc.edu

K. Koile
MIT Center for Educational Computing Initiatives, Cambridge, MA, USA
e-mail: kkoile@mit.edu

creating a picture of a situation, then counting the objects in the picture. She notes that if students need to draw multiple copies of the same object, they often begin to simplify the drawing, leaving out unnecessary features that might have been important in an artistic context, but become cumbersome in a mathematical context. Woleck also regards students' drawings as "springboards for the talking of mathematics," a way for students to share their mathematical thinking and their further questions.

Fosnot and Dolk [1] examine the role drawing can play in students' learning of multiplication and division. In multiplication, students need to be able to count groups, each of which contains multiple objects. This need requires students to make a major shift in perspective from looking at individual objects to focusing on the group of objects as an individual entity, a process called *unitizing*. Fosnot and Dolk describe drawings, either presented by teachers or created by students, that support this unitizing process by depicting objects grouped "naturally," e.g., people sitting at tables of six, games packed ten to a box, or apples in boxes of six. Similarly, Smith [4] describes how children drew multiple copies of an object (in this case, candy bars) to support their thinking about a division problem.

Drawing many identical images, however, can end up being a tedious distraction from the mathematical focus of a problem, and students often make unintentional errors by drawing one too many or one too few copies. A pen-based system has just the right affordances to simplify the creation of multiple copies of a drawn image. The INK-12 project has been investigating the use of a pen-based classroom interaction system in upper elementary math and science classes for the past four years [2]. As part of this project, we designed and implemented *stamps*, digital structures that could be used to create multiple, identical "stamped" images that we hypothesized would support students' learning of multiplication and division concepts. This paper reports on the use of the INK-12 stamp technology in a special education class of 4th and 5th graders who were learning multiplicative reasoning.

The research reported in this paper is part of a broader research question about ways in which digital tools can enhance students' ability to express their mathematical and scientific understandings through drawing. By providing students with the ability to easily make multiple copies of an image, our software, which we call Classroom Learning Partner (CLP), adds structure to the digital drawings students create, without taking away the creativity and ownership freehand drawing confers. Another advantage of this added structure is that it aids automatic interpretation of student drawings, as described in a companion paper Koile et al. [3].

6.2 Method Employed

The classroom setup in which we investigated this tool is as follows: Students and teacher each had a tablet computer, and a tablet was connected to a projector. At the start of a lesson, students logged in and were automatically connected to a wireless peer-to-peer network. They loaded the lesson's electronic notebook, which had been created using an authoring system we have implemented. Students worked through the lesson and wirelessly submitted their responses to the teacher's machine. Students used the pen to write number sentences, draw on a stamp, and make copies of the drawn image using a "handle" on the stamp (see illustrations below). Details of the design and use of the stamp tool, as well as teachers' viewing of student responses, are described elsewhere [3].

The results reported here are from 10 sessions of between 45 minutes and an hour in a class of eight 4th and 5th grade students with disabilities in a working-class suburb of Boston. Students were assigned to this class based on having IQs below 70 as determined by district and/or state tests. The class included two students who had limited knowledge of English and others who had difficulties with focus and attention. The teacher had been working with the students on their multiplication facts, but did not have the curriculum resources to work on building conceptual understanding of the operations. Accordingly, we designed a series of lessons that focused on the idea of multiplication as an operation on equal groups, using stamps as one way to visualize groups. In creating students' notebooks, we had the option of either including pre-made stamps, as in Figs. 6.1 and 6.2 below, or a blank stamp on which the student would draw, as in Figs. 6.3 through 6.8. In general, we used more pre-made stamps early in the lesson sequence as a way to scaffold students' thinking about groups, and let students draw their own stamps in later lessons.

Pre- and post-assessments with multiplication and division items were administered, both orally and in written form, to all the students in this class. Items included multiplication and division computation, solving story problems, and problems involving visualization, e.g., If there are three tennis balls in one can, how many are there in 4 cans?

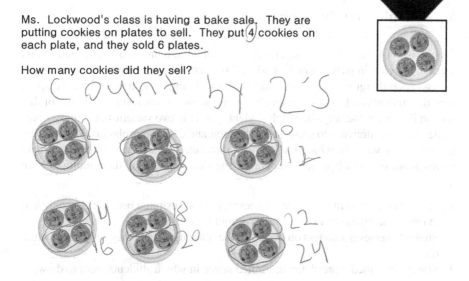

Fig. 6.1 Mickey's work using stamps for 4 × 6

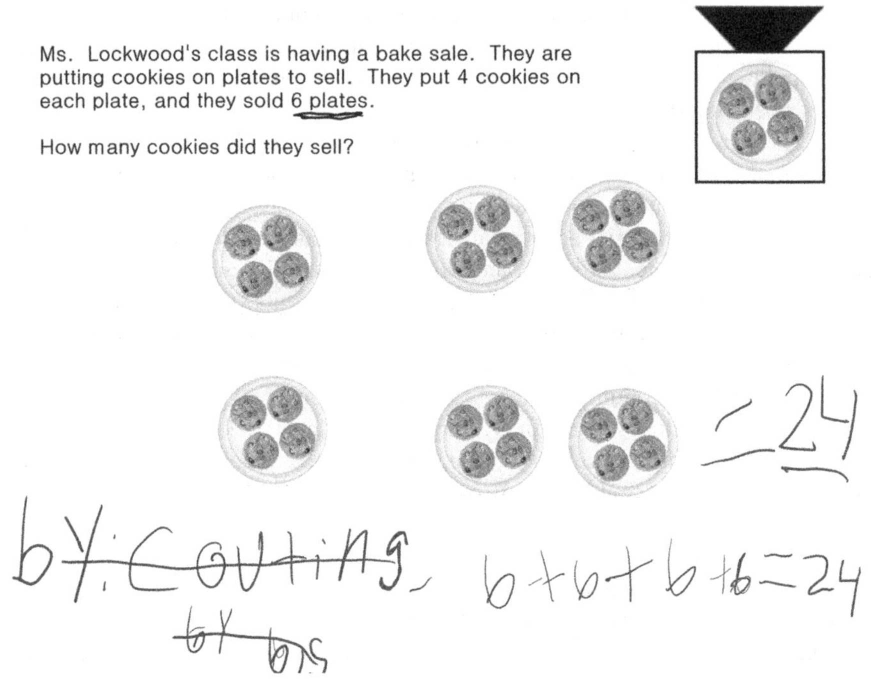

Ms. Lockwood's class is having a bake sale. They are putting cookies on plates to sell. They put 4 cookies on each plate, and they sold 6 plates.

How many cookies did they sell?

= 24

by counting
by ones

6 + 6 + 6 + 6 = 24

Fig. 6.2 Eliza's work using stamps for 4×6

6.3 Results and Evaluation

Comparison of pre- and post- test results, described in more detail at the end of this section, showed improvement in students' understanding of multiplication, which we considered significant considering both the limited amount of time we spent with the students and their relatively low math achievement levels. The bulk of this section illustrates the ways in which students used the two varieties of stamps—pre-made and hand-drawn—to solve multiplication and division problems. We describe the following ways in which the stamps contributed to students' ability to create representations, which in turn supported the development of their multiplicative reasoning.

1. Students with fine motor control issues were less frustrated because they only had to draw one image and could erase without leaving a mess.
2. Students perseverated less on details of the drawings, since they only had to draw once.
3. Stamps provided a pre-defined, limited space in which students were to draw.

Ms. Lockwood's class was looking at the school parking lot. They saw 7 cars.

How many wheels did they see?

Fig. 6.3 Hector's work using a car stamp he drew

4. Students could first create, then move, stamped images, organizing their representations as they went along.
5. Pre-drawn stamps modeled unitizing.
6. Students created unitized drawings on stamps, modeled on pre-made examples.
7. Drawing in a stamp was a clear first step for problem-solving, especially useful for these students, who often struggled with how to begin working on a problem.

In the first lesson, students used a pre-made stamp, with the object in the story already drawn. The first stamps students encountered explicitly modeled unitizing by including the group of objects to be counted on the stamp, as in Figs. 6.1 and 6.2. The group consists of four cookies; it is further made into a single "object" by being on a single plate. Most of the students were easily able to create a well-organized picture of six plates of cookies, then use it to count the total number of cookies. Mickey,[1] whose work in shown in Fig. 6.1, counted by 2's to solve the problem. Other students, such as Eliza, used the stamps and repeated addition to solve the problem, as shown in Fig. 6.2.

After students had some experience with pre-made stamps, problems were introduced in which students drew their own image on the stamp. The students were

---

[1] All student names are pseudonyms.

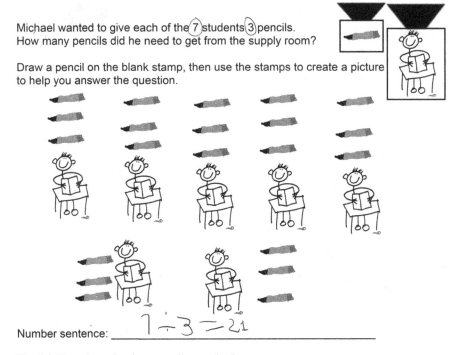

Michael wanted to give each of the ⑦ students ③ pencils.
How many pencils did he need to get from the supply room?

Draw a pencil on the blank stamp, then use the stamps to create a picture
to help you answer the question.

Number sentence: _____ 7 ÷ 3 = 21 _____

Fig. 6.4 Hector's work using a pencil stamp he drew

highly engaged by being able to make their own representations. The teacher reported that in addition to engaging the students, the stamps helped students organize
their representations and kept them from perseverating over details of the drawing.
She also noted that, while these students often had trouble deciding what to do when
presented with a word problem, drawing their own stamp provided a useful first step.
Not only did it give them something specific to do, but the act of drawing the stamp
required them to think about the quantities in the problem in a way that seemed to
prepare them for the next step—that of creating multiple stamped images.

The students with a limited knowledge of English did particularly well when they
were able to draw their own stamps. Hector created a stamp of a car with four wheels,
made several copies of it and used repeated addition to solve a multiplication problem
about wheels, as shown in Fig. 6.3. When he had been asked a similar wheel problem
orally on the pre-test, he had not been able to solve it. Hector also used a combination
of a pre-drawn stamp (the person) and one he drew himself (the pencil), as shown
in Fig. 6.4, to solve a problem in which he had to group objects, rather than having
them automatically "grouped" by virtue of being part of the same object, such as the
car in Fig. 6.3. Although he did not write the number sentence correctly (using the
symbol for division instead of multiplication), he represented the problem correctly
and knew what all of the parts meant.

There are 8 people in the class.
Ms. Lockwood wants to give each person 3 star stickers.

How many stickers does she give out?

Use the stamp to create a picture to help you answer the question.

Ms. Lockwood gives out ___24___ stickers in all.

Fig. 6.5 Alfonso's work with a drawn stamp

Alfonso, another student with limited English proficiency, had more success drawing his own stamps, as opposed to using the pre-made stamps. He had some fine motor control difficulties with the pre-made stamps, which frustrated him, especially if he had to create a large number of stamped images. When he created his own stamp with three stickers on it for the problem, "If each student gets three stickers and there are eight students, how many stickers are there in all?" he was able to represent and solve the problem correctly, as shown in Fig. 6.5. Note that by creating a stamp with three stars on it, Alfonso seems to be showing some awareness of unitizing; he could have created a stamp with a single image on it (and some other students did). By creating a stamp with three stickers on it, he only had to create eight stamped images, rather than the 24 he would have had to create with a stamp of just one sticker. Alfonso also was able to use his drawings to correctly solve some division problems, as shown in Fig. 6.6, even though when we started working with the class, he did not understand what division was and was unable to answer any division questions on the pre-assessment.

For another student, Kordell, exposure to and practice with the stamps appear to have helped him organize his work. In the first example, Fig. 6.7, he seems to have lost track of the number of cars whose wheels he is counting, and he arrives at the wrong answer. In the second example, Fig. 6.8, which occurred after several days of using stamps, he was able to systematically organize the images for a more complex problem and arrive at the correct answer.

Nael wants to play basketball. There are 25 students. Each team has 5 students.

How many teams will there be?

Use the stamp to create a picture of the students. Draw a circle around each team of 5 students.

Number sentence: _____25 ÷ 5 = 5_____

Fig. 6.6 Alfonso's work on a division problem

The pre- and post-assessments suggest that the students from this special needs class made real progress in solving multiplication and division problems through their experience using CLP's stamps. On the post-assessment, they were more confident in their ability to solve problems. They all had a strategy for each problem, even if it was counting by 1's, and were more likely to explain how they got an answer than they had been on the pre-assessment. For example, on the post-assessment:

1. For $20 \div 5$ one student said that she put cubes in her head, indicating that she put 20 in 5 groups of 4.
2. For 4×3, one student said, "I know 3×3 is 9," and then he said, "10, 11, 12."
3. One student solved $10 \div 2$ by remembering that $5 + 5 = 10$ and reasoning that there were 2 groups of 5 in 10.
4. One student said "$36 \div 6$ is 6 because $6 \times 6 = 36$."

As there had been during the class sessions, there was considerable variability in students' ability to connect representations with number sentences on the post-assessment. Although a few students were able to connect representations with number sentences on the post-assessment, others were not. For example, for 7×3, some students drew 7 things and 3 things, as opposed to 7 groups of 3, but had the correct number sentence. Despite this variability, and especially given the difficulties these students often have with mathematics, we believe the affordances of the stamps are worth further exploration with this population, as well as with non special-needs students.

Fig. 6.7 Kordell's incorrect work

Michael and Nael see 4 cats and 2 birds on the playground.

How many animal legs do they see in all?

Draw a cat stamp and a bird stamp. Then use the stamps to create a picture to help you answer the question.

They see _____ animal legs in all.

Fig. 6.8 Kordell's correct work

6.4 Future Work

We are interested in supporting students' growth in mathematical reasoning beyond the single-digit multiplication tables, so we are designing tools that enable students to visualize more complex multiplication problems. One such tool would let students draw and partition arrays. Array-based representations can be used to help students envision how to think about a problem such as 24 × 36 as the sum of four simpler problems: 20 × 30, 20 × 3, 30 × 2, and 4 × 6. We will try out these new tools with non-special-needs students in the coming year. We also will continue working with special needs students on single-digit multiplication and division using stamps.

Acknowledgments This research is funded by NSF DRK-12 collaborative awards DRL-1020152 (Koile), DRL-1019841 (Rubin); many thanks to program officers Michael Haney and Robert Gibbs for their support. The authors gratefully acknowledge the contributions from the MIT CLP research group: Steve Diles, Claire DeRosa, Eryn Maynard, Jessie Mueller, and Kelsey Von Tish; Lily Ko at TERC; Katie Sawrey at Tufts; and David Reider at Education Design, Inc.

References

1. Fosnot, C. T., & Dolk, M. (2001). *Young mathematicians at work: Constructing multiplication and division*. Portsmouth: Heinemann.
2. Koile, K., Reider, D., & Rubin, A. (2010). INK-12: A pen-based wireless classroom interaction system for K-12. In R. Reed & D. Berque (Eds.), *The impact of tablet pcs and pen-based technology on education: Evidence and outcomes*. West Lafayette: Purdue University Press.
3. Rubin, A., Storeygard, J., & Koile, K. (2013). *Supporting special needs students in drawing mathematical representations*. In Proceedings of WIPTTE 2013.
4. Smith, S. P. (2003). Representation in school mathematics: Children's representations of problems. In J. Kilpatrick, W. G. Martin, & D. Schifter (Eds.), *A research companion to principles and standards for school mathematics* (pp. 263–274). Reston: NCTM.
5. Woleck, K. R. (2001). Listen to their pictures: An investigation of children's mathematical drawings. In A. Cuoco (Ed.), *The roles of representation in school mathematics* (pp. 215–227). Reston: National Council of Teachers of Mathematics.

Chapter 7
Animated Mathematical Proofs in Elementary Education

Kimberle Koile and Andee Rubin

Abstract The ability to prepare and present a mathematical argument, or proof, is a key component of the mathematical competence students need to achieve in elementary school. A proof for elementary students is not the highly structured deductive mathematical argument seen in high school algebra classes. Elementary students can, however, create mathematical arguments about equivalence using vocabulary appropriate for their level of understanding. The goal of the *Technology to Support Mathematical Argumentation* project is to develop computational tools with which elementary students can construct and share mathematical arguments. This chapter reports on the development of array manipulation and animation creation tools that are extensions to our tablet-based Classroom Learning Partner (CLP) software. It also describes our experience in a Boston third grade classroom in which students were able to successfully create animations to demonstrate mathematical arguments about equivalence.

7.1 Problem Statement and Context

The ability to prepare and present a mathematical argument, or proof, is a key component of the mathematical competence students need to achieve in elementary school. Developing this skill serves three distinct purposes for elementary math students: It supports and scaffolds their learning of computation, it prepares them for upcoming courses in algebra by introducing them to algebraic reasoning, and it begins the process of teaching them how to formulate and justify claims. Learning how to construct persuasive mathematical arguments can be challenging, however, and many students struggle with the subject matter. We believe that appropriate computational tools can help students develop their ability to fashion convincing proofs. In the NSF-funded *Technology to Support Mathematical Argumentation* project we are collaborating

K. Koile (✉)
MIT Center for Educational Computing Initiatives, Cambridge, MA, USA
e-mail: kkoile@mit.edu

A. Rubin
TERC, Cambridge, MA, USA
e-mail: andee_rubin@terc.edu

© Springer International Publishing Switzerland 2015   67
T. Hammond et al. (eds.), *The Impact of Pen and Touch Technology on Education*,
Human-Computer Interaction Series, DOI 10.1007/978-3-319-15594-4_7

with leading mathematics educators who study early algebraic reasoning in order to design and implement computational tools with which students can construct and share mathematical proofs. These tools are being developed and tested within an existing tablet-based software system called Classroom Learning Partner (CLP), which supports the creation and sharing of student work as a basis for class discussion [1–3]. With CLP, students use the tablet computer's pen to interact with computational tools and to create inscriptions—handwritten sketches, notes, etc.—in an electronic notebook. Students share their work by means of the tablet computers' wireless networking. The teacher views and projects student work, using it to guide classroom discussion about alternate representations and problem-solving strategies.

Key to our development and research is the work of Russell, Schifter, and Bastable [4] and Schifter [5], which explored the idea of representation-based proofs, i.e., proofs about the behavior of arithmetic operations that employ representations of quantities rather than algebraic symbols. Many of the representation-based proofs described by these authors involve an initial representation of a quantity or quantities, a manipulation of that representation, and a final state. The "proof" is contained in the observation that, even though the structure of the representation has changed, the quantity represented in the initial and final state has remained the same. That is, there is a story to the proof. As one of the students in Schifter's work says, "It's like you replay it in your mind, and now it makes sense." [[5], p. 79] One of the affordances of the pen-based tablet technology we are exploiting is the ability to record, save, and replay a series of actions on a representation, thus creating a *dynamic* representation.

We are designing the new computational tools by engaging mathematics educators who have studied how students develop mathematical argumentation skills, but who have little experience using technology to support mathematical thinking. To date, we have designed and implemented tools that allow students to create and communicate mathematical arguments about numbers and operations. We have identified the following design goals for these tools: (1) offer enough flexibility for students to create *novel representations*, (2) support creation of not only *static* representations but also *dynamic representations* that illustrate process as part of the argument, and (3) facilitate recording *explanations,* either oral or written, to accompany the representations. Below we describe the tools we have developed, our experience with them in a third grade classroom, reflections on our design criteria, and plans for next steps.

7.2 Method Employed

7.2.1 Classroom Setup

In a CLP classroom, students and teacher each have a tablet computer, and a tablet is connected to a projector. At the start of a lesson, students log in and are automatically connected to a wireless peer-to-peer network. They load the lesson's electronic notebook, which the teacher has created using an authoring system. Students work

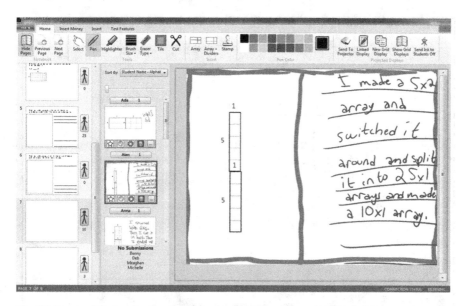

Fig. 7.1 Teacher UI: thumbnails of pages are on the *left*, student submissions for a page are to the *right* and accessed via the person tab for the page, student work is displayed in the main window

through the lesson—individually, in groups, or as a class—and wirelessly submit their responses, which appear on the teacher's machine. The teacher views student work while circulating through the classroom, identifying students who need help. She also conducts class discussion focused on student work examples that she has selected and sent wirelessly to the projector to be displayed anonymously. The teacher's UI is shown in Fig. 7.1. The student's UI is shown in Fig. 7.2. In both versions of the UI, users select commands by tapping on icons on the top command bar with pen or finger. Thumbnails of notebook pages are shown in the panel on the left, which the user can hide from view. In addition, the teacher can view student work for a particular page by tapping on the person tab associated with a page. By tapping on icons below each page of student work, the teacher can tag work so that it can be sorted by those tags. In addition, the teacher can create and project displays showing multiple examples of student work at the same time. The student version has a *Send to Teacher* button for submitting notebook pages to the teacher.

7.2.2   Software Development

To support teaching and learning of mathematical proofs, we added two new features to CLP: a new math tool and an animation tool.

New Math Tool The new *Cut* tool enables students to split CLP's mathematical representations, e.g., an array, into two objects. Such a cutting tool is necessary for

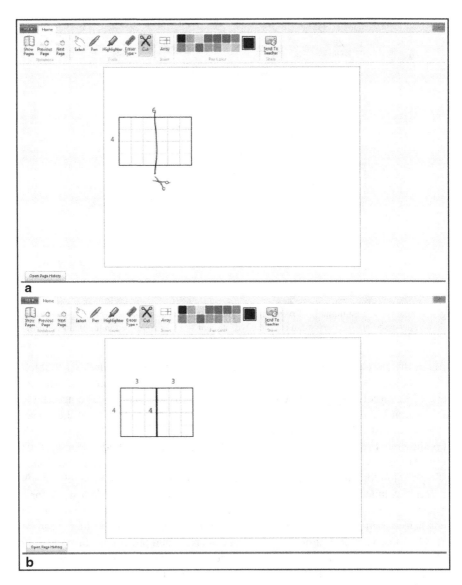

Fig. 7.2 a To cut an array, student taps on the *Cut* tool then draws a line at a cut location. **b** Result of cutting an array is two new arrays, each of which can be moved independently

the kinds of mathematical proofs that are prevalent at the elementary grade level, e.g., showing mathematical equivalencies such as $4 \times 6 = 8 \times 3$. For such a proof, a student could create a 4×6 array, cut it into two 4×3 arrays, then move one of the 4×3 arrays below the other one to show an 8×3 array. Shown in Fig. 7.2a, 7.2b are the beginning steps in such a proof. To use the *Cut* tool, a student taps on

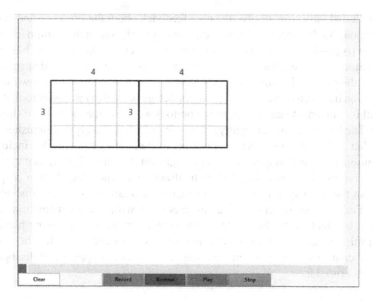

Fig. 7.3 CLP page for creating and playing animations using controls at the bottom of the page

the ✂ icon in the top command bar and uses the tablet pen to draw a continuous stroke across the object where he or she wanted to split it, as shown below. While the line is being drawn, the cursor is a scissors icon.

Animation Tool To enable elementary students to create a dynamic representation that illustrates a mathematical proof, we designed and implemented a simple animation tool. With such a tool, students have an artifact of their work that can be easily replayed and shared with other students and the teacher. Having an animation also avoids a problem with paper-based animation proofs: Having separate representations of the initial and final state of a proof represents the quantity in question twice, rather than having a single representation that is modified.

In order to avoid having animation controls on the command bar, where they would be available on every page and might prove distracting to students, we created a new kind of CLP notebook page with animation controls at the bottom of that page, out of students' way. The new Animation Page with controls is shown in Fig. 7.3.

In designing the animation controls, we wanted to have a UI that was intuitive and easy for students to use, so we patterned our UI after that of a general media player, which students are likely to have seen before. As shown in Fig. 7.3, it has a *Record* button that is used to indicate when actions would begin to be recorded to create an animation. It also has *Rewind*, *Play*, and *Stop* buttons for the animation. To create an animation, a user taps the *Record* button, manipulates objects on the notebook page, then taps *Stop*. Tapping *Rewind* then *Play* replays the animation. Stopping an animation at any point during playback then tapping *Record* records over any animation that follows the stopping point.

We included indicators to give the user feedback about the presence and state of an animation: An *Animation Present* indicator—a small box on the bottom left of the animation page—is white when no animation is present on the page and blue when an animation is present. An *Animation Progress* bar is a yellow bar that spans the bottom of the page, indicating the user's location in the animation, i.e., how much of an animation has been played back. An initial design proved to have buttons that were too small for students to easily tap, so the buttons were enlarged to the size shown in Fig. 7.3. The buttons also are brightly colored in order to be easily distinguished from one another and to help make the UI appealing to elementary students. We included a *Clear* button after observing in an initial design that students often wanted to try out several versions of an animation before finalizing one. The *Clear* button is spaced away from the other control buttons in order to decrease the chance of accidental tapping. Finally, after observing that students often wrote their explanations while recording, we made contiguous text appear on the screen at once during playback. Without this feature, when a teacher replays a student's animation for the class to see, significant time may be spent watching a student's ink appear and disappear if the student erased it.

7.2.3 Classroom Trials

Our classroom observation of students using the new CLP features took place in two Boston-area classrooms—four days in a classroom with 25 third grade students and two days in a classroom with five fourth and fifth grade special needs students. Described here is our experience in the classroom of 25 students.

The classroom was at the Mattahunt School in Boston, MA, an inner-city school with students of predominantly African-American, Latino, and Caribbean backgrounds. We spent four days in this classroom with class durations between 60 and 90 min. The class had participated in the NSF-funded project *Using Routines as an Instructional Tool for Developing Students' Conceptions of Proof*, led by Russell, Schifter and Bastable, so the students were familiar with the process of using representations to prove generalizations about arithmetic operations. On the first day, students spent 15 min getting used to navigating through pages in a CLP notebook, inking, submitting work to the teacher, and creating arrays. They spent the remainder of the class using CLP to create and discuss representations that employed arrays to visualize multiplicative relationships, e.g., showing all the ways to use arrays to represent the number 32. On the second day, students used array creation, cutting, and animation tools to divide large arrays into smaller ones and to discuss the mathematical relationships between the large and small arrays. On the third and fourth days, the students worked on proofs that required them to coordinate use of all the tools they had employed on the previous days. The student work discussed below is from the fourth day.

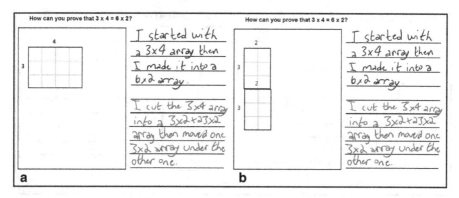

Fig. 7.4 a AL's proof for problem 1: Beginning. **b** Ending

Problem 1: How can you prove that $3 \times 4 = 6 \times 2$? In order to solve this problem, students had to create either a 3×4 array or a 6×2 array, cut it in half and rearrange the halves to create the other array, recording the transition from one shape to the other in an animation. The proof of the equality of the two expressions is inherent in the fact that, while the shape of the array has changed, the representation still contains the same number of units. Several student responses are shown below. AL's response, shown in Fig. 7.4a, 7.4b, is typical. She began with a 3×4 array, cut it into two 3×2 arrays and moved one of the smaller arrays under the other small array to create a 6×2. Her explanation reads, "I started with a 3×4 array, then I made it into a 6×2 array. I cut the 3×4 array into a $3 \times 2 + a\ 3 \times 2$ array, then move one 3×2 array under the other one."

Some students wanted to show the array transformation in both directions, i.e., from 3×4 to 6×2 and from 6×2 to 3×4. One example is DO's work shown in Fig. 7.5a, 7.5b. Before starting her recording, she created a 3×4 array, a 2×6 array and two 3×2 arrays. Her final screen shows just two arrangements: a 6×2 made up of two 3×2 arrays and a 3×4 made up of two 3×2 arrays. Her written explanation—"I did a 3×4 then I move the cube under the other cube now it's a 3×4. Now I made a 6×2. I cut it in the middle and put to a long stick."—is a little hard to follow, partly because of her use of some vocabulary that had been developed in her classroom, e.g. "stick" to mean arrays that are much longer than wide. Her oral explanation in class, however, was quite clear.

While few students actually wrote down a statement that "the quantity had not changed, just the arrangement of the arrays," the teacher led the class discussion in that direction and at least one student included the following in his work, "The arrays are different sizes but have equal numbers." (By "size," he means "shape.")

All but three students were successful in creating animations to prove this equivalence. (One student with behavioral problems did not want to participate; a second student could create animations but did not understand the math; a third student showed that $3 \times 4 = 12 \times 1$, rather than 6×2.) Several students went on to make up their own similar problems, creating animations showing, for example, that $5 \times 2 = 10 \times 1$, or $6 \times 6 = 12 \times 3$.

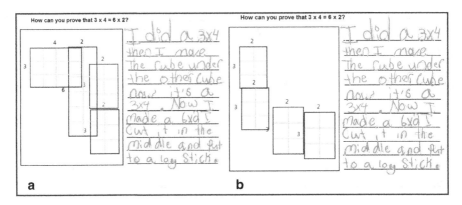

Fig. 7.5 a DO's proof for problem 1: Beginning. **b** Ending

Problem 2: What happens when you subtract 1 from one of the factors in a multiplication problem? Create an animation to show what happens. While this problem was stated as a general question, we decided in consultation with the teacher to pose it about a particular multiplication problem, namely 6 × 4. We planned to move to the more general problem statement if we had time, but we did not.

The key insight we hoped students would have in working on this problem is that subtracting 1 from one of the factors can be modeled by subtracting a row or a column from the array representing the original multiplication problem. Some students initially thought that they could model "subtracting 1 from a factor" by subtracting 1 from the product. In fact, for better or for worse, our software made this impossible, since using the *Cut* tool on an array automatically cut off some number of rows or columns. However, we observed at least one student (JA) trying—unsuccessfully—to cut off a single unit from an array. Her eventual solution to the problem is presented in Fig. 7.6a, 7.6b, which show the beginning and end of the animation she created. She cut off one column from the 6 × 4 array and moved it to the side. Her written explanation offers a window into her struggles: "I notice that if you take away 1 your answer would be 1 more less and if you take away 4 your answer would be 4 more less."

While many of the students created animations similar to JA's, cutting off and moving either a row or a column, several students saw an additional level of complexity in the problem and realized that they could subtract one from *either* factor, ending up with two different array manipulations. ME, for example, created two 6 × 4 arrays, cut a row off one and a column off the other and wrote, "I started with 6 × 4. I cut one of sides of 6 × 4 and made it in to a 5 × 4. When I cut the other one I took the top one and it made 6 × 3." Starting and ending states of his animation are shown in Fig. 7.7a, 7.7b.

Another student added a dramatic flair to his solution by cutting off a row, moving it away from the original array, then deleting it. During the class, he was adamant that we display his work on the projector, so in the last few minutes of class we did—and the disappearance of the cut-off row was greeted with appreciative laughter from the other students and the teacher.

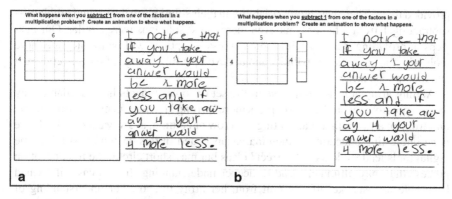

Fig. 7.6 a JA's proof for problem 2: Beginning. **b** Ending

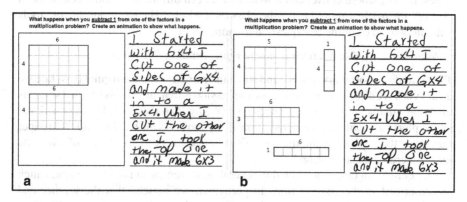

Fig. 7.7 a ME's proof for problem 2: Beginning. **b** Ending

All but four students were able to create animations for this proof. (One again did not want to participate; one forgot to tap *Record*, but was nonetheless successful in cutting and moving arrays to demonstrate the proof; two did not understand the math, though they could create animations.)

7.3 Results and Evaluation

Our reflections are organized around our three design goals: *novel representations, dynamic representations*, and *explanations*.

• Were students able to create *novel representations*?

Students were able to use the tools quite facilely (and enthusiastically), but their solutions had only minimal variability, due to the narrow range of tools that we provided them. There was more variability in their solutions to the second problem—subtracting 1 from a factor—but even there, most solutions were similar. Our next steps in providing students with more expressive options will be to integrate more tools with the animation capability and to develop a fuller range of tools to construct and manipulate arrays.

Adding array construction tools to the set of tools students have available may make it possible for students to express more "wrong" ideas, e.g., cutting off a single unit from an array, rather than cutting off a row or column, as JA wanted to do. There is an interesting educational dilemma encapsulated in this design question: Some digital tools lead students to "correct" ideas but may short circuit the re-conception process that may ultimately lead to deeper understanding. In this case, if JA had been able to just take off one unit from her array to show her understanding of "subtracting 1 from a factor", which she would have been able to do with physical cubes, the classroom conversation would have been different. Would this have been "better" for her learning? Or for the class as a whole? Having more flexible tools will allow us to examine this question in more depth.

• Were students able to create *dynamic representations*?

The animation tools worked well, and students learned to use them quickly. While we do not yet have direct comparisons, our impression is that these tools enabled students to express mathematical equivalences more easily than they could with pencil and paper, physical manipulatives, or static drawing tools. As the teacher said, "On paper they draw the beginning and the end. It's so much easier to see the proof when the kids can create the animation."

Our classroom observations led to several improvements in our UI design, which are described in the next section. In particular, we noticed that the teacher and students would sometimes want to forward/rewind an animation to a specific spot, and sometimes the students lost track of what they were doing with an animation (rewinding, editing, replaying, etc.). In addition, the teacher sometimes wanted to vary the speed at which an animation played back. For more complex animations, the teacher would want to play them back slowly so that students could see exactly what was taking place, but for simpler animations, she wanted to play them back more quickly.

• Did the tools facilitate both written and oral *explanations*?

We had originally hypothesized that adding the ability for students to record an audio explanation to accompany an animation would enhance their ability to explain their thinking, but we did not implement such a feature for two reasons. First, we realized in the design phase that it would be difficult for students to synchronize their verbal explanations with the animation. In general, the animations for the number proofs in our curriculum are brief and last a far shorter time than it takes for a student to describe what is happening in the animation. As described above, the issue of playback speed was a complicating factor, and we decided that integrating audio at this point would be more of a burden than a help to the users. Second, we had discovered in previous experiments with audio explanations that it was quite difficult for an entire class to

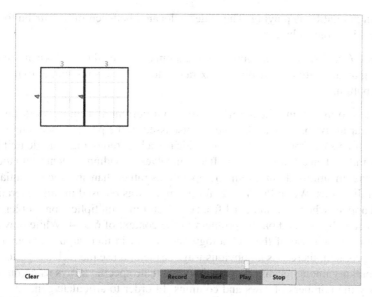

Fig. 7.8 New features: location slider (on *yellow progress bar*) and variable playback speed (*below progress bar*)

hear an explanation played on a student's or teacher's machine. In our trials with the animation tool, the students' written explanations were sufficient to support oral class-wide discussions about their proofs.

There are students, however, who find writing daunting, and they may benefit from an audio recording capability. Such audio recordings may be especially helpful when a teacher will be reviewing work outside of class when students are not available to describe or answer questions about their animations.

7.4 Current and Future Work

The current version of the animation software has three new features, the first two of which are shown in Fig. 7.8.

Location Slider We added a location slider, overlaid on the animation progress bar, that allows a user to play an animation by moving the slider back and forth, until she gets to a specific location. The slider allows a user to forward an animation past uninteresting or repetitious sections.

Variable Playback Speed Initially we attempted to decide on an optimal average speed for animation playback, but it is better to create a user control, implemented as a slider, that allows the teacher and students to change in real time the speed at which an animation is playing. The slider is located between the *Clear* button and the animation control buttons.

Recording Cue We made the border of the animation area flash red when users are recording an animation, providing an extra cue to help users remember to press the *Record* button.

In addition to modifying the animation tool, our current and future work involves making our array tools more flexible, as discussed in the previous section, e.g., to enable students to express more "wrong" ideas such as removing a single unit from an array rather than a row or column. It also involves providing students with tools to prove generalizations about arithmetic operations rather than specific instantiations of generalizations. While Problem 2, for example, was phrased in full generality— "What happens when you subtract 1 from one factor in a multiplication problem?"— students actually worked on the problem in the context of 6×4. While they were successful in their use of the technology and cogent in their arguments about the specific problem, there was no obvious way for them to use the technology to make the general argument because they could only create specific arrays using our tools to specify the numbers of rows and columns. In order to articulate general proofs, elementary students need a representation that achieves what "x" and "y" do in formal algebraic proofs—in this case, a representation that enables students to indicate that the actual numbers of rows and columns do not matter. Using such a representation, students then could state proofs about the structure of numbers and the effect of manipulations on that structure. One such representation can be modeled after what students do when using physical manipulatives such as Unifix cubes to state a proof about numbers: The Boston teacher reported that when her students talk about proofs, they sometimes use their hands to cover part of their representation in order to indicate that it doesn't matter how many cubes are in the "covered" part of the number. We are designing for CLP a similar software "hand" that will allow students to cover parts of an array to distinguish between the critical parts of the structure of a number, i.e., those parts that are important to the proof and those indeterminate parts that are "variable." We plan to observe the use of this new feature in our next classroom trials.

Acknowledgments The authors are listed in alphabetical order. This research is funded by NSF Cyberlearning collaborative awards IIS-1250362 (Rubin), IIS-1250802 (Koile). Many thanks to program officer Janet Kolodner for her support. The PIs gratefully acknowledge the contributions from Tim Mwangi and Steve Diles, members of the MIT CLP research group; and Lily Ko and Judy Storeygard at TERC.

References

1. Koile, K., Reider, D., & Rubin, A. (2010). INK-12: A pen-based wireless classroom interaction system for K-12. In R. Reed & D. Berque (Eds.), *The impact of tablet PCs and pen-based technology on education: Evidence and outcomes* (pp. 93–101). West Lafayette: Purdue University Press.
2. Koile, K., Reider, D., & Rubin, A. (2010). INK-12: a pen-based wireless classroom interaction system for K-12. In R. Reed & D. Berque (Eds.), *The impact of tablet pcs and pen-based technology on education*: Evidence and outcomes. West Lafayette: Purdue University Press.
3. Koile, K., & Rubin, A. (2013). *Machine interpretation of students' hand-drawn mathematical representations*. In Proceedings of WIPTTE.
4. Russell, S. J., Schifter, D., & Bastable, V. (2011). *Connecting arithmetic to algebra: Strategies for building algebraic thinking in the elementary grades*. Portsmouth: Heinemann.
5. Schifter, D. 2009. Representation-based proof in the elementary grades. In D.A. Stylianou, M. L. Blanton, & E. J. Knuth (Eds.), *Teaching and learning proof across the grades: A K-16 perspective* (pp. 71–86). New York: Routledge.

Part III
Emerging Technologies—Tutoring Systems

Chapter 8
LogiSketch: A Free-Sketch Digital Circuit Design and Simulation SystemLogiSketch

**Christine Alvarado, Andy Kearney, Alexa Keizur, Calvin Loncaric,
Miranda Parker, Jessica Peck, Kiley Sobel, and Fiona Tay**

Abstract This paper presents LogiSketch, a system that recognizes hand-drawn digital logic diagrams and then allows students to simulate those diagrams. LogiSketch is one of few complete sketch recognition systems (and the first in its domain) that allows the student to draw freely, without drawing style constraints. LogiSketch employs novel recognition feedback and active support for error correction. Additionally, LogiSketch incorporates behind-the-scenes, user-targeted learning that improves recognition that requires no additional effort from the student. A pilot study reveals that LogiSketch succeeds in engaging students, even though it is not yet a suitable replacement for menu-based tools. Study results also reveal what is most important in the interface and functionality of a sketch recognition tool for education.

8.1 Problem Statement and Context

Even in today's technology-enabled classrooms, drawing remains a central activity for students in design-oriented classes. Drawing allows students to think about their designs and to focus on learning the discipline rather than on learning to use a potentially complex tool.

Of course, drawing on paper does not allow students to see the behavior of their designs, so students usually transfer their designs to a computer tool after drawing them on paper. This two-stage process is cumbersome and does not allow the computer tool to provide assistance to the student as they are initially creating their designs, when they are likely the most confused. On the other hand, having students work

C. Alvarado (✉) · A. Kearney · A. Keizur · C. Loncaric · M. Parker · J. Peck · K. Sobel
Harvey Mudd College, Claremont, CA, USA
e-mail: alvarado@cs.ucsd.edu

C. Alvarado
University of California, San Diego, CA, USA

F. Tay
Pivotal Labs, San Francisco, CA, USA

© Springer International Publishing Switzerland 2015
T. Hammond et al. (eds.), *The Impact of Pen and Touch Technology on Education,*
Human-Computer Interaction Series, DOI 10.1007/978-3-319-15594-4_8

83

directly with point-and-click menu-based tools removes drawing from the learning process, which could have negative consequences, as drawing has been found to be a critical part of the design process [4, 11].

Recently deployed pen-based computer systems in the fields of statics [8, 12] and discrete math [3] have shown learning improvements by integrating drawing and interaction into a single tool. Following in the vein of these tools' successes, we developed LogiSketch, a system that allows students to freely draw and then simulate digital logic circuit diagrams. LogiSketch makes three central contributions to the field of pen-based educational tools. First, it is the first pen-based simulation tool for the domain of digital circuit design. This complex domain presents many new challenges: sketches can be quite large, many of the symbols in the domain are visually similar, and drawing styles vary significantly between users. Second, LogiSketch implements delayed recognition of unconstrained sketches in a complex domain, and provides novel recognition feedback and adaptive error correction. Third, LogiSketch incorporates behind-the-scenes user-targeted learning that improves recognition as a student uses the system.

We deployed LogiSketch in a pilot study in an introductory computer science course at Harvey Mudd College during a lab on digital circuit design. However, we categorize LogiSketch as an emerging technology rather than deployed system because of the scope of the tool and the complexity of the domain. Our pilot study upheld our central premise—that students would find value in being able to freely draw and then simulate their circuits—but it also showed that LogiSketch is not yet a suitable replacement for point-and-click menu-based simulation tools.

8.1.1   Related Work

LogiSketch is one of many sketch-based simulation tools for education targeting a variety of domains. These previous systems are distinct from one another and from LogiSketch not only in their domain of focus, but also in the interaction techniques they employ to aid recognition. Some systems place constraints on the way users must draw, for example requiring the user to draw each shape with an individual stroke, or to pause between symbols [2, 7, 8]. These restrictions are appropriate for some domains but do not match the way students draw digital logic diagrams [1]. Other tools, such as Mechanix [11] and ChemInk [9], allow users to draw more freely, placing few, if any, restrictions on the user. LogiSketch takes a similar approach, but unlike these previous systems, we focus not only on recognition algorithms, but on recognition feedback and error correction mechanisms that are essential in an interactive tool. Finally, there are a growing number of systems to support mathematical equation recognition and exploration [3, 6]. Because of the domain, these systems tend to be fairly different from tools that support two-dimensional drawing and simulation in both their interface and their recognition algorithms.

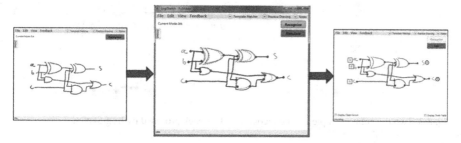

Fig. 8.1 An overview of the LogiSketch interaction process: drawing (*left*), recognizing (*middle*) and simulating (*right*) a circuit

8.2   Method Employed

We had three central goals in the design of LogiSketch. First, we wanted to allow students to sketch freely, just as they would on paper, and then simulate these sketches directly. We found in previous work that students prefer not to be interrupted by recognition feedback while they are designing a circuit because this feedback is distracting [13]. Informally we have also observed that the experience of having a drawing literally come to life can be very engaging for a user. Second, we wanted to provide a seamless pen-based interface to support drawing, error correction, editing and simulation. Third, we wanted to allow the creation of circuits up to the complexity students would see in the 1st month of a circuit design course. After this time, circuits typically become complex enough to require alternate tools such as scripting languages.

Figure 8.1 shows the interaction process with the LogiSketch interface, which runs on a Tablet PC. On the left, the student draws her circuit diagram. When the student is finished drawing, she presses the red "Recognize" button in the upper right corner of the window. LogiSketch then interprets her diagram and gives her recognition feedback, which is shown in the middle pane in Fig. 8.1 and in more detail in Fig. 8.2. When the student is satisfied that the system has recognized her sketch correctly, she presses the green "Simulate" button, which appears underneath the "Recognize" button once the drawing has been recognized as a legal circuit. Once the student begins simulating the circuit (Fig. 8.1 right, and Fig. 8.4), she can interact with the circuit in a variety of ways, as described below.

8.2.1   Recognition Feedback and Error Correction

LogiSketch gives feedback through multiple channels at both the symbol level and the circuit level to help students understand how their drawings have been interpreted and how they can correct recognition errors. The system provides symbol level feedback by coloring the strokes with a unique color for each symbol and by

Fig. 8.2 Two different examples of the recognition feedback provided by LogiSketch

a   b

Fig. 8.3 The edit menus that appear when the user hovers the pen over a shape while nothing is selected (*left*) and while a set of strokes is selected (*right*)

Fig. 8.4 The simulation interface in LogiSketch

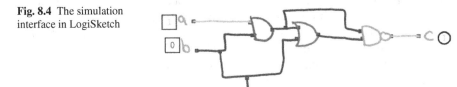

overlaying recognized shape templates on top of the user's strokes in the case of gate recognition (Fig. 8.2, left). These "ghost gates" not only help the user understand what symbol was recognized, but also help the user see when a gate's orientation has been recognized incorrectly, as in Fig. 8.2, left. Additionally, hovering the pen over any recognized object will display the name of the recognized shape (Fig. 8.3, left).

LogiSketch also provides feedback about the recognition of the circuit at a higher level. Wire endpoints are highlighted as either small green circles, meaning that they are connected to another component in the sketch, or red x's, meaning that they are not connected to any other component in the sketch. When LogiSketch detects circuit errors that prevent it from simulating a user's sketch, it highlights these errors and displays a message about a potential way to fix the errors (Fig. 8.2, right). Finally, LogiSketch provides wire *mesh highlighting*: when the user hovers her pen over either a wire or a gate, LogiSketch highlights the wires and gates that are directly connected to that component by thickening the strokes that comprise these objects (e.g., Fig. 8.2 (right) where the wire and AND-gate are thickened as the user hovers over the wire).

LogiSketch supports efficient error correction both by providing a suite of pen-based interaction mechanisms for correcting errors as well as by leveraging the user's input to perform additional corrections automatically. As in previous systems (e.g., [12]), our modeless editing interface comprises a ring of buttons that appears when the user hovers her pen over the tablet screen for a few seconds (Fig. 8.3). If the user is not intending to edit, she can ignore these buttons and continue to draw. If she clicks on one of the buttons, she enters a temporary editing mode where she can perform the selected action with the next stroke and then she automatically returns to drawing mode. These hover menus are context sensitive, depending on which shape the user is hovering over and which strokes (if any) are highlighted.

To help the user efficiently correct recognition errors, the system performs eager re-recognition in response to the user's explicit input. For example, if the system has misrecognized both a gate and the wire connected to that gate, and the user corrects the recognition of the gate, the system (usually) will automatically correct the recognition of the wire using the new context supplied by the correct interpretation of the gate. Additionally, to correct recognition errors, often it is enough for a user simply to indicate which strokes are supposed to belong to the same symbol using the "Group" menu option shown in Fig. 8.3 (right). Once the strokes are correctly grouped, LogiSketch is usually able to determine the correct interpretation for the symbol. Simply clicking "Group" is much faster than selecting the correct interpretation from a list.

LogiSketch also allows users to correct errors by directly manipulating feedback objects in the sketch. The user can drag the red "x"s that appear at the ends of unconnected wires to a shape in the sketch to create the connection between the wire and that shape. The user can also directly rotate the ghost gates to indicate the proper orientation of a symbol.

8.2.2 Simulating Circuits

Once a circuit is recognized correctly, a user can interact with it in a number of ways. When she presses "Simulate", values appear next to the inputs and outputs of the circuit (Fig. 8.4). She can toggle input values by clicking on them with the pen, and see the output values change. LogiSketch also displays data flowing through the circuit by coloring wires carrying a 1 with light blue and wires carrying a 0 with dark blue. The user can also open the truth table that corresponds to the circuit. Highlighting a row in the truth table shows the corresponding data in simulation.

8.2.3 Personalized Recognition

LogiSketch uses a multi-stage recognition process that first groups strokes into individual shapes and then recognizes those shapes as individual symbols. Finally, recognized symbols are linked together into a complete circuit diagram. As part of the initial grouping process, each stroke group is categorized as a wire, text, or a gate (details can be found in [10]). Wire strokes are simply passed on to the circuit recognition algorithm. Text strokes are recognized using the Microsoft Ink Analyzer.

For gate recognition, we needed an algorithm that allows the user to understand the underlying recognition model and that is easy to adapt to a particular user's style using few examples. To meet these goals, we use the image-based nearest-neighbor classifier described in [5]. In other words, we compare each user-drawn symbol visually to a set of pre-populated examples and choose the label of the example that looks the most similar to what the user drew. We initially train (populate) the system with five relatively clean examples from each type of gate, but we add examples as the user draws, as described below.

We expose the recognition model to the user in the hope that understanding the underlying model will make users less frustrated when they encounter recognition errors and better able to subtly adapt their drawing style to reduce errors. We expose the model in two ways. First, the ghost-gates are created by drawing the gate in a way that matches the templates that the system is initially trained on. Second, we provide an interface that allows users to hover over a shape and see the template that it was matched to during the recognition process.

LogiSketch also adapts to individual users' styles without requiring users to explicitly train the recognizer. When the user re-labels a gate, the recognizer adapts by adding the drawing to its database of templates. To prune the database of templates, we keep track of how often each template in the database was matched to the user's strokes to yield both correct and incorrect recognition results. We remove the templates that are least likely to yield correct recognition.

8.3   Results and Evaluation

We deployed LogiSketch in an introductory computer science class at Harvey Mudd College during the lab on circuit design. During this lab students use the Logisim—a drag and drop circuit simulation tool—to design and implement circuits of increasing complexity, starting with a simple XOR circuit up to a ripple carry adder. 21 volunteers chose to use LogiSketch instead of Logisim to complete their lab and then completed a short survey about their experience.

Our results showed promise for our tool. 73 % of participants stated that they enjoyed using LogiSketch either "somewhat" or "quite a bit." Only 5.6 % said they did not enjoy using it at all, despite LogiSketch's limitations in the context of this lab, described below. When asked what one thing they enjoyed most about LogiSketch, almost half of the students cited the intuitiveness or ease of sketching, and about a fourth of the students reported that using the interface was fun.

On the other hand, our study also revealed that LogiSketch is not yet ready to replace menu-based tools. While most students (73 %) successfully completed the XOR circuit, only 33 % were able to complete the ripple-carry adder.

Our study revealed two central limitations to LogiSketch that must be addressed. First, the (perceived) recognition rate is simply too low to be practical. Only 29 % of users reported that LogiSketch correctly interpreted their sketch most of the time (90–100 %). 56 % of users felt LogiSketch understood their sketch only about half the time or less. While most users (84 %) felt it was relatively easy to understand the recognition feedback LogiSketch provided, over half (55 %) of users felt it was at least somewhat difficult to correct recognition errors. Many users (56 %) felt that LogiSketch's recognition improved its recognition as they used it, but given the low starting point, this improvement was not enough to be useful. The second main problem users had with LogiSketch is that their drawings would become too messy as their circuits got larger. While it's nice to allow users to sketch freely and to simulate these sketches directly, we must better leverage the computer's ability to help organize the user's own strokes as she draws.

8.4 Future Work

Our pilot study showed the promise of LogiSketch, and we are actively working to improve both the system's recognition and its interface, particularly for large circuits. One of the central challenges to recognition is that digital logic symbols all look visually very similar. We are looking into algorithms that could pinpoint salient features in the shape (e.g., the curved back of an OR gate vs. an AND gate) to and weight these features more prominently in the recognition process. On the interface side, we are exploring methods for organizing the user's strokes while still leaving them "rough" so that the user still has the experience of their drawing coming to life.

We plan to assess LogiSketch's impact on students' learning once LogiSketch's ease of use approaches that of Logisim. In addition, we suspect based on comments from our pilot study that the fun that students have with LogiSketch might make the learning process more enjoyable.

8.5 Additional Resources

For videos and downloads see https://sites.google.com/site/logisketchucsd/home

Acknowledgements   This work is supported by NSF grant number 0546809.

References

1. Alvarado, C., & Lazzareschi, M. (2007). Properties of real world digital logic diagrams. In Proceedings of 1st International Workshop on Pen-based Learning Technologies.
2. Buchanan, S., Ochs, B., & LaViola, J. (2012). CSTutor: A pen-based tutor for data structure visualization. Proceedings of the 43rd Technical Symposium on Computer Science Education (SIGCSE 2012), pp. 565–570.

3. Cossairt, T. & LaViola J. (2012). SetPad: A sketch-based tool for exploring discrete math set problems. Proceedings of the Ninth Eurographics/ACM Symposium on Sketch-Based Interfaces and Modeling (SBIM 12), pp. 47–56.

4. Do, E., & Gross, M. D. (1996). Drawing as a means to design reasoning. In Proceedings of Artificial Intelligence in Design '96 Workshop on Visual Representation, Reasoning and Interaction in Design, Palo Alto, CA.

5. Kara, L. B., & Stahovich, T. F. (2005). An image-based, trainable symbol recognizer for hand-drawn sketches. *Computers & Graphics, 29*(4), 501–517.

6. Labahn, G., Lank, E., MacLean, S., Marzouk, M., & Tausky, D. (2008). MathBrush: A system for doing math on pen-based devices. In Proceedings of the Eighth IAPR International Workshop on Document Analysis Systems, Washington, DC, USA, IEEE Computer Society.

7. LaViola, J., & Zeleznik, R. (2004). MathPad2: A system for the creation and exploration of mathematical sketches. *ACM Trans. on Graphics (Proc. SIGGRAPH), 23*(3), 432–440.

8. Lee, W., de Silva, R., Peterson, E. J., Calfee, R. C., & Stahovich, T. F. (2008). Newton's pen: A pen-based tutoring system for statics. *Computers & Graphics, 32*(5), 511–524.

9. Ouyang, T. Y., & Davis, R. (2011). ChemInk: A Natural Real-Time Recognition System For Chemical Drawings International Conference On Intelligent User Interfaces, IUI.

10. Peterson, E., Stahovich, T. F., Doi, E., & Alvarado, C. (2010). Grouping strokes into shapes in hand-drawn diagrams. In Proceedings of the 24th AAAI Conference on Artificial Intelligence.

11. Ullman, D. G., Wood, S., & Craig, D. (1990). The importance of drawing in the mechanical design process. *Computer & Graphics 14*(2), 263–274.

12. Valentine, S., Vides, F., Lucchese, G., Turner, D., Kim, H., Li, W., Linsey, J., & Hammond, T. (2012). Mechanix: A sketch-based tutoring system for statics courses. In Proceedings of Innovative Applications of Artificial Intelligence (IAAI 12). Toronto, Canada.

13. Wais, P., Wolin, A. & Alvarado, C. (2007). Designing a sketch recognition front-end: User perception of interface elements. In Proceedings of Eurographics Workshop on Sketch-Based Interfaces and Modeling (SBIM). Riverside, CA.

Chapter 9
Mechanix: A Sketch-Based Tutoring System that Automatically Corrects Hand-Sketched Statics Homework

Stephanie Valentine, Raniero Lara-Garduno, Julie Linsey, and Tracy Hammond

Abstract With the rise in classroom populations—in both physical classrooms and online learning environments such as massively open online courses—instructors are struggling to provide relevant and personalized feedback on student work. As a result, many instructors choose to structure their homework assignments and assessments via multiple-choice questions or other more automatable techniques, rather than assign complete problems and diagrams. In this work, we aim to provide a new solution to the instructors of introductory engineering courses. We leveraged the power of sketch-recognition and artificial intelligence to create Mechanix, a sketch-based system that tutors students through drawing and solving free-body diagrams. Mechanix can support problems that have only a single answer, as well as questions for which many answers might apply (i.e. *design this* vs. *solve this*).

Over the last 3 years, besides deploying Mechanix in multiple classrooms at three different universities, we have presented the system to over 150 high school and university teachers, where they themselves stepped through the problems as a student would. This paper summarizes the system that was tested by multiple educators during the 2012 ASEE Workshop, the 2014 TAMU Teacher's Summit, and the You-Try-It Strand during WIPTTE 2014. We found that even physics teachers could use a reminder of the concepts, and by changing our first problem set to be a tutorial of the concepts, the teachers were much happier with the software and able to solve the problems much more quickly.

S. Valentine (✉) · R. Lara-Garduno · T. Hammond
Sketch Recognition Lab, Department of Computer Science & Engineering,
Texas A&M University, College Station, TX, USA
e-mail: valentine@tamu.edu

R. Lara-Garduno
e-mail: raniero@tamu.edu

T. Hammond
e-mail: hammond@tamu.edu

J. Linsey
Georgia Institute of Technology, Atlanta, GA, USA
e-mail: julie.linsey@me.gatech.edu

© Springer International Publishing Switzerland 2015
T. Hammond et al. (eds.), *The Impact of Pen and Touch Technology on Education*,
Human-Computer Interaction Series, DOI 10.1007/978-3-319-15594-4_9

9.1   Introduction

As the number of students enrolled in large universities steadily grows, underclassman class sizes are likewise growing. Introductory classes in engineering, calculus, logic, and many more subjects can contain upwards of 200, even 300 students in a single lecture. Instructors of large classes struggle to assign and provide essential feedback on hand-written homework assignments, so they instead rely on multiple choice or otherwise limited-response assessments. These assignments are easier to grade and require less-detailed feedback. While these options do reduce grading time, hand-drawn diagrams and homework assignments have been shown to significantly improve learning spatial reasoning skills [5], which are essential for students' future careers as mechanical engineers, architects, etc.

Therein lies the problem we aim to solve through this work: *How can instructors assign pedagogically valuable hand-drawn assessments and provide timely and constructive feedback, while still respecting the time constraints of professors in such large classrooms?*

We believe this problem affords sketch recognition and pen-based computing as a solution. We present Mechanix, a sketch-based homework system intended for students enrolled in statics courses (which are generally required in the freshman year of engineering and physics curriculums). In statics courses, students learn how to calculate forces exerted on structures, and particularly the forces at play on trusses. Trusses are used in the construction of nearly every structure, like bridges, roofs, furniture, etc. Mechanix allows students to draw trusses and other free-body diagrams directly into the software application, and will tutor students through the process of solving for reaction forces and other values. Mechanix can provide feedback on statically determinate trusses that can be analyzed using method of joints analysis. Mechanix can grade and provide feedback to students in real time, thus allowing students to quickly learn from (and remedy) their mistakes.

9.1.1   Related Work

There exist multiple computer systems designed for tutoring and homework grading beyond traditional multiple-choice implementations. Widely used systems are mostly commercial software such as McGraw Hill's Connect Engineering [7], which is a web-based system that provides students with partially completed solutions and asks them to fill the remaining components. Like Mechanix, Connect Engineering provides step-by-step instructions and some degree of contextualized feedback, but does not allow students to sketch their solution from scratch and, more importantly, does not allow instructors to create additional problems using only sketching. Other systems that provide partial solutions include WinTruss [2], a stand-alone computer application, and Bridge Architect, a mobile phone application. They too share the same drawbacks from Connect Engineering with regards to restrictions on student and instructor input.

Other systems improve on these shortcomings, such as the Andes physics tutoring system [12] and the Free Body Diagram Assistant [8] that allows a student to complete diagrams without relying on partially completed solutions by choosing components from a palette and dragging them into the answer space. InTEL [9] is a 2D or 3D physics-based tutoring system where the student is shown a completed diagram or 3-dimensional model and he or she is tasked with correctly labeling the resulting forces. These solutions, however, do not support pen sketching, which is a more universal and pedagogically effective method of sketch creation. Mechanix's full support of beginning-to-end sketching is more reflective of paper diagram creation and helps students better prepare for written examinations.

Sketch Worksheets [14] and Newton's Pen [6] support beginning-to-end freeform sketching, which more closely aligns with Mechanix's educational and interface goals. Sketch Worksheets [14] does not use sketch recognition, rather it applies spatial analysis, generating data on "facts", through which the instructor then chooses as the most important components of that problem's answer. However, creating new problems using this system requires extensive knowledge of Sketch Worksheets' internal language of these spatially-analyzed "facts". Newton's Pen [6] supports sketching with no requirement on "fact" generation, but the system is restricted to the proprietary pen and accompanying FLY pentop computer limitations. Additionally, the system requires that students draw the correct sketch in an exact order, which restricts students and is unrealistic of the paper-and-pen drawing experience.

9.2   Mechanix: System Overview

As described above, Mechanix is a sketch-based tutoring system intended to facilitate learning, assessment, and feedback for students in introductory engineering courses. We designed Mechanix with the express intention of making the interface as similar to pencil and paper as possible, thus minimizing the learning curve required to learn new software. We wanted the student's focus to be on learning engineering concepts, rather than learning the intricacies of software with elaborate menus.

When using Mechanix, a student can draw his or her diagram directly into the program using a tablet and pen. Those who lack tablet technologies can use a simple computer mouse to draw their diagrams. As a user draws, the strokes are automatically recognized by the Mechanix system. Generally, the first few strokes a student will draw make up the truss or free-body (though Mechanix does not require diagram elements to be drawn in any specific order). Mechanix will not only recognize whether the strokes make *a truss*, Mechanix recognizes and communicates to the user whether or not they've drawn *the correct truss* as specified by the course instructor in the problem. Correctness is communicated by auto-labeling of nodes— if colored circles and node labels appear after completing a truss drawing, then the truss was correctly drawn and recognized within the Mechanix system. Likewise, users can draw force arrows (which change color when recognized as being attached to a node), axes, and other shapes as necessary for their diagrams.

In an effort to keep the Mechanix interface simple and unobtrusive, we decided not to perform any beautification of sketches. According to Varley [13], people use sketches as extensions of their short-term memories. If we chose to beautify the sketch, then the transition will be jarring, and the student will have to re-conceive the new beautified diagram in short-term memory, halting the design process. Furthermore, it would make using Mechanix less like using a pen and paper, since beautified, precise images are associated with CAD software.

Mechanix provides two modes of interaction, one for the students and one for the instructors. Instructors may open the Mechanix instructor client (which automatically connects to the server) and create any number of assignments with any number of problems. The instructor is free to type problem statements and provide reference images. For comparison-based problems, an instructor can provide any number of possible solutions to the problem by freeform sketching the correct free body diagrams. The process for instructors to enter questions is almost identical to the process that students use to solve them. In order to support free-response questions, instructors are able to specify more general requirements instead of providing reference solutions. More detailed information about Mechanix' instructor mode can be found in Sect. 2.2.

To complete assignments, students simply open the Mechanix student client (which automatically connects to the server) and begin solving problems. The server stores not only the student's final solution but also a log of any mistakes that the student made while solving the problem. These logs may be used for assigning grades or, more importantly, determining problem areas where students struggle with understanding the material.

9.2.1 Student Interface

The student interface (as shown in Fig. 9.1) aims to be clear and intuitive consisting of clearly defined panels and toolbars the users can use to interact. These multiple sections were chosen based on their functionality after interviews with education, civil engineering, and mechanical engineering professors. Below, we briefly describe each of the sections of the interface.

a. **Problem Description**: This panel shows text containing the description of the problem to be solved. The problem can be accompanied by an image that allows clicking to zoom in for more detail.
b. **Tool Panel**: This panel contains the buttons that trigger useful functions to help edit the sketches. The buttons (from left to right) are undo, redo, clear, open, save and erase.
c. **Check List**: The checklist provides step-by-step guides to assist students to finish the problem.
d. **Note Taking Panel**: Students can use this panel to make notes when they are working any problem

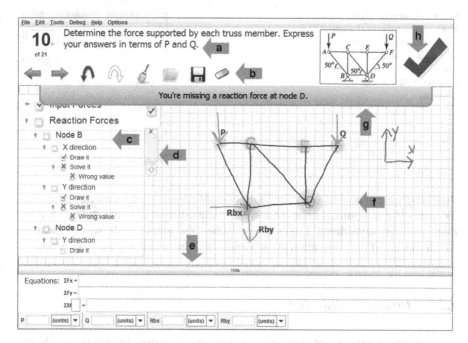

Fig. 9.1 Student Interface. The student interface is composed of different parts. **a** Problem Description. **b** Tool Panel. **c** Checklist. **d** Note Taking Panel. **e** Equation Panel. **f** Drawing Panel. **g** Feedback Panel. **h** Submit Button

e. **Equation Panel**: Students use this panel to enter the required equations and values of reaction forces. Then the system compares these inputs with correct answers.

f. **Drawing Panel**: This is the drawing canvas on which students sketch their diagrams. Each pen-down motion is captured and processed by our software.

g. **Feedback Panel**: The system gives feedback by showing a helpful and informative message. In Fig. 9.1, Mechanix has alerted the student in the checklist and also in the drop-down feedback message (in orange) at the top of the screen. Mechanix does not provide the answers to the students but does tell them if their answers are correct or incorrect.

h. **Submit Button**: Whenever students want to check their solutions, they can simply click the submit button to see whether their answers are correct.

There is also a round pop-up menu that provides context-sensitive functionality, which will appear when the pen is hovering over or when right-clicking on a drawn shape. This menu provides functionality for deleting a particular shape or stray mark from the screen as well as the ability to assign a label to forces and other applicable shapes. Besides the round pop-up menu, we also provide some gesturing functionality such as using scribbles for erasing, tapping on a shape for labeling, and click and holding to move a shape.

Sketches are also logged on the server each time the erase, clear, or undo functions are used. This allows our developers to determine whether the students erased their

Fig. 9.2 Instructor mode
looks very similar to student
mode. The problem text is
now editable, and there is an
extra set of buttons to add and
remove problems and
solutions

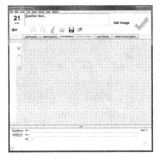

strokes because of poor recognition. This allows Mechanix team members to improve
the geometric recognizers to better accommodate different drawing styles that they
might not have considered. Logging of sketches also allows professors to identify
which aspects of the curriculum the students are frequently being misunderstood.

9.2.2 Instructor Interface

To create new problems for their students, TAs and professors use Instructor Mode.
Instructor Mode (shown in Fig. 9.2) is directly based on the same interface that
students use to solve problems. It offers the same affordances for drawing trusses or
free bodies and their required components. Because of this, instructors can focus on
creating problems for students instead of learning the software needed to do so. Any
number of questions can be specified in an assignment set and multiple solutions can
be created for each of these questions.

9.2.2.1 Creating a New Problem

To outline the ease of use and functionality of Mechanix's Instructor Mode, consider
the following task. A TA wishes to add an additional problem to a new homework
assignment for her students. In our experience, TAs follow the same process to input
the solution to a problem as students follow to derive the solution for that problem.
We present the steps to enter a problem in that favored order. However, Mechanix
does not require or enforce such an ordering.

1. First, the TA will type the question text directly into the area where it will be
   displayed to students. She will then select an image from her computer to give
   the question more context.

2. The TA enters the solution diagram. This is done in exactly the same manner that a student would draw their submission: by drawing in the graph paper area. Once the TA has drawn the truss, she can give each node a label based on the question text or image. Alternatively, Mechanix can automatically label the nodes with arbitrary values. We can use this information to automatically label the nodes for the student, to show the student that their truss or body is drawn correctly as they work on the assignment.

3. Next, the TA draws the input forces as described in the question text and image. Input forces are specified exactly in the problem statement and can be labeled with their value and units. In the case that the value of an input force is to be computed by the student, the TA can select the "Add Target Force" button from the shape's round menu after that force has been given a label. This action adds a Target Force Answer Panel to the answer pane where the TA can then specify the correct value and units. The TA will choose a descriptor for the new special force: "minimum", "maximum", or exact "value", that is used to remind the student what they should solve for.

4. The TA now draws the reaction forces. Mechanix identifies reaction forces based on the label given. If a force is labeled with at least two characters beginning with either 'F' or 'R', it is identified as a reaction force, and a new panel is created for the TA to enter its correct value and units.

5. As the TA added labels to the truss nodes in step 2, Mechanix automatically created panels for each member force. Not every problem involves solving for member forces. Accordingly, these panels are initially disabled and grayed out. If the TA chooses to specify the correct value and units for a member force, it will be enabled and marked as required. Only required member forces will be shown to students when they are solving the problem.

6. Finally, for this particular question, the TA wants to have her students calculate the Factor of Safety for the truss, a dimensionless value describing how many times the current input load could be applied before the truss collapses. All previous components of the question that the TA has specified were based on parts of her sketch. Because there is no shape that corresponds to the Factor of Safety, Mechanix provides instructors with an "Extra Answer" option. The TA clicks the corresponding button and then supplies the name, value, and units (if needed) for the extra answer. The Factor of Safety is dimensionless, so the TA simply selects the "No Units" drop-down option.

A fully-specified problem can be seen in Fig. 9.3.

It is important that instructors complete step 2 before the other drawing steps. Because the truss is the focal point of the question, the forces must be attached to the truss. There is no order dependence for step 1, but in practice it serves as a valuable reference for the other steps. Steps 3–7 can be completed in any order; this preferred order is based on the steps taken to solve such a problem.

Removing or editing a problem that is already a part of an assignment is as straightforward as creating one. Each problem in an assignment set will open and redisplay all of the set information that the instructor specified when she initially

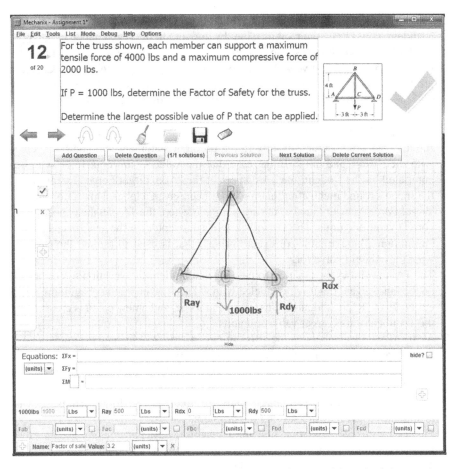

Fig. 9.3 A fully specified problem. In this case the instructor does not wish to check the equations as an intermediate step. Note that when instructors do not enter an axis, the standard axis is assumed by default

created it. For instance, if a professor realizes that one of her member forces has the wrong value she can open the assignment, find the correct problem, and change the value. Once she saves the new version of the solution, any student who then attempts to solve this problem will have their submission checked against the latest version of the solution file. An instructor can remove a question by clicking the "Delete Question" button while in Instructor Mode.

9.3   Instructor Presentations

9.3.1   ASEE 2012 Workshop

At the American Society for Engineering Education (ASEE) conference in 2012, we had the privilege of presenting Mechanix to nearly 20 engineering educators. To begin the 3-hour workshop, we briefly discussed the design and functionality of Mechanix. However, the educators spent most of the workshop working hands-on with the system. The educators solved problems in Student Mode and also created problems in Instructor Mode.

Overall, the educators were pleased with the system and excited about the potential benefits such a system could have for their students. The educators provided us with very constructive feedback, such as suggestions for the improvement of arrow recognition, improvements in the intuition of the instructor interface, and, most importantly, the addition of a mechanism to remind both students and instructors of the steps required to solve free-body diagrams.

Despite our intention to design the Mechanix user interface to be as intuitive as possible, students in our classroom deployments, as well as the Instructors who vetted the system at ASEE, expressed an interest in learning the software through a demo-like atmosphere. So, we took this opportunity to create a tutorial, which can be used for future presentations and classroom deployments. The intention of this assignment is not only to provide students with an environment in which they are free to experiment and try every function of the interface, but also to learn about how the system grades student problems and provides feedback. Additionally, it provides us with a valuable demonstration tool at workshops and conferences, where attendees can quickly and easily complete sample problems while learning about the basic components of Mechanix.

9.3.2   2014 Teachers Summit

At the 2014 Teachers Summit for educators in STEM fields, we had the opportunity to present Mechanix and our new tutorial to each of the 100+ attendees. The structure of this workshop was similar to the ASEE workshop, but, due to the 50-minute time slots for each workshop, we were only able to discuss the student interface, rather than both the student and instructor interfaces. Most all of the Teachers Summit attendees were able to successfully complete the tutorial. Any issues encountered by participants stemmed from unfamiliarity with the technologies used (i.e. Windows 8 on a Surface Pro 2). Attendees were very interested in using Mechanix in their own classrooms, and as such, they provided very constructive comments regarding better feedback of successful recognition (like changing the colors of shapes once successfully recognized) and finer-grained progression of the questions in the progress of the tutorial. Following this feedback, we made some modifications to our tutorial in order to make the questions more clear and the progression more appropriate for presentations of this kind.

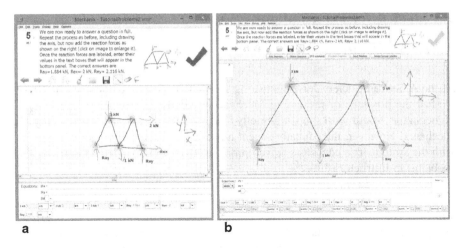

Fig. 9.4 a A question from the first iteration of the Mechanix tutorial we developed. **b** The same tutorial question, as viewed from Instructor Mode

9.3.3 WIPTTE 2014

Finally, we had the opportunity to present Mechanix as a You-Try-It Workshop at WIPTTE 2014. We presented Mechanix and our newly polished tutorial to both faculty in academia and industry researchers at a hands-on workshop in similar style to the ASEE Workshop and 2014 Teachers Summit. Feedback was similar to that of the previous presentations, with constructive critiques of the interface and a universally enthusiastic reception of the concept and implementation.

Faculty expressed interest in the system's capability to assign and automatically grade free-response diagrams and seemed open to the concept of assigning homework in such a system. Some confusion arose from the bottom panel in the Mechanix interface, where participants were unsure as to how to enter reaction force errors and units. A few participants also reported issues with the recognition, where the participants believed they entered the correct answer, but Mechanix marked it as wrong. From this, we learned that we still need to better communicate to users when correct recognition takes place in the system (color changing, etc.).

9.4 Description of Tutorial

The tutorial we developed for Mechanix focused on practicing drawing basic shapes and getting acquainted with the style of sketched answers that Mechanix expects. Emphasis is placed on learning the interface instead of knowledge in statics, so most question prompts supply students with the answers so that they can practice entering them in the correct format (Fig. 9.4).

We present a description of each of the seven questions in our first Mechanix tutorial:

1. The first question explains the intention of this tutorial, invites students to learn about the main function buttons via reading their mouse hover description, asks them to draw a square shape, and invites them to check their work by clicking on the large green check mark, thereby walking students through the process of submitting a basic sketch answer.
2. The second question asks students to draw their first truss. The question explains the definition of a truss, how students are expected to draw one, and how Mechanix automatically labels the truss nodes when it recognizes a structure.
3. The student is asked to re-draw the same truss as Question 2, and this time they are also asked to draw an incoming reaction force at a specific node and label it. This teaches students to enter reaction forces common in statics problems. Students from this point forward are asked to re-draw most of their sketch from the previous problem and build on it with the intention to have students practice their sketching.
4. Students are asked to repeat their process from Question 3, this time drawing an "axis" shape. The "axis" shape is required in nearly every statics problem in order for the student to identify the x and y directions. It is incidentally also the most complex shape for Mechanix to recognize, so repeated practice of this particular shape is imperative for students to successfully finish graded homework.
5. Question 5 repeats the process of Question 4, and this time students are asked to label more nodes with reaction forces. They are also asked to enter text-box values at the bottom of the interface for the first time. They are given the correct numerical values, as the focus in this problem is not to solve the statics problem but rather learn the interface.
6. Question 6 switches to a different problem, adding more beams to the truss with different input forces. Students are asked to draw the reaction forces, axis, and this time also asked to solve the force equations at the bottom of the interface. The answers are not given in this question, since some students asked for an ungraded sample problem for them to solve.
7. Question 7 repeats the process from Question 6, but this time the student is asked to calculate the moment at a specific node. As with Question 6, the answer is not given.

9.5 Classroom Deployment

For nine semesters and across three universities, we have tested the Mechanix software in university classrooms. Through these deployments, we learned that Mechanix significantly improves student understanding of static concepts (over pencil and paper). Particularly, we learned that Mechanix helps to engage and retain at-risk students—students who are underprepared for college or otherwise at risk to fail the course. At-risk students using Mechanix were more likely to complete their homework than those who used only pencil and paper. More information regarding Mechanix and its implementations in the classroom can be found in [1, 3, 4, 10, 11].

9.6   Conclusion

At WIPTTE 2014, we presented a tutoring system that allows students to annotate their sketches to produce precisely specified diagrams. Designed to be no more difficult to use than pencil and paper, Mechanix recognizes student's hand-drawn diagrams and provides helpful feedback regarding processes and correctness in order to aid the learning of engineering statics concepts. We have implemented and deployed our system in large classrooms with our intended population, undergraduate Engineering students. Further, we have trained over 150 teachers on how to use Mechanix in their classrooms. These exercises allowed us to receive valuable feedback that we have used to improve Mechanix.

Acknowledgments   The authors thank the many other contributors to Mechanix, specifically Hong-Hoe Kim, David Turner, Chris Aikens, Kourtney Kebodeaux, Francisco Vides, and Martin Field, as well as other members of the Sketch Recognition Lab and the IDREEM Lab (Innovation, Design Reasoning, Engineering Education and Methods Lab). This research is funded in part by Google and the National Science Foundation under Grant Nos. 0935219, 0942400 and 1129525.

References

1. Atilola, O., Valentine, S., Kim, H.-H., Turner, D., McTigue, E., Hammond, T., & Linsey, J. (2014). Mechanix: A natural sketch interface tool for teaching truss analysis and free-body diagrams. *Artificial Intelligence for Engineering Design, Analysis and Manufacturing, 28*(02), 169–192.
2. Callahan, J., Hopkins, D., Weiser, M., & Shneiderman, B. (1988). *An empirical comparison of pie vs. linear menus*. In Proceedings of the SIGCHI conference on human factors in computing systems, pp. 95–100. New York, NY, USA, ACM.
3. Field, M., Valentine, S., Linsey, J., & Hammond, T. (2011). *Sketch recognition algorithms for comparing complex and unpredictable shapes*. In Proceedings of the Twenty-Third International Joint Conference on Artificial Intelligence. Barcelona, Spain.
4. Kebodeaux, K., Field, M., & Hammond, T. (2011). *Defining precise measurements with sketched annotations*. In Proceedings of the Eighth Eurographics Symposium on Sketch-Based Interfaces and Modeling. SBIM '11. ACM, New York, NY, USA, pp. 79–86.
5. Kozma, R. B. (1994). Will media influence learning reframing the debate? *Educational Technology, 42*, 7–19.
6. Lee, W., de Silva, R., Peterson, E. J., Calfee, R. C., & Stahovich, T. F. (2008). Newton's pen: A pen-based tutoring system for statics. *Computers & Graphics, 32*(5):511–524.
7. McGraw Hill. (2011). McGraw Hill connect. http://connect.customer.mheducation.com/. Accessed: 1 Sept 2012.
8. Roselli, R. J., Howard, L., Cinnamon, B., Brophy, S., Norris, P., Rothney, M., & Eggers, D. (2003). *Integration of an interactive free body diagram assistant with a courseware authoring package and an experimental learning management system*. In Proceedings of the American Society for Engineering Education.
9. Rosser, S. V. (2007). InTEL: Interactive toolkit for engineering learning. http://intel.gatech.edu/index.php. Accessed 24 Feb 2010.
10. Valentine, S., Vides, F., Lucchese, G., Turner, D., Kim, H., Li, W., Linsey J., & Hammond, T. (2012). *Mechanix: A sketch-based tutoring system for statics courses*. In Proceedings of AAAI.

11. Valentine, S., Vides, F., Lucchese, G., Turner, D., Hong-Hoe, K., Wenzhe, L., Linsey, J., & Hammond, T. (2013). Mechanix: A sketch-based tutoring and grading system for free-body diagrams. *AI Magazine, 34*(1), 55–66.
12. Vanlehn, K., Lynch, C., Schulze, K., Shapiro, J. A., Shelby, R., Taylor, L., Treacy, D., Weinstein, A., & Wintersgill, M. (2005). The Andes physics tutoring system: Lessons learned. *International Journal of Artificial Intelligence in Education, 15*(3), 147–204
13. Varley, P. & Company, P. (2008). *Automated sketching and engineering culture.* VL/HCC Workshop: Sketch Tools for Diagramming September, pp. 83–92.
14. Yin, P., Forbus, K. D., Usher, J., Sageman, B., & Jee, B. (2010). *Sketch worksheets: A sketch-based educational software system.* In Proceedings of the 22nd AAAI Conference on Innovative Applications of Artificial Intelligence. Menlo Park, CA: AAAI Press.

Chapter 10
Sketch Worksheets: A Brief Summary

Kenneth D. Forbus, Jeffrey Usher, and Maria Chang

Abstract Sketch worksheets are a new kind of sketch-based education software designed to facilitate spatial learning. Each worksheet represents a particular exercise, which the student does on a computer. Students get feedback, based on automatic comparison of their sketch with a hidden solution sketch. A software gradebook, which uses scoring rubrics in the solution sketch, is intended to help instructors in grading. Sketch worksheets have been used in classroom experiments with college students, high school students, and middle-school students. They are domain-independent, requiring only that the exercise involves visual distinctions that the software can understand. They rely on cognitive models of human visual/spatial representations and a model of human analogical matching. An authoring environment enables domain instructors to create new sketch worksheets on their own. CogSketch is freely available for download.

10.1 Background

Pencil and paper worksheets are commonly used in education to give students practice with new ideas and to assess how well they understand them. The flexibility of paper means that assignments can potentially include sketching. However, sketching assignments are often avoided, since they are difficult and time-consuming to grade. With Sketch Worksheets [1], our goal is to use advances in AI and Cognitive Science to create a new technology that provides immediate feedback for students, anytime, anywhere, and automatic grading for instructors, to make sketch-based assignments more attractive and practical.

Sketch worksheets are built on top of CogSketch [2], an open-domain sketch understanding system. By open-domain, we mean that it does not rely on domain-specific vocabulary or recognition techniques. Instead, it models aspects of human visual processing, so that, ideally, the software sees sketches in ways that are similar

K. D. Forbus (✉) · J. Usher · M. Chang
Qualitative Reasoning Group, Northwestern University, Evanston, IL, USA
e-mail: forbus@northwestern.edu

© Springer International Publishing Switzerland 2015
T. Hammond et al. (eds.), *The Impact of Pen and Touch Technology on Education,*
Human-Computer Interaction Series, DOI 10.1007/978-3-319-15594-4_10

to the way people see them (e.g. [3]). A model of human analogical matching is used to compare a student's sketch with one or more solution sketches, with feedback provided based on differences perceived in them. CogSketch is being developed by the Spatial Intelligence and Learning Center [4], both as platform for cognitive science research and for new kinds of educational software.

There have been a number of experiments with CogSketch in classrooms; we summarize two recent ones here. Using Sketch Worksheets developed in collaboration with Maria Chang, Brian Miller at Temple University showed that middle-school students did better on two out of three post-tests after using Sketch Worksheets. Bridget Garnier, a geoscience graduate student at Wisconsin, authored over a dozen Sketch Worksheets for use in their introductory geoscience class. While instructors currently do not give sketching assignments in these classes, due to their large size, Garnier also created equivalent pencil and paper worksheets, and measured student performance on unit-level pre/post tests for both Sketch Worksheets and the pencil and paper versions. Overall, learning gains were the same for both groups, with Sketch Worksheets doing slightly better for some units, and pencil and paper doing slightly better for others. This is evidence that Sketch Worksheets can improve student learning, and in a more scalable way, since grading effort is greatly reduced. We find these results very encouraging and are using the data from these experiments to further improve Sketch Worksheets and support their widespread use.

Acknowledgements CogSketch is being developed by the NSF-sponsored Spatial Intelligence and Learning Center, and is freely available on-line.

References

1. Yin, P., Forbus, K., Usher, J., Sageman, B., & Jee, B. (2010). Sketch worksheets: A sketch-based educational software system. Proceedings of the 22nd annual conference on innovative applications of artificial intelligence.
2. Forbus, K., Usher, J., Lovett, A., Lockwood, K., & Wetzel, J. (2011). CogSketch: Sketch understanding for cognitive science research and for education. *Topics in Cognitive Science, 3*(4), 648–666.
3. Lovett, A., & Forbus, K. (2011) Cultural commonalities and differences in spatial problem solving: A computational analysis. *Cognition, 121,* 281–287.
4. http://spatiallearning.org/

Chapter 11
Increasing Student Confidence in Engineering Sketching via a Software Coach

Jon Wetzel and Ken Forbus

Abstract Sketching is an important skill for engineering design students. A serious problem found by Northwestern instructors is that students are afraid to sketch. We are tackling this problem by developing the Design Coach, which enables students to practice explaining their designs via a combination of sketching and language, to reduce their anxiety about communicating via sketching. This paper summarizes the overall operation of the Design Coach and reports on a classroom experiment providing evidence that the Design Coach does in fact reduce student anxiety, compared to a control group that did not use it.

11.1 Introduction

Sketching is an important skill for students in the STEM disciplines [1]. Sketching is a powerful means of thinking and communicating spatial ideas, and spatial abilities play an important role in STEM success [10]. Unfortunately, students are often afraid of sketching in engineering classes. At Northwestern, a required course for first-year students is Design Thinking and Communication. Its students tackle design problems, typically for real clients. They start by working with their client to figure out what the problem really is, through sketching out initial ideas and refining them, and building prototypes. Instructors view sketching as essential in engineering practice, yet they find that most students lack confidence when sketching in an engineering context. They view this as one of the most significant pedagogical challenges that they face. Working with these instructors, we came up with the idea of using a software environment to enable students to practice explaining designs via sketching, without the social pressure that comes with sketching in class and in their working groups. Thus the Design Coach was born.

This is a challenging application, for three reasons. First, sketching is used during the early stages of design, what is known as conceptual design. In these early stages,

K. Forbus (✉) · J. Wetzel
Qualitative Reasoning Group, Northwestern University, Evanston, IL, USA
e-mail: forbus@northwestern.edu

J. Wetzel
e-mail: jw@northwestern.edu

© Springer International Publishing Switzerland 2015   107
T. Hammond et al. (eds.), *The Impact of Pen and Touch Technology on Education*,
Human-Computer Interaction Series, DOI 10.1007/978-3-319-15594-4_11

precise shapes and values are not yet known: The purpose of sketching is to think through whether the idea makes sense. There is not enough information to make traditional numerical simulation feasible, nor would it be appropriate: The explanations that count at this stage are qualitative, focusing on the kinds of behaviors that will (and will not) occur. Second, the software must be able to understand a student's explanation in human-like ways, so that its feedback will be appropriate. Third, the solutions to design tasks are open-ended: Students should be able to sketch any reasonable solution and have the software figure it out. Moreover, the design tasks change from quarter to quarter, depending on what clients sign up. As outlined below, we tackle the first two problems by using qualitative reasoning, including both qualitative spatial reasoning, to abstract the important aspects of shapes from the messy hand-drawn ink that students produce, and qualitative mechanics, to understand the interactions of forces, shape, and motion. To handle the third problem, we limit the use of the Design Coach to design problems where the key aspects of any design involve the kinds of mechanical principles it can understand[1].

This paper reports on a classroom experiment that provides evidence that Design Coach does indeed reduce student anxiety. We start by explaining the relevant aspects of CogSketch, the approach to open-domain sketch understanding [7] that we use. We then summarize how the Design Coach works, using an extended example for illustration. Then we describe the experiment and its results. We conclude with related work and future work.

11.2 CogSketch

The Design Coach is built on CogSketch [7], a sketch understanding software platform for cognitive modeling and educational applications. In CogSketch, the ink users draw is grouped into *glyphs* that represent something. Typically a glyph is drawn by clicking a "finish glyph" button when they are finished, but they are free to merge and split their ink in defining glyphs. In Design Coach, all of the parts of a student's design are drawn as glyphs. The meaning of a glyph is described via concepts from CogSketch's knowledge base, which is derived from OpenCyc. For example, in Design Coach, a student might label a glyph with the concepts "spring" and "compressed", indicating that it represents a compressed spring[2]. Glyphs are also given names, which are used to refer to them in the rest of the interface, including explanations that students construct and feedback provided about them. Figure 11.1 illustrates.

CogSketch automatically computes a variety of visual representations between glyphs. Moreover, it can automatically segment glyphs into edges, identifying qualitative segments even within hand-drawn shapes. This visual processing capability

---

[1] A prior survey suggests that mechanical solutions suffice for roughly 40 % of DTC problems [11]. Our collaborating instructors are happy with that degree of coverage.

[2] While students see English terms, underneath there are formal representations for these concepts, supporting qualitative reasoning about them, as outlined below.

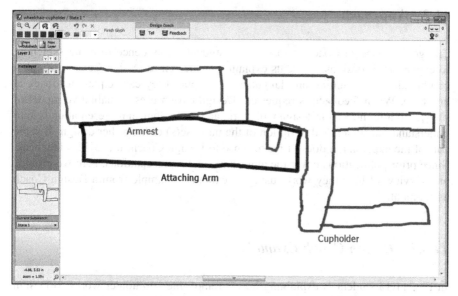

Fig. 11.1 A Design Coach sketch of a removable cup holder for a wheelchair in CogSketch

Cupholder Attached **causes** Cupholder Removed

Fig. 11.2 The metalayer view of the removable cup holder design

is used both in constructing qualitative spatial representations and in qualitative mechanical reasoning in Design Coach.

Most designs involve more than one distinct state or behavior. For example, a key aspect of a removable cup holder is that it has at least two states, attached and detached. CogSketch supports sketches with multiple *subsketches*, each of which can be used to describe a specific behavior. Moreover, all of the subsketches can be viewed as glyphs on the *metalayer* for the sketch (see Fig. 11.2). Since they can be thought of as a generalization of a comic strip, with each subsketch being a panel, we call these descriptions *comic graphs*. Users can add new glyphs to the metalayer. In Fig. 11.2, for example, a relation glyph is used to express a causal relationship between the two states of the design. Relation glyphs always depict binary relationships between other glyphs. CogSketch does attempt to recognize arrows in relation glyphs (note the yellow arrow overlay in Fig. 11.2), but if that recognition fails, the user can still assign which glyphs are intended to be related by it.

Finally, annotation glyphs enable additional information to be added to a glyph. Sometimes annotations are purely numerical, such as the weight of a part. Other times they have associated directions, such as forces and torques, as illustrated in Sect 11.3.

11.3 Approach

The goal of Design Coach is to improve students' confidence in using sketching to explain their designs. Students explain their design to Design Coach through a combination of sketching and language-like input. They can request feedback at any time. When feedback is requested, Design Coach uses a qualitative model of physics to infer how their design will work, and a teleological representation [13] to understand the student's description of the purpose(s) of his or her design. If some part of the explanation doesn't make sense to Design Coach, it provides feedback. Since prior publications cover the algorithms and representations, here we provide an overview of how they work, using an extended example from a Design Coach assignment.

11.3.1 Design Coach Example

In Fig. 11.1a student is explaining how a removable cup holder works to Design Coach. She begins by drawing the parts of the design and labeling them with concepts. In this assignment, she starts with a photograph (Fig. 11.6 below) of an existing design as a first step. She names the leftmost object "Armrest" and labels it with the concepts "rigid object" and "fixed object" to tell the system that it is rigid and it does not move in the frame of reference. Once the first sketch is complete, the student moves to the metalayer to depict a subsequent state of the design. She starts by cloning her first subsketch, called "Cupholder Attached", to create a new state, which she called "Cupholder Removed". She then edits the new subsketch to reflect the intended relationships in it, by moving the cup holder out and up from the attaching arm. The relationship between the two subsketches is then indicated by drawing a relation glyph (Fig. 11.2).

The student's explanation consists of both sketched and language-like input. Students enter the language part using the Design Coach Tell Window (Fig. 11.3). The Tell Window has two parts. The first is a text box for writing a plain English description for instructors. The Design Coach ignores this information. The second part is an interface that lets students construct what looks to them like English sentences, with a constrained grammar. The options for subjects, verbs, objects, and other constituents of the sentence are drawn from the objects in the sketch and the formal concepts used to reason about them (e.g. the idea of preventing something). When a sentence is complete, its meaning to the system is constructed by creating one or more facts from it, in the underlying knowledge representation used by CogSketch. Students can switch between sketching and constructing sentences as they choose.

In Fig. 11.4, the student requests feedback. Design Coach uses two algorithms to generate feedback [12] about the student's explanation of her design. One algorithm processes the internal representations of the sentences in order, checking to see if each one is consistent with knowledge from the sketch and the sentences before it. The

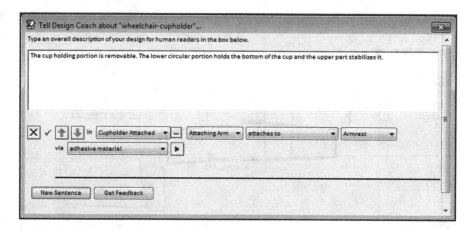

Fig. 11.3 Students add information to their explanation using the tell window. In this example, the student explains that the device will attach to the armrest using an adhesive material.

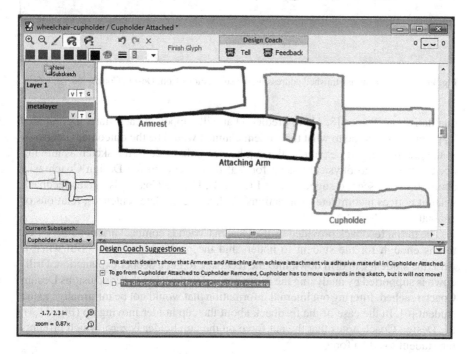

Fig. 11.4 Feedback appears at the bottom of the sketching window. Students may click on some feedback items to learn why Design Coach gave the feedback it did.

sentence in Fig. 11.3 says that the attaching arm attaches to the armrest via adhesive materials. But there is no adhesive material in the sketch, so feedback is generated (i.e., first suggestion in Fig. 11.4). The other takes as input the comic graph and uses

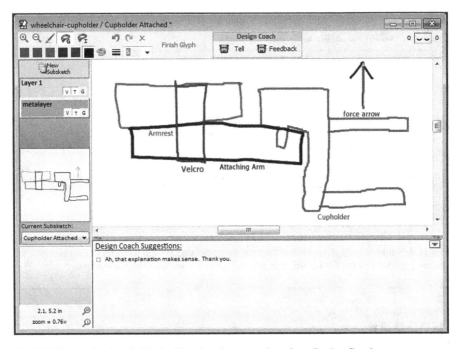

Fig. 11.5 The student has finished addressing the suggestions from Design Coach.

qualitative mechanics [8, 11] to predict what will happen in each state. It compares its predicted outcome to what the student claimed would be the outcome, via arrows in the graph. Here, for example, the cup holder is depicted in the sketch as moving up, but there is no physical reason for that movement, so the Design Coach asks about this (i.e., second suggestion in Fig. 11.4). Design Coach also gives feedback when it notices incomplete explanations, such as incomplete sentences, relations or annotations.

The initial feedback provided by the Design Coach is compact and concise. Often this is enough for the student to understand the problem and fix it. But when it isn't, the student can drill down into the feedback to get a deeper explanation. Drill-down is supported by analyzing the dependencies underlying the conclusions Design Coach reached, filtering out internal information that would not be informative to the student [6]. In the case of the feedback about the cup holder moving up (Fig. 11.4), the Design Coach notes that the net force on the cup holder is zero, which prompts the student to add a force.

Forces are depicted using annotation glyphs. Since forces have direction, CogSketch expects them to be drawn as arrows. In Fig. 11.5, the student adds a force to show how the cup holder moves, and some velcro straps to show how the armrest and connecting arm are attached. The next time the student asks for feedback, the Design Coach reports that it is satisfied (see Fig. 11.5).

11.3.2 Deployment in Design Thinking and Communication course

Pilot testing of Design Coach with DTC students began in Fall 2009 with pull-out studies. By Fall 2011 it was robust enough that homework assignments were given using it in some sections. Feedback from students and instructors led to improvements in both the Design Coach user interface and its feedback [12, 13], setting the stage for the experiment described next.

11.4 Experiment

What we are dealing with might be thought of as *sketching anxiety*, analogous to the well-known phenomena of math anxiety. Beilock et al. have shown the harmful impact of anxiety on math skills in different situations [4]. With the help of Beilock and one of her students, we adapted one of their surveys [4] for measuring math anxiety to measure sketching anxiety. The survey used the following questions to measure anxiety:

- In the past two weeks, how nervous would the following situation make you feel?
  - Joining a group which put you in charge of sketching the design of their engineering concept
  - Getting an assignment asking you to draw an engineering design to scale
  - Being asked to sketch an idea you have just suggested in brainstorming
  - Being asked to draw an oblique view of a model
  - Being asked to draw an isometric view of a model
  - Being asked to draw an orthographic projection of a model

For each item, students ranked their anxiety using a five point Likert scale, using one of the following values: Not at all, A little, A fair amount, Much, or Very Much. These values were then were converted to scores of 0–4. An individual student's anxiety rating is the mean of their choices on the anxiety item.

In the Fall 2012 offering of DTC we conducted the following experiment. Two sections of 16 students each were given a homework assignment using Design Coach, described below. Before and after the assignment, online surveys were opened to the entire class (including the sections not using Design Coach) to measure their self-reported anxiety with sketching. The online surveys were our measurement device, the two sections using the Design Coach formed the Design Coach group, and the rest of the class formed the control group. Our prediction was that the Design Coach group would have reduced anxiety, and the control group would not.

Fig. 11.6 The wheelchair cupholder design, as pictured in the homework assignment

11.4.1 Design Coach Homework Assignment

The instructors, with help from us, created a homework assignment where students used Design Coach on a real but constrained design problem. Here is how it worked:

1. Students first learn to use the Design Coach by taking the two built in tutorials.[3] The first tutorial explains how to make and edit the three types of glyphs, use the metalayer, enter sentences, and get feedback. The second tutorial explains how to describe rotation using two types of annotation glyphs.
2. Explain a given design to Design Coach, e.g. the design in Fig. 11.6.
   a. Draw a sketch (comic graph), type up description in English for instructor and construct sentences for the Design Coach in the Tell Window.
   b. See if Design Coach understands your explanation, and if not, improve it until it does.
   c. Record your thoughts on the program in a separate provided space for notes
3. Think of an improvement for the given cupholder design, and then repeat step 2 with the improved design.

11.5 Results

We received 16 survey responses from the Design Coach group in the pre-test, and 21 in the post-test. We received 30 survey responses from the control group in the pre-test, and 16 in the post-test. The anxiety results are shown in Figs. 11.7, 11.8, and 11.9.

The mean anxiety rating is shown for each group, pre and post Design Coach activity. The error bars show the error margin for 95 % confidence. We used the Wilcoxon rank sum test to determine significance. We found that the difference between the Design Coach group pre/post was significant ($P < 0.05$) in Fall 2012 and Fall 2013 quarters, while the difference between the control group pre/post was only significant in the Fall 2013 quarter. Indeed, the mean of the control group actually increased in the first two quarters, though the change was not significant in either case.

---

[3] http://www.qrg.northwestern.edu/software/cogsketch/index.html.

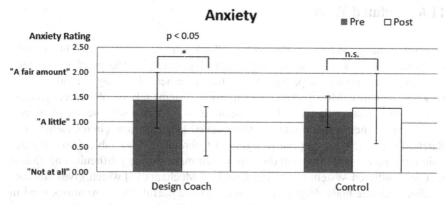

Fig. 11.7 Sketching anxiety survey results, Fall 2012 DC: $N_{pre} = 16$, $N_{post} = 21$, $p = 0.043$ Control: $N_{pre} = 30$, $N_{post} = 16$, $p = 0.644$

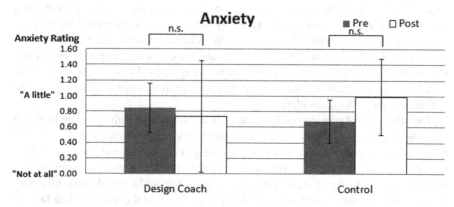

Fig. 11.8 Sketching anxiety survey results, Winter 2013 Design Coach: $N_{pre} = 15$, $N_{post} = 7$, $p = 0.478$ Control: $N_{pre} = 24$, $N_{post} = 12$, $p = 0.211$

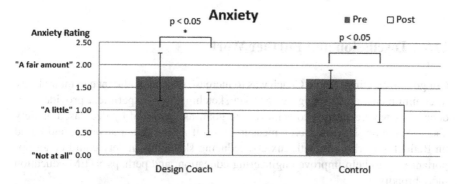

Fig. 11.9 Sketching anxiety survey results, Fall 2013 Design Coach: $N_{pre} = 17$, $N_{post} = 14$, $p = 0.026$ Control: $N_{pre} = 91$, $N_{post} = 27$, $p = 0.004$

11.6   Related Work

The value of providing on-demand feedback during learning has been well-established in the intelligent tutoring system literature [2]. The problem has been providing such advice for pedagogical situations where sketching is a primary interaction modality. Most sketch-based tutoring systems rely on object recognition. That is, they restrict the domain of discourse to involve a specific set of objects (e.g. organic chemical formulae in OrganicPad [9], electrical circuit elements in Kirchoff's Pen [5]) so that the recognition technology is tractable. This requires building a new system for each domain, which makes scaling difficult. The closest recognition-based system to Design Coach is Mechanix [3],which gives students feedback on free-body diagrams of trusses. While useful, the conventions used in such diagrams are quite specialized, compared to the problem Design Coach faces. For Design Coach, the space of objects and designs that students may draw is open-ended, making the training of recognizers infeasible. The open-domain approach of CogSketch sidesteps the need for recognition, drawing on the observation that when people sketch with each other, they typically use language to identify what they are drawing, rather than counting on recognition. While the CogSketch interface is not as fluid as speaking to another person, it enables the system to operate in a wider variety of circumstances than recognition-based systems. For example, we do not need to train the system to recognize all the possible shapes that a student might use in their design for a cup-holder.

The other type of educational application being developed with CogSketch, *sketch worksheets* [14], uses a very different technique. Sketch worksheets contain one or more instructor-generated sketches, representing a correct answer (and sometimes multiple correct answers, or common misconceptions). These instructor sketches are compared against what a student has drawn via a human-like analogical matching process, and the differences are used to give feedback to the student. The lack of domain-specific reasoning in the critiquing process means that sketch worksheets are more broadly applicable than Design Coach, but at the cost of not giving as deep feedback as Design Coach can within its domain.

11.7   Discussion and Further Work

Our goal in creating Design Coach was to increase student confidence in their ability to communicate engineering designs via sketching. Our experiment provides evidence that we are starting to achieve that goal, as measured by decreased anxiety about sketching. Having such a measure is itself an important advance, and based on Beilock's work with math anxiety, reducing sketching anxiety could be an important way to help engineering education, and perhaps STEM education more broadly.

We see three main lines of future work. First, we plan on conducting more in-class experiments and gathering more data. Second, we want to see if we can develop other measures, such as the degree to which students use sketching in different phases of design, as a complement to the sketch anxiety measure, and to provide a way to calibrate it. Finally, another problem DTC instructors have that is not unrelated is that students currently learn drafting via pencil and paper assignments, e.g. drawing something in orthographic perspective. Such assignments are difficult to grade and result in delayed feedback, often a week or more. In collaboration with instructors, we are exploring using Sketch Worksheets for such assignments. This could both have the direct advantage of providing students with immediate on-demand feedback during those homework exercises and also reducing the learning curve for later usage of the Design Coach, due to the systems using almost the same interface.

Acknowledgements   This research was supported by the Spatial Intelligence and Learning Center, NSF SLC Grant SBE-0541957. We thank Bruce Ankenman, John Anderson, Stacy Benjamin, Jee Rim, and Keith Tyo for their feedback and help, and for allowing us to work with their EDC students. We also thank Dr. Sian Beilock and Gerardo Ramirez for their help with the survey used in this work. Finally, we thank CogSketch team members Jeff Usher and Maria Chang for their support.

References

1. Ainsworth, S., Prain, V., & Tytler, R. (2011). Drawing to learn in science. *Science Magazine, 333,* 1096–1097.
2. Anderson, J. R., Corbett, A. T., Koedinger, K. R., & Pelletier, R. (1995). Cognitive tutors: Lessons learned. *The Journal of the Learning Sciences, Lawrence Erlbaum Associates, Inc., 4*(2), 167–207.
3. Atilola, O., Field, M., McTigue, E., Hammond, T., & Linsey, J. (2011). *Evaluation of a natural sketch interface for truss FBDs and analysis.* In: Conference on Frontiers in Education.
4. Beilock, S. L., Gunderson, E. A., Ramirez, G., & Levine, S. C. (2010). Female teachers' math anxiety affects girls' math achievement. *Proceedings of the National Academy of Sciences, 107,* 1860–1863.
5. De Silva, R., Bischel, T. D., Lee, W., Peterson, E. J., Calfee, R. C., & Stahovich, T. F. (2007). *Kirchhoff's Pen: A penbased circuit analysis tutor.* In: Proceedings of the 4th eurographics workshop on Sketch-based interfaces and modeling.
6. Forbus, K. D., Whalley, P., Everett, J., Ureel, L., Brokowski, M., & Baher, J., et al. (1999). CyclePad: An articulate virtual laboratory for engineering thermodynamics. *Artificial Intelligence, 114,* 297–347.
7. Forbus, K., Usher, J., Lovett, A., Lockwood, K., & Wetzel, J. (2011). CogSketch: Sketch understanding for cognitive science research and for education. *Topics in Cognitive Science, 3*(4), 648–666.
8. Nielsen, P. E. (1988). *A qualitative approach to rigid body mechanics.* Technical report, no. UIUCDCS-R-88-1469; UILU-ENG-88-1775. University of Illinois at Urbana-Champaign, Department of Computer Science.
9. Pargas, R., Cooper, M., Williams, C., & Bryfczynski, S. (2007). *OrganicPad: A Tablet PC based interactivity tool for organic chemistry.* In: International workshop on pen-based learning technologies.
10. Wai, J., Lubinski, D., & Benbow, C. P. (2009). Spatial ability for STEM domains: Aligning over 50 years of cumulative psychological knowledge solidifies its importance. *Journal of Educational Psychology, 101,* 817–835.
11. Wetzel, J., & Forbus, K. (2009). *Automated critique of sketched designs in engineering.* In Proceedings of the 23rd international workshop on qualitative reasoning. Ljubljana, Slovenia.

12. Wetzel, J., & Forbus, K. (2010). *Design buddy: Providing feedback for sketched multi-modal causal explanations*. In Proceedings of the 24th international workshop on qualitative reasoning. Portland, Oregon.
13. Wetzel, J., & Forbus, K. (2012). *Teleological representations for multi-modal design explanations*. In Proceedings of the 26th international workshop on qualitative reasoning. Los Angeles, California.
14. Yin, P., Forbus, K., Usher, J., Sageman, B., & Jee, B. (2010). *Sketch worksheets: A sketch-based educational software system*. In Proceedings of the 22nd Annual Conference on innovative applications of artificial intelligence.

Chapter 12
Enhancing Instruction of Written East Asian Languages with Sketch Recognition-Based "Intelligent Language Workbook" Interfaces

Paul Taele and Tracy Hammond

Abstract For American higher education students studying one of the major East Asian languages in Chinese, Japanese, and Korean (CJK) as a second language, one of the major challenges that students face is the mastery of the various written scripts due to those languages' vast contrasts from written English. Conventional pedagogical resources for written CJK languages frequently rely on language instructors, who provide in-class demonstrations of the written scripts and real-time assessment of their students' written input: paper workbooks, which offer guided instructional drills and supplementary knowledge on the written component; and practice sheets, which enable students to absorb components of the written scripts through repetitious writing practice. Unfortunately, these techniques also present their own inherent disadvantages: language instructors are constrained by time in teaching the written components to students for typical classroom sizes, workbooks are static instructional materials that lack real-time intelligent feedback and assessment, and practice sheets result in monotonous practice to students and are vulnerable to students erroneously practicing potential mistakes repeatedly if left unsupervised.

In this paper, we describe our work behind "intelligent language workbook" interfaces, which combine the benefits of stylus-driven tablet devices and state-of-the-art sketch recognition algorithms for developing intelligent computer-assisted instructional interfaces catered towards written CJK language instruction. We evaluated our interfaces on their capabilities to provide instructor-emulated feedback and assessment on the visual structure and writing technique of users' written input for two distinct written scripts, and our findings demonstrate strong results for supporting the incorporation of educational applications supporting written CJK instruction.

P. Taele (✉) · T. Hammond
Sketch Recognition Lab, Department of Computer Science & Engineering,
Texas A&M University, College Station, TX, USA
e-mail: ptaele@cse.tamu.edu

T. Hammond
e-mail: hammond@tamu.edu

© Springer International Publishing Switzerland 2015
T. Hammond et al. (eds.), *The Impact of Pen and Touch Technology on Education*,
Human-Computer Interaction Series, DOI 10.1007/978-3-319-15594-4_12

12.1 Problem Statement and Context

For the major East Asian languages consisting of Chinese, Japanese, and Korean (CJK), the written scripts that make up those languages' written component greatly differ from written English for reasons including the vast quantity, diverse variety, and visual complexity of their symbols (i.e., letters, characters). As a result, American higher education students enrolled in CJK language courses and lacking prior knowledge of related languages understandably struggle when first exposed to their written component. In order to address these difficulties, CJK language instructors employ different techniques that take advantage of the inherent properties of the written component. Some of those commonly-employed techniques include stroke order and direction, which constrains how the strokes of those symbols should be written for reducing the burden of memorization; brute force memorization, which repeatedly introduces the symbols so that they may more effectively be retained in long-term memory; and knowledge of subcomponents, which introduces the meanings or sounds of the inner components within CJK symbols so that they may be more intuitively understood [1, 3].

The traditional curriculum resources for assisting students in the mastery of the written CJK languages largely rely on a variety of sources. Language instructors are able to assist students by providing in-class demonstrations of the symbols' proper written technique (i.e., stroke order and direction) with accompanying explanations and insights for better understanding those symbols, as well as providing proper real-time assessment on students' written input. Paper workbooks serve as supplementary educational materials, which provide guided instructional drills for students to test their knowledge on the actual meaning and usage of those symbols. Moreover, practice sheets enable students to repetitiously practice writing the symbols in order to positively affect the muscle memory in writing them and absorb large quantities of symbols into their memory more effectively. While these resources have been consistent staples in the written CJK language curriculum, they also have their limitations [9]. Restricted classroom time for typical student class sizes constrains instructors from sufficiently assisting students with expert feedback and assessment of their input, and from more comprehensively demonstrating writing of the symbols. The static nature of paper notebooks means that students would not be able to receive real-time feedback of their written responses, and instructors would not be able to gauge the written technique correctness of students' delayed written responses. Furthermore, drilling students with repetitiously writing characters on practice sheets is a monotonous task for students and also increases the risk of students repetitiously practicing and memorizing potential mistakes in their writing if left unsupervised.

As a result of the existing limitations of conventional educational resources for written CJK language instruction, we explored three related key research questions in this paper. In response to the time constraint issues of language instructors, how do we achieve the benefits offered from valuable in-classroom instruction of written CJK language instruction by instructors beyond their existing time constraints? In response to the static nature of paper workbooks, how do we incorporate feedback on students' written input onto existing supplementary educational resources employed outside of the classroom? In response to the lack of oversight from practice sheets, how do we assist students in properly assessing the correctness in the visual structure and written technique of their written input absent input from human language instructors?

12.2 Method Employed

12.2.1 Stylus-Driven Tablet Environment

In order to address the core aspects of the key research questions, we propose a solution that is defined through an "intelligent language workbook" interface, combining the accessibility aspects offered by paper workbooks and practice sheets with the feedback capabilities of human language instructors. As a result, we chose to develop such an educational tool on a stylus-driven tablet environment for several reasons: it provides flexibility for use in various environments such as with instructor supervision within the classroom, from instructor assistance within the language lab, or through self-study outside the classroom; it maintains the prehensile skills and sketching surfaces already extant in writing symbols on paper; and it enables the use of state-of-the-art sketch recognition algorithms for developing tablet-based intelligent user interfaces to emulate human instructor-level feedback [6].

12.2.2 Sketch Recognition Techniques

For symbols in the written CJK languages, the properties of visual structure (i.e., how they look) and written technique (i.e., how they are written) are heavily emphasized by language instructors in order for students to effectively understand those languages' written component. As a result, instructors provide valuable feedback and assessment to students on improving the correctness of and preventing bad writing habits in their written symbols' visual structure and written technique. In developing the "intelligence" aspect of our proposed intelligent language workbook interfaces for the written CJK languages, we adopted a sketch recognition-based approach over alternative handwritten recognition-based approaches, since the former allows for students' written symbols to be recognized more stringently on their visual structure correctness and can differentiate the correctness of their written technique [6].

12.2.3 Visual Structure Recognition

We observed that symbols contained within the several written scripts in the CJK languages—especially those introduced in the novice language courses—demonstrate strong visual geometric structure, so we designed our approach to

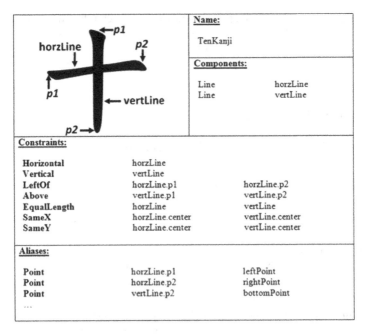

Fig. 12.1 A shape description for classifying students' written input of a specific kanji

determine the visual structure correctness of students' written input by comparing their input to geometric properties inherent in the intended symbol. This insight motivated us to employ the LADDER sketching language [2] to classify students' written input based on shape descriptions that define such geometric properties. Shape descriptions in LADDER (see Fig. 12.1) are composed of various specifications including *components*, which are either primitive geometric shapes or simpler user-defined shapes (e.g., inner components of existing symbols) and which we chose to label by either their orientation or their meaning, respectively; *constraints*, which define the physical spatial relationships between those geometric shapes; and *aliases*, which provide alternative label names to the components' original label names and which we chose to alias by their enumerated stroke order for later exploitation in the written technique recognition stage.

After constructing shape descriptions that correspond to target symbols for a particular lesson, we can determine visual structure correctness of the students' written input by first processing the original strokes of the students' written input into their interpreted geometric representation; then locating corners from various metrics of the original stroke's spatial and temporal information using the Sezgin recognizer [5], and finally extracting the written input's recognized composition of primitive geometric shapes from their located corner information using the PaleoSketch recognizer [4]. From this extracted geometric structure, our approach determines the visual structure correctness by comparing the processed original strokes of the students' written input to the components and constraints in the target shape description.

If the original strokes' recognized geometric components and constraints match the target shape description, then our approach determines the students' written input to have correct visual structure; otherwise, the written input is determined as having incorrect visual structure.

12.2.3.1   Written Technique Recognition

For visual structure recognized as correct, our approach proceeds to determining the written technique correctness by the correctness of the stroke order and direction. In LADDER shape descriptions, each recognized *component* of the students' written input is assigned a given label name with pre-defined endpoints. We also previously assigned for each stroke an *alias* label name with their stroke order enumeration in the shape description (see Fig. 12.1). This LADDER feature is exploited by first retrieving and sequentially sorting the timestamps of when each stroke was written by the user, then extracting and listing each stroke's corresponding *alias* label names, and finally checking if the enumerations from each stroke's *alias* label name is in correctly ordered sequentially to determine if correct stroke order was followed. We similarly check for correctness in stroke direction with assigned alias label names for the defined starting and ending stroke endpoints. If the students' written input is recognized as having correct stroke order and direction, then it is subsequently recognized as having correct written technique.

12.2.3.2   The "Intelligent Language Workbook" Interfaces

Based on our proposed methodology and additional feedback received from several East Asian language faculty members at our university, we developed two specialized "intelligent language workbook" interfaces that focus on distinct separate written CJK language scripts with little linguistic and visual overlap: Hashigo for the instruction of the Japanese kanji character script instruction, and LAMPS for the instruction of the Chinese zhuyin phonetic script. The general format of our intelligent language workbook interfaces—which also summarizes the overall structure shared by our specialized instances of Hashigo and LAMPS—consists of two main parts: the sketch layout, where users write the prompted symbols; and the feedback layout, which provides automated feedback and assessment of the users' written input.

When users first begin using the intelligent language workbook interfaces, they are prompted to first choose a lesson, which consists of a set of symbols taken from an existing textbook chapter; and a mode, which either enables (i.e., practice mode) or disables (i.e., review mode) accompanying information on the symbols prior to each prompted question. After the selections have been made, the user is taken to the sketch layout with a canvas to write the solution and a sidebar to prompt the task. After the user completes and submits their written input, the user is taken to the feedback layout that provides a critique of the user's performance in terms of visual structure and written technique correctness, an animation of the expected

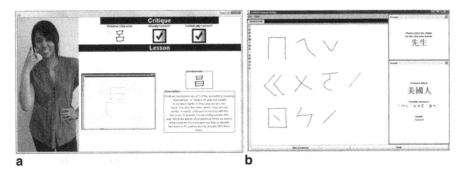

Fig. 12.2 Screenshots of developed "intelligent language workbook" interfaces. **a** Hashigo for Japanese kanji instruction [7] and **b** LAMPS for Chinese zhuyin instruction [8]

solution, and an accompanying paragraph that provides instructor-level assessment of the user's performance. The user continues through each question until completion, where a final feedback window grades the entire performance of the user for that particular lesson (Fig. 12.2).

12.3 Results and Evaluation

We summarize here the separate evaluations of our Hashigo and LAMPS intelligent language workbook interfaces on their effectiveness of several metrics, with our first metric being visual structure correctness. For Hashigo, we recruited eleven international graduate students fluent in the characters of the domain, since we desired the benchmark of our model input to match those of expert users. The result of our preliminary study for a set of nineteen characters from a selected textbook chapter using cross-validation yielded 93 % accuracy, which was on par with alternative handwriting recognition techniques. A similar study was performed with nine distinct users of similar demographics, expertise, and parameters for LAMPS and yielded 95 % accuracy.

Our subsequent metric was on written technique correctness, and we conducted a study on a group of five users—all of whom lacked prior knowledge of writing characters in the domain—to write a set of characters from a textbook chapter with only the visualization of those characters and no information on how they are supposed to be written. While the users achieved 99 % accuracy on the visual structure of those characters given the accompanying visual aid, they achieved 6 % accuracy on their written technique that we attributed to their lack of familiarity of the characters. We received similar results when the study was conducted again for LAMPS.

As a subsequent study to the written technique correctness, we conducted a pilot study of Hashigo on the metric of learning tool viability using the same set of novice users by using the interface three complete times (i.e., preview, learn, and review) for a particular textbook chapter lesson. Following their third use, we analyzed the interface's critique of users' written input for visual structure and written technique correctness. Their results showed that the users were 100 % accurate on their visual correctness and 97 % accurate on their written technique after using our interface. These results showed the potential of Hashigo's viability as a learning tool since these novice users improved their written technique correctness during those sessions from 6 to 97 %.

12.4 Future Work

Promising results from our emerging technology research work related to our initial intelligent language workbook interfaces encourage us to continue working with East Asian language faculty members at our university on possible next steps for initial deployment of these interfaces in the classroom and language lab settings. We also strongly desire for our interfaces to complement the instructors' existing curriculums as opposed to replicating their existing pedagogical methods, so we aim to coordinate more directly with the faculty members in our university for our interfaces to better accommodate the instructors' and their students' existing needs. Additionally, we would like to expand our intelligent language workbooks to incorporate other CJK language scripts such as the Korean phonetic written script and the remaining Japanese written scripts.

Acknowledgements We thank all our study participants for their time and input. We thank the members of the Sketch Recognition Lab for their insight. We thank NSF for funding in part through the REU program as well as inspiration from EEC 1129525 and EXP 1441331.

References

1. Banno, E., Ohno, Y., Sakane, Y., & Shinagawa, C. (1999). *Genki I: An integrated course in elementary Japanese I*. Japan: The Japan Times.
2. Hammond, T., & Davis, R. (2003). Ladder: A language to describe drawing, display, and editing in sketch recognition. In G. Gottlob & T. Walsh (Eds.), IJCAI-03: Proceedings of the eighteenth international joint conference on artificial intelligence, Palo Alto, 9–15 August 2003.
3. McNaughton, W., & Ying, L. (1999). *Reading & writing chinese: Traditional character edition*. Rutland: Tuttle Publishing.
4. Paulson, B., & Hammond, T. (2008). PaleoSketch: accurate primitive sketch recognition and beautification. In IUI '08: Proceedings of the 13th international conference on intelligent user interfaces, New York, 13–16 January, 2008.
5. Sezgin, T. M., Stahovich, T., & Davis, R. (2001). Sketch based interfaces: Early processing for sketch understanding. In PUI '01: Proceedings of the 2001 workshop on perceptive user interfaces, New York, 15–16 November, 2001.
6. Taele, P. (2010). Freehand sketch recognition for computer-assisted language learning of written East Asian languages. Master's Thesis, Texas A&M University.
7. Taele, P., & Hammond, T. (2009). Hashigo: a next-generation sketch interactive system for japanese kanji. In IAAI-09: Proceedings of the twenty-first innovative applications in artificial intelligence conference, Palo Alto, 14–16 July, 2009.

8. Taele, P., & Hammond, T. (2010). LAMPS: A sketch recognition-based teaching tool for mandarin phonetic symbols i. *Journal of Vis. Language Computer, 21*(2) (Apr. 2010), 109–120.
9. van Dam, A., Becker, S., & Simpson, R. M. (2005). Next-generation educational software: Why we need it and a research agenda for getting it. EDUCAUSE Review, 40, 2 (Mar/Apr. 2005), pp. 26–43.

Chapter 13
Classroom Uses for BeSocratic

Sam Bryfczynski, Roy P. Pargas, Melanie M. Cooper, Michael Klymkowsky, Josiah Hester, and Nathaniel P. Grove

Abstract This paper describes how BeSocratic can be used to improve learning and class interaction. BeSocratic is a novel intelligent tutoring system that aims to fill the gap between simple multiple-choice systems and free-response systems. The system includes a set of interactive modules that provide instructors with powerful tools to assess student performance. Beyond text boxes and multiple-choice questions, BeSocratic contains several feedback driven modules that can capture free-form student drawings. These drawings can be automatically recognized and evaluated as complex structures including Euclidean graphs, chemistry molecules, computer science graphs, or simple drawings for use within science, technology, engineering, and mathematics courses. This paper describes three use-cases for BeSocratic and how each scenario can improve learning and class interaction throughout the curriculum. These scenarios are: (1) formative assessments and tutorials, (2) free-response exercises, and (3) in-class real-time activities.

S. Bryfczynski (✉) · R. P. Pargas · M. M. Cooper · J. Hester
Clemson University, Clemson, SC, USA
e-mail: sbryfcz@clemson.edu

R. P. Pargas
e-mail: pargas@clemson.edu

M. M. Cooper
e-mail: cmelani@clemson.edu

J. Hester
e-mail: jhester@clemson.edu

M. Klymkowsky
University of Colorado, Boulder, CO, USA
e-mail: michael.klymkowsky@colorado.edu

N. P. Grove
University of North Carolina at Wilmington, Wilmington, NC, USA
e-mail: nathaniel.grove@uncw.edu

© Springer International Publishing Switzerland 2015
T. Hammond et al. (eds.), *The Impact of Pen and Touch Technology on Education,*
Human-Computer Interaction Series, DOI 10.1007/978-3-319-15594-4_13

13.1   Problem Statement and Context

Since the early days of personal computing, software has been developed for educational purposes. The number of such applications continues to increase, and the sophistication of the systems is constantly evolving. There exists a wide spectrum of educational software meeting needs from Pre-K to industry.

Today, most higher education institutions use broad learning management systems such as Blackboard, Moodle, or Instructure Canvas to aid in assessment. Additionally, specialized systems (such as the Mastering software series, OWL, etc.) exist for individual disciplines and courses. A subset of these systems includes intelligent tutoring software such as MathTutor and CogTutor, which provide students with step-by-step guidance during problem solving. While these systems have been shown to enhance student learning in a range of domains [4–6], they tend to be difficult to author, and the majority of questions they can ask fall into one of two categories: free-response text-based questions or multiple-choice/matching questions. Free-response systems allow teachers to ask meaningful questions that require students to have a deep understanding of the subject in order to answer correctly; unfortunately, they are difficult to assess quickly and without bias. Multiple choice and matching questions are more restrictive by nature, and research has suggested that these questions cannot be used to properly assess deep knowledge on a subject since the exercises often only involve memorization [2, 3, 7, 8].

Which system a teacher uses generally depends on the amount of time available to evaluate student solutions. Free response systems require teachers to manually check each submission; this is too time-consuming for teachers to perform on a regular basis. Because of this, teachers instead rely on using multiple-choice or matching questions that can be quickly or automatically evaluated. The ideal system combines the best parts of both question types: for example a teacher would be able to pose questions that require students to have a deep understanding of the material and allows students to reply in an intuitive free-form manner. Upon completion of activities, student responses would be automatically evaluated, analyzed, and made available to the teacher.

13.2   Method Employed

With this motivation, we built BeSocratic, an online intelligent tutoring system that contains a variety of question types that are free-form in nature yet well-defined to the point in which they may be automatically evaluated and analyzed [1]. BeSocratic's interactive tutors are referred to as *activities*. Each activity is made up of one or more slides. And just as slides in a slide-show have various content elements within them (e.g., text, images, videos), BeSocratic slides contain one or more *modules*.

BeSocratic modules are divided into two general categories: *non-interactive* and *interactive*. Non-interactive modules, which include text boxes, images, videos, ink canvases, and 3D molecular models do not provide students with feedback. These

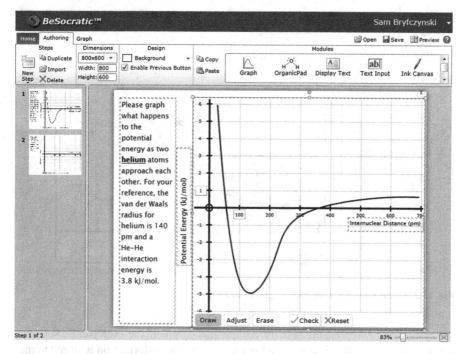

Fig. 13.1 BeSocratic's activity authoring tool

are generally used to convey information and/or instructions to students or are used
to gather information for manual analysis. Interactive modules, on the other hand,
allow BeSocratic to pose free-form questions, provide automatic response-driven
feedback to students, and enable automatic analysis for teachers. These modules
currently include SocraticGraphs, OrganicPad, and GraphPad. All of these modules
may be used together within slides to build rich, interactive activities.

Teachers construct activities from the modules in BeSocratic's Activity Authoring
Tool. Since it has been shown that tutor authoring is often a difficult and time-
consuming task, BeSocratic's Activity Authoring Tool has been designed to resemble
Microsoft PowerPoint using the Microsoft Ribbon interface, as seen in Fig. 13.1.
Similar to PowerPoint, modules are added to activities by dragging a module from
a list onto a slide; then teachers can customize the look and behavior of the module
by changing various options. The Authoring Tool also contains a preview function
for the teacher to preview how the activity will appear to the students. This allows
teachers to quickly prototype various configurations for the activity.

Once an activity is created, teachers specify a roster along with start and end dates
so that students in the roster may log into BeSocratic and complete the activities
within the time allotted. Activities and their student data are stored in the BeSocratic
database so the teacher may access them from any computer's browser connected
to the Internet. After a teacher makes an activity available, students can log into

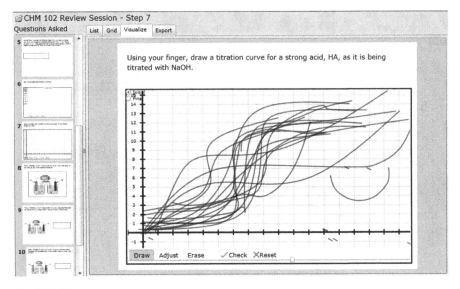

Fig. 13.2 Visualization of many student graphs drawings

the system and complete the activity. As students complete the exercise, BeSocratic records each action that is performed in the system. This information is stored to the database upon completion of each slide for analysis later. BeSocratic contains a set of powerful analysis tools that allow teachers to view, replay, and visualize individual student submissions as well as groups of student submissions as seen in Fig. 13.2.

BeSocratic currently runs on a variety of devices with varying levels of functionality. The activity authoring and analysis tools requires the Microsoft Silverlight plug-in to run inside of most common browsers (e.g., Internet Explorer, Chrome, Firefox, and Safari) on Windows and Mac computers. In its current form, BeSocratic is targeted for use with Tablet PCs and touchscreens; however, it is by no means necessary to use either. In addition, we have also developed a prototype iOS application. A screenshot of the app is shown in Fig. 13.3. This application only contains the student's viewing tool. We feel that because of the fine control needed to author a BeSocratic activity, iOS devices are not yet appropriate for tutor authoring.

The next three sections detail the primary ways teachers have been using BeSocratic: (1) formative assessments and tutorials, (2) free-response exercises, and (3) in-class real-time activities.

13.2.1   Formative Assessments and Tutorials

The primary goal of BeSocratic is the creation of intelligent tutors with the most natural interface possible. We are able to achieve this goal using our interactive modules. They enable the construction of representations (such as Euclidean graphs,

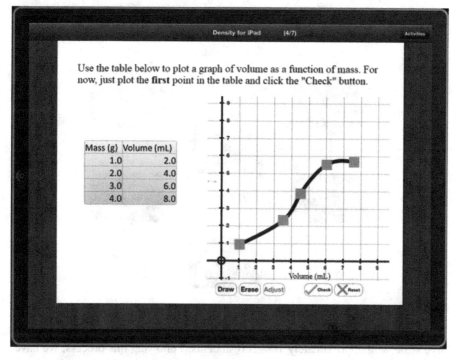

Fig. 13.3 Student completing a question on the iPad

organic chemistry molecules, computer science graphs, and simple drawings) using free-form input (via pen, finger, or mouse) while still being able to respond with tiered contextual, Socratic feedback. Teachers compose this hierarchy of rules (with associated feedback) visually, trying to address different failure areas as well as gently guiding students toward a correct understanding. The end result of this work is an effective, formative assessment system that can serve a wide range of student populations in many STEM disciplines.

We have created many formative assessment and tutorial activities using a process similar to that shown in Fig. 13.4. To start, a topic is selected with the intent to improve or assess student understanding. Once the topic for the activity has been chosen, the first step in the construction process is to interview students in order to determine specific problem areas and identify gaps in understanding. The information obtained from these interviews is used to build the initial version of the activity. This preliminary version is then tested using one-on-one interviews with students to observe how they interact and navigate through the activity; from these observations further refinements are made to address the students' comments and feedback. The revised version of the activity is then pilot tested with approximately 20–40 students to evaluate how a larger group of students progress through the activity. This is an attempt to determine if there are any issues that have not been previously addressed. Once any problematic areas have been worked out, the activity is administered on a

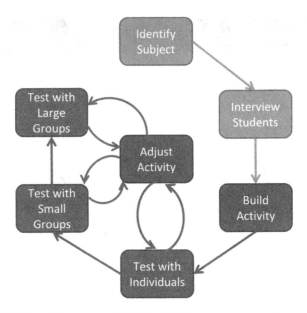

Fig. 13.4 Typical BeSocratic assessment activity creation process

large scale with approximately 100–200 students. Following this process, we have developed many rich, formative assessment activities for introductory chemistry, molecular biology, and computer science courses.

13.2.2 Free Response Exercises

While the formative assessments provide students with a high level of interactivity, we recognize that they are time-consuming to construct and test. Constructing an effective hierarchy of rules paired with feedback requires a lot of time, energy, and piloting. Often teachers want to quickly create an activity that asks students questions that don't necessarily require Socratic feedback. We have been doing exactly that by frequently having students complete short free-response homework assignments. Using just the non-interactive modules, teachers can rapidly author and deploy interesting homework questions. While these activities cannot be graded automatically, teachers can project interesting student answers (anonymously) from the homework assignment as a means to teach by example. While other systems are capable of similar features, BeSocratic has a greater number of customizations that can be utilized to tailor the interactivity of the assignments. In particular, we find that teachers are asking many ink-based questions which require students to answer questions through drawings. Teachers can then project the student submissions during lecture and have discussions on the merits of various answers. In our opinion, having students discuss answers that they have generated themselves leads to improved student engagement.

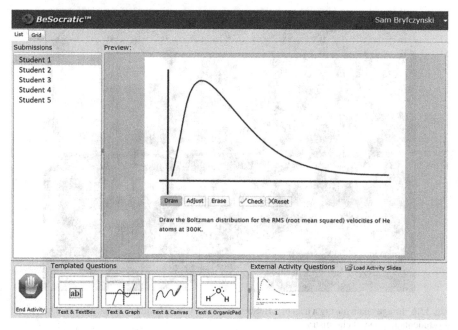

Fig. 13.5 BeSocratic's uRespond system

13.2.3   uRespond Classroom Activities

The functionality described so far has been asynchronous in that teachers create activities, student complete activities and then teachers analyze the student submissions; however, BeSocratic also contains a system called uRespond which provides a way for teachers to interact with students in real-time. This work is part of collaboration with the University of North Carolina at Wilmington. In a manner similar to Clicker systems, uRespond's goal is to allow teachers to ask BeSocratic questions and receive real-time responses from students. This allows teachers to identify misunderstandings and address them in class instead of having to wait until tests or assignments to identify and fix problems.

Internally, the uRespond system works in a similar fashion to the standard BeSocratic activity model. Teachers start by initializing a uRespond session with a name, save location, and roster. This starts an initially empty activity. Once students have loaded the blank activity associated with the uRespond activity, the teacher may either send students previously created activity steps from other activities or send predefined template questions. Figure 13.5 displays an example of the teacher's view during a uRespond session. Template questions and previously-created activity steps are shown along the bottom of the figure. Clicking one will send the question to all the students (Fig 13.6).

Fig. 13.6 Image taken during a trial of a BeSocratic activity in a chemistry class. This trial included 93 students in general chemistry

Students respond using the same activity completion tool that was previously described. When a student responds, a new entry into the submission table is added with the student's user key, replay and final submission. The teacher's uRespond client periodically polls the database for any new submissions for the current question. If new submissions are found, the teacher's view is updated with the new submissions as seen along the left side of Fig. 13.4. The student's activity also polls the database for additional questions added by the teacher. If a new question is found, it is downloaded and presented to the student.

uRespond is a powerful teaching tool that allows teachers to be extremely flexible. By flexible, we mean that questions during a uRespond session can be mixed and matched depending on the feedback received from students. For example, teachers may have a series of planned questions that they create in the authoring tool ahead of class. As they send students these questions and start seeing the answers that students respond with, the teacher may want to change the plan and ask a follow-up question that had not initially been planned on. This is where the teachers may select from a template question, such as a question with text and an ink canvas where teachers ask students to draw something. Alternatively, teachers can load an appropriate question from another activity or quickly create a new question altogether with the authoring tool. Using uRespond in this manner, teachers can control the flow of class by recognizing difficult concepts and immediately addressing them.

13.3   Results and Evaluation

BeSocratic has been implemented in chemistry, molecular biology, and computer science courses in three different universities (Clemson University, the University of Colorado Boulder, and the University of North Carolina at Wilmington) and has collected over 200,000 student submissions. Instructors are using BeSocratic inside the classroom with lecture sizes sometimes exceeding 100 students. We are currently pilot-testing a variety of formal assessment and tutorial activities. Several of the pilot tests show positive learning gains with students; however, further testing and refinement is required to verify the results. In addition to these assessment activities, we are testing BeSocratic's effectiveness as a homework management system in several chemistry courses at Clemson University. We have found that the ability to quickly and easily record and project student drawings without the need to collect paper-based assignments is particularly appealing. uRespond is undergoing pilot-tests at the University of North Carolina Wilmington where it has been used with students during review sessions before chemistry exams.

13.4   Future Work

Our current primary focus is evaluating the effectiveness of the activities we have created. Further testing is required before results can be properly reported. So far, BeSocratic activities have primarily been created for chemistry, molecular biology, and computer science classes. We have begun developing activities for physics and mathematics courses as well and believe that properly developed exercises could improve student learning in these disciplines.

As mentioned in Sect. 3, BeSocratic was created with the Microsoft Silverlight framework. Unfortunately, Microsoft has recently indicated that it will not be updating Silverlight in the future. Because of this we have been actively developing a standards based, HTML5 web application to emulate portions of the BeSocratic system. We believe moving to the HTML5 platform will ensure BeSocratic's future on the plugin-less web; especially since the technologies that comprise HTML5 are nearly universally supported on all devices by their native browsers. Emerging devices such as the Apple iPad, Android Tablet, Kindle Fire, and Microsoft Surface each use a different software development kit yet each of these devices has a built-in web browser capable of running HTML5 applications.

Acknowledgements   We would like to acknowledge and thank the NSF for providing funding for this project (TUES-1043707, TUES-1122472). We would also like to acknowledge our collaborators at Clemson University, the University of Colorado at Boulder, and the University of North Carolina at Wilmington.

References

1. Bryfczynski, S., Pargas, R., Cooper, M., & Klymkowsky, M. (2012). *BeSocratic: Graphically assessing student knowledge.* IADIS International Conference on Mobile Learning. Berlin, Germany.
2. Glaser, R. (1988). *Cognitive and environmental perspectives on assessing achievement.* In Assessment in the service of learning ETS Invitational Conference, Princeton.
3. Glaser, R. (1991). Expertise and assessment. In M. Wittrock & E. Baker (Eds.), *Testing and cognition.* Englewood Cliffs: Prentice-Hall.
4. Koedinger, K. R., Anderson, J. R., Hadley, W. H., & Mark, M. A. (1997). Intelligent tutoring goes to school in the big city. *International Journal of Artificial Intelligence in Education, 8,* 30–43.
5. Lesgold, A., Lajoie, S., Bunzo, M., & Eggan, G. (1992). Sherlock: A coached practice environment for an electronics troubleshooting job. In J. Larkin & R. Chabay (Eds.), *Computer assisted instruction and intelligent tutoring systems: Shared goals and complementary approaches* (pp. 201–238). Hillslade: Erlbaum.
6. Mark, M., & Greer, J. E. (1995). The vcr tutor: Effective instruction for device operation. *The Journal of the Learning Sciences, 4*(2), 209–246.
7. Resnick, L. B., & Resnick, D. P. (1992). Assessing the thinking curriculum: New tools for education reform. In B. R. Gifford & M. C. O'Connor (Eds.), *Changing assessments: Alternative views of aptitude, achievement and instruction* (pp. 37–76). Boston: Kluwer Academic.
8. Shepard, L. (1991). Interview on assessment issues with Lorrie Shepard. *Educational Researcher, 20*(2), 21–23.

Part IV
Emerging Technologies—Collaboration, Learning, & Best Practices

Chapter 14
Use of Layers and User Manipulation to Improve Group Environments

Christopher Findeisen and Page Heller

Abstract Collaborative learning systems benefit from the ability of multiple students to interact with each other in an online workspace. However, collaborative clutter can occur when multiple students overwrite, erase and add side notes to the workspace. This paper offers a system and method for use of layering, user manipulation, and client-side service to control multiple user interaction and make online collaborative workspace useful. Early results indicate that the solution is seamless and intuitive, allowing individual users control over their own environments in a collaborative system.

14.1 Problem Statement

Internet-based eLearning tools are changing the way teachers interact with students. Schools set up virtual classrooms where one teacher can reach many remote students. Teachers present course materials and exercises online for local students. In addition, courses are being offered as online learning systems that allow for self-paced advancement and mastery.

The vast resources of the Internet are changing the way students study as well. Students spend more time online than ever before. A study conducted by the Pew Research Center's Internet & American Life Project indicates that close to 100 % of all college students and 92 % of non-students 18–24 years of age use the Internet [1].

To date, however, students have had few choices to work in collaboration with other students to enhance their study process. As a result, most online study time is spent working individually or in social tools designed only for communication and with little support for studying.

C. Findeisen (✉)
Department of Computer Science & Engineering, Texas A&M University, College Station, TX, USA
e-mail: cfindeisen7@gmail.com

P. Heller
HopesCreek, College Station, TX, USA
e-mail: pageheller@hopescreekconsulting.com

© Springer International Publishing Switzerland 2015   139
T. Hammond et al. (eds.), *The Impact of Pen and Touch Technology on Education*,
Human-Computer Interaction Series, DOI 10.1007/978-3-319-15594-4_14

Now, however, virtual group environments are beginning to enter the scene and are ubiquitous in the social sphere. Lately, there has been a push to introduce collaborative themes into the education system to expand the capacity of classrooms [2]. These include distance education, webinars, online office hours, conferencing, and meeting support systems.

As such systems are made available to students they also come under scrutiny. As author Nicholas Croft points out [3]:

> The physical and temporal separation of tutor and student, and between students themselves, can lead to feelings of isolation. The lack of interaction and discussion between students lessens the richness of the learning experience and omits a significant element of the constructivist approach to learning.

It is thus important to maintain the ability of students to interact with one another. One of the most important areas of student interaction is during times of study.

A small number of new entries in collaborative support for education include online whiteboards that multiple students may use for working problems or creating designs. Graphical interfaces are important within these virtual group environments. With three or four students working on a whiteboard in the same online space, the graphics can quickly become hard to manage. Overwriting, erasing and adding side notes can make the workspace unreadable.

The proposed system is conceived to make graphical interfaces within virtual group environments more effective, particularly with larger groups of users. The system involves the server/client relationship, data storage, and user privileges. It operates such that each user can manipulate and control their own workspace, but in conjunction with others.

The system groups data within layers, which provides for methods to efficiently filter out noise and individually prioritize important information for each user within a group. These layers also maintain the integrity of each user's work by limiting write control.

We believe that this system is most meaningful and useful within a whiteboard environment, where a collaborative space is shared. Thus, our system pairs well with pen and touch technologies, because they excel within these graphical environments.

14.2 Method

We propose a layering system and method allowing cooperative graphical interaction between spatially diverse individuals. The system functions to permit several users to interact with a virtual group environment under control of remote computers or mobile devices to manipulate a virtual display.

Each user has read-write control of an individual layer within the virtual group environment and may stack and view layers of other participating users in an arbitrary read-only fashion to form a customized display view associated with individual user layer ordering preferences. Each user may also simplify the view by temporarily removing or deactivating one or more layers belonging to others or themselves.

A web server coordinates with the system by storing the layers in a database and interacts over the Internet with remote user computer systems to permit updates of individual user layers and dissemination of read-only views to remote user computer systems.

Others have suggested the use of layers for evaluating online collaborative learning interactions by collecting statistical use information for user interaction, task performance and group functioning [4]. The application described in the aforementioned work, however, is used to assess a student's participation and interaction in a collaborative session.

The collaborative system and method described here is designed to alleviate the "collaborative clutter" and improve the content management for multiple users editing the same environment. Precisely, this system is devised to best complement graphical interfaces for use in online collaborative environments.

14.2.1   Layers

The system invokes layers to organize data and sets privileges across entire layers. Thus, users are able to manipulate the way they view and edit data intuitively from a high level of abstraction.

When the environment is created, separate layers are created and assigned to each of the initial users. As a new user later joins the environment, they are also assigned a unique new layer.

Each user has read-write control over their own layer and read control over all other layers within the virtual group environment. Thus, all of the work or interaction made by a given user is attached to their assigned layer and carry the user privileges according to that layer.

Each user interaction or edit made gets sent to the database, placed on the appropriate layer, and then the change is disseminated to all connected clients.

14.2.2   Manipulation

The client-side impact of this layering system is visible in the methods that manipulate these layers. Layers are ordered differently for each user. Particularly, each user's display prioritizes their layer and places it on top. The order of other layers is arbitrary. The user can adjust and order layers according to their preference. Perhaps the most critical method of the layering system permits the user to prioritize which layers are relevant and hide the layers that are not. This is valuable in many settings, but the value is readily seen in large groups where only some individuals' work may be relevant.

This system and method is exceptionally good at grouping and filtering uninteresting "noise," which can be different for individual users. The layering system is crucial for this function, because it groups objects according to ownership. This grouping is a tool that allows the system to quickly and efficiently assign privileges, coordinate updates, and disseminate changes to each independent user display.

14.2.3   Server-Client Relationship

The client-side computer system detects user interaction and reports valid updates to the server. The server identifies the client and assigns the update to the proper layer. It then stores the change within the server's database. Although this relationship certainly is not new amongst web applications, our system is particular in the ownership of objects based upon layers.

The server then updates all other clients with the change and identification for that layer. The client stores the update locally and only updates the user's display if that layer is currently "shown" (i.e. not hidden) on that user's computer system.

14.3   Evaluation and Results

The layered collaborative whiteboard was released under beta version control in October of 2013 to a select group of students at Texas A&M University and the University of Texas at San Antonio. We targeted STEM majors, and we selected students through multiple STEM organizations at Texas A&M. We chose to target STEM majors because we believe that they will gain the most value from our tool. This hypothesis is proposed based on two observations. First, STEM subjects cover a high number of symbols and diagrams not supported by traditional text editors, and second, their studies often require group work.

As of this writing, there are approximately 150 students using the beta version of the online study tool. Of these, we estimate that about 70 % of users are undergraduate students within STEM majors. The other 30 % of users have been adopted through general marketing, and their demographic identity is not consistent.

Students were asked to provide feedback through direct questions, open-response, and through a simple voting tool within the web app. An examination of collected feedback indicates that a large percentage of users were interested in the layering controls. However, though many users regularly used the layer controls, we received feedback reporting that some users did not understand how to access or use the layer controls. Visibility was usually the issue—the layer controls were contained in a side-panel, and they were not initially visible for the users.

Results indicate early success, despite some reports of confusion. We suspect that increased visibility and/or user education would have increased the usage of the layer controls.

14.4   Conclusion

The system outlined within this paper was conceived to improve the effectiveness of virtual group environments, particularly intended within the sphere of education. The system presented will greatly increase the effectiveness of a virtual group environment by permitting multiple users to collaborate with greater control and filter information independently according to preference. The system leverages the classification and use of layers to permit users to manipulate displays at a high level.

References

1. Smith, A., Rainie, L., Zickuhr, K. (2011). College students and technology, Pew Report, July 11.
2. Wagner, E. (2006). Adobe systems, delivering on the promise of eLearning. http://www.adobe.com/government/pdfs/promise_elearning_wp.pdf.
3. Croft, N., Dalton, A., & Grant, M. (2011). Overcoming isolation in distance learning: Building a learning community through time and space, Center for Education in the Built Environment working paper N0. 18, University of the West of England, Bristol.
4. Snásel, V., & Abraham, A., et al. (2012). A layered framework for evaluating on-Line collaborative learning interactions. *Journal of Computational and Theoretical Nano-science, 9*, 1–18.

Chapter 15
VText: A Tablet Based E-Textbook Framework

John Cristy and Joseph G. Tront

Abstract The VText framework is designed to provide many of the desired features of an e-textbook in such a way that it provides pedagogical value rather than just convenience for students. Many so-called e-textbook solutions available today provide few features beyond those possible with hardcopy textbooks. The VText framework is built as an add-in to Microsoft's note-taking program, OneNote. The add-in provides features which facilitate the use of OneNote as a reader and educational tool while leaving in place OneNote's strengths in note-taking, collaboration, and search.

This paper discusses the necessary features of e-textbooks, the user experience of VText, and the planned evaluation of VText. The evaluation will consider factors such as usability, student learning performance, and satisfaction. The main areas of interest for the evaluation include effective note-taking in the e-text, rehearsal skills, facilitation of collaboration, ease of use for the student, improvements in integrating lectures and individual study, and the general utility of tools included in the plug-in such as the Bluetooth Scanner, which allows pictures to be inserted into OneNote from an Android device. The results will be used to generate suggestions for further improved work in this area.

15.1 Problem Statement and Context

15.1.1 Literature Review

Computers, particularly tablet computers, provide a potential new platform for delivering textbook content to students. Shepperd et al. found in 2008 that students who tried the e-textbook, in their case simply the same as a paper copy but in digital form, spent less time studying although they performed as well as the students using

J. Cristy (✉) · J. G. Tront
Bradley Department of Electrical & Computer Engineering, Virginia Polytechnic Institute and State University, Blacksburg, VA, USA
e-mail: jcristy@vt.edu

J. G. Tront
e-mail: jgtront@vt.edu

© Springer International Publishing Switzerland 2015
T. Hammond et al. (eds.), *The Impact of Pen and Touch Technology on Education,*
Human-Computer Interaction Series, DOI 10.1007/978-3-319-15594-4_15

a paper copy [8]. They also found that while students found the e-textbook easy to use, they did not find it convenient nor would they use it or recommend it in the future. However, based on their findings as well as those of an earlier study by Aust, it seems likely that computer screens are not fundamentally more difficult to study on then paper and using computers may increase the efficiency of studying [1]. While these results seem positive, the results of a more recent study by Daniel seem to suggest that electronic formats are not more efficient, though again not detrimental to performance [2]. Daniel found that e-textbooks tended to cause more multi-tasking and therefore longer study periods, contrary to Shepperd's findings of less time spent studying.

While the previous research found that simple e-textbooks are nearly equal to paper copies, other research shows the potential for feature-rich e-textbooks to be much greater. Guess reports findings that note-taking and highlighting were the major features that students were interested in [3]. Snowhill also identified note-taking as an important feature as well as multi-media, full text searching, reference linking, convenience, and portability among others [9]. A discussion at WIPTE 2010 identified many of the same features as desirable as well as text-to-speech, collaboration, internal and external searching, and individualized tutoring and assessment [10]. Work by Kiewra [4] and Martinez [7] also demonstrates the importance of note-taking for student achievement and the effect of difficult-to-use platforms on proper note-taking. This problem is best solved on digital systems by allowing free-form notes, including a variety of possible inputs, such as typing, pen, audio, and video. However, while there is agreement on useful features, there has been little testing of the affects of feature rich e-Textbook platform use on student performance.

15.1.2   Previous Efforts

One of the earlier featured e-textbook candidates tested in college classrooms was the Kindle DX. In 2008, a pilot study was performed at many schools across the country. The study at Reed College found that the Kindle DX provided students with a usable form factor, legible display, long battery life, convenient delivery mechanism, and paper savings [6]. However, there were few pedagogical improvements. The Kindle DX did not allow students to annotate and highlight content in PDF files, a feature identified as being of particular pedagogical importance. Students and faculty also complained about difficult distribution of reading materials beyond the course text. While Amazon had helped to ensure the textbooks would be available, many of the supplementary readings were only available as PDFs. Other issues included poor image display due to low resolution and lack of color, slow changing between pages and books, difficulties for the visually impaired, and cumbersome note-taking.

Another attempt at creating an e-textbook was the Kno tablet. The Kno was a promising, full-featured e-textbook hardware and software solution [5]. There were originally two systems proposed, one with a 14.1 inch touch screen and the other with two of the screens hinged together. This form factor would have allowed a paper-book-like experience with the benefits of a computer. The hardware also allowed for

Bluetooth devices, such as a keyboard, to connect to the system. The software for textbooks included many features such as note-taking, highlighting, and search that would have made the Kno fit many of the requirements of a fully featured device. There was even a planned SDK for developers to extend the system including Google Documents, now Drive, and Microsoft Office Live support. Unfortunately, the project was cancelled in April 2011 in favor of a software only approach. The current Kno software is web-based and includes annotations and highlighting, however, no pen support. There is also no easy, built-in way to view two pages at one time as the two screened tablet would have allowed.

15.2 Method Employed

VText is an e-textbook platform built as an add-in for Microsoft OneNote. The goal is to provide the tools and capabilities desirable in an e-textbook as identified by previous efforts while allowing OneNote to remain one of the most fully featured note-taking programs available today. By doing so, the add-in, along with OneNote, can improve both individual study and the lecture experience. VText also considers the role of publishers and authors by including mechanisms, in addition to those included by OneNote, to import various formats of material without losing capabilities. This project also intends to perform a formal analysis of the benefits of a fully featured e-textbook compared to simple e-textbooks and paper copies.

Since OneNote is not intended for textbook display, some changes had to be made to meet users' expectations for interacting with textbooks. The add-in adds controls, gestures, and screen configurations. One allows users to flip through the pages with simple motions while another lets users easily choose how their screen real estate should be used based on the size and style of their device. To automatically have two windows open side-by-side, top-to-bottom, or have only one window containing the contents of the book, the user simply clicks one of three buttons added to OneNote's ribbon interface. It is also possible to have these two separate windows synchronized so that when one changes, the other is also changed, creating a book like environment. Multiple windows can also be unsynchronized, allowing the two windows to display content from different sections or different books entirely.

To ease the flipping of pages while preserving screen real estate taken up by the default OneNote UI, two mechanisms have been added to support users on both standard laptops and tablets. For those on tablets, gestures can also be used. Simply moving a finger, pen, or the mouse left or right along the bottom of the window will flip the page backwards or forwards through the book. The user can configure which input devices trigger page flips via the add-in's settings. For those on standard laptops, two buttons can be added to the screen to allow easy flipping back and forth between pages. This works in both synchronized and unsynchronized modes by offering one or two sets of buttons, respectively. Navigation within a single page is provided by OneNote's included drag-to-pan and pinch-to-zoom functionalities.

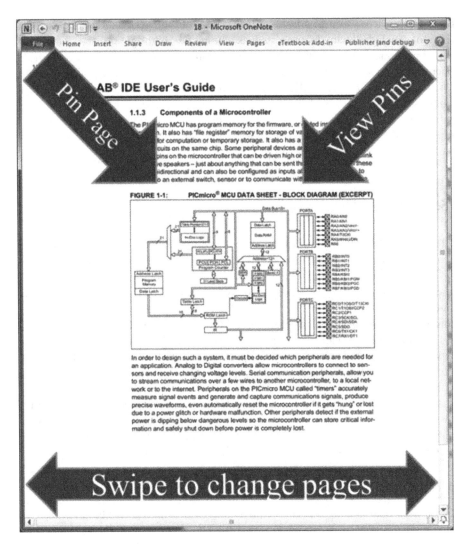

Fig. 15.1 VText's gestures

VText provides two more gestures to allow for quick navigation and bookmarking. By moving a finger from the top left corner of the window in a diagonal direction down and right, a page will be pinned. To view the pinned pages, a user simply drags their finger from the top right in a diagonal direction down and left. This will bring up a window with a list of all pages that have been pinned allowing a user to quickly return to the page or remove it from the saved list. These functions can also be controlled through the Ribbon interface for those without touch or pen enabled devices. Figure 15.1 shows the gestures provided by VText.

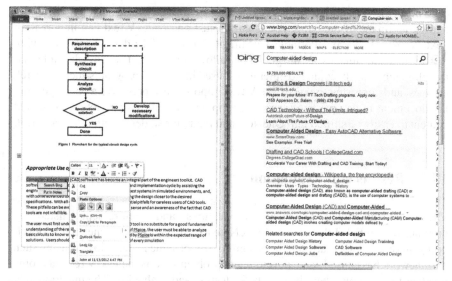

Fig. 15.2 Example of the *search* the web feature

While OneNote already provides a mechanism for searching the contents of hand-written notes, images, and text inside any book, VText adds a mechanism to search the web using popular search engines such as Google, Yahoo, and Wikipedia for any text content in the books quickly and easily. This feature, shown in Fig. 15.2, can be accessed by selecting the desired search terms, then pressing and holding or right clicking to launch the add-in's context menu which includes an option to "Search the Web". This operation can also be accessed by clicking the button added to the ribbon interface.

VText adds the ability to aggregate important text from a chapter into a notes page. To add a note to the notes page, a user selects the text, presses and holds with their finger or right clicks, then selects "Add to Notes" on the add-in's context menu. The selected text is then automatically copied to the notes page located at the beginning of the chapter or book. This should allow students to easily see sections they felt were important when reading the book or excerpts they felt they needed to review further.

By utilizing OneNote, a student will have access to all of their notes on all of their devices. This can also be used to share notes from lectures and readings with other students. The add-in includes a mechanism to allow all students to synchronize the page they are viewing with their instructor allowing them to seamlessly follow along with discussions in the text. These abilities have potential to improve collaboration between students both in and out of the classroom. VText also enhances the lecture experience with a mechanism to quickly insert pictures into their digital notebook from an Android device via Bluetooth. For instance, a student may wish to include notations on a chalkboard or handwritten notes if using a non-pen enabled tablet.

While OneNote allows for a document to be printed into OneNote, essentially putting an image of the entire document on just one page, VText can import Rich Text Format (RTF) and Portable Document Format (PDF) documents preserving text as text and images as images. This allows the content to be selectable and therefore more easily copied to other notes, used in external programs such as search engines, and converted to voice. The VText importer also preserves a one page from the document to one page in OneNote mapping. This allows previously generated content to easily be shifted into OneNote and ready for students with minimal effort.

15.3 Results and Evaluation

VText has attempted to meet the features and requirements listed by previous research. While the use of OneNote as a base has been beneficial in developing this e-textbook platform, the design control of some features lost by using such a framework has caused some development problems. Nonetheless, VText has come together to the point where it is ready for testing and evaluation. The intention is to evaluate the effectiveness of both VText and other feature-rich e-textbook platforms by using it as a tool in an introductory programming course in the spring of 2013.

A baseline will be established to provide information about the students' opinions of e-textbooks. The initial survey will ask student's for insight in to their willingness to try e-textbooks, their technical background, and their experiences with traditional books. While these questions will be individual Likert items, there will be open ended questions for students to provide additional concerns about using e-textbooks. These questions intend to find insight into students' current opinions and also to see if these opinions change after using VText. Data about their personal hardware will be collected as part of the survey to see if there are trends that should be taken into account in further development.

To assess improvements in learning, the final survey will ask students to consider how VText affected their coursework. Students will be asked if they believe VText encouraged them to spend more time reading, read more effectively, interact with other students and professors more often, and develop a more complete understanding of course materials. The student's will be asked to evaluate these traits as individual Likert items. Students will also be asked to assess the utility of various features, such as the Bluetooth scanner, through open ended and multiple choice questions. Finally, students will be asked to re-answer some questions from the baseline survey to see if their perception of e-textbooks has changed. Faculty will be asked to make similar assessments as well as to evaluate improvements, both perceived and objectively, in student understanding, participation, and performance.

The data provided by the students and faculty will be used to determine beneficial improvements for the tool from both an operational and pedagogical perspective. This evaluation will be used to determine the direction for VText as well as advise future e-textbook development.

References

1. Aust, R., Kelley, M., & Roby, W. (1993). The use of hyper-reference and conventional dictionaries. *Educational Technology Research and Development, 41*(4), 63–74. http://link. springer.com/article/10.1007/BF02297512#page-1.
2. Daniel, D. B. E-textbooks at what cost? Performance and use of electronic v. Print texts. *Computers & Education.* http://www.citeulike.org/group/13454/article/7136283. Accessed 1 Nov 2012.
3. Guess, A. (2008). E-textbooks—For real this time? *Inside higher education.* Accessed 1 Nov 2012.
4. Kiewra, K. A., & Benton, S. L. (1988). The relationship between information-processing ability and notetaking. *Contemporary Educational Psychology, 13*(1), 33–44.
5. Kno. http://www.kno.com. Accessed 2 Nov 2012.
6. Marmarelli, T. (2010). The Reed College Kindle study. https://reed.edu/cis/about/kindle_ pilot/Reed_Kindle_report.pdf. Accessed 1 June 2012.
7. Martinez, A. (2010). Amazon.com's Kindle fails first college test. *The Seattle Times.* http://www.seattletimes.com. Accessed 1 July 2011.
8. Shepperd, J. A., Grace, J. L., & Koch, E. J. (2008). Evaluating the electronic textbook: Is it time to dispense with the paper text? *Teaching of Psychology, 35*(1), 2–5
9. Snowhill, L. (2001). E-books and their future in academic libraries: An overview. *D-lib.* http:// www.citeulike.org/group/13454/article/7136283.
10. Tront, J. (2010). Operations needed in e-textbooks of the future. http://filebox.ece.vt.edu/ ~jgtront/wipte/e_textbook_functionality.pdf. Accessed 21 Feb 2011.

Chapter 16
Embodied Interaction Through the Fingers: Ebooks for the Blind and Navigation in Virtual Spaces

Francis Quek

Abstract We shall explore interaction on a touch surface in two domains. In the first, we shall look at a system that enables Individuals with Blindness or Severe Visual Impairment (IBSVI) to read at their own pace. We show how reading and information access are inherently embodied activities, and how touch interaction can support reading for IBSVI. In the second project, we will investigate one of the challenges of spatial knowledge acquisition while moving through large virtual spaces. The widespread availability of consumer HDTVs with 3D capability have brought them within reach of use in classroom and other learning environments. We demonstrate how transferring walking action to the hand and fingers can enable virtual navigation with benefits in the form of route knowledge, survey knowledge, and perceptual gains over traditional virtual navigation techniques. The technique is lightweight and suitable for widespread use for learning.

16.1 Introduction

This paper explores how embodied interaction theories may inform new and innovative use of tablet and touch technology. Consequently, these innovative uses of tablet and touch technology grounds embodied interaction research by providing concrete instances where embodiment theory has produced systems and applications that demonstrate clear benefits.

We will first contextualize our work by elucidating our perspective of embodiment. We follow this up by discussing two very different lines of research that share a common thread of employing 'embodied thinking' as the fountainhead of their conceptualization. The first project is on supporting Individuals with Blindness or Severe Visual Impairment (IBSVI) to read. The second project is on effective lightweight navigation in large virtual reality spaces that support enhanced spatial learning and awareness.

F. Quek (✉)
Department of Visualization, TAMU Embodied Interaction Laboratory (TEILab),
Texas A&M University, 77840 College Station, TX, USA
e-mail: quek@tamu.edu

© Springer International Publishing Switzerland 2015
T. Hammond et al. (eds.), *The Impact of Pen and Touch Technology on Education*,
Human-Computer Interaction Series, DOI 10.1007/978-3-319-15594-4_16

153

16.2 Embodiment, Thought, and Interaction

The basic tenet of our approach to embodied interaction is the idea that human thinking itself is grounded in the machinery of mind (cognitive, perceptual, sensory) that enables our function in the physical, temporal, social, and affective world that we inhabit [1]. The key issue is not whether a particular interaction methodology is explicitly physical. Adding a humanoid avatar to an interaction does not, for example, necessarily make an interface more 'embodied' from this perspective. Our interest is in how embodiment may engage mind for activity that may or may not even employ overt physical action. In the words of Michael Polanyi, *"we can know more than we can tell"* [2]. For Polanyi much this knowledge is *"in the body"* and is 'tacit' in that we find difficult to explain or articulate what this knowledge comprises. The mental machinery of embodiment is engaged, for example, in language [3, 4], mathematics [5], and imagination [6]. In the words of Margaret Wilson, instead of the body serving as a slave of mind *"... we find the body (or its control systems) serving the mind. This takeover by the mind, and the concomitant ability to mentally represent what is distant in time or space, may have been one of the driving forces behind the runaway train of human intelligence that separated us from other hominids."*

We do not imply that that there is a single cognitive principle or perceptual model that constitutes embodiment. That the human mind is embodied does not mean that there is a single model that explains all embodied thought and function. At issue are the cognitive, perceptual, and sensory strategies and resources for our physical-spatial, temporal-dynamic, social-cultural, and affective-emotional function that we appropriate for abstract thought and language. An analogy may help to explain the significance of this 'purpose-oriented' approach to embodied interaction. For our analogy, consider the GPGPU approach to computing [7, 8] where high-speed architectures designed for graphics are appropriated for general purpose computing. There is no single model behind the way memory, processor pipelines, and buses are designed for particular GPUs. They are designed for the purpose of the kinds of processes needed for modern graphics computation. To understand why certain non-graphics algorithms are more easily implemented or more or less efficient on GPU architecture, the programmer cannot ignore the purpose for which the architecture was designed in the first place. Similarly, understanding how underlying embodied functions and strategies of mind may be appropriated for higher thought may be important in our design of technology that supports that mind in its function.

In the design of technologies to support of human learning, especially, it is important for us to consider this embodied perspective. In the rest of this paper, we shall show how this consideration may be operationalized in two designs and uses of tablet and touch technologies to support reading for IBSVI and for spatial knowledge acquisition when navigating in large virtual reality spaces.

16.3 Design of an E-Reader for IBSVI

Our first project is in the design of e-Readers for IBSVI [9–13]. The underlying premise of this project is that books are information designed for embodied humans with sight. In fact, the very form of the information itself is organized for visual access. Walter Ong, in his highly influential work "Orality and Literacy: The Technologizing of the Word" [14] argued that before the invention of printing and widespread literacy, all information was designed for aural consumption. Alliteration, rhyme, and orally-oriented organization permeated all literature. After the advent of printing, information became increasingly organized with the expectation of visual access in its very fabric. When paper became the dominant form of storage, transfer, and representation of knowledge, spatial organization, prosaic form, and visual markings (e.g., varying fonts and typestyles) have become the coin of the realm for information organization.

16.3.1 Understanding the Problem

To understand this, consider reading this paper without the ability to look back a paragraph or two, or even to skip back to the introduction to see what the fundamental premise of this paper is. The problem for IBSVI is that Braille, invented in 1824, is still the only information format that supports spatial reading. Unfortunately Braille literacy is declining in the USA for various reasons, and the current Braille literacy level stands at 10 % [15]. Various forms of refreshable Braille are limited to very small arrays of no more than eight lines of 40 characters each at maximum. Just as importantly, Braille is cumbersome. "Harry Potter and the Order of the Phoenix" is 870 pages in the paperback version, and the Braille it is thirteen 14" × 11" volumes that makes a two-foot high stack.

Currently, the most viable alternative to Braille is the audio book that renders text into audio streams. The IBSVI has limited control to play, pause, and rewind the audio, but do not have the ability to read and reread in the random order that is trivial for the sighted. Various solutions that translate printed books using OCR technology essentially proffer the same solution. They obliterate space, and render information as linear streams of ephemeral information borne by vibrating molecules of air. The problem is that the information was designed for visual access, and IBSVI is left with the task of maintaining all context, organization, and prior information in memory. While audio books may be suitable for leisure reading, few sighted people would entertain studying for an examination using an audio book. This may explain why very few IBSVI advance through high school and beyond.

The introduction of slate-type devices and large form-factor smart phones threatens to widen the information divide for the IBSVI as information becomes more readily available to the sighted more rapidly. Conceptually, we address the spatial nature of informational media itself. Informational resources are not conceived or designed in a vacuum. They are optimized for consumption by embodied beings, and in this case, typically endowed with vision. An apropos analogy may be a world endowed with staircases designed because we are bipedal (as opposed to wheeled or arboreal) beings. Such a world is biased against individuals with paraplegia. The differences in the information/media world from this analogy are twofold. First, the spatial nature of the media bias is not as obvious, and so, not as well studied or understood. Consequently, the importance of visuo-spatiality for information access is undervalued. Second, unlike the staircase analogy, the solution is not as straight-forward as building ramps between floors. The entire design of floors would be an impediment if the analogy were to hold. Individuals deprived of a visuo-spatial sense do not just have an input-output problem. The entire conceptualization of information is permeated with this spatial formulation. It is not just an information repackaging issue, because the repackaging would have to involve a complete information re-design. Rather, one has to think of providing individuals without vision with an alternate means to access space and not just information bits.

16.3.2 STAAR Solution Overview

Figure 16.1 pictures our Situated Touch Audio Annotator and Reader (STAAR) e-Reader designed to provide spatial access to textual information for IBSVI. Figure 16.1-left shows an iPad with text rendered in it. The STAAR e-reader can handle any PDF document. As the IBSVI moves her finger across the text, as she touches each word the reader sounds the word. The system tracks the finger, and speaks the word at the anticipated rate at which the IBSVI moves across a line of text—in essence giving her control of her own reading rate. Figure 16.1-right shows an embossed overlay with a tactile pattern that provides the IBSVI with landmarks and the haptic feedback needed to stay on line and to maintain place across the iPad [11]. A set of tactile buttons allows for a limited set of page and reading controls. The vertical lines allow the IBSVI to more rapidly find a position on a line, and the vertical ruler on the left side of the overlay allows the IBSVI to locate lines of text. A minimal set of sonifications is designed to provide the IBSVI with some awareness of page structure (e.g., where the white space is).

The STAAR system thus provides a spatial tactile landmark grid for textual read-ing, and an audio system that renders the information on the page by location of touch. The IBSVI is able to fuse both of these modes of sensing to gain an under-standing of the structure of the page, and to read and reread at her own pace and under her control.

16.3.3 STAAR Design

Figure 16.2 provides a graphical overview of the subsystems that make up the STAAR e-Reader. The left of the figure shows the Basic System Components of the system

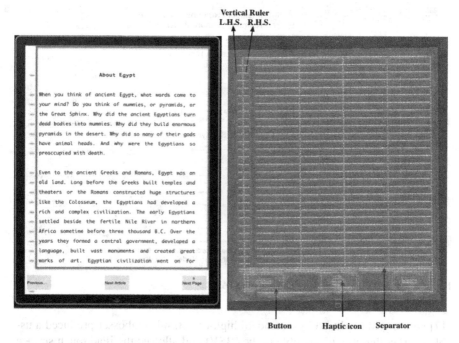

Fig. 16.1 STAR reader with touchable text and overlay

architecture, page layout and description, and overlay design. The top right of the figure shows the design for Intelligent Runtime Reading Support that helps the IBSVI to stay on a horizontal line during reading. The bottom-left of the figure shows the sub-systems for audio support. While the detailed design is beyond the scope of this paper, we shall provide a high-level overview of these system components to elucidate the functioning of the e-Reader system, and how it addresses the requirements and provides the functionality discussed earlier.

16.3.3.1 Basic System Components

The system architecture has four major subsystems that (1) Interprets standard PDF documents; (2) Models the page/document to be rendered spatially on the iPad; (3) Tracks the actions of the IBSVI on the touch surface of the iPad; and, (4) Produces the audio to render the page dynamically.

We include the basic document presentation and overlay designs as Basic System Components. A series of careful studies with IBSVI participants allowed us to determine effective document scales and layout of the overlay [16]. After some prototyping-testing iterations we determined that a material known as 'embossables'

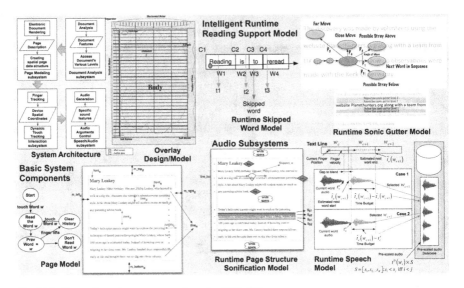

Fig. 16.2 Situated touch annotator and reader (STAAR)

[17] with a grid produced by a standard high-end Braille embosser produced a usable overlay that was perceptible to the IBSVI and allowed the iPad touch surface to function. A key finding concerning the document scale and overlay layout to be related here is that IBSVI are able to use the tactile overlay as a landmarking grid even when there is no one-to-one correspondence between the grid lines and text lines. There is a requirement, however, that the grid be denser than the text lines.

16.3.3.2 Intelligent Runtime Reading Support

In a usability study with 16 IBSVI, we found a high occurrence to "Wandering Between Lines" incident despite the existence of the horizontal landmarks on the overlay [10]. Hence STAAR is designed with dynamic reading support features [9]. If the system determines that the IBSVI reader is in the process of reading a line of text, the line-reading support is activated. This support comprises two components. First, to augment the tactile grid, a 'sonic gutter' is activated. This is a kind of sound fence that produces a rustling sound when the reader strays off the center of the current text line. Two levels of audible signals are used on each side of the text for closer, and farther deviations. At the same time, a probabilistic decision system estimates if the user intended to stay on line, and is merely straying, or if she intended to move to a different line. In the first case, the system reads the 'intended next word' even if the user's finger had strayed onto an adjacent line (still within the range of the sonic gutter). The sonic gutter provides feedback that the deviation has occurred and allows the user to self-correct. If the system determines that the user intended to leave the line, or if she moves beyond the bound of the sonic gutter, the line reading support feature disengages and the user is free to explore the document. What this essentially does is 'fatten the line' that is currently being read to account for motoric uncertainty.

Two other reading support features are designed into STAAR. The first is the 'skipped word notification system' that produces a click if the reader moves so fast that the audio system cannot keep up [10]. Each word skipped results in an audible click to alert the IBSVI to the fact. The second other support is that STAAR estimates which is the intended 'reading finger' and only renders words touched by that finger. This allows the IBSVI to use a trailing touch point as a physical reference, or to touch the iPad surface with the heel of the palm while reading.

16.3.3.3   Audio Subsystem

The final component block in STAAR handles the production of audio. The runtime page structure sonification produces audible cues concerning page spatial structure. This is a minimal set of sonifications designed to provide the IBSVI with spatial information on the page. These include whitespace (rustling sound when whitespace is touched), end-of-line (a typewrite-style 'ding' when the last word is read), skipped word (a click is heard if the IBSVI reads too quickly for the system to keep up, and a word is skipped), and line location (as the user moves her finger along the left vertical margin, a click is heard when the finger crosses a line of text—this allows the reader to know where to begin reading a line).

Finally, to enable self-paced reading, we had to implement a variable-speech-rate reading sub-system. This makes it impractical to use a text-to-speech (TTS) system directly because it is very hard to vary the vocalization duration of each word dynamically within a sentence or range words being rendered. To address this, we developed a system where TTS output is pre-sampled and pre-scaled for playback.

16.3.4   STAAR e-Reader Results and Discussion

The STAAR e-Reader was developed in collaboration with a cadre of IBSVI participants who served as our early testing participant designers and advisors [16]. The components described in Fig. 16.2 were developed over multiple cycles of 'design-prototype-test with IBSVI-glean lessons learnt—redesign' cycles. To give a sense of the functionality of the STAAR system, we summarize the results of an extended Experience-Sampling Method [18] study [10]. This was after the third cycle of our design loop. We seeded 7 IBSVI with the STAAR system to use for two weeks in their own homes and workplaces. Each participant was given 27 pages to read, and a set of reading and comprehension benchmark tests were administered at the beginning and end of the period. The results were very promising, with all readers completing the reading and able to answer questions on content and comprehension with minimal error. In fact three of the participants completed all the readings in seven days, and requested more. There was marked improvement over all similar benchmarks administered in the second cycle tests. This and a subsequent study uncovered the need for the *Intelligent Reading Support* subsystem described above. This led to our final design-prototype-test cycle where we implemented and validated the subsystem [9].

With respect to this paper's basic premise, the STAAR project shows how embodied theory and thinking informed and motivated a direction of research employing tablet and touch technology to support reading and learning for an important special population. The understanding of the nature of information as being designed intrinsically for embodied/sighted individuals determined how we approached the problem. This allows us to employ modern slate technologies with multimedia and touch capabilities to address a fundamental problem encountered by IBSVI. As we discussed, the embodied conceptualization served to motivate and guide the research, but many rigorous technical, design and validation steps were needed to fully explore the implications of the concept and lead to a usable technology.

16.4   Design of a Navigation Technique for VR

Our second project relates to the use of virtual reality (VR) technologies in education. The rapid fall in prices and the increasing capabilities of regular 3D-capable HDTV and even ultra-high definition HDTVs [19] portends opportunities for their expanded application in education [20]. These consumer-priced technologies make possible the widespread the application of VR to support learning. Through these technologies students may be able to explore distant places, mathematical forms or biological anatomies 'from the inside' by navigating through these structures. The goal is to give the student an understanding of the structure and spatial relationships of the subject matter.

It has, however, been shown that visual interaction with conventional VR interfaces alone do not provide sufficient support for such spatial knowledge acquisition [21]. An approach proposed to address this problem is to employ more embodied approaches to navigation using walking-like interfaces [21, 22] such as walking-in-place [23–25], redirected walking [26, 27], and walking on treadmills [28]. The argument is that the embodied experience of body-based walking and moving through space provides the user with richer information to reason about space. However, such body-based walking-like interfaces require significant space, are often cumbersome to implement, and incur user fatigue with extended use.

Our approach to the problem of extended VR navigation is to design and implement a more light-weight embodied interaction approach that retains the capacity for users to engage their broader embodied perception, sensing, and cognition resources to acquire 3D information. The Motor Equivalence Theory [29] states that humans are able to engage the majority of their neural resources for a well-learned task even when the task is performed by a different body part. For example, individuals deprived of the use of their dominant hand may learn quickly to write with

FWIP Approach

Fig. 16.3 Walking & turning on a touch surface (from xx). **a.** Walking on a touch surface. **b.** Pivot turn

the non-dominant hand and access the majority of the neural and nervous machinery for writing. This motor-equivalence phenomenon has been verified through brain imaging studies [30, 31].

We investigate a novel Finger-Walking-in-Place (FWIP) [32–34] approach that replaces full-body bipedal walking with 'finger walking' where users simulate walking with their fingers on a tablet or smartphone touch screen while they navigate within a large VR environment. The question is whether users will experience any gain in 3D spatial knowledge acquisition over commonly used VR navigation approaches, and how may these results compare with simulated full-body bipedal walking.

16.4.1 FWIP Approach

Figure 16.3 illustrates the finger-walking technique that we designed and implemented. Figure 16.3a shows how the approach employs analog interaction where the simulated walking action was directly coupled to the movement of the user through the virtual space. It supports forward, reverse, and directional walking in direct response to finger action on the touch surface. To address the biomechanical operation of human wrist movement that limits the amount of rotation of the approach, we developed the pivot-turn methodology illustrated in Fig. 16.3b. In operation, the user experiences visual stimulus from the VR system in direct response to the FWIP finger actions.

16.4.2 3D Spatial Knowledge Acquisition

Common approaches to assessing one's acquisition of spatial information involve considering the dimensions of route and survey knowledge [35]. The former involves a user's ability to recall or navigate routes or pathways within a virtual space. The latter relates to one's ability to acquire a 'bird's-eye' knowledge of an environment where one is able to estimate the direction to a remote target after, or in the course of, navigating through the space.

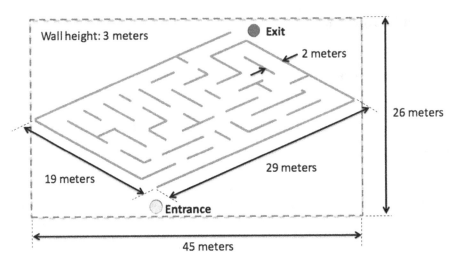

Fig. 16.4 Virtual maze for route and survey knowledge tests

A key tenet of the human perceptual system is that it is active in that sensing, perception, and action are tightly coupled [36, 37]. If our hypothesis that simulated finger walking on a touch surface activates the major neural pathways of well-learned bipedal walking, then we might expect that there would be concomitant perceptual improvements through associated activation of perceptual pathways.

To assess the benefits of FWIP for enabling the student to acquire spatial knowledge while navigating through a VR environment, we conducted two kinds of tests. The first involved assessing route and survey knowledge acquisition as a user navigates a maze in VR. The second involves testing a user's ability to estimate spatial information of a distal scene that is viewed within a VR space from a distance. Although space does not allow full discussion of these studies, we will nevertheless overview these studies to advance our discussions on embodiment and novel touch-based interaction on touch surfaces. Details may be found in [32].

16.4.3 Maze Studies

Figure 16.4 shows the virtual maze which is used for our maze navigation studies for our route and survey knowledge tests. We used a Linux-based Cave Automatic Virtual Environment (better known by the recursive acronym CAVE) system. The specific CAVE [38] used in our studies comprised three 10 by 10 ft walls and a floor on which stereo video data was projected. Each projection was of 1920 pixels by 1920 pixels resolution. A commercial tracking system was used for head tracking.

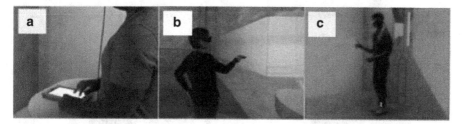

Fig. 16.5 a FWIP. b Conventional navigation. c WIP

16.4.3.1 Participants and Test Conditions

Sixty college-age participants were divided into three groups that are balanced for gender and spatial ability. Figure 16.5 shows the three interaction technology conditions to which the groups are assigned. In Fig. 16.5a, the participant uses the FWIP approach for navigation. In Fig. 16.5b, the participant navigates using a conventional wand-and-joystick (thumb joystick) device. In Fig. 16.5c, the participant employs a walking-in-place technology that tracks his orientation and the up-down movements of his feet.

The study is divided into two phases. First the participants follow way-point markers (colored cones) along three paths through the maze. The paths are designed so that together, they cover the entire maze. In the course of their navigation, they encounter two recognizable landmarks (e.g., a guitar object placed in the maze) in each of the three paths. The landmarks were included to aid the participant in remembering the otherwise visually-impoverished maze. The order of presentation of the three way-point-marked paths were counterbalanced.

16.4.3.2 Route and Survey Knowledge Acquisition Tests

The participants navigated each path thrice with the waypoints and landmarks in place. They were asked to retrace the path with the waypoints and landmarks removed on their fourth traversal through the maze. Since the three routes shared some corridors, the 'route learning' evaluation was done only for the first route (i.e., the participants at that point would have repeated the first path three times with way-points and landmarks, and were asked to replicate the path on the fourth traversal as the route test).

After traversing the maze twelve times (four for each prescribed route), the participants were asked to explore the maze again to locate all six landmarks (no way-point markers are present for this exploration). The participants were then permitted to explore the maze freely to get a sense of the structure of the maze. For the survey-knowledge acquisition test, the participants were presented with six maze drawings each, and were asked to pick the correct one.

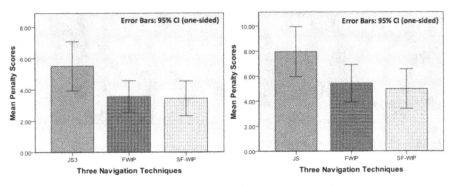

Fig. 16.6 Penalty measures with $P_{ms} = 1/2$ & $P_{ms} = 1.0$ respectively

Table 16.1 Penalty scores of FWIP and WIP vs JS

P_{ms} Value	FWIP vs JS	WIP vs JS
0.5	$p < 0.05 (= 0.04)$	$P < 0.05 (= 0.035)$
1.0	$p < 0.05 (= 0.043)$	$P < 0.05 (= 0.024)$

16.4.3.3 Route-Knowledge Acquisition Results

To evaluate the 'correctness' of a maze traversal with respect to a reference route, we employed a *route-penalty* measure:

$$S_{penalty} = P_{ms}N_{ms} + P_a N_{ms,\, a} + P_b N_{ms,\, b}$$

The measure sums the scores of three kinds of errors along a route. $P_a N_{ms,a}$ measures contribution of missed segments at 3-way junctions (forks with the possibility of backtracking) with P_a set at 1/3, and $N_{ms,a}$ is the number of misses at forks. Similarly, P_b is set at 1/4, and $N_{ms,b}$ is the number of misses at 4-way junctions. For segments that are missed entirely, P_{ms} set at 1/2 or 1.0, and N_{ms} is the number of misses. The *penalty-scores* for all three configurations at with $P_{ms} = 1/2$ and $P_{ms} = 1.0$ are shown in Fig. 16.6.

We employed a single-tail t-test for the hypothesis that both the FWIP and WIP would produce better route learning than the wand/joystick configuration for P_{ms} at 1/2 and 1.0. Our results, summarized in Table 16.1, show that both FWIP and WIP outperform the traditional joystick (JS) in the route replication or route-learning task. No significant difference was found between FWIP and WIP.

When we take travel time into consideration by including task time as a covariate, our ANCOVA (analysis of covariance) results (summarized in Table 16.2) were more telling. Both FWIP and WIP far outperformed the joystick interaction in supporting route knowledge acquisition, and no significant difference was found between FWIP and WIP.

Table 16.2 ANCOVA results with task time as a covariate

P_{ms}	FWIP vs JS	FWIP vs WIP	WIP vs JS
0.5	$p < 0.05$ (= 0.000)	$p > 0.05$ (= 0.546)	$p < 0.05$ (= 0.002)
1.0	$p < 0.05$ (= 0.006)	$p > 0.05$ (= 0.903)	$p < 0.05$ (= 0.007)

Table 16.3 Survey knowledge acquisition test results

	χ^2	p-value	p-value (generalized Fisher's exact test)
FWIP	26.955	< 0.05 (= 0.000)	< 0.05 (= 0.000)
JS	2.543	> 0.05 (= 0.111)	> 0.05 (= 0.128)
WIP	11.514	< 0.05 (= 0.001)	< 0.05 (= 0.003)

16.4.3.4 Survey Knowledge Results

Our survey knowledge tests was a multiple-choice test where the participants were asked to identify which of six maze drawings represented most accurately the maze they just explored. The number of correct responses for FWIP, JS, and WIP were 12, 6, and 9 respectively. We wanted to know if these correct answers were significantly better than a chance selection. For each selection, the chance of randomly picking the correct answer is 1/6. Hence, for 20 participants per group, the expected number of correct answers of purely chance selections is 3.3. This falls below the suggested minimum number of chance correct answers for a simple one-sample Chi-square (χ^2) goodness-of-fit test. Hence, we employed the Fisher's exact test method that entertains smaller sample sizes. Our test results are summarized in Table 16.3. As with the route knowledge acquisition test, FWIP showed similar performance to WIP. This suggests that both WIP and FWIP are able to engage body-based resources for virtual navigation when compared with the conventional wand and joystick navigation approach.

16.4.4 Perceptual Gains from FWIP

Figure 16.7 illustrates the experimental configuration for our perception-navigation test. The participants viewed objects in three virtual glass boxes. They were free to 'move' virtually within the physical CAVE space to gain a better sense of the three-dimensional structures in the glass cases. Our goal was to determine if participants using FWIP gained a better perceptual accuracy in estimating the structure of the objects in the glass cases as compared to those using the conventional wand-joystick interaction methodology. Since the viewing geometry and VR system are identical between the FWIP and JS conditions, any perceptual gain would have to be related to the navigation methodology.

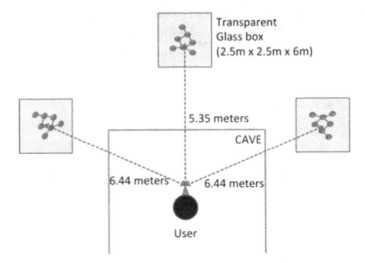

Fig. 16.7 Distal perception test configuration

Fig. 16.8 Molecule structure objects for perceptual tests

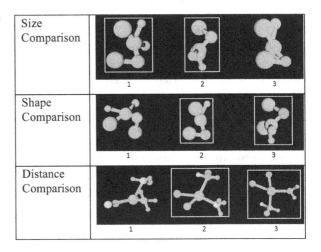

16.4.4.1 Participants and Object Comparisons Test

Twenty participants who were balanced for gender and spatial ability were assigned to each of the FWIP and JS groups.

We tested the participant on their estimation of shape, size, and distance between object components of the objects in the virtual glass cases. Figure 16.8 shows the molecule-like objects that are viewed. Three molecule structures are presented in the three virtual glass boxes, and the participant is asked to identify the two that match in the specific dimension being queried. For *size*, the participants are first presented with one molecule structure and asked to focus on its size. Two other molecule models

Fig. 16.9 Presentation of molecules in the virtual glass boxes

are then shown in the other two glass boxes (positions are randomized) and asked to select the one of similar size to the first molecule shown. The *shape* task was similar to the *size* task except that the participants are told to focus on the angles of the links between the molecule balls. For *distance*, the participants are first presented with one molecule structure in which two balls are highlighted in a different color. Two other molecule models with a pair of highlighted balls each are then presented in the other virtual glass boxes, and the participants are asked to select the one whose highlighted balls are separated by the same distance as the first molecule presented. Figure 16.9 shows a view of the three glass boxes as seen by the participants.

The participants were administered two training phases to familiarize them with the system and the test conditions. In the first phase, they familiarized themselves with the navigation methodology by moving freely within the 'viewing box' shown in Fig. 16.7. In the second phase, they were shown the different color balls and were presented with a sample of each of the *size*, *shape*, and *distance* tests.

16.4.4.2   Perceptual Test and Results

The perceptual tasks were broken into three sub-sections, one for each of the *size, shape*, and *distance* tests. Each sub-session comprised eight molecule triplet presentations as described. The participants had 1.5 min to move around the viewing area for each molecule triplet presentation. There was a break between each sub-session and as requested by the participants. The mean number of correct answers and standard deviations are shown in Table 16.4. A significance difference was found for the distance estimates ($F(1, 38) = 10.537$, $p < 0.05$ ($= 0.002$)).

That we found a significant difference (advantage) only for distance and not for size and shape is not surprising in light of our embodiment hypothesis. A major embodied cognition/perception theory advanced by J.J. Gibson may have predicted this result. Gibson's *ecological psychology* [39] principle that "perception is for action" suggests that one's perceptual acuity would be optimal for the action that best suits the perceptual scenario. In the configuration shown in Fig. 16.7, the molecules

Table 16.4 Perception test results

Tasks	FWIP	JS
Size	$M = 5.15, SD = 1.755$	$M = 4.55, SD = 1.36$
Shape	$M = 4.25, SD = 1.45$	$M = 4.6, SD = 1.85$
Distance	$M = 5.1, SD = 1.2$	$M = 3.85, SD = 1.23$

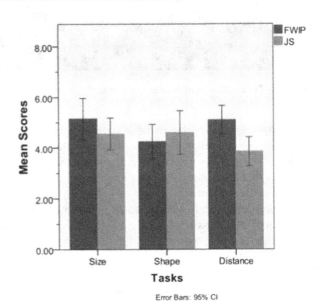

Fig. 16.10 Perception test results (Error bars CI = 0.95)

are distal to the participants such that they would not be able to manually affect the objects. Hence, there would have been no advantage to assign perceptual resources to the *shape* and *size* of the molecules. *Distance* estimate at that standoff that may be enhanced by bipedal locomotion would support an opportunity for action (e.g., to cast a projectile at the object or to jump over an obstacle at that distance or to plan a footfall on the run). Hence, this result lends support to our hypothesis that FWIP engages body-based action and perception (Fig. 16.10).

16.5   Conclusion

In this paper, we presented a theoretical basis that may inform new and innovative applications of tablet and touch technology. We have shown how the embodied interaction perspective can suggest novel designs and anticipate the benefits that those designs can yield.

We tendered two specific tablet and touch-based applications in the domains of e-reading for *Individuals with Blindness or Severe Visual Impairment* and navigation in virtual spaces. The broad utility of the embodied cognition/perception/sensing perspective to design is reinforced by the difference between the application areas.

In the e-reader for IBSVI project, we proceeded on the premise that reading and the very organization of information itself is grounded in human embodiment, and that solutions to support reading for IBSVI needs to address the challenges that visual deficits bring to access this information. In the FWIP project, we based our design and approach on the idea that body-based activity would yield advantages in spatial knowledge acquisition and that this body-based activity may be transferred to alternate body parts to yield the same advantages. Both projects were informed, motivated, and guided by the embodiment perspective and embodiment theory. However, both projects also involved rigorous iterative design and validation research approaches to fully understand the implications of the embodiment perspective on the specific application.

Finally, we showed how the embodiment perspective can support design for education and learning systems.

Acknowledgments   The research presented were partially supported by National Science Foundation grants IIS-1117854 and IIS-1059398. The e-reader for IBSVI project was done as part of the doctoral thesis of Yasmine Elglaly supervised by the author, and the FWIP research was done as part of the doctoral thesis of Ji-Sun Kim that was jointly supervised by the author and Dr. Denis Gracanin.

References

1. Quek, F. (2011). Embodiment: We're just human. In CHI 2011 Workshop on embodied interaction: Theory and practice in HCI. Vancouver, British Columbia.
2. Polanyi, M. (1967). *The tacit dimension* (p. 108). New York: Anchor Books.
3. Goldin-Meadow, S. (2003). *Hearing gesture: How our hands help us think.* Cambridge: The Belknap Press of Harvard University Press.
4. Quek, F., McNeill, D., Bryll, R., Duncan, S., Ma, X., Kirbas, C., & McCullough, K.-E. (2002). Multimodal human discourse: Gesture and speech. *ACM Transactions on Computer-Human Interaction, 9*(3), 71–193.
5. Lakoff, G., & Nunez, R. (2000). *Where mathematics comes from: How the embodied mind brings mathematics into being.* New York: Basic Books.
6. Pelaprat, E., & Cole, M. (2011). Minding the gap: Imagination, creativity, and human cognition. *Integrative Psychological and Behavioral Science* (Springer), *45,* 397–418.
7. Fung, J., & Mann, S. (2004). Using multiple graphics cards as a general purpose parallel computer: Applications to computer vision, In Proceedings of the Pattern Recognition, 17th International Conference on (ICPR'04) Volume 1– Vol. 1., IEEE Computer Society.
8. Park, S., Cao, Y., Watson, L., & Quek, F. (2012). Performance analysis of a novel GPU computation-to-core mapping scheme for robust facet image modeling. *Journal of Real-Time Image Processing,* 1–16.
9. Elglaly, Y. N. (2013). *Spatial reading system for individuals with blindness, in computer science.* Blacksburg: Virginia Polytechnic Institute and State University.
10. Elglaly, Y. N., Quek, F., Smith-Jackson, T., & Dhillon, G. (2012). Audible rendering of text documents controlled by multi-touch interaction. In ACM International Conference of Multimodal Interaction, USA.

11. Elglaly, Y. N., Quek, F., Smith-Jackson, T., & Dhillon, G. (2013). Touch-screens are not tangible: Fusing tangible interaction with touch glass in readers for the blind. In ACM International Conference on Tangible, Embedded and Embodied Interaction (TEI). Barcelona, Spain.
12. Quek, F., Elglaly, Y., & Oliveira, F. (2013). Supporting learning for individuals with visual impairment. in Multimedia and Expo Workshops (ICMEW), 2013 IEEE International Conference. IEEE.
13. El-Glaly, Y. N., Quek, F., Smith-Jackson, T., & Dhillon, G. (2012). It is not a talking book; It is more like really reading a book! In Proceedings of the 14th International ACM SIGACCESS Conference on Computers and Accessibility. Boulder, USA.
14. Ong, W. J. (1982). *Orality and literacy: The technologizing of the word*. London: Methuen & Co.
15. Stephanidis, C. (2009). Universal access in human-computer interaction. In Applications and Services: 5th International Conference, UAHCI 2009, Held as Part of HCI International Applications, incl. Internet/Web, and HCI). San Diego, CA, Springer.
16. Dhillon, G. S., El-Glaly, Y. N., Holbach, W. H., Smith-Jackson, T. L., & Quek, F. (2012). Use of participatory design to enhance accessibility of slate-type devices. In Proceedings of the Human Factors and Ergonomics Society Annual Meeting. SAGE Publications.
17. American Thermoform Corporation. (2012). Embossables. http://www.americanthermoform.com/brailon.htmembossables. Accessed 1 Jan 2013.
18. Larson, R., & Csikszentmihalyi, M. (1983). The experience sampling method. *New Directions for Methodology of Social and Behavioral Science, 15,* 41–56.
19. Inagaki, K., & Cheng, J. (2014). Inexpensive ultra high-definition TVs on horizon, In The Wall Street Journal. Wall Street Journal: New York. http://online.wsj.com/news/articles/SB10001424052702304361604579292630876600834. Accessed 1 Jan 2013.
20. Gukbransen, S. (2011). New HD technology means enriched education for kids. http://technorati.com/technology/gadgets/article/new-hd-technology-means-enriched-education/. Accessed 1 Jan 2013.
21. Ruddle, R. A., & Lessels, S. (2009). *The benefits of using a walking interface to navigate virtual environments. ACM Transactions on Computer-Human Interaction (TOCHI), 16*(1), 5.
22. Ruddle, R. A., Volkova, E., & Bülthoff, H. H. (2011). Walking improves your cognitive map in environments that are large-scale and large in extent. *ACM Transactions on Computer-Human Interaction (TOCHI), 18*(2), 10.
23. Feasel, J., Whitton, M. C., & Wendt, J. D. (2008). LLCM-WIP: Low-latency, continuous-motion walking-in-place. In 3D User Interfaces 2008, 3DUI 2008. IEEE Symposium on. IEEE.
24. Wendt, J. D., Whitton, M. C., & Brooks, F. P. Jr. (2010). Gud wip: Gait-understanding-driven walking-in-place. in Virtual Reality Conference (VR), 2010 IEEE.
25. Slater, M., Usoh, M., & Steed, A., (1995). Taking steps: The influence of a walking technique on presence in virtual reality. *ACM Transactions on Computer-Human Interaction (TOCHI),* 2(3), 201–219.
26. Razzaque, S., Kohn, Z., & Whitton, M. C. (2001). Redirected walking. In Proceedings of Eurographics. Citeseer.
27. Steinicke, F., Bruder, G., Jerald, J., Frenz, H., & Lappe, M. (2010). Estimation of detection thresholds for redirected walking techniques. *Visualization and Computer Graphics, IEEE Transactions, 16*(1), 17–27.
28. Souman, J. L., Giordano, P. R., Schwaiger, M., Frissen, I., Thümmel, T., Ulbrich, H., Luca, A. D., Bülthoff, H. H., & Ernst, M. O. (2011). CyberWalk: Enabling unconstrained omnidirectional walking through virtual environments. *ACM Transactions on Applied Perception (TAP), 8*(4), 25.
29. Lashley, K. S. (1930). Basic neural mechanisms in behavior. *Psychological Review, 37*(1), 1.
30. Rijntjes, M., Dettmers, C., Büchel, C., Kiebel, S., Frackowiak, R. S., & Weiller, C. (1999). A blueprint for movement: functional and anatomical representations in the human motor system. *The Journal of neuroscience, 19*(18), 8043–8048.

31. Swinnen, S. P., Vangheluwe, S., Wagemans, J., Coxon, J. P., Goble, D. J., Van Impe, A., Sunaert, S., Peeters, R., & Wenderoth, N. (2010). Shared neural resources between left and right interlimb coordination skills: the neural substrate of abstract motor representations. *Neuroimage, 49*(3), 2570–2580.
32. Kim, J.-S. (2013). *Action-inspired design approach of navigation technique for effective spatial learning in 3-D virtual environments, in Computer Science.* Blacksburg: Virginia Polytechnic Institute and State University
33. Kim, J.-S., Gracanin, D., & Quek, F. (2010) The meaning of the action of locomotion techniques on spatial knowledge acquisition in virtual environments. In review. doi:DIS 2010 2010.
34. Kim, J.-S., Gračanin, D., Matković, K., & Quek, F. (2010). The effects of finger-walking in place (FWIP) for spatial knowledge acquisition in virtual environments. In R. Taylor, et al. (Eds.), *Smart graphics* (pp. 56–67). Berlin: Springer.
35. Richardson, A. E., Montello, D. R., & Hegarty, M. (1999). Spatial knowledge acquisition from maps and from navigation in real and virtual environments. *Memory & cognition, 27*(4), 741–750.
36. Herwig, A., Prinz, W., & Waszak, F. (2007). Two modes of sensorimotor integration in intention-based and stimulus-based actions. *The Quarterly Journal of Experimental Psychology, 60*(11), 1540–1554.
37. Elsner, B., & Hommel, B. (2001). Effect anticipation and action control. *Journal of experimental psychology: Human perception and performance, 27*(1), 229.
38. VT-VISIONARIUM. VisCube. Virginia Tech Visionarium. 2010. https://snoid.sv.vt.edu/visionarium/. Accessed 18 April 2014.
39. Gibson, J. J. (1979). *The ecological approach to visual perception.* Hillsdale: Lawrence Erlbaum Associates.

Chapter 17
Beyond 'Apps' on Tablets: Making Sense of Learning Within Technology Ecologies

Sharon Lynn Chu and Francis Quek

Abstract The vision of Vannevar Bush and Douglas Englebart of using computers to augment the human intellect more than half a century ago has been taken to heart by technology designers and computer scientists. Much technological progress has been made that allows the rampant use of laptops, desktops, tablets and smartphones in daily tasks to help us in thinking and learning. However, the single device can only go so far to facilitate higher-level thinking. We advance that the possibilities of the augmentation of human intellect by digital technologies are limited unless we design for the various technologies to function together in ecologies. In this paper, we present a theoretical foundation using Lev Vygotsky's sign mediation theory to articulate a design framework identifying key processes that should be supported to assist higher-level thinking. We also provide examples of affordances that can help the design of effective technology ecologies within our framework.

17.1 Introduction

At the very beginnings of the computing revolution, both Vannevar Bush in 1945 and Doug Englebart in 1962 presented visionary essays positing that machines may one day 'augment the human intellect,' extending the powers of the mind to make knowledge more accessible. Since then the computer has been developed to enable the manipulation of numbers, databases, texts, simulations, artificial intelligence, etc.

As Bush and Englebart contemplated at the dawn of our computing era, we are at a point of critical mass of development of computation and connectivity to revisit the question of how computation may extend our capacity to think and learn. If we look at the current landscape of computing technologies, the modern computer has taken on many different forms from the notecard-sized smartphone to the book-sized tablet and to the whiteboard-sized large screen displays. We propose in this paper that all

S. L. Chu (✉) · F. Quek
TAMU Embodied Interaction Lab (TEILab), Departments of Visualization
& Architecture, Texas A&M University, College Station, TX, 77840, USA
e-mail: sharilyn@tamu.edu

F. Quek
e-mail: quek@tamu.edu

© Springer International Publishing Switzerland 2015
T. Hammond et al. (eds.), *The Impact of Pen and Touch Technology on Education*,
Human-Computer Interaction Series, DOI 10.1007/978-3-319-15594-4_17

of these technology and devices need to function in ensemble to truly augment the human intellect.

In her seminal book 'Inventing the new medium,' Murray listed four unique affordances or properties of the computer that characterize the power of this digital method of representation: procedural, participatory, encyclopedic, and spatial [1]. Modern computing devices and technologies vary on a spectrum of Murray's properties of procedural, participatory, encyclopedic, and spatial, but functioning together they can empower the user to think more deeply and learn more broadly in a pervasive fashion throughout daily life. We explore how computing devices, especially tablet and touch devices, functioning in concert in *technology ecologies* [2, 3] may augment the user's mental capabilities throughout the entire workflow of knowledge-based tasks. We present a theoretical and a design framework for how technology ecologies augment human thought based on our reflections, observations, and results of exploratory studies.

17.2 Technology in Education

Why is it so significant to understand and to design the next wave of computing technologies such that they function within technology ecologies? After all, we have already come a long way from Bush's vision of 'memex' and can already use our smartphone to look up a Wikipedia page whenever we want to know something and our laptop to store searchable databases of research papers. The problem we address is how operating singularly, each device or technology is limited to isolated instances of 'intellect augmentation,' that although still beneficial, does not necessarily extend across the broader panoply of our thinking. After each episode of technology use or information access, we go back to relying on the use of our human memory and inherent mental capabilities to make use of the information or knowledge gained.

Nowhere is this isolated use of computing technologies more apparent than in education and learning environments. The dominant current paradigm of using the computer in the classroom is characterized by learning within the confines of single devices. An embodiment of this paradigm is the one-on-one tablet programs that are rapidly gaining popularity across the country. School districts that are investing large amounts of resources on distributing an iPad to every student [4–9] face problems not only in the form of loss of devices, hacking [10], or loss of precious classroom time on tech support, but also in the failure of the transformative change in education that the devices were expected to bring.

Users of the various devices typically construct their own workarounds to transcend the bounds of single device silos. People email themselves and each other relevant files, keep their files on online services, discuss ideas on instant messaging. They use online storage not primarily as storage but as data bridges across devices, and use attachment features of social media to foster 'data dialogs' with themselves and each other to move data between laptops, iPads, android devices, smartphones and the like. For learners with single devices these workarounds are cumbersome and many students do not discover how to break the device silos. With well-designed and thought-out integration of technologies, the level of intellect augmentation that could result from the use of technologies designed to interact and function in concert can far exceed what is capable by the single computer.

17.3   Technology Ecologies

A range of research has hitherto applied the metaphor of a biological ecosystem to human activities with technology. However, this body of work does not always form a coherent whole, and it is a challenging undertaking to present either a commonly agreed definition or a comprehensive synthesized account of the work. The overall message underlying the different positions of technology ecologies in the literature is that artifacts, devices, systems, and products cannot be studied in isolation but can only be truly understood when seen in the broader perspective of the universe they inhabit. Depending on the position taken, the universe can consist of one's physical context, other artifacts used, or one's practices and culture using technology. From our perspective, a technology ecology is characterized by three key principles:

• The technology engages all devices within the environment,
• The technology addresses the entire workflow of the task being undertaken,
• The technology provides an experience of flow to the user.

Prior notions of technology ecologies can be classified into three categories: theoretical or philosophical positions, empirical study results, and technical frameworks enabling the implementation of ecologies. Figure 17.1 summarizes some of the main concepts of technology ecologies in prior research. Our conception of technology ecologies distinguishes itself in three ways. First, it specifies not only interrelationships among devices to be important, but also the support of human thinking as it deals with digital information from one subtask to another across space and time. Second, we think of technology ecologies as the environment inhabited by information and information objects. The technology ecology supports the manipulation, manifestation (through display and outputs), and movement of these information objects. Third, we emphasize that this engagement of the user with the various devices has to occur within flow—seamless interaction with digital information.

Our task of focus in this paper is learning. There has been little research that evaluates the effects such ecologies on learning or other higher thought processes in relation to the devices used. Rick [11] points out the importance of a classroom ecology, but does not provide any supporting study. Coughlan et al.'s [12] investigation informs the design of ecologies by studying transitions in foci across devices (a tabletop computer with a mirrored projection, laptops, a telephone) in three short controlled activities, carried out in a "technologically-enhanced indoor space." Communication across devices was provided by a Central Management System and instant messaging. The focus of their study was on how device ecologies can support collaboration. Their study results presented a set of "seams" that represent disconnects in a device ecology that can affect users' behaviors. Their study however gave little

	Author	Year	Concept
THEORETICAL	McLuhan	1962	Media ecology
	Altheide	1994	Ecology of communication
	Nardi & O'Day	1999	Information ecology
	Krippendorf	2005	Ecology of artifacts
	Tungare & al.	2006	Personal information ecosystem
	Rick	2009	Classroom ecology of devices
EMPIRICAL STUDIES	Huang, Mynatt & Trimble	2004	Display ecology
	Enquist, Tollmar & Corry	2007	Interaction ecology
	Dearman & Pierce	2008	Computing with multiple devices
	Jung et al.	2008	Personal ecology of interactive artifacts
	Forlizzi	2008	Product ecology
	Bailey & Barley	2011	Teaching-learning ecologies
	Coughlan et al.	2012	Device ecology
	Chu et al.	2012	Technology ecology of displays and devices

Fig. 17.1 Concepts of technology ecologies

indication of how one can understand whether or how learning has occurred within the context they constructed.

Jung et al. [13] studied one's network of personal artifacts through the lens of 'factors' and 'layers' within a 'personal ecology of interactive artifacts,' described as a "set of all physical artifacts with some level of interactivity enabled by digital technology that a person owns, has access to, and uses." They make use of two methods called the Personal Inventory, based on a simplified version of the Repertory Grid Technique, and the Ecology Map, which consists of sketching using sticky notes to probe a person's device ecology. Their exploratory study with ten graduate students found that perceived attributes of an artifact can be classified into two categories, designed properties (physical, functional, informational, interactive aspects) and subjective values (experiential, emotional, social). They further specify the different types of relations that artifacts in a personal ecology can have, based on: purpose of use, context of use, or subjective meaning. Their study results, although very helpful to understand the nature and types of technological ecologies, again do not consider the process of learning.

Perhaps the area that comes the closest to studying the process of higher level thinking in an environment of multiple devices is that of visual analytics. Visual analytics [14] aims to understand how people make sense of and integrate (digital) information from various sources to solve a problem or to gain insight to a particular scenario, most often an intelligence analysis task. Research in visual analytics has resulted in interesting models of the human sensemaking process that may help us to understand how levels of thought at each stage is augmented by current technologies, for instance, the well-known Pirolli and Card's [15] sensemaking loop. However there remain two large gaps: First, what is the exact mechanism by which the user interacts with a device to augment cognition in a learning context? Second, in what ways can various devices work together to reinforce the augmentation of cognition? In this paper, we draw on psychological and learning theories to answer the first question, and present a design framework that illuminates the second.

17.4 The Thinking Process

17.4.1 Sign Mediation Theory

Vygotsky [16, 17] proposes a way by which things in the environment may be brought into the very process of thinking in the form of the sign mediation theory. Similar to Kirsh's 'Thinking with external representations' [18], that posits that human thinking may be mediated or enhanced by psychological tools called signs or symbols [16, 19]. Signs may be defined as self-generated linguistic stimuli [20] that extend the operation of human cognition beyond the confines of the strictly biological system.

While thought is distinct from language, Vygotsky conceived of language as a tool for thought. 'Signs' are language units that relate to units of thinking to allow the building of higher-level and more abstract thinking. Signs are more than just encapsulations of thought objects or idea chunks that support more effective use of human short-term memory [21]. Signs are a kind of psychological 'handle' that allows the learner to grasp and manipulate concepts mentally or through such externalizing mechanisms as the sound of words either covertly or overtly expressed. Hence, they can function as building blocks with which we can build more complex thought objects. Figure 17.2 illustrates Vygotsky's sign mediation theory and an example of a student learns the concept of 'Average' or 'Mean' of N numbers: $\sum^{N} a_i / N$. She understands and is able to perform the operation. However, if she had to think of details of the concept each time she applies it, the limits of her memory, attention, and mental processing would make further advancement untenable. Thus, she encodes this concept as a mental sign—the concept of 'Average.' She is able to think of the operation simply through the sign, and to employ this in further learning (e.g., *Average* of sample means). As the sign becomes 'internalized', it becomes in essence the object in her thinking. She can 'unpack' the sign as needed to attend to the details.

Signs may take the form of both internal (e.g., the word *Average* that represents the mental concept of the sum of a set of numbers divided by how many numbers are

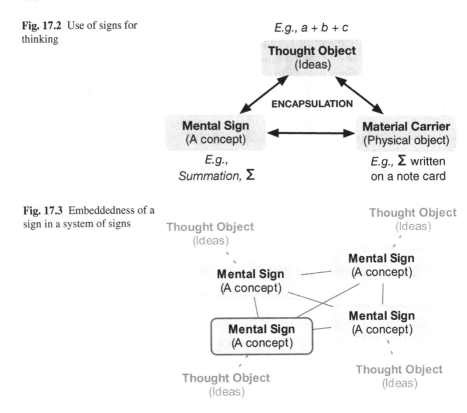

Fig. 17.2 Use of signs for thinking

Fig. 17.3 Embeddedness of a sign in a system of signs

in the set) or external forms (e.g., the sound of the word *Average*). Vygotsky talks of a stick between a child's legs becoming his horse, a block representing an idea [16]. Externally instantiated signs have been referred to as 'material carriers' of thought [22]. One can think of them as essentially 'physical, tangible signs.' Any perceivable object (spatial location, gestures, objects or even sounds) in the environment can opportunistically and temporally be appropriated for use as material carriers to assist thinking thus bringing spatial ability and perception into play. In theory thus, the material carrier can be anything that may or may not resemble the mental object.

17.4.2 Higher-Level Thinking

According to Vygotsky [17], the formation of concepts, and thus the creation of meaning and true understanding, is achieved only when a sign is embedded within a 'system of signs,' as illustrated in Fig. 17.3. He gives the following example: "The relationship of the word "flower" to the object is completely different for the child who does not yet know the words rose, violet, or lily than it is for the child who does."

Similar mediated models of cognition has been advanced by others as well apart from Vygotsky. The theory of distributed cognition, first proposed by Edward Hutchins [23], based on his study of airline cockpits, holds that we 'offload' cognition (thinking) onto tools, artifacts, people and processes. The theory of situated cognition, from the work of Lave and Wenger [24] in situated learning and apprenticeships, maintains that people act and learn in context, reinforcing he inextricate link between thinking and the contexts in which it occurs. Last but not least, activity theory [25] from Leont'ev and Engestrom has as its basic premise that any activity is goal-directed and mediated through the use of tools or artifacts.

17.5 Augmenting the Intellect

Using the theoretical framework of the sign mediation theory, we propose that at least three key processes need to be supported to allow higher-level thinking to occur. Augmenting human's thinking capabilities may work through the facilitation of the:

- **Creation of material carriers:** Binding a thought object to a physical object;
- **(Re-) Access to signs:** Uptaking the signs through the material carriers to avoid memory overtaxation;
- **Manipulation of signs through their material carriers:** Manipulation means higher level processes such as association, extension, pattern recognition, inferencing, abstraction.

In the paper world, we have developed a range of material innovations, processes, and procedures that can support each of these three processes in various ways persistently across time: A notecard allows one to quickly and easily create a recognizable material carrier for a particular concept. The notecard, or physical proxy of the sign, can then be picked up whenever, carried around, and referenced at one's convenience; and across space: A series of notecards representing distinct signs can be manipulated (turned upside down, sideways, etc.), laid out spatially to facilitate manipulation of signs to which they are associated. Information on note cards can cross-reference other repositories of personal information (e.g., referencing notebooks and journal entries) and knowledge encoded in broader society. The concept of 'archival publications' book indices, and the entire domain of 'library studies' were designed around the primacy of paper as the chief extender of human intelligence beyond a single episode of thought, a single person, a single community, a single society, a single generation, and a single epoch.

While advancements of computation and connectivity are challenging the hegemony of paper as the chief augmenter of human thought, the promissory note of their potential remains mostly unclaimed. Unlike paper, the interface between digital technology and human thinking and learning has not had centuries of combined evolution across communities. With our model of augmentation, we seek to contribute to understanding of how tablets and touch interaction may be key elements in human intellectual augmentation.

Fig. 17.4 Sign mediation
with digital technologies

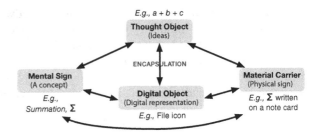

17.6   Digital Technology in Single Devices

With digital technologies, mental signs can be manifested not only through physical objects or material carriers, but also in the form of digital, non-tangible objects (see Fig. 17.4). Digital technologies have near infinite ability to encode and represent information, and modern display/output technologies can manifest information in multiple ways (e.g., as an icon, a text blurb, a graph, a diagram). In the language of *Sign Mediation Theory*, digital objects can describe the concept encoded by the sign. Digital objects come with both benefits and costs. Murray's four affordances of the computer illustrates well some of the benefits that the digital medium provides, for e.g., searchable databases enabling quick re-access to particular signs. The digital information object can instantaneously be linked to an existing system of concepts, e.g. clicking on a term opens up its Wikipedia page describing the history and related terms, double-clicking on a filename opens up a PDF document with an explanation of a term or a picture illustrating the concept, thus making the acquisition of the significance of the sign much easier. Furthermore, the digital object can be designed to look like anything that would support easier access to the attached thought object. The malleability of the digital world is relatively unbounded as compared to the physical world.

The design of digital interfaces has unfortunately throughout its history, for the most part, failed to fully harness that flexibility we just described. During the first forays of interface design for instance, the desktop metaphor [26] was conceived as a model to design easy-to-use interfaces. The general space for document placement is called the 'desktop' modeled after the office desktop. Icons of folders look like the paper document folder. In the "Myth of the paperless office," Sellen and Harper [27] suggest that instead of trying to mimic or reproduce exactly the affordances of paper for the design of technologies, paper should be used only as an analytical resource or inspiration.

The tremendous flexibility of individual computational devices may, ironically, be one of the hindrances to the realization of its promise for augmenting human thinking and learning. Because a single device can serve multiple purposes, it resembles a 'Swiss-army-knife' in supporting human intellectual activity. This one-size-fits-all thinking can be as limiting as a do-it-yourselfer who thinks that a single Swiss-army-knife can be his entire carpenter's toolbox. In educational technologies such thinking is evidenced in the app-oriented model where tablets and laptops are imbued with different capabilities by the simple launching of a different app.

This single device conceit does not exist in the physical paper world where devices, by design and by necessity, have different capabilities and are based on different paradigms. To give an example, while two pairs of scissors may be designed differently, they both satisfy the basic function of cutting.

17.7 Augmenting the Intellect with Technology Ecologies

Two key dimensions that the paper world has learned to handle well over its long process of design evolution are space and time. To deal with space limitations, we have created various forms of accessories ranging in size and portability from index cards to notebooks to large whiteboards. To deal with time limitations, we have bookmarks, indices, cross-references, and libraries that allow one to pause and come back to a book that one is reading or to access information at different times. Moreover paper has the advantage of being inherently persistent across time. A paper placed on a desk will remain there unless moved. This persistence over time is a natural, and necessary property of things in the physical world [28] that resonates with our sense of the world.

Digital technologies, on the other hand, are typically manifested only within the confines of a screen, irrespective of the size of the display, and persist only for a particular session of working with the document. Even when documents are not 'closed' after each session, they switch out of interaction focus and typically become obscured by other application windows. They disappear as the device is switched off or put to sleep. We argue that this ephemerality of digital presentation (as opposed to for e.g., the persistence of paper) can compromise the suitability of their use as *material carriers* to support thinking. A technology ecology, if properly designed, may expand tremendously the opportunities of the manifestation of digital objects within the constraints of space and time to support the creation, access and manipulation of signs.

17.7.1 Scenario of Learning/Thinking with Signs and Things

We shall use a real-life scenario description how students may think and learn using multiple technologies to illustrate our idea of the relationship between signs, material carriers, and learning (see the Sign Mediation Theory described earlier). A student, Tom, is given an assignment to produce a group report on the influence of ancient Japan on modern Japan. He works in a team of three students over a period of two weeks. On the first day of the assignment, Tom's team holds a group meeting to discuss about possible ideas for the direction of the report. In the meeting room, they brainstorm keywords related to the topic and write them on a whiteboard. They distribute the list of keywords among the team members for further research. At the end of the meeting, Tom quickly jots down his allocated keywords on a small notepad, and the group decides to go for lunch together. Over lunch, Tom casually discusses with his teammates and something that his teammate mentions advances his thinking about the assignment topic. He takes out his notepad and scans the list of keywords that he jotted down. He adds a related point next to one of the keywords. At home he does an Internet search for material relevant to his assigned keywords on his notepad. He browses through a few papers and saves them in a temporary folder on his laptop. When the group meets a few days later to review the material that they have gathered. Tom brings along his laptop and plugs it to the large screen display in the meeting room. He goes through each paper that he found with the team so that they can decide as a group which ones are relevant for the direction that they want to take for their project. He moves the relevant ones to a project folder and deletes the non-relevant ones.

This scenario describes some key tasks of part of the workflow of the creation of a group report. Tom uses a combination of the paper and the digital technology to satisfy his needs in this workflow. Figure 17.5 traces examples of signs that are created during our sample episode and re-accessed across key processes of the sensemaking workflow of Pirolli and Card [15] mentioned earlier. Space/location, time, and form in which the creation and access of signs occurs are shown in between square brackets. As can be seen, signs across space and time can vary greatly. The variance in the place and time of creation and access of signs requires the use of different devices and forms that are also noted in Fig. 17.5. One can further imagine Tom's notepad being replaced by the smartphone or the tablet for notetaking to make his experience more techno-centric.

17.7.2 Mapping to Principles of Ecology

We can now map aspects of our example and analysis into the three principles of a technology ecology discussed earlier. First, a technology ecology seeks to address the entire workflow of a task. The key stages of the sensemaking workflow in the context of the production of a report in our scenario clearly shows how integrating across workflow processes would support a student's understanding of the material transforms from surface-level relationships (e.g., facts that come from an author, things that happen close to each other in time) into more meaningful concepts [19]. This process is similar to that of 'incremental formalism' where systems of concept relationships take shape over time through interaction [29]. The workflow can further be mapped to the levels of Blooms' taxonomy of learning (see Fig. 17.5), which specifies the different depths of thinking and types of skills desired in education.

Second, a technology ecology integrates all devices within an environment. By necessity, the user presently makes use of many ad-hoc ways to integrate information across devices and across the different processes of the workflow (e.g., typing in keywords taken down in the notepad during the meeting into the laptop at home).

Workflow process	Bloom's Taxonomy	Creation of signs	Access to signs	
Brainstorming	Knowledge, Comprehension	Keywords *[Meeting room; Day 1 morning; Oral]* Additional Keywords *[Foodcourt ; Day 1 lunch; Mental]*	Recording of keywords *[Meeting room; Day 1 morning; Whiteboard]* *[Food place; Day 1 lunch; Notepad]*	
Information foraging	Knowledge, Comprehension	PDF files *[Home; Day 1 night; File icons]*	Written keywords *[Home; Day 1 night; Written in notepad]* File naming *[Home; Day 1 night; Text string on laptop]*	Transfer of signs
Drawing relations	Application, Analysis	Notes, Annotations, Comments *[Meeting room; Day 3 morning; Oral, Notepad]*	File names *[Meeting room; Day 3 morning; Text string on laptop]* PDFs *[Meeting room; Day 3 morning; Large display]* Folder structure *[Home; Day 3 night; File explorer on laptop]*	
Schematizing	Application, Analysis	Mindmap, Write up	File naming	
Hypothesis building	Synthesis	Report/Presentation outline	File naming	
Presenting story	Synthesis	Report, Presentation	File naming	

Fig. 17.5 Examples of sign creation and access throughout workflow

Within a technology ecology, devices and information flows should be designed so that the student is able to focus on the manipulation of signs (higher-level thinking) throughout without having to worry about how to move representations across the different device and application barriers. Without such support the thinking and learning process becomes as cumbersome as having to devise different ways to join pieces of cloth while trying to make a tapestry.

And third, the experience from brainstorming to story presentation is a coherent flow of engagement in higher thinking instead of spurts or fragmented episodes.

17.8 Designing Technology Ecologies

17.8.1 Fundamental Principles

The first section of this paper has presented a theoretical framework from which to understand the mechanism by which human intellect can be augmented by technology ecologies, i.e., how we can be supported to engage in higher-level thinking through technology. In this section, we draw out the implications that this important theoretical basis provides us for the design of technology ecologies. As was pointed out before, higher-level thinking such as synthesis, inference, and abstraction. occurs

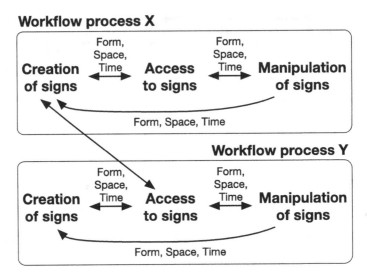

Fig. 17.6 Design framework for technology ecologies

through the manipulation of signs. We have also described previously how the presence/creation of a 'system of signs' is necessary for such manipulation of signs to take place. To do so, one must be able to hold multiple signs in mind simultaneously.

Using Fig. 17.6 that illustrates how the creation and access of signs are embedded within workflow processes, we can derive fundamental principles for the design of technology ecologies that can effectively mediate thinking:

- Each step of the thinking process, including the *creation of signs* of different forms, the storage and quick retrieval *(access) of created signs*, and the simultaneous persistence of multiple signs to enable *sign manipulation*, must be made as easy, transparent and fast as possible within itself.
- Transfer of signs from previous stages necessary for a stage to occur must be made as seamless as possible, including the conveyance of the *space* and *time* context of signs and transformation of the *form* of the sign if needed.
- Transfer of signs from other workflow processes necessary for a workflow process to complete successfully must be made as seamless as possible (this is shown as the red diagonal arrow in Fig. 17.6).

17.8.2   Design Affordances

The difficulty of implementing technology ecologies is that every part or whole of the framework in Fig. 17.6 can be carried out on a different device. The creation of a sign, for example, can happen on a tablet, and later re-access of the sign may be made on a laptop for workflow process X, and on a desktop computer for workflow process Y. It

Fig. 17.7 Levels of a
technology ecology

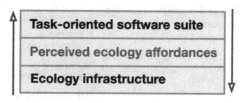

is challenging to identify design affordances that are generalizable across varying sets of technology ecologies, e.g., a set consisting of a Mac laptop, a Windows desktop, an Android smartphone *vs* a set with an iPad, a large screen TV and a laptop running Linux. It is not only a question of platforms, but also of form factors, user interfaces, applications, processor capabilities, etc. We propose that any technology ecology consists of three levels, as shown in Fig. 17.7. The bottom-most level of 'ecology infrastructure' involves the basic method by which connection is established among different devices. Much of this ecology infrastructure nowadays is set up through the Cloud. Of main interest to us is the second level of 'perceived ecology affordances,' which involves characteristics that are designed into the various device interfaces to enable the user to perceive the possibilities of interaction among the devices. The top level of 'task-oriented software suite' represents characteristics that are given to the interface of a device in the ecology at any one particular time based on the task that is being performed, e.g., when a word processing application is opened on a laptop. Generalizable affordances for technology ecologies can be made only at the second level, where the interface is not dictated by task-specific needs or by current state-of-the-art in computer network architectures.

We have conducted an exploratory study [3] collecting interview and self-reported questionnaire data of twelve students using a basic testbed technology ecology (an iPod Touch, an iPad, and a 27" iMac) to produce a knowledge discovery report on the topic of 'physical computing.' The focus of this paper is not to report on the study but we will use the findings of the study here to provide examples of design affordances for technology ecologies. Using qualitative coding methods of data analysis, the study findings uncovered five main affordances, two applicable within devices and three across devices. These are summarized in Fig. 17.8 together with associated design features:

Within device: **Iconicity and Atomization**
Iconicity specifies that the form of the digital object or physical object used to anchor the mental sign can facilitate or hinder the creation, access, and manipulation of signs. The greater the fidelity of the material carrier to the sign (i.e., how much the material carrier resembles the behavior, appearance or certain characteristic of the sign), potentially the easier the binding of the signs to the digital/physical object, and the easier the recall of the mental sign from perception reuptake of the material carrier. The use of file renaming and organization of folder structure are examples of instances when iconicity helps specific digital objects to be used as proxy for mental signs and thought objects. Thus, providing functionalities in device interfaces that facilitates the control of structure, mnemonicity, and customization may help with the handling of iconicity.

Fig. 17.8 Examples of design affordances for technology ecologies

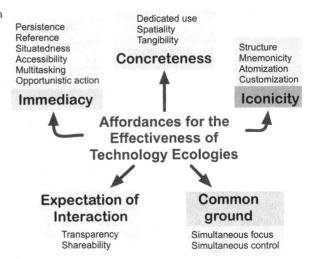

Atomization is a related feature that supports the association of digital objects to mental signs. A mental sign is typically an atomic concept at some level of abstraction, in the same way that a 'unit of analysis' specifies an entity that is a coherent whole at a certain level. Take the idea of 'Average/mean' in our earlier example. A Wikipedia page on 'Means' would be an apropos digital object for the concept, but a whole book on mathematics would not (even if it contains a section on 'Average'). Features to support atomization may include, for instance, enabling bookmarking of individual components larger text documents at different levels of abstraction.

Within device: Concreteness
In our study we saw how the whiteboard that affords the use of space and how the iPad that runs applications using the full screen real estate aid information to become what Heidegger [28] calls a 'thing,' something tangible for the student to grasp in her thinking process. **Concreteness** is the extent to which the physical object or digital object that is appropriated to anchor a mental sign is physically manipulable or tangible like a wooden block would be as a material carrier. Concreteness aids in the (re-)access of signs by for example providing focus of attention, and in the manipulation of signs through spatiality, change of perspectives, etc. The kinds of design features that can help to instill the sense of concreteness in technological devices and digital objects may be an interesting research question for one to empirically pursue.

Across devices: Immediacy
Immediacy concerns features that allow the user to convey signs to himself across space (from one device to another) and time (at a later point in time), and to others. Digital objects must be able to be transferred and shared across devices without going through one or more indirect actions. Essentially, immediacy attempts to minimize the 'cost' of information [30]. For example, if a user has a physical paper that she wants a friend to read, she drops it on the table in front of him. However, if she had the

document on her laptop, she may have to put it into a cloud storage location and tell him where to get it before they can discuss its contents. The lack of immediacy then hinders the opportunistic use of the document as a focus of discussion or thought.

Transparent interoperability across platforms may support immediate action as do consistency of interaction techniques (consistent ways to move and manipulate digital objects across platforms is critical to support their use as material carriers of signs). In our study, participants used persistence to allow information to stay immediate: on the laptop, they aligned their Word document and the PDF papers side by side. Others used their iPad as a 'persistent' secondary display for the PDFs.

Across devices: Expectation of interaction

It is key that components of technology ecologies are able to not only interoperate in some way, but also provide an **expectation of interaction** to users. Users should be able to expect that the creation of a sign at any one particular moment or place will not impede its re-access and later use for higher-level thinking through sign manipulation at other times and places, or for later parts of the workflow. For example, one can read what has been written on a sticky note at any time anywhere. Of course, the paper ecology is constrained by materials and physical laws (e.g., we do not have to worry about book 2.0 falling through the surface of Table 3.1 because of incompatibilities) while all interactions in technology have to be designed and implemented. Also, the cultural longevity of paper has built expectations and constraints (e.g., pencils do not work on leather portfolios) into the user community that digital technologies cannot always rely on.

In our study for instance, the students reported that they decided to use the whiteboard for brainstorming particularly because they knew that they would be able to take a picture of it with their iPad cameras later on. Conversely, a clear example of failure of the user's expectation of interaction in our study is one instance where the students spent one entire meeting only to set up shared Dropbox [31] folders and Evernote [32] notebooks.

Across devices: Common ground

The technology should provide support for students to easily share digital objects with the potential to become *common material carriers*. A common digital object may not necessarily be the proxy for the same mental signs for two different people. This is essentially the question of inter-subjectivity [33]. Physical things inherently allows for several users to have simultaneous focus and control. A page on the table can be seen by everyone around the table; several users can write on the whiteboard at the same time. In digital technologies however, the students always needed a separate 'situating channel' (e.g., speech, instant messaging, comment lines) to establish and maintain **common ground** with the 'information channel', where work is carried out.

17.9 Summary

This paper advanced that the possibilities of the augmentation of human intellect by digital technologies are limited unless we design for technologies to function in ecologies. Further, our aim was to fill the gap in our understanding of a mechanism by which technologies ecologies may then augment the human intellect. The contribution of this paper is at least three-fold: (i) we provide a theoretical framework using sign mediation theory to understand higher-level thinking; (ii) we derive principles that can guide the design of technology ecologies from the theoretical foundation; and (iii) we describe an initial set of design affordances of technology ecologies that can be translated into device features.

In a nutshell, our theoretical framework proposed that thought is encapsulated within and mediated by mental signs. We anchor signs onto external objects to help higher-level thinking, which consists of the creation of a 'system of signs.' External objects that are used to anchor signs can be either physical objects or digital objects. This framework suggests that three key processes need to be supported for higher-level thinking: the creation, access, and manipulation of signs. Integrated into a technology ecology whose aims is to integrate all devices within an environment, address all processes throughout a workflow, and engage the user in an experience of flow, technology ecologies should facilitate each of the three key processes of thinking, the transfer of signs across the three processes, and the transfer of signs across workflow processes. Examples of technology affordances are iconicity, concreteness, immediacy, expectation of interaction, and common ground.

17.10 Conclusion

The paradigms of learning and education have not developed in tandem with progress in technology, as epitomized in the tablet one-to-one programs. A major reason is that our understanding of how to design technologies that integrate well into the learning process is currently insufficient. While we are intuitively still making headway into the implementation of technologies that are necessary for the formation of technology ecologies such as cloud computing and peer-to-peer communication networks, we have yet to grasp the broader vision of how new technologies may be harnessed for deeper learning and thinking. A firm theoretical foundation and systematic derivation of design principles can go a long way to help in our quest to further augment the human intellect beyond the vision of Vannevar Bush and Doug Englebart.

Acknowledgments This work has been partially supported by NSF grants # IIS-0954048 and IIS-1059398.

References

1. Murray, J. (1997). *Hamlet on the Holodeck: The future of narrative in cyberspace* (p. 324; Anonymous. Vol. 1997). Cambridge: The MIT Press.
2. Chu, S., Quek, F., Endert, A., Chung, H., & Sawyer, B. (2012). The physicality of technological devices in education: building a digital experience for learning. *Advanced Learning Technologies (ICALT), 2012 IEEE 12th International Conference on*. IEEE, 2012.
3. Chu, S. L., & Quek, F. (2013). Information Holodeck: Thinking in Technology Ecologies. In *Human-Computer Interaction–INTERACT 2013* (pp. 167–184). Berlin: Springer.
4. Blume, H. (2014). L.A. school board moves forward with computer effort. http://articles. latimes.com/2014/jan/14/local/la-me-lausd-20140115. Accessed 15 April 2014.
5. AppleInsider Staff. (2014). Los Angeles school district earmarks $ 115M for additional iPads. http://appleinsider.com/articles/14/01/15/los-angeles-school-district-earmarks-115m-for-additiional-ipads. Accessed 18 March 2014.
6. Campbell, A. (2011). At a U. of Kentucky Dorm, a Live-In iPad Experience. 2011 Sept. 23rd [cited 2011 December 27th]. http://chronicle.com/blogs/wiredcampus/at-a-u-kentucky-dorm-a-live-in-ipad-experience/33380?sid=wc&utm_source=wc&utm_medium=en. Accessed 18 Dec 2011.
7. Ferenstein, G. (2011). Apple's iPad officially passes the higher education test. 2011 Feb. 14th. http://www.fastcompany.com/1727292/apple-ipad-officially-passes-the-higher-eduction-test-exclusive. Accessed 27 Dec 2011.
8. Hu, W. (2011). Math that moves: Schools embrace the iPad. New York Times 2011 Jan. 4th. http://www.nytimes.com/2011/01/05/education/05tablets.html?pagewanted=all. Accessed 27 Dec 2011
9. Seton Hill University. (2011). iPad2 for everyone. http://www.setonhill.edu/techadvantage/index.cfm. Accessed 27 Dec 2011
10. Lopez, S. (2013). New problems surface in L.A. Unified's iPad program. http://www.latimes.com/local/la-me-0929-lopez-ipad-20130929,0,2398142.column—axzz2yyzmZPy6. Accessed 15 April 2014.
11. Rick, J. (2009). Towards a classroom ecology of devices: Interfaces for collaborative scripts. In Workshop at 8th international conference on Computer Supported Collaborative Learning (CSCL2009): "Scripted vs. Free CS collaboration: Alternatives and paths for adaptable and flexible CS scripted collaboration". Rhodes, Greece.
12. Coughlan, T., et al. (2012). The conceptual framing, design and evaluation of device ecologies for collaborative activities. *International Journal of Human-Computer Studies, 70*(10), 765–779.
13. Jung, H., Stolterman, E., Ryan, W., Thompson, T., & Siegel, M. (2008). Toward a framework for ecologies of artifacts: How are digital artifacts interconnected within a personal life? In *Proceedings of the 5th Nordic conference on Human-computer interaction: Building bridges* (pp. 201–210). ACM.
14. Andrienko, G., et al. (2010). Space, time and visual analytics. *International Journal of Geographical Information Science, 24*(10), 1577–1600.
15. Card, S.K. and Pirolli, P. (2005). Sensemaking processes of intelligence analysts and possible leverage points as identified through cognitive task analysis. In international conference on intelligence analysis.
16. Vygotsky, L. S. (1978). *Mind in society: The development of higher psychological processes.* Cambridge: Harvard University Press.
17. Vygotsky, L. S. (1986). In A. Kozulin (Ed.), *Thought and language*. Cambridge: MIT Press.
18. Kirsh, D. (2013). Thinking with external representations. In *Cognition beyond the brain* (pp. 171–194). London: Springer.
19. Vygotsky, L. S. (Ed.). (1987). In A. Kozulin (Ed.), Thought and language (Edited and translated by E. Hanfmann and G. Vakar). Cambridge: MIT Press.

20. Vygotsky, L. S. (1978). Internalization of higher psychological functions. In M. Cole et al. (Ed.), *Mind in society: The development of higher psychological processes* (pp. 52–57). Cambridge: Harvard University Press.

21. Miller, G. A. (1956). The magical number seven, plus or minus two. *Psychology Review, 63,* 81–97.

22. McNeill, D., et al. (2008). MIND-MERGING. In E. Moresella (Ed.), *Expressing oneself/expressing one's self: Communication, language, cognition, and identity: A festschrift in honor of Robert M. Krauss (11/8/07).* Abingdon: Taylor & Francis Pubs.

23. Hutchins, E. (1995). *Cognition in the wild.* Cambridge: MIT Press.

24. Lave, J., & Wenger, E. (1991). *Situated learning: Legitimate peripheral participation* (1st ed.). Cambridge: Cambridge University Press.

25. Halverson, C. A. (2002). Activity theory and distributed cogntion: Or what does CSCW need to do with theories? *Computer Supported Cooperative Work, 11,* 243–267.

26. Erickson, T. D. (1993). Working with interface metaphors. In B. Laurel (Ed.), *The art of human-computer interface design* (pp. 65–73). Chicago: Addison-Wesley Publishing Inc.

27. Sellen, A. J., & Harper, R. H. (2003). *The myth of the paperless office.* Cambridge: MIT press.

28. Heidegger, M. (1962). In J. Macquarrie (Ed.), *Being and time.* New York: Harper & Row Publishers.

29. Shipman III, F. M., & Marshall, C. C. (1994). Roles, characteristics, and affordances of spatialized information. In Proceedings of the ACM ECHT '94 workshop on spatial metaphors, ACM European Conference on Hypertext.

30. Card, S. K., Robertson, G. G., & Mackinlay, J. D. (1991). The information visualizer, an information workspace. In Proceedings of the SIGCHI conference on human factors in computing systems. ACM.

31. Dropbox. (2011). Dropbox. http://www.dropbox.com/. Accessed 8 Dec 2014.

32. Evernote. (2011). Evernote. http://www.evernote.com/. Accessed 8 Dec 2014.

33. Gillespie, A., & Cornish, F. (2010). Intersubjectivity: Toward a dialogical analysis. *Journal for the Theory of Social Behaviour, 40,* 19–46.

Part V
Technologies in Practice—K-12 Classroom Models

Chapter 18
Improving Student Understanding with Video Grading

Walter Schilling

Abstract It is known that students exhibit different learning styles. Good instructors adapt their teaching style to target the appropriate style(s) for their students, and by doing so achieve significant improvements in student outcomes. The same approach, however, does not hold true for submitted assignments. Due to logistics, most submitted assignments are graded in the same fashion: providing numeric feedback (i.e. a grade) and written comments. This article describes a different approach, an approach which is designed to aid visual and audible learners to obtain better feedback from submitted assignments.

18.1 Problem Statement and Context

It is well known within the educational community that students exhibit different learning styles. Overall, there are six prominent learn style models in the literature [1]. One of the most commonly cited models is the VARK model developed by Neil Flemming [2]. Based upon this model, students are classified as either a visual learner who learns best by seeing pictures or slides, an auditory learner who learns best from through listening, a reading and writing learner who prefers to learn from both reading and writing, or a kinaesthetic learner who learns best by touching or doing. The Kolb Experiential Learning Theory model indicates that learning is a set of continuous processes, starting with concrete experience and evolving to active experimentation [3]. The Gregorc model states that individuals have natural predispositions toward learning in four different dimensions, including abstract and concrete perception, sequential and random ordering, deductive and inductive processing, and separative and associative relationships [4]. Felder and Silverman have expanded upon this premise and performed extensive analysis within the engineering field, developing a 5 dimensional model of learning [5] which incorporates student perception, input modality, organization, processing, and understanding. The Dunn and Dunn learning style model represents the most complex model, in which five stimuli are analyzed

W. Schilling (✉)
Milwaukee School of Engineering, Milwaukee, WI, USA
e-mail: schilling@msoe.edu

© Springer International Publishing Switzerland 2015
T. Hammond et al. (eds.), *The Impact of Pen and Touch Technology on Education*,
Human-Computer Interaction Series, DOI 10.1007/978-3-319-15594-4_18

across multiple dimensions. Lastly, the Revised Approaches to Studying Inventory model (RASI) uses three dimensional scales to model the interaction between a learner and the learning environment [6].

Effective teachers employ multimodal approaches to ensure that material is both taught and reinforced using different methods. These approaches work well in the traditional classroom. However, at some point, every instructor has an assignment that needs to be graded, and while the classroom dynamic is important to ensuring student achievement, providing students with high quality feedback on submitted work is equally important. Hounsell states:

> It has long been recognized, by researchers and practitioners alike, that feedback plays a decisive role in learning and development, within and beyond formal educational settings. We learn faster, and much more effectively, when we have a clear sense of how well we are doing and what we might need to do in order to improve [7].

Feedback has been shown to be the single most powerful influence on student success [8]. For feedback to be meaningful, it must meet many criteria, including being applicable to the student, delivered in a timely fashion, engaging to the students, and relevant to the topic at hand [9]. With all of the importance placed on feedback, student feedback has generally remained unchanged over the years. Written comments make up 79 % of feedback received by students, though 45 % of students report that they rarely received individual written feedback on assignments [10], and many students admit that they do not read written comments [11].

18.2 Method Employed

Electronic ink has ushered in a new realm of capabilities for the classroom instructor. In the area of grading, electronic ink has been used to mark up [12, 13] submitted assignments, and has been viewed favorably by both students and faculty. However, like traditional paper based grading, this mechanism suffers from several weaknesses. Due to the medium, feedback is almost entirely in the form of written comments, mirroring traditional feedback from paper submissions. Excluding the improvement in timeliness and accessibility, this form of feedback offers little improvement over traditional paper based feedback.

To improve the effectiveness of feedback, it is imperative that, just like classroom teaching, multiple dimensions be used. For many years, audio commentary has been used to evaluate student performances in the musical and arts forms, as it was convenient for an evaluator to speak into a tape recorder while judging the event. Oral comments have also been used informally in class and in team settings for an instructor to "coach" a team. In research studies, students have shown a preference for audio commentary over written comments [14].

While beneficial, audio commentary does not aid the visual learner. A visual learner needs to see things in context in order to understand their meaning. Thus, while audio commentary is an improvement over written feedback, it still is not optimal. To truly reach all student learning styles, feedback to the students must also incorporate visual feedback. Thus, the concept of video grading.

Video grading starts in much the same manner as any other form of electronic grading. A student submits to an instructor an electronic document. While in this particular process a PDF document format was chosen for portability purposes, any electronic format could be employed. Prior to the instructor grading the assignment, the instructor runs a screen capture program[1] and dons a headset microphone. As the instructor reads, interprets, and marks up the document, a stream of consciousness capture of the instructor's thoughts is captured on the audio track, allowing the student to see the progression of markups in the document as well as hear verbal comments. If written comments are made on the document, the instructor can either verbally repeat the comments or provide more rationale for their inclusion. Overall the process is shown in Fig. 18.1.

One distinct advantage of this process is that in addition to aiding visual learners, it really helps the students see the non-linear process of assessing a submission. For example, when an instructor grades an assignment, they may refer back to a previous page if something contradictory is found later on or if a duplicated point is found. With this approach, since the student is visualizing exactly what the instructor saw when the assignment was graded, the student sees the instructor returning to the previous location and clearly can follow the reference.

18.3   Results and Evaluation

The described method was employed in a software requirements and specification course during the Fall of 2012. In this course, students work in teams to develop a requirements specification for a software product. Activities that the students conduct include preliminary research, stakeholder identification, interviewing stakeholders, drafting a requirements document, and developing storyboards. While the students do give oral presentations, a significant amount of their grade involves effective written communication, which has always been evaluated in a traditional manner using written comments as well as standardized grading rubrics. Overall, there were three major assignment submissions that were graded using video grading techniques, resulting in the average video lengths shown in Fig. 18.2.

At the end of the course, students were given a brief, 10-question survey that assessed their perceptions of video grading. In particular, there was a strong desire to determine if the students watched the videos and if they found the videos to be helpful. If the students did not watch the videos, then the videos would clearly be no more effective than written comments, which are ignored. If the students watched the videos but did not feel the feedback was worthwhile, then again the video system would not be effective. Results of the survey are provided in Table 18.1. On all

---

[1] In this particular instance, Microsoft Expression Screen Capture utility was used, but any program which does screen capturing could be used.

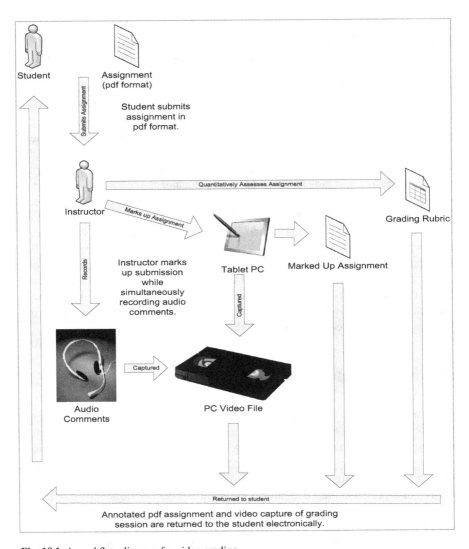

Fig. 18.1 A workflow diagram for video grading

Fig. 18.2 Average video
lengths for graded
assignments

Assignment ▼	Average Video Length ▼
Assignment 1	0:22:08
Assignment 2	0:11:44
Assignment 3	0:20:41

questions, the majority of the students either agreed or strongly agreed with the
statements, and the majority of students watched all of the videos. Reaction was
mixed to the length of the videos, as half of the students felt that they were too

Table 18.1 Student survey results

	MSOE SE3821 Software Requirements and Specification				
	All	2	1	0	
How many of the videos did you watch?	57%	29%	14%	0%	
	Strongly Agree	Agree	Neutral	Disagree	Strongly Disagree	
I found the video format more helpful than traditional paper-based assignment feedback.	29%	43%	29%	0%	0%	*The only downside is the time it takes to listen to the videos, unavoidable but still nice to hear what you're thinking.* *It was nice to see the thought process of your grading, as you're grading.*
I found the audio commentary more helpful than traditional written comments.	43%	43%	14%	0%	0%	*Audio comments, while taking longer, provide much more in-depth feedback as well as including feedback that is not easily included in written feedback. I believe that the rubric and summary are important parts of the feedback process, however.*
I was able to read the text on the video.	71%	14%	14%	0%	0%	*The length was long, but less time would make the video feedback far less useful*
I was able to clearly see what was being described in the video.	67%	17%	17%	0%	0%	
I prefer video feedback to traditional feedback in computer courses.	20%	40%	20%	20%	0%	*Easier to reread paper than go back in video.*
	Way Too Long	Too Long	About Right	Too Short	Way too short	
I felt that the length of the videos were:	0%	50%	50%	0%	0%	Perhaps a 5 minute limit
In what way(s) could video grading be improved to make it more useful for you?	If different professors were involved in the video grading process collaboration for improving the process might help; I have no suggestions at this time.				
Please enter any other thoughts or comments that you may have about video grading.	In a course like Software Req+Specs, video grading is nice to have, but actually seems it might be more trouble than it's worth. There's no product after labs that we need to demonstrate, just a report, so there's not much to talk about - either we reported something correctly, or we didn't. In order to keep the video short, you had to skip over a lot of content of reports, only taking samples of the overall work. I don't think this helps overall - what if you skip over a really big mistake? Then you'll have to resort to looking through the report and handwriting the comments anyway, which seems to defeat the purpose of doing video grading in the first place. Should be continued Good idea, takes a little long but insightful comments make the value about the same as written.				

long.[2] The response rate was 38 % out of a potential of 18 students. Overall, students viewed the videos very positively, and a slight majority indicated a preference for video grading versus traditional grading.

To be more effective, it is important that some of the technical issues with this approach be resolved. While the actual time spent grading was very comparable to that spent grading in a traditional manner, there was a significant overhead associated with assignment return. While the output of the tablet was an annotated PDF file, the initial output of the Expression Screen capture utility needed to be encoded using Microsoft Expression. This added approximately 15 min of processing after grading was completed in order to create a video format which could be distributed to the students. The files themselves were also very large. Some of the videos approached 35 MB in size, too large to return by e-mail. Thus, a dedicated website was setup to allow the students to log on and view their videos. While these techniques were not insurmountable, they may preclude less technically savvy instructors from adopting the procedure.

---

[2] This was a somewhat expected response, as even the instructor felt the videos were a bit too long. However, the assignments had 25 or more pages in the report that was to be reviewed, and significantly reducing this time was not deemed feasible for the assignments.

18.4 Future Work

There is obviously much more research to be done to assess the effectiveness of video grading. The scope of this project was small and the sample size was very limited. However, it is believed that this is an acceptable way for assessing student work that offers unique advantages in the digital age.

The assignments given in this class were very static in nature, and grading on paper would probably convey most of the relevant information. Could this technique be applied to other aspects of the software and computer engineering curriculum? An area of exploration is in the design and execution of computer programs. With this technique, and an appropriate split-screen approach, an instructor could markup a design while simultaneously executing the program. Preliminary work has already started in this area in another programming course.

It is also important to look at learning gains with this technique. While it was not possible for the instructor to compare learning outcomes from this class with previous offerings, it is important to compare student achievement with this method versus more traditional approaches.

Further research needs to be done on the length of the videos as well. It is known that humans have limited attention spans. Clearly the 20 min videos used may have been too long, just as a 50 min lecture without appropriate active learning exercises can be too long. What is the appropriate length for a custom video? This length may be highly variable based on the assignment context.

Lastly, it is important that this approach be tried in different disciplines. Mathematicians could verbally explain mistakes in a mathematical proof or numerical computation. Chemists could easily show mistakes in a chemical equation; other disciplines of engineering could easily perform a design review of a product and capture the thoughts of the reviewers.

References

1. Hawk, T. F., & Shah, A. J. (2007). Using learning style instruments to enhance student learning. *Decision Sciences Journal of Innovative Education, 5*(1). doi:10.1111/j.1540-4609.2007.00125.x.
2. Fleming, N. D., & Mill, C. (1992). Not another inventory, rather a catalyst for reflection. *To Improve the Academy, 11*, 137–155.
3. Kolb, D. (1984). *Experiential learning: Experience as the source of learning and development, Englewood Cliffs.* Englewood Cliffs, NJ: Prentice-Hall.
4. Gregorc, A. F., & Ward, H. B. (1977). A new definition for individual: Implications for learning and teaching. *NASSP Bulletin, 401*(6), 20–23.
5. Felder, R. M., & Silverman, L. K. (1988). Learning and teaching styles in engineering education. *Journal of Engineering Education, 78*(7), 674–681.
6. Duff, A. (2004). Approaches to learning: The revised approaches to studying inventory. *Active Learning in Higher Education, 5*(1), 56–72.
7. Hounsell, D. (1987). Essay writing and the quality of feedback. In J.T.E. Richardson, et al. (Eds.), *Student learning: Research in education and Cognitive psychology Milton Keynes* (pp. 109–119). SRHE & Open University Press.

8. Hattie, J. (1987). Identifying the salient facets of a model of student learning: A synthesis of meta-analyses. *International Journal of Educational Research, 11,* 187–212.
9. Gibbs, G., & Simpson, C. (2004). Doies your assessment support your studens' learning? *Journal of Teaching and Learning in Higher Education, 1*(1), 3–31.
10. Rowe, A., Wood, L., & Petocz, P. (2008). Engaging students: Student preferences for feedback. In *Proceedings of the 31st HERDSA Annual Conference*, Rotorua.
11. Rowe, A., & Wood, L. N. (2008). What feedback do students want? In Australian Association for Research in Education (AARE) International Education Research Conference, Fremantle.
12. Hermann, N., & Popyack, J. L. (2003). Electronic grading: When the tablet is mightier than the pen. *Syllabus: Technology for Higher Education, 16,* 1–16.
13. Castles, R., Scott, E., Lo, J., & Lohani, V. (2009). A Tablet-PC-Based electronic grading system in a large first-year engineering course. In ASEE Annual Conference, Austin.
14. Wallace, I., & Moore, C. (2012). Providing in-depth and personalized feedback to online students using audio recording. In 3rd International Conference on e-education, e-Business, e-Management, and e-Learning, Singapore.

Chapter 19
"Kids teaching Kids": Student-Created Tablet-based Mathtrain.TV Tutorials For A Global Audience

Eric J. Marcos

Abstract This paper details the benefits of empowering students to create video tutorials. For the past 6 years, middle school students at Lincoln Middle School in Santa Monica, California have adopted a "kids teaching kids" model. The students use a Tablet PC to create short mathematics tutorial lessons ("screencasts") based on classroom material. Their voice and writings are recorded simultaneously using screen-recording software and produced as a video file. The student-created tutorials are shared with their peers during class instruction, on the class iTunes podcast, YouTube channel, as well as YouTube EDU, our student created mobile apps, and archived on their own Mathtrain.TV video Web site. A global audience emerged as students, parents/guardians, teachers, and the general public across the country and world began accessing this on-line library of freely available lessons. Students enthusiastically spend hours after school, on their own time, collaborating with other students, as they contribute to the library of student-created tutorials. They are self-motivated and never receive a grade or extra credit for these screencasts. Over 155 countries have accessed Mathtrain.TV. Students of all levels are having fun while taking an active role in their own learning and recognizing its global impact.

19.1 Problem Statement and Context

19.1.1 The Classroom Tablet PC

For over 6 years, my middle school students have been creating video tutorials on our Tablet PC and sharing them as part of our "kids teaching kids" Mathtrain Project. This paper focuses on the powerful effects of a classroom Tablet PC, emphasizing student creation of content and the beneficial impact that student-created video tutorials have on education.

In 2006, I bought my first Tablet PC and began using it with a projector for classroom instruction as an upgrade to the clunky overhead projector. It was a convertible

E. J. Marcos (✉)
Lincoln Middle School, Santa Monica, CA, USA
e-mail: mathtrain@gmail.com

© Springer International Publishing Switzerland 2015
T. Hammond et al. (eds.), *The Impact of Pen and Touch Technology on Education*,
Human-Computer Interaction Series, DOI 10.1007/978-3-319-15594-4_19

201

Tablet PC, which allowed the laptop screen to twist around and rest flat on top of the keyboard. An active digitizer stylus was used to interact with the computer. Students were instantly captivated by its ability to enable one to write directly onto the screen. This generated a marked increase in classroom participation. Students enthusiastically raised and waved their hands, hoping to be called upon so they could come up and use the Tablet PC. In several of my classes, it became necessary to keep a tally of students whom had and had not already come to the front of the class to answer questions. Several students who were previously distracted or inattentive became engaged in the lessons.

In an effort to capitalize on the exceptionally high-level of student interest with the Tablet PC, I decided to trust my students and let them actually try out and use the Tablet PC. They were visibly excited since students are sometimes not allowed to use the teacher's computer or technology. The decision to allow and encourage students to use the Tablet PC was a major turning point as it allowed our student-created tutorials and "kids teaching kids" model to evolve.

Student interest in the Tablet PC continued to flow beyond the class period and throughout the school. Students of all levels, backgrounds, grade level, and other classes stopped by before school, between classes, during lunch, and after school for a chance to use the Tablet PC. Each day, groups of middle school students huddled around the Tablet PC waiting for their turn while observing their peers drawing, creating fonts, solving a mathematics problem, or exploring the physics simulation program. They found common ground as they collaborated and learned from each other. This "kids teaching kids" collaboration made me recognize what a great, useful resource the students can be to each other. I realized they were natural collaborators and their power to teach and share their knowledge should not be underestimated.

Students visiting my classroom after school would stay for hours using the Tablet PC. Although they were often content with just doodling or drawing, they also enjoyed working on mathematics problems on the Tablet PC. The allure of the Tablet PC itself increased student engagement. But it proved to be even more valuable. The Tablet PC transformed our teaching and learning after I discovered the screen-recording software, Camtasia Studio. This software enabled the Tablet PC to create handwritten video tutorials, revolutionizing how content information could be accessed and shared.

19.1.2   The Power of Tablet PC Screencasts

One late afternoon, one of my students needed help on a homework problem. Using our class Web site messaging system on Mathtrain.com, the student asked for assistance. Ordinarily, I would use Microsoft Word or e-mail to explain mathematics problems when on remote locations. But that is not always an ideal way to tutor or assist a student. Those mediums can be difficult to follow for several reasons. For example, fractions do not always stack properly, equations are difficult to line up, mathematical notations can get messy and at the time it was not easy to insert sketches or drawings. Fortunately, I had just discovered the screen recording software, Camtasia Studio, which enabled the creation of dynamic videos using natural handwriting and voice. Instead of typing the instructions, I tried a new strategy, creating a video tutorial explaining the homework problem. It only took a few minutes to create a diagram and explain the mathematics problem on my Tablet PC as Camtasia Studio simultaneously recorded my computer screen and voice. The resulting video file was then e-mailed back to the student.

Within the hour the student replied that she now understood the problem and then requested, "Can I have another one?" It was the first time she had received a personalized video tutorial explanation of a mathematics problem, or for any subject. The next day in class, other students heard about the video and suggested they could have benefited from it as well. So, the tutorial was posted onto our class site. Other students began requesting homework videos. The demand and interest soon lead me to begin actively creating daily tutorial videos to assist students with each night's homework and to upload them onto our class Web site, Mathtrain.com.

19.1.3 Student-Created Tutorials

The idea of developing student-based mathematics tutorials evolved and became a reality after our Winter Break in 2007. Students continued to be fascinated with the Tablet PC and continued to request new teacher screencast tutorials. That could have been the end of a positive story right there, where "teacher creates personalized video tutorials to help students with mathematics concepts and homework." However, through trusting my students and allowing them to use the Tablet PC, a more important and unexpected, story was born.

In February 2007, a student came after school and asked if she could create a video tutorial. She wanted to produce a screencast that explained how to solve proportions. This student proceeded to create a short tutorial on the Tablet PC. The student-created video was shared in my mathematics classes the next day. The students reacted positively and suddenly other students began showing up after school to now create mathematics tutorial videos. The students never received a grade or extra credit for these screencasts. They were self-motivated to produce them.

As the number of student-created tutorials grew, it became necessary to have one location that stored them all. In addition to posting the tutorials onto our class Web site, Mathtrain.com, we had also been uploading the videos onto YouTube and a few other sources. But YouTube was blocked at our school and posting blog links onto our class site was becoming inefficient and difficult to navigate. To alleviate these issues, we launched our own YouTube-clone video site, Mathtrain.TV, to house our growing amount of student-created content.

19.2   Method Employed

19.2.1   Overview

The student videos we produced are also known as "screencasts." We use a Tablet PC with an active digitizer to write and screen recording software Camtasia Studio. Our videos were not created using an external video camera pointed at our hands nor are they the type of video one might create at a wedding or birthday party. Instead, as one wrote and explained the mathematical problem, Camtasia Studio simultaneously recorded both what was written onto the Tablet PC screen and the accompanying audio. This enabled the students to write and speak naturally. In an effort to protect the identity of the students, their faces and real names were not used in the tutorials. Students would choose an alias prior to recording. Camtasia Studios' recording and editing features were easy for students to use and made it simple to create a video file that could be easily shared on a Web site or e-mailed. Many of the videos were produced as ".swf" and ".flv" flash formatted files. Today, in an effort to be playable on the most devices possible, we mainly produce ".mp4" and "H.264" video files.

19.2.2   Steps for Creating a Student Tutorial

When a student wanted to record a screencast, they would come after school to my classroom with an idea of which mathematical concept or lesson they wanted to produce. On the Tablet PC, we used a drawing program such as the free Windows Journal or the OneNode program as the canvas area to write onto with the active digitizer stylus. We used an active digitizer stylus because it mimicked true hand-writing the best, as it was sensitive to pen pressure. Each of these drawing programs allowed the background color to be changed as well as multiple pen and highlighter colors and thicknesses. This facilitated student creativity, personalization and the overall comprehension of the video. After observing the teacher or a peer create a tutorial screencast, the students would be empowered to run the entire process themselves. The student would usually begin by writing a title and then opening the screen recording software, Camtasia Studio. They would then select the area that would be recorded and check the microphone level. If more than one student was collaborating, they would check the microphone level for each student. Once they were ready to go, the student would push the big red "record" button, watch it count down and begin their tutorial.

When finished, the student would stop the recording and preview what was just recorded. If there were major errors or issues, they would delete the file and start over, re-recording everything. If there were minor errors or no issues at all, the student would save the clip and display the recording in an editing window. In the editing window, students could add pop up messages, arrows and other effects using a feature called "call outs". Any undesired audio could be easily removed, making the screencast easier to follow, shorter in length, and smaller in file size. Background, intro/outro music could also be added to the clip. Usually, opening and ending titles would be added as bumpers. The opening title would include the topic about to be taught and the ending title would usually thank the viewers for watching.

Once satisfied, the student selected "Produce" and the clip would be rendered into a freestanding video file. This video file was then shared with their peers during class instruction, and with a global audience on our class Mathtrain iTunes podcast, YouTube channel, including YouTube EDU as well as archived on our own Mathtrain.TV video Web site.

19.2.3 Microphone

Although most Tablet PCs have a microphone installed, we found it advantageous to use an external microphone. It made the audio sound clearer. The factory-installed microphone will pick up every click and scribble sound you write onto the Tablet PC screen. In our first few years, we used an inexpensive RadioShack microphone leftover from my cassette player days. It turned out the students enjoyed holding the microphone, because they felt like they were on American Idol. Eventually, we replaced that microphone with an inexpensive desktop microphone. This freed up the student's hands and allowed them to collaborate more easily.

One mistake I made was purchasing an expensive microphone. The issue was not because of the students handling it. The problem with an expensive microphone is that they are built to be spoken into directly and cut out ambient noise from the sides. The problem is that students do not sit with the microphone directly in front of them at a constant and consistent distance. They are often animated as they are when called to the front of the class to solve a problem. A cheaper microphone is more forgiving and is often designed to pick up audio in a less directional and more cardioid area. We want to capture an authentic representation of the students explaining their concepts, not a robotic narration, so we opted to use an inexpensive desktop USB microphone that offered more student mobility during the recording process.

19.2.4 Unscripted

One of the most important aspects of our student-created videos is that they are unscripted. Conventional wisdom is that narrated videos should be planned and scripted. We certainly planned out each video in that the student knew ahead of time which concept was to be taught and knew what the expected answer or answers would be. But we never scripted the dialog. If one listens to a scripted video, it can sound lifeless and artificial as the narrator is concentrating on reading the right words in the correct order at the right time instead of focusing on delivering the overall multimedia message.

Our goal was to capture an authentic representation of the student's explanation. For example, when a student is called to the front of the class to answer a question on the chalkboard or whiteboard, that student does not usually craft a scripted discourse as he or she approaches the front. Instead, the student might bring their paper or notebook with them and use that as a guide as they explain their reasoning or answer. Another benefit of keeping our videos unscripted is that we hear the student's own voice or, "kid language" as one student called it. Students have reported they often prefer a peer's explanation to another adult's or teacher's.

19.2.5 Captioning

We continue to caption our student content and are passionate about making our content viewable and useful to as many people as possible. All users can benefit from captions.

19.2.6 Mathtrain.TV

Although we share our student-created tutorials in multiple locations, our main location is our own video Web site, Mathtrain.TV. When we first began creating videos, YouTube was blocked at many schools, including ours. This led to the creation of our own site. Mathtrain.TV runs on free software, called PHPMotion, where videos are categorized by groups, genres and tags to make search easier and efficient. The site is free to use and ad-free. No login is required, unless a user wants to comment on a video or upload their own content. Mathtrain.TV also offers numerous sharing options, including embed codes and links to social networking sites.

19.2.7 Other Devices

Our main workhorse for creating student screencasts has been a convertible Tablet PC. We have also had success using SmartBoards, Wacom Tablets, and iPads for creating student content. The iPad has offered some encouraging results due to its mobility and apps. Free iPad apps such as ScreenChomp and Educreations and ShowMe have been useful. The most promising app is Doceri. With its Doceri GoodPoint Stylus connected, which has a palm rejection feature, students are able to nearly replicate an actual Tablet PC experience (minus pen pressure).

19.3   Results and Evaluation

Whether created on a Tablet PC or iPad, it is exciting to watch how students naturally develop their presentation skills. The students enjoy creating and do their best because they know their tutorials have purpose. As mentioned above, students never receive a grade or extra credit for creating a tutorial, yet they are self-motivated to produce them. Students continue to come after school, on their own time, to contribute to our growing library of tutorials. At Mathtrain.TV, middle school students of all levels who desire to take an active role in their own learning, drive our unscripted student-created tutorials. They learn skills such as the importance of empathy as they compose their screencasts with helpful arrows, highlighting, "white space" and organization. Students are even eager to caption our videos on their own time as we continue to develop closed caption versions of our student videos for deaf and hard of hearing with assistance from the DCMP "Described and Captioned Media Program" [1]. Our students understand the value and need to make the videos as accessible as possible.

Several of my students (accompanied by their parents) have co-presented with me at education conferences across the country (e.g. Boston, Philadelphia, San Diego) and participated in interviews or Skype sessions with classes in New York City and podcasts such as the EdTechCrew in Australia. We have also been featured on EuroNews, which was broadcast to over 155 countries and translated into 11 languages. It is empowering to the students to know their video tutorials are being watched by real people-students, families, educators and even universities, who often e-mail us or post meaningful comments about their work.

Students will spend hours on one tutorial, where they may only spend minutes on a homework question, because they find creating screencasts to be fun. When the first iPhone was released, one student was motivated to create an iPhone app for our student content. Shortly after, another student created an Android version of the app.

Today, our student-created videos are shared with a global audience [2]. The instructional tutorials are also used as authentic assessment and flipping or double flipping classrooms (including our own). The student who creates a tutorial certainly benefits. Instead of just being consumers of content, they are also creators of content. As one student pointed out, the best way to learn something is to teach it. There are times when a student producing a video has to pause the recording because they realize they do not know why they are performing a mathematical step. The student might collect their thoughts, ask a peer in the room or go seek out the reasoning and try recording the next day. It is a wonderful self-learning tool.

Internationally-recognized education technology leader, Alan November, helped spread our student's Mathtrain.TV tutorials in his keynotes, TEDx Talk and presentations across the world. Mr. November inspires others to set up student Tutorial Designers in every classroom, based on our Mathtrain.TV model. He also featured Mathtrain.TV and interviewed several of our students in his recent book, "Who Owns the Learning?" [3]

The student-created math tutorials have been an inspiration to other students and educators across the globe. Our YouTube channel gets an average of 1000 views per day and 29,000 views per month. One student tutorial, "Egyptian Multiplication", has been viewed over 30,000 times on YouTube and over 7000 times on our very own MathTrain.TV. Mathtrain.TV receives an average of 766 views each day. Each month, MathtrainTV gets about 23,000 visits and 750,000 hits. Over 155 countries and every continent have accessed our student tutorials. Students are contributing to not only the mathematics community, but to the education community at large.

19.4   Future Work

This project was achieved with limited personal resources. I look forward to future school and district support. We will continue our quest to create a student-created mathematics tutorial lesson for every topic we cover in class. In addition, it would be valuable to continue studying how on-line collaboration influences mathematical understanding.

Acknowledgements   Thanks to Aleya and Camilla Spielman, Tiana Kadkhoda and all my students for their inspiring contributions to this project and to the mathematics community. Thanks to the late Dianne Talarico; to Dave McCollom, Daniel Foster, Troy Stein and the entire TechSmith staff; to Alan November and all at November Learning whose encouragement helped broaden the scope of our work; to Richard McKinnon; to Dr. Eric Hamilton; and to Elaine and Frank Marcos.

References

1. Jones, K., & Marcos, E. J. (2008). Google video in the classroom. Described and captioned media program. http://www.dcmp.org/caai/nadh217.pdf. Accessed 21 Nov 2012.
2. Marcos, E. (2008). Kids Teaching Kids. In K. McFerrin et al. (Eds.), Proceedings of Society for Information Technology & Teacher Education International Conference 2008 (pp. 4510–4514). Chesapeake, VA: Association for the Advancement of Computing in Education (AACE).
3. November, A. (2012). *Who owns the learning? Preparing students for success in the digital age.* Bloomington: Solution Tree Press.

Chapter 20
Using Technology to Pair Cognitive Demand of Tasks to Its Appropriate Community in a Math Classroom

Wendi Klaiber

Abstract How is the mathematics teacher to best utilize the latest accessible advancements in technology to motivate and foster perseverance and tenacity in students? Pedagogically, which approaches will yield the most fruitful dynamic as regards the balance between class time (community) and homework (individual), given that many students benefit more from the struggle within a community of learners when first facing new, incrementally more difficult material, and when the normal amounts of conventional class time allotted are rarely adequate?

To what degree can the integration of technology as such enhance learning? Would a given teacher's individually created multimedia (e.g., videos with pen and tablet technology, screen casting, and reflective questionnaires within Google forms) effectively create more time such that the students can address higher cognitive tasks more often while in the classroom community?

20.1 Problem Statement and Context

High-school students entering a given AP calculus course often struggle in applying skills and knowledge to new problems. Generally, calculus students have succeeded in their previous math classes by following the algorithmic processes that were modeled by their teachers (e.g., knowing and memorizing procedures). But when they begin the study of calculus, a markedly different set of skills is required of them. Students are expected to analyze, interpret, conjecture, justify, and apply their skills verbally, graphically, and analytically. Such higher-order thinking requires perseverance and tenacity. To teach, model, and give opportunity for the students to develop these higher-order thinking skills [4] the instructor needs to free up classroom time by spending less of it delivering direct instruction on knowledge-based content. Similar to the teaching dynamic often utilized in humanities classes, AP calculus teachers can—and this paper will argue *should*—assign lessons for students to study outside of class, and then, in the classroom, engage students in tasks and discussions

W. Klaiber (✉)
Oaks Christian High School, Westlake Village, CA, USA
e-mail: wklaiber@oakschristian.org

© Springer International Publishing Switzerland 2015
T. Hammond et al. (eds.), *The Impact of Pen and Touch Technology on Education*,
Human-Computer Interaction Series, DOI 10.1007/978-3-319-15594-4_20

that require interpretation, analysis, and the overall more intensive levels of content creation. Normally in the mathematics discipline, this model would be more difficult to implement because of (1) time limitations, and (2) the need to present and model content; however, innovations in easily accessible technology (such as virtual pen and tablet technologies) make it possible for students to access a given teacher's presentations of assigned content outside of class. Pragmatically speaking, the AP calculus instructor thereby *creates* time, or at the least, reaps a far more effective use of the time allotted.

20.2 Method Employed

In spring of 2011, I awoke to the disheartening reality of being a twentieth century educator teaching mathematics in a twenty-first century world. An ever-increasing deluge of advances in accessible technology had raced so far ahead of me that I was missing opportunities to more fully engage my students. In March of 2011 I attended my first annual conference of Computer-Using Educators (CUE) where I learned the benefits of tools like virtual screen casting, Google documents, and Flip-teaching. In July, I attended a weeklong session at Pepperdine University with the organization Teachers Create where I was introduced to the tools, skills, and opportunities necessary to create curriculum related videos, which would align with my content standards. Continuing this path of professional development during the ensuing academic year I attended monthly meetings with Teachers Create, the annual CUE conference in March 2012, a summer session with Teachers Create, and a subsequent CUE conference in July 2012. These experiences challenged me to rethink my pedagogy as regards designing units of study and using technology as a tool to more effectively develop students who are tenacious problem-solvers.

For example, I have been using pen and tablet technology as a tool to pair the learning activity with the learning community. As presenter and teacher, Ramsey Musallam, suggests [2], I examine the level of cognitive demand (as aligned to Bloom's taxonomy) of given content tasks in a unit and pair it/them appropriately with either the classroom community or the individual setting. Where a skill or concept can be learned through direct instruction without requiring the classroom community, I will create and upload a student accessible video using pen and tablet technology, assigning the viewing of the video and student reflection as a homework assignment. The next class will include a short discussion analyzing individual student responses to the video followed by a task(s) of higher cognitive demand that requires, and benefits, the classroom community.

While planning a unit on solving optimization word problems in my Calculus class, for example, I examined the content objectives, the assessments, the research on problem solving, and representative problems. I then aligned it to Bloom's taxonomy as diagrammed below (Fig. 20.1) [3].

For the knowledge-based skills (e.g., finding the derivative and using critical points to find the extremas of a function) I used a SMART board to record several

Create	
Evaluate	• Optimization project – create a product with given conditions • Given a new optimization problem, students are able to apply knowledge of derivatives, solve, and interpret their answer.
Analyze	
Apply	• Model given information with a function • Apply the problem-solving process
Understand	• Understand that extrema occur at critical points • Find the derivative of a function
Know	• Learn the problem-solving process of Question, Clarify, Strategize & Solve, and Check.

Fig. 20.1 Bloom taxonomy for solving optimization word problems

lessons for the students, which gave examples with solutions already worked out. In the past I have also used a Wacom Tablet or iPad to record my lessons. I subsequently upload these videos to our class website for student access. After viewing the videos, the students are then responsible for submitting responses to a Google form that I created, which is embedded on the class's website. The questions in the Google form require students to reflect on their understanding of derivatives and critical points and to solve problems similar to those presented in the video. Their responses provide an excellent starting point for class discussion on the following day. As a class, the students will engage in error analysis as I display their responses to the Google form on the SMART board, and I can address any misconceptions in their understanding prior to applying the skills that day.

I also used pen and tablet technology to create instructional videos introducing a problem solving protocol and modeling the implementation of this protocol in solving optimization word problems. In my research on teaching problem solving, one of the consistent elements of student success is that students are taught a protocol based on reading-comprehension and given ample opportunity to use this protocol in problem solving. By creating these videos, the students then come to class the next day with a foundational understanding of the problem-solving protocol and how to solve optimization word problems. Classroom time is then freed up so that students can spend this time solving new problems in a collaborative environment.

I also use pen and tablet technologies to hold virtual conferences for review sessions at the end of a chapter. Typically, I will plan on using one class session to review content prior to a chapter test, however, during this time, there is always conflict between the students and myself as to how to spend the time. I want to facilitate student groups collaborating on cumulative problems [1] as they review the learned skills of the unit. The students typically want to spend the time asking individual questions to assigned review problems. As a result, the review sessions end up stretching to two class sessions instead of one class session. In order to maximize the effectiveness of class time, I have started using an online application, Canvas by Instructure, as a tool to host review sessions at the end of a chapter. This is a free resource for teachers. I create a class, invite my students to join the class, and then set a date and time for a virtual conference. In the sessions, students can log in and can ask questions. I upload a blank page to the site and use a Wacom tablet to answer the mathematical questions of my students. As a result, I can meet the needs and desires of both the students and myself by spending one class session working on cumulative problems and one virtual session answering the individual student questions.

I have repeated this cycle of unit planning for several units this semester.

20.3   Results and Evaluation

While the anecdotal evidence constituted by students' thank you notes and their affirming reports to fellow teachers and parents indicates how helpful the videos have been, it is difficult to directly, or conclusively, link or quantify perceived gains (academic and otherwise) to the technologically enhanced approach to teaching discussed herein—at least it is for me at this time. However, scores on my chapter tests rose about 5 % this year over last, and my most recent AP Calculus AB results are historically high for our school, but these results could, of course, also be affected by other variables.

As of this writing, in the second quarter of my current classes, I still have students complaining about "how hard AP calculus is," and how they know the rules but have a difficult time answering the questions.

After the first month of originally implementing this technologically enhanced approach to teaching, I had observed that it was necessary for students to not only do problem-solving in the collaborative community of the classroom but also independently (outside of class). My initial mistake in this regard was having the students do most of the problem solving in class and very little at home. The students thereby gained confidence while working with their classmates, but when given individual assessments, their individual scores did not align with their level of competency demonstrated in the classroom. So I adjusted the pacing and homework assignments to include more individual practice of problems similar to those that I observed being solved in class.

20.4   Future Work

Given the wide accessibility of the technologies discussed herein I envision a multifaceted expansion of technologically integrated methods and memes, including students' use of technology (and whatever follows in its wake) to create their own collections of instructional videos. For instance, prior to an Advanced-Placement exam, I would like to assign free response questions to pairs or groups of students where they create a video, which presents their solution(s). Such groups would also benefit by creating an accompanying questionnaire to each video. Subsequently one might even have students provide feedback evaluating their classmates' videos probably based upon a teacher-created rubric.

References

1. Heller, P., Keith, R., & Anderson, S. (1992). Teaching problem solving through cooperative grouping (Part 1): Group versus individual problem solving. *American Journal of Physics, 60*(7), 627–636.
2. Musallam, R. (2010). *The effects of using screencasting as a multimedia pre-training tool to manage the intrinsic cognitive load of chemical equilibrium instruction for advanced high school chemistry students*. Doctoral dissertation, The University of San Francisco.
3. Ferguson, C. (2002). Using the revised taxonomy to plan and deliver team-taught, integrated, thematic units. *Theory into Practice, 41*(4), 239–244.
4. Hackathorna, J., Solomon, B. E. D., Blankmeyer, K. L., Tennialb, R. E., & Garczynski, A. M. (2011). Learning by doing: An empirical study of active teaching techniques. *The Journal of Effective Teaching (JET), 11*(2), 40.

Chapter 21
The Flipped Classroom: Touch Enabled, Academically Proven

Stacey Roshan

Abstract In a classroom-based intervention utilizing the flipped classroom model, students showed increased performance and satisfaction. During a 2-year experiment in an 11th and 12th grade AP Calculus course, the teacher recorded lectures to be watched at home via the Internet and used class time for problem solving, reversing the standard educational model. Compared with the previous year, average student AP score increased, as did the percentage of students who earned scores eligible for college credit. In a qualitative survey, students unanimously preferred the new format and reported lowered stress and anxiety levels related to homework and learning. Implications for instructional technology, classroom pedagogy, and future technological advances are discussed.

21.1 Problem Statement and Context

Pen and touch technology appear to present exciting applications for educators. This paper explores the potential impact on student learning and satisfaction through the use of tablet PCs and screencasting. In particular, this chapter examines the impact of one implementation of the flipped classroom model in AP Calculus AB.[1] High school mathematics classrooms often deserve the commonly held notion of a boring, rigid learning environment where the teacher lectures and the students repetitively practice problems from a textbook until the skill is mastered. The problem is that lecturing to a classroom full of students is not a meaningful discussion; it does not require students to participate in their learning process.

The motivating factor for change in this project was to reduce students' stress levels. Anxiety undermines a student's ability to reach his/her full potential and master challenging AP level mathematics. An unreasonable amount of anxiety and

---

[1] The success of the flipped classroom model in the AP Calculus Classroom has garnered attention from a number of media sources including: USA Today, The Washington Post, and CNN.

S. Roshan (✉)
Bullis School, Potomac, MD, USA
e-mail: staceyroshan@gmail.com

© Springer International Publishing Switzerland 2015
T. Hammond et al. (eds.), *The Impact of Pen and Touch Technology on Education*,
Human-Computer Interaction Series, DOI 10.1007/978-3-319-15594-4_21

apprehension exists among high stakes courses, such as AP Calculus, particularly at high performing schools. The pressure to achieve at the highest levels to stay competitive in the college admissions process is ever growing. To allow enough time to work problems in the classroom, with the rigorous and fast-paced AP Calculus curriculum, the solution identified was to eliminate and replace the lecture. The flipped classroom provides a means of testing this solution: by pre-recording lessons and sending the teacher-driven lecture home, we hoped to see whether students would regain a voice in the classroom and whether the classroom environment could be transformed into a more calm, excited, inspiring atmosphere where learning can truly thrive.

21.1.1   What is the Flipped Classroom?

The flipped classroom changes the traditional classroom dynamic by shifting the method of instruction delivery. In an effort to best support students, class time is spent having students solve problems, where they are surrounded by the help of their peers and teacher, rather than doing this work alone at home without guidance. An effective use of the flipped model in the math classroom is to have the students view an instructional video for homework and use class time to work through their questions and engage in authentic, lively discussions.

21.1.2   The Changing Role of the Teacher and Student

The student-centered classroom requires students to be resourceful and independent in the learning process. By providing customized learning time in the classroom, students take more ownership of their learning and can focus on individual needs. As students work collaboratively through problems in the classroom, stronger students naturally begin teaching peers instead of the teacher being required to do the majority of instruction. The teacher's role thus shifts from driver to facilitator and learning coach. By observing and listening to students' conversations, the teacher is able to direct and guide discussions and immediately catch misconceptions.

21.1.3   Shift in Classroom Culture and Climate

The successful, prepared student of today is imaginative, creative, and curious. However, in the traditional lecture-based classroom that remains prevalent in the U.S., there is little room for these essentials. The flipped classroom challenges the current format of classrooms by shifting the culture to one of discussion and playing with ideas, providing an inspiring, innovative, and collaborative classroom climate where learning can truly thrive. By alleviating student stress, students have an increased ability to apply and abstract. Additionally, the flipped classroom is a participatory learning environment. When students come into class having previewed material, they are able to engage in an authentic discussion. Pen and touch technology enables the teacher to create video content as a means of moving one-way lecture outside of the classroom and replacing class time with an interactive discussion.

21.1.4 Technology as a Means of Bringing Compassion Back to the Classroom

There is a common misconception that technology is an ice-cold, robotic, and automated thing. Instead, technology should be viewed as a way to individualize and customize learning. Flipping the classroom can bring the compassion back into an otherwise overly stressed environment by freeing time for the teacher to walk around, observe, support, and get to know students as individuals during class. Providing students the time to feel their questions can be heard and answered and allowing class time for one-on-one work, the flipped classroom transforms the relationships that the teacher is able to build with students.

21.2 Method Employed

The experiment consisted of two groups of students: Control and Treatment. In the 2009–2010 school year, seventeen 11th and 12th grade students participated in AP Calculus AB taught in the traditional style, with in-class lectures and out-of-class problem sets as homework (Control). In the 2010–2011 and 2011–2012 school years, thirty-one 11th and 12th grade students participated in the same class taught in a flipped classroom, with in-class problem sets and out-of-class video lectures as homework (Treatment). All students were required to sit for the AP Exam.

21.2.1 Teacher Created Videos

Video lectures, created by the teacher, are used to deliver content for students to watch at home.[2] The Power Point lessons that would traditionally serve as the basis for instruction in the classroom are the basis for the video lessons. The screencast is created using a Fujitsu tablet PC to ink and Camtasia Studio to record (Fig. 21.1).

Seeing a teacher work through a problem, step-by-step, is a critical piece in making the video lecture easily digestible. Pen technology is essential in providing flow to

---

[2] Teacher-created content example: http://www.screencast.com/t/vKNtUTgRH.

Fig. 21.1 Teacher created
content using tablet PC with
Camtasia studio

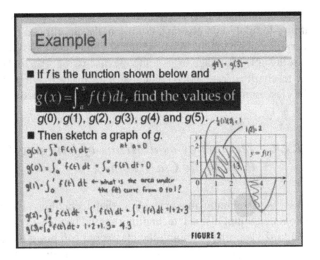

the lecture, enabling teachers to fluidly present their thought process (overlaid with voiceover). Simply speaking over a presentation of static slides would not create a similar interactive, comprehensible experience. Students taking notes along with the teacher's inking in the video is a very important component to making the experience less passive.

After recording the lesson, the editing process allows the teacher to not only clean up and consolidate work, but also to add in engaging elements. Current tools available in Camtasia Studio include embedded quizzes and callout boxes.

The quizzing provides a way for students to engage in an interactive activity yielding immediate feedback, for both teacher and student. A variety of question formats can be asked: multiple choice, fill-in-the-blank, and short answer. The benefit of the first two options is automated, instant grading for student feedback while the advantage of the latter option is the ability to assess beyond recognition. In addition to being a tool to help students self-assess, the quiz results provide teachers with a quick snap-shot of areas that need more attention in the classroom. Possible uses for these results include: setting the tone for full-class discussion, grouping students based on need, and as a way of pre-identifying necessary one-on-one work. Finally, teachers can use the feedback to assist in improving video lessons by recognizing which concepts are not being grasped. To track student data, videos with embedded quizzes ask students to enter a name and email address. Videos are viewable on both computers and tablets.

Callout boxes are another way of increasing engagement by zoning students attention and providing a visual clue to important talking points. Much like margin notes or highlighted definitions are used in a textbook, callout boxes can be used to call attention to key concepts.

21.2.2 Student Created Content

Moving lecture outside of the classroom creates valuable time in the classroom. One effective use of class time is giving students the opportunity to teach their peers. For example, students can be made responsible for creating video responses for test preparation. Instead of the teacher standing at the board, students work individually or in pairs to create video solutions to questions. The videos are then uploaded to the Internet, where they can be tagged and archived to create a library of student-created content for future reference.

Beginning in the 2011–2012 school year, students were asked to create video content. To ensure quality, students were asked to prepare a "script", reviewed by the teacher, before recording was allowed. This was often a collaborative process, involving the teacher and other students. Students were then given an iPad to record, using the ScreenChomp app and a BoxWave sylus. The value in this exercise was found to be multifold: providing large-scale peer-to-peer teaching opportunities, creating a lasting resource of content created by learners, and offering a value opportunity for the teacher to assess thought process and target the source of a misunderstanding. Most powerfully, this activity enhances higher-order thinking and a deep understanding; effectively explaining a topic requires a thoughtful, step-by-step process rather than a more procedural solution.

One of the main problems faced by students when using the iPads to create video solutions was the ability to write legibly on the iPad. The problem became more pronounced over the course of the year as Calculus equations became more complex. One solution was to have students solve the problem on a piece of paper, neatly written, below a copy of the problem itself and then to take a picture of the work using the iPad. The picture was then placed into the ScreenChomp app as a background. In recording, students provided a voiceover to explain the steps in the written work, while using the stylus to circle, shade, and draw quick sketches or equations (Fig. 21.2).[3]

21.3 Results and Evaluation

Before exploring the results of the flipped classroom experiment, it is important to recognize the limitations of the study. First, classes are not only non-randomized but carefully selected: only students with strong prior performance in mathematics can enroll in the AP Calculus AB class. While there was no explicit change in the selection criteria used between the class years, the potential nonetheless exists that implicit differences exist. Second, because the Control and Treatment groups come from different class years, there are potential cohort effects. Some attempt is made to address this point in the analysis, but it remains an important drawback of the study.

---

[3] Student-created content example: http://youtu.be/Y48s16qRCP0.

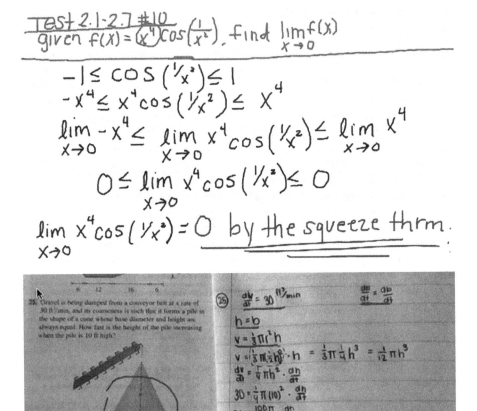

Fig. 21.2 Two examples of student-created content that were created using the iPads

Limitations aside, there are two key components to understanding the impact of a flipped classroom on students: quantitative academic performance and qualitative reviews of the learning experience.

To address quantitative performance, the study benefits from the standardized, third-party review process of the Advanced Placement tests operated by the College Board. At the conclusion of all classes, all students were administered the Advanced Placement Calculus AB test. Scored between 1 (no recommendation) and 5 (extremely well-qualified), the exam is independently evaluated by the College Board.[4]

---

[4] The exact scoring method used by the College Board changed somewhat prior to the 2011–2012 academic year (between the Control and Treatment administrations), removing penalties for wrong answers. However, the national distribution of scores was nearly identical for both tests, suggesting that the score comparison remains robust.

Participants in the Treatment condition had higher AP scores ($M = 4.065$, $SD = 0.892$) than did participants in the Control condition ($M = 3.588$, $SD = 1.176$), $t(46) = -1.58$, $p = .121$, indicating a rise in quantitative academic performance in the flipped classroom. While this increase did not reach conventional levels of significance, the restricted range of the AP exam and large ordinal differences would necessitate a sample size beyond that available in this limited case study for anything but the most but the largest effect size.

Qualitative performance was also measured by in-class student performance. For comparison, students in the 2010–2011 Treatment group were given the identical assessments and homework assignments as those in the Control.[5] The mean grade for students in the Treatment condition was higher in all three trimesters, by 2, 3, and 4 %, respectively. Not only was there an increase in grades using the flipped classroom format, but there was also a trend upwards over the course of the year. One reason may be that there was some learning curve to getting used to the format of class and the video lectures.

As noted earlier, the subjective experience of the students is also an important part of the flipped classroom model. To test for differences in student experience, 16 students in the 2011–2012 class completed anonymous questionnaires indicating their agreement on a 1–5 scale for a series of statements.[6]

One important pattern that emerges from the responses is an emphasis on individual pacing and instruction. Students strongly endorsed statements like "I felt that instruction was more individualized because the lectures were watched at home." ($M = 4.13$) and when asked their favorite part of the class, 12 out of the 16 students identified the ability to rewind and review video lectures at their own pace and, importantly, on their own schedule.

A reasonable explanation might be that academic performance increased because students spent more time at home watching lectures in a flipped class than a traditional one. Students, however, showed strong endorsement for opposing statements ("I felt that the format of class helped reduce my homework load.", $M = 4.19$; "The format of class helped reduce my anxiety about homework.", $M = 4.13$), which suggests that lowered stress, not increasing workload, is a more salient instructional characteristic of flipped classrooms.

Finally, students overwhelmingly preferred the flipped class structure ("I would prefer to go back to the 'normal' format that other classes use.", $M = 1.63$; "Overall, I preferred the format of this class.", $M = 4.75$) but were also conscious that it may only be appropriate in certain environments; when asked what type of class the format would work for, the majority of the students (9) responded "Only AP and Honors Classes".

---

[5] Both the textbook and teacher remained unchanged throughout the study.
[6] The survey was only administered in the 2011–2012 academic year.

21.4 Discussion

In the flipped classroom model, the problem solving activity is brought inside the classroom, inciting authentic thinking questions and allowing teachers to monitor understanding, performance, and to immediately pick up on misconceptions. Time spent actively interacting and engaging with students provides evidence of student comprehension before assessments—one of the key reasons underlying increased student achievement. Other factors include in-class time for one-on-one instruction to target individual gaps and collaborative problem solving. Finally, access to online lectures for students to re-watch (in part or in full) after in-class discussion and problem solving allows students to tailor homework to their needs.

Pen and touch technology provides fluidity and natural flow to videos, significantly increasing students' ability to independently follow the thought-process being conveyed. Asking students to take notes in the viewing process increases engagement and provides students with a reference to bring to the classroom. This framework has been an essential component to successful implementation of the flipped model.

In conclusion, changing the type of work performed at home has been a means of reducing student stress and re-energizing the classroom experience. Alleviating student anxiety has been an important component in stimulating higher-order, critical thinking in class. The results have yielded increased student satisfaction and higher AP scores. In flipping the dynamic, the teacher's role in the classroom transitions to guide and learning coach, emboldening students with a stronger voice. By shifting the classroom culture to a collaborative, student-centric space and providing students with a resource bank of teacher and student-created instructional content, students become empowered learners.

Chapter 22
A More Inclusive, Less Distracting, and Engaging Learning Environment Through Smartsync

Alicia Gonzalez, Hiroo Kato, and Jose Israel Ramirez Gamez

Abstract This paper documents some of the initial experiences of using synchronization technology via networked tablet computers in a high school classroom setting. It addresses some of the rudimentary issues of how instructional time is lost by physical motion; how student teacher confidentiality affects student feedback; and how whole class interruptions can do more harm than good. The networked tablet computers allow students to freely communicate with teachers in a more private and personalized study environment, and can be done without the teacher having to move around the classroom. Initial findings suggest a high level of student engagement, less downtime for students, faster and more frequent teacher responses, enhanced communication between teacher and student, and better behavior.

22.1 Problem Statement and Context

The current public high school math classroom has approximately 30 students. With class time ranging from 40 min to 80 min, and an ever increasing curriculum load, students have much content to consume and in less time, among their many peers within a classroom. While there have been many advances in pedagogy, there are many aspects of classroom teaching that hinder or slow down student progress. Because the classroom format allows one teacher to address the entire class, there have been strategies and structure for teaching such as peer teaching, collaborative work, project-based learning, use of IT, and cross-curricular content integration, which

---

J. I. R. Gamez (✉)
Spring Valley High School, Las Vegas, NV, USA
e-mail: jramirez-gamez@interact.ccsd.net

A. Gonzalez
Santa Monica High School, Santa Monica, CA, USA
e-mail: a.gonzalez@smmusd.org

H. Kato
Pepperdine University, Malibu, CA, USA
e-mail: hiroo.kato@pepperdine.edu

© Springer International Publishing Switzerland 2015
T. Hammond et al. (eds.), *The Impact of Pen and Touch Technology on Education*,
Human-Computer Interaction Series, DOI 10.1007/978-3-319-15594-4_22

are among things that are integral or complementary to the learning environment. Despite advances in pedagogy, there are simple issues that still prevail in a traditional classroom environment.

22.1.1 Time Is Lost as the Teacher Moves Around the Classroom

While it is good practice to check student progress and address individual student needs by physically moving around the classroom, teacher movement takes away from students and teachers' time. As the classroom teacher addresses each student individually, time elapses in moving from one end of the classroom to another. This creates "pockets" of "wait-time" for the remaining students waiting to address their own needs with the classroom teacher, and increases the time it takes for the teacher to address all student needs. During this wait-time, students tend to become disengaged from the content or lesson activity, as their questions become obstacles to their successfully progressing through the lesson activity. As a result, student focus and attention become swayed from the intended instruction of the lesson activity, leading to off-task behavior (and possibly even misbehavior) and significant loss of learning opportunity, especially considering the limited time 40–80 min students have with their classroom teacher. Furthermore, the physical structure of a classroom can also facilitate or hinder the teacher's ability to navigate around a classroom, potentially leaving certain locations more accessible and others more inaccessible.

22.1.2 Students that are Less Comfortable Speaking Publically Naturally Receive Less Attention

Students have varying level of comfort in addressing their needs/concerns in a classroom environment. The engagement level and confidence level changes in differing settings, and in a traditional classroom setting, those who can speak up invariably get more attention (including those that are not engaged in the prescribed work), and the classroom is a place where those who lack confidence or who struggle are less likely to be addressed given their quiet nature. Much of the teacher's response is based on the feedback that students provide (whether verbal, body language, facial expression, signal tools, etc.), and in the absence of such a voice, teachers find it more difficult to address their needs. Consequently, the teacher's ability to ensure that all students get the academic support they need becomes nearly impossible. Student hesitation in addressing their needs in the classroom may be due in part to the lack of privacy that students have, and the fear they perhaps experience in exposing their mistakes or weaknesses. In addition, students may also have limited language skills (both linguistically and technically) to address their needs with the teacher.

If technology can provide a way in which students can communicate their individual needs, without publically doing so, teachers can provide feedback in a way that effectively provides specific academic support to each student while maintaining each student's comfort level. This would increase the extent to which the teacher can gain insight as to students' level of mastery/struggle with the content.

22.1.3   Teacher Tendency to Interrupt the Whole Class When Addressing Questions of Individuals

As the classroom teacher addresses individual student needs, the teacher becomes aware of commonalities and often stops the entire to class to address a seemingly common misunderstanding that the majority of students are showing. This may seem justified by the number of students making the common error, or perhaps by how misguided the errors are to the goal of the lesson. For the teacher, these interruptions serve the purpose of preventing the other students from making the same errors or holding the same misconceptions. However, this "mass correction" may not have the intended outcome, and may miss its goal altogether as the interruption occurs during different "places" of engagement for each student. As students work at their own pace, the information shared by the teacher during the interruption may bear no relevance to many of the students if they have not yet reached a point in the lesson activity where such a "mass correction" will be beneficial. Consequently, this not only takes away that immersive experience and engagement in the work that some were experiencing, but also is an unnecessary stoppage of work for those that don't require the intervention.

Trying to ensure that all students get the most out of the classroom experience requires a delicate balance of maximizing instructional time while minimizing distractions and obstacles. The result is often a uniform "one-size-fits-all" experience, where student voice is mostly limited. With these constraints and the limited time that students have in the classroom, creating a learning environment with less wait time, fewer interruptions and more equitable distribution of teacher attention is sure to facilitate greater student engagement in their classroom activities and sure to create more effective learning environments.

22.2   Method Employed

In this study, we investigate the impact that networked tablet computing devices can have in a high school mathematics and physics classroom. The study took place in a public charter high school in Los Angeles, where the students were juniors and seniors, mostly first-generation college bound students, who lived locally.

Each classroom was provided with 10–20 pen and touch ready tablet computers, where students paired up and shared one tablet per pair. There was also one tablet (sometimes two tablets) provided to the teacher. The tablet devices were wirelessly networked and configured in a way so that the teacher was able to see the screen of

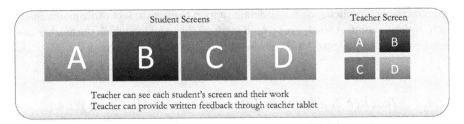

Fig. 22.1 Screen setup

all student tablets in real-time on the teacher tablet, using the SMART Sync software provided by SMART Technologies. All written work by the students was done on the tablet device using a stylus, where the tasks were given in the form of electronic worksheets, and the teacher was able to see exactly what each pair was writing into their tablets. The configuration also allowed for the teacher to directly write into the teacher tablet in a way that would show on the student tablet, thus enabling written feedback to appear for students to see. Figure 22.1 below depicts the relationship between screens.

The classes were video-recorded with a camcorder on a tripod, capturing student-teacher interactions and conversations as well as peer dialog. In addition, a teacher reflection was recorded subsequent to the class (and later transcribed), and also student debriefs took place for feedback. Students also provided written feedback about their experiences using the tablets.

22.3 Results and Evaluation

22.3.1 Elimination of Physical/Social Constraints Leads to Faster and More Frequent Teacher Response

The SMART Sync software eliminated the need for the teacher to move in order to check in with students and address their needs. As a result of the teacher's ability to view all of the student's work on the teacher tablet, less time was spent on physical movement and more time was afforded to addressing student needs. This led to a greater number of student-teacher interactions, and allowed the teacher to address a greater number of questions during the same classroom time period. While the teacher initially expressed frustration in not being able to physically move, and that there was a feeling of 'disconnect' due to lack of physical proximity, the teacher expressed that with practice, talking to the student while checking student work on the tablet alleviates that feeling. In a particular lesson, there were a total of 134 interactions (See Fig. 22.2 for an example of what is understood by an interaction) between the students and the teacher within a period of 71 min, where more than half (72 to be exact) were initiated by the tablets. Since there was no control group for comparison, it is difficult to attribute any significance to this figure, although the

Fig. 22.2 Interaction

> **Definition of a single interaction:**
> It is a set of question(s) and answer(s) (including immediate
> follow-ups)
>
> **Example of one interaction**
> Student: does 'x' have to be written in a curly funny way?
> Teacher: preferably, but it is up to you.
> Student: and what font is it if I have to type it up?
> Teacher: I am not sure. You would have to look it up.
> End of interaction

video showed very little downtime by the teacher and the conversation continued to flow. Feedback from students also point to quicker teacher feedback: "It was quicker for the teacher to help the students when they have a question." "One thing that I like very much is how the teacher is able to see what you are doing wrong and answer questions much more faster."

Additionally, the elimination of teacher movement also eliminates the physical constraints of the classroom environment that may normally limit teacher movement, accessibility, and the ability of the teacher to ensure that all students reach the learning target of the lesson. This means that teachers had equal access to each pair of students. Since communication is facilitated by the SMART Sync tablet, the teacher can still use "virtual physical proximity" to see student work, and can still address students' needs by writing to them on the teacher screen and allowing the students to see the teachers response on their own tablet screen, keeping communication as confidential (and individualized) as needed. This enables the teacher to reach every student in the classroom, no matter what the physical arrangement of the classroom is. Not only is the teacher not limited by the classroom space, but the teacher also can continue the practice of checking in with students even when they do not have concerns to address. The use of the tablet, allows the teacher to view student work on the teacher screen to informally assess progress, level of understanding, productivity, and points of confusion. In this manner, the teacher is able to assess individual and overall levels of student engagement, understanding, and misconceptions that may need to be addressed. As a result, the teacher is better able to equitably distribute attention to all students in the classroom and is able to do so more effectively by individualizing that attention.

22.3.2 *Student-Teacher Confidentiality Allows Enhanced Communication*

The SMART Sync and pen and touch technology created a vehicle for all students to communicate their individual needs. Specifically, the students were able to share their questions privately with the teacher (as only the teacher could see their screens), creating an experience where students felt more comfortable asking questions or merely asking for help. This resulted in a classroom experience more rich in student voice, as all students (those usually shy to ask for help, those comfortable asking for help, and even those with limited language skills) were able to use the pen and touch technology to write their needs on the tablet screen, thereby communicating with the teacher in an effective and confidential manner.

Furthermore, the SMART Sync software allowed the teacher to create a learning activity that with the help of the pen and touch technology made it easier for students to address their needs with more preciseness. In this study, the students worked through an activity that, facilitated by the use of the pen and touch technology, allowed them to pinpoint precise areas to address with the teacher. Guided by a "digital document" that students viewed and "wrote on" using the tablet screen and stylus pen, the teacher could see their work on the teacher screen and have greater information as to their points of confusion. Students could also use the language of the document to phrase their questions, making it easier to use precise (both content specific and accurate) language to address their needs with the teacher. Students voiced their experiences on how the technology facilitated their learning: "I think it is easier for students and allows for more educational interaction." "Also it made working more easier having the teacher check our progress. It was interactive and fun. Seems it can be easier to learn." "Is also easier to write and fix your work that you are trying to complete." "I enjoyed using this tablet because it was easy to use and working with a partner made it easier to figure out each problem."

22.3.3 Individualized Pacing Leads to Increased Engagement, Less Interruption, and Better Behavior

The use of the SMART Sync software allows the learning environment to become more individualized to student learning needs. While students are able to work on the lesson activity at their own individual pace, they also maintain the ability to address their individual needs and receive the specific support they need regardless of their "place" in the learning activity. This eliminates the teacher's desire to interrupt the entire group, as all students can communicate their questions and the teacher can still check in with all students, particularly students with more specialized learning needs (such as English learners, or students who tend to need higher levels of academic support). With fewer interruptions and more individualized support, the learning experience can flow at the appropriate rate for each student (not too fast for those that need more time and not to slow for those that need less time), creating a more individualized learning environment. Specifically, in this study, students reported that working in the SMART Sync classroom using pen and touch technology and tablets was a more enjoyable experience, increased their ability to focus and their sense of independence while learning. "You get to ask us questions and check up on our work without interrupting anyone else in the class." "I enjoy using the tablets it is very helpful to me and I am able to concentrate much more when using tablet". "I really enjoyed working this way because you have more flexibility, and you get to work with your partner, and when you have a question the teacher can look at your screen and tell you where you not doing well. This method helps a lot." "I like how we are able to help each other out. This makes learning more interesting." In addition, in one of the recorded lessons, there was only 1 classroom management prompt by the teacher in a 71 min learning segment of the lesson, where the teacher asked some students to get back to work in the last 5 min of the segment. This not only is indicative of a high level of student engagement on the prescribed tasks, but is also an indication that the teacher can focus on engaging students to learn instead of spending time on behavioral issues.

While the observed outcomes and reflections on the use of pen-and-touch tablets here are in no way conclusive, they suggest significant and optimistic implications. The challenge of creating the most effective, individualized and successful learning environment for each and every student that enters a typical high school math class is not one that is easily met. While the pedagogy of teaching combined with teacher creativity can meet this challenge with success, there is no predetermined pedagogy for how technology can aid in overcoming such challenges fast enough to address their urgency. Therefore, it is important to consider how using technology, such as the pen and touch tablets, created an experience where significant classroom constraints became almost nonexistent, and the conditions for effective learning experiences prevailed. More specifically, it is important to further consider what unique capabilities pen and touch technology coupled with the SmartSync software offer to the learning environment and how these unique capabilities accommodate the classroom environment to make it a more effective learning environment. The implications for qualitatively better use of class time, for increasing access for all students, and for creating a uniquely individualized learning experience open the door for further possibilities and questions. These and other considerations necessitate further investigation, however, it is certain that the observed benefits to the classroom make such investigation a worthwhile and pressing endeavor.

22.4 Future Work

This study is based on the analysis of video footage from a learning environment, as well as feedback emerging from personal reflections and debriefs. Comparison with a control group may be one step in identifying the degree of significance of the findings in this study. In addition, while this study provides insights into the gains of working in a new physical and relational setting in a classroom, some of the possible drawbacks have yet to be addressed. Lastly, this study can address what such a new environment means for professional development of teachers, as maintaining such a classroom setting entails considerable attention to detail and engagement on the part of the facilitator.

Acknowledgement The authors gratefully acknowledge the Institute for Education Sciences [1], National Science Foundation [2], Microsoft Research [3] and Pepperdine University in supporting this project.

References

1. Hamilton, E., & Harding, N. (2008). "Agent and library augmented shared knowledge areas (ALASKA)". Institute for Education Sciences Award 305A080667.
2. Hamilton, E. (2010). PREDICATE Project: Targeted research on teacher creativity at the intersection of content, student cognition, and digital media. National Science Foundation award 1044478.
3. Hamilton, E. (2007). Virtual and face-to-face workshops to organize the international distributed learning and collaboration (DLAC) research network, Microsoft Research USA.

Chapter 23
Make it Mobile: Best Practices for Science Courses in iTunes U

Eric A. Walters and Katherine Krueger-Hirt

Abstract iTunes U provides K-12 educators a straight-forward yet dynamic way to design, implement and deliver complete courses that are supported by pedagogically-sound video, audio, web content, iTunes content, and Apps. Moreover, the iPad provides educators a unique opportunity to move learning into a true mobile environment. The challenge for educators is evaluating and curating content from a variety of sources, while ensuring that specific learning objectives are addressed. iTunes U, for example, offers students an opportunity to engage in "meaning-making" through the acquisition of both continuous and discontinuous content. Moreover, students can connect with and interact with their peers and their environment anywhere, anytime. The key question: how do you transform an "analog curriculum" to a "digital curriculum"?

This chapter reviews the transformation of two 12th grade electives, AP Physics C: Mechanics and Molecular Biology, from traditional classroom courses to mobile-based, iPad courses on iTunes U. Methodology for course design and curriculum development, including App integration; innovative mobile learning activity design; student collaboration opportunities in a mobile environment; teacher-published MultiTouch textbooks; and effective formative, summative and laboratory assessment mechanisms will be addressed through the lens of current research on digital and mobile learning.

As a "work in progress," quantitative and qualitative evidence of student success as well as impact on student learning, based on a transformative learning model, will be reviewed.

E. A. Walters (✉) · K. Krueger-Hirt
Marymount School of New York, New York, NY, USA
e-mail: ewalters@marymountnyc.org

K. Krueger-Hirt
e-mail: kkrueger@marymountnyc.org

© Springer International Publishing Switzerland 2015
T. Hammond et al. (eds.), *The Impact of Pen and Touch Technology on Education,*
Human-Computer Interaction Series, DOI 10.1007/978-3-319-15594-4_23

23.1   Problem Statement and Context

Mobile learning was defined by O'Malley et al., early on, as "Any sort of learning that happens when the learner is not at a fixed, predetermined location, or learning that happens when the learner takes advantage of learning opportunities offered by mobile technologies" [1]. Yet, as Mike Sharples notes, "Every era of technology has, to some extent, formed education in its own image. For the era of mobile technology, we may come to conceive education as conversation in context, enabled by the continual interaction through and with personal and mobile technology" [2].

Yet, as Pachler et al. suggest, "by using mobile technologies and convergent media, and by working with pieces and fragments of distributed contents and information, learners generate contexts" [3]. The content that both educators and students appropriate "be it continuous or discontinuous [is to be used] for the purpose of construction of individualized meaning."

The challenge for the authors was to redesign two senior level electives, Molecular Biology and AP Physics C: Mechanics as mobile learning courses. We wanted our students to approach the curriculum from a constructivist approach, while drawing on resources from a variety of sources. As such, we needed to consider the following:

1. Mobile devices are part of the users' creation of contexts.
2. They enable them to connect different contexts but also create their own contexts for learning.
3. How to utilize our everyday life-worlds as learning spaces.
4. Being able to operate successfully in, and across, new and ever changing contexts and learning spaces with and through the use of mobile devices.
5. Focus on the process of meaning making

Our goal was to develop our courses in such a way that each "relieves the recipients from passivity and affords them the role of active and constructive individuals who engage in meaningful media reception and the production of meaning individualized contents" [4]. Students need to be actively engaged in the learning process as teachers serve as facilitators of learning and curators of content.

Moreover, we needed to "select those resources that are relevant for them in their meaning-making process" that allowed users to "construct new structures and contexts which are, in turn, meaningful in relation to already existing structures and in relation to the users' life-worlds" [5].

23.2   Method Employed

23.2.1   Program Implementation Process

As this program was being implemented in a K-12 setting, a modified version of Gary Woodill's *Mobile Learning Implementation Roadmap* was used to assist in content design and development process. Table 23.1 outlines the implementation process.

Table 23.1 Application of mobile learning implementation roadmap

Roadmap step	Description	Program implementation
2	Identify stakeholders	Molecular biology
		AP Physics C: Mechanics
5	Identify types of mobile content for project	Apptivity model used
6	How will content be developed?	Teacher generated content
		Student generated content
		iTunes U content
		Apps
		MultiTouch Books
13	How will mobile project work with IT	Project is self-managed by teachers
17	Select mobile device for project	iPad 3
21	List all project costs	24 iPads
23	Prepare project budget	$ 50 App allowance per device
26	Budget approved	$ 20 App allowance per student
		Budget approved: 6/8/12
41	Create and update content	Summer/Fall 2012
42	Develop policies on use of mobile devices	Acceptable use policy for iPad published, 8/31/12
45	Have regular evaluations and collect usage data	Ongoing

23.3   Content Development

Each course was hosted on our school's iTunes U site; course content was curated through the iTunes Course Manage. Links to each course are posted in the Resources section. The following information was posted for each course:

- Course Overview
- Instructor Information
- Course Outline
- Course Calendar

Specific content in iTunes U is curated as a Post. Each post includes a topic/title (connected to the course outline), message (often a list of learning objectives) and assignments. Assignments and curated content takes the form of web links, iTunes Store links, Apps, eTextbook readings, or teacher generated content.

Course posts were developed using Apple's Apptivity Model for mobile learning with the iPad. A sample Post development using this model is shown in Table 23.2. A screen capture of the iTunes U Post is shown in Fig. 23.1.

Table 23.2 Post development for AP Physics C: Mechanics topic—free fall motion

Step	Curriculum development	Post information
1	Overview and objectives	Write expressions for velocity, position for object in free fall motion
		Use kinematic equations to solve problems involving free fall motion
		Derive expressions for which acceleration as a function of time for an object under influence of drag
2	Workflow	
3	Content and resources	Textbook reading, 2.5 on iPad
		Preview Video: a victim of gravity
		Review Video: Walter Lewin free fall lecture on iTunesU
		Homework problems
		Lab experiment: free fall motion & drag
4	Apps	Tom Daley diving App

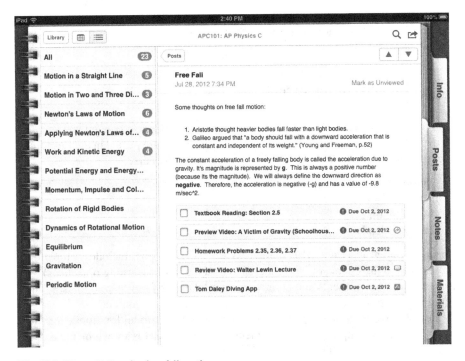

Fig. 23.1 iTunes U Post for free fall motion

23.3.1   Curriculum in Action: Molecular Biology

The portable nature of the iPad allows for a truly mobile curriculum. Furthermore, the touch aspect of the iPad allows for a truly interactive curriculum. The learning activities here deftly weave hands-on learning, mobile computing and touch learning into the curriculum.

In Molecular Biology, students apply scientific practices during a hands-on, inquiry-based investigation into the principles of Mendelian genetics. Students study the plant life cycle from seed to seed as they investigate the method of inheritance of an albino mutant phenotype by designing, testing, and analyzing models of inheritance.

Brassica rapa B3 is a variety specifically bred for use in classrooms and laboratories. It is outwardly similar in phenotype and growth habit to the Wisconsin Fast Plants (WFP) variety of rapid-cycling *B. rapa* that completes its life cycle in about 60 days, but differs in one way that enables teachers and students to take an integrated approach to Mendelian and molecular genetics. The essential difference between B3 and WFP is that B3 is self-compatible and tolerates inbreeding (via self-pollination, or 'selfing') with no consequent inbreeding depression. B3 has been extensively inbred: seeds prepared for distribution were derived from plants that had progressed through seven generations of single-seed descent by selfing. Since in each such generation the residual heterozygosity is reduced by one-half, we estimate that B3 is homozygous at more than 99 % of all loci in the genome, and is therefore true-breeding.

The recessive albino mutant allele of rapid-cycling *B. rapa* B3 can be clearly distinguished from the tall, green, wild-type siblings several days after planting, thus demonstrating Mendel's Law of Segregation in the observable 3:1 ratio. The albino mutants will continue to grow, but at a diminished pace, so students will not be available to perform a standard test cross to determine the genotype of the wild-type plants.

The albino mutant activities provide multiple opportunities to discuss the nature of scientific research, including how scientists use data to either prove a hypothesis or support a hypothesis, depending on the type of question being researched. Students will have the opportunity to prove that a parent is a heterozygous for one or more genes that confer an albino phenotype by self-pollinating the parent and observing albino offspring. Additionally, the students will create an inheritance model (that a single recessive mutation accounts for the albino phenotype) and gather evidence that statistically (within the 95 % confidence required by the scientific community) supports, but does not prove, their model.

Students were given *B. rapa* B3 seeds at the beginning of the school year and were asked to plant and grow the seeds and document their experience. Students were unfamiliar with gardening and thus explored how to best grow *B. rapa* B3 seeds using their iPad a research tool. When documenting the growth and progress of their year long experiment, students have created short films (using iMovie for iOS), stop animation films (using the Stop Motion App), photo galleries (using iPhoto), laboratory reports and charts in Pages on their iPad. Once the plants began

Table 23.3 Learning activities for projectile motion in AP Physics C

App	Learning activity
iTunes U	Watch LaTrobe University Physics Vodcast on two-dimensional motion
Pearson eText	Read Sect. 3.3. Take reading notes within eText App
Explain everything, part 1	Textbook problems. Use explain everything to complete voiceovers of problem solutions
Angry birds	Apply concepts of projectile motion to answer the question: "Does angry birds take place on earth?"
Tom Daley diving	Analyze diver motion for projectile quantities and relate to conservation of energy principles
Vernier graphical analysis	Collect projectile motion using Vernier projectile launcher. Data analysis in graphical analysis
Explain everything, part 2	Share data analysis with peers, teacher

to grow, students were informed that they were given a lot of seeds that had a mutant gene. Using the data they had collected and through the use of debating skills, students settled on the idea that the mutation was an albino mutant. Students gather evidence to support their albino mutant hypothesis. For the next 4 months, students planned out crosses, harvested seeds that were artificially selected for and planted new generations of *B. rapa* B3 plants. Using statistical analysis and their collective observations and data, students will present their findings before finishing the class.

23.3.2   Curriculum in Action: AP Physics C

Learning activities in AP Physics C: Mechanics are centered on a prescribed list of learning objectives outlined by the College Board. For the study of two-dimensional motion, the College Board offers the following learning goals:

1. Students should understand the general motion of a particle in two dimensions so that, given the functions $x(t)$ and $y(t)$ which describe this motion, they can determine the components, magnitude and direction of the particle's velocity and acceleration as functions of time.
2. Students should understand the motion of projectiles in a uniform gravitational field so they can (a) write down expressions for the horizontal and vertical components of velocity and position as functions of time, and sketch and identify graphs of these components, and (b) use these expressions in analyzing the motion of a projectile that is projected with an arbitrary initial velocity. (Source: College Board AP Physics Course Description, Effective Fall 2011) [4].

Using the iPad and a suite of Apps, students construct their own knowledge of projectile motion. The necessary learning activities are outlined in Table 23.3.

Table 23.4 Survey results—access to iTunes U

Question 1: how many times per week do you access iTunes U?

Once	Two to four	Five to seven	> Seven	
0 %	0 %	77 %	23 %	

Question 2: what information do you access on your iTunes U course? (more than once answer accepted)

Calendar	Posts	Apps	Documents	eText
100 %	100 %	100 %	100 %	68 %

The above learning activities again leverage the touch aspect and mobile aspect of the iPad. All of the students' learning activities are completed on the iPad, including homework and data analysis.

23.4   Results and Evaluation

As this is a "work in progress," much of our evidence of success is anecdotal. We cite the following qualitative evidence of success.

- "Having my own iPad is definitely helpful because I can now access my textbook anywhere. Having our coursework on iTunes U is also helpful because it keeps me organized in what I need to learn and in an interactive way."—Sophia L., Class XII.
- "Having an iPad in class for labs and classwork has really allowed me to visualize the concepts we are learning. As a very visual learner, I believe the Apps we use really allow the material to jump off the page, so to speak."—Paige B., Class XII
- "This has made my learning more compact, convenient and engaging, since I can find all of my assignments, textbook, videos and useful Apps in one place. It's so effective, that I think Apple will be true to their word when it comes to killing the high school textbook."—Emma H., Class XII

The authors also surveyed the students participating in the pilot program (Tables 23.4, 23.5, 23.6, and 23.7).

Some points to note about the survey results.

1. Students access all content with substantive frequency to support their learning.
2. Students tend to prefer PDFs and actual documents in contrast to multimedia content. The outlier for this survey question is Apps.
3. eTexts tend to be only moderately important. Students in Molecular Biology do not use an eText. Students in AP Physics C use their eText in conjunction with other learning activities.
4. Students view the iPad as both an effective mobile learning tool and an interactive/touch tool to support their learning.

Table 23.5 Survey results—usefulness of materials

Question: which types of learning materials on iTunes U do you find helpful to your learning?

	Very imp. (%)	Important (%)	Mod imp. (%)	Of little imp (%)	Not imp
Vodcasts	14	68	14	5	0
Podcasts	14	68	14	5	0
YouTube	27	45	18	9	0
Apps	73	18	9	0	0
PDFs	91	9	0	0	0
Web links	68	23	9	0	0
EText	9	27	46	18	0

Table 23.6 Survey results—effectiveness of learning

Question: iTunes U and the iPad have been—in learning course content.

Very important	Important	Mod important	Of little import
82 %	9 %	9 %	0 %

Table 23.7 Survey results—effectiveness of youch and mobile learning

Question: which aspect of the iPad has been most effective in supporting your learning?

I can learn anytime, anywhere	I am interacting with my iPad through touch	Both aspects are affective to me
14 %	14 %	72 %

23.5　Additional Resources

Molecular Biology on iTunes U:
https://itunes.apple.com/us/course/molecular-biology/id561110059
AP Physics C: Mechanics on iTunes U
https://itunes.apple.com/us/course/ap-physics-c/id541642666

References

1. O'Malley, C., Vavoula, G., Glew, J., Taylor, J., Sharples, M., & Lefrere, P. (2003). Guidelines for learning/teaching/tutoring in a mobile environment. Mobilearn project deliverable. http://www.mobilearn.org/download/results/guidelines.pdf. Accessed 2 July 2012.
2. Sharples, M. (2005). Learning as conversation: Transforming education in the mobile age. *Proceedings of conference on seeing, understanding, learning in the mobile age* (pp. 147–152). Budapest, Hungary.
3. Pachler, N., Cook, J., & Bachmair, B. (2010). Appropriation of mobile cultural resources for learning. *International Journal of Mobile and Blended Learning, 1*(2), 1–21.

4. The College Board. (2011). *Physics course description*. Princeton: College Board. http://www. farraguttn.com/science/milligan/apphys/ap-physics-course-description.pdf.
5. Seipold, J., & Pachler, N. (2011). Evaluating mobile learning practice: Towards a framework for analysis of user-generated contexts with reference to the socio-cultural ecology of mobile learning. *Medien Padagogik*.

Chapter 24
Using Shared Microsoft OneNote "Binders" to Create a School Environment for Sharing, Continual Formative Assessment, & Information Organization

Cal Armstrong and Jason Llorin

Abstract This past academic year saw the implementation of structured OneNote notebooks throughout the middle and high school campuses, across all academic departments and extracurricular activities. Dynamically provisioned, stored, and secured server-side, teacher notebooks are visible to all students in the course (and their parents) with integrated student notebooks that are visible by the author, parent, and teacher; collaborative team-based notebooks were created as needed. An assignment dropbox and digital portfolio were included in each course for each student. There were enormous increases in teacher's use and adaptation of OneNote along with parallel increases in the embedded technologies, including audio & video resources, and improvement in parental involvement and awareness of classroom progress. The community had a breadth of opinions on the growth in use and potential of always-connected students' notebooks; this feedback informed changes for the following school year.

24.1 Problem Statement and Context

With teacher and students working in a 1:1 tablet computer environment, there is an overarching desire to be paperless. We would like teachers to create materials that can be provided to students, who can then create, modify, and build on the work and then deliver it to the teacher and other students in a feedback and assessment loop, but all in a digital space. Paper is remarkably flexible: it accommodates structured content, tables, images placed anywhere on the page, and is easily distributed back and forth to another person nearby. We wanted a similar situation to exist on our

C. Armstrong (✉) · J. Llorin
Appleby College, Oakville, ON, Canada
e-mail: carmstrong@appleby.on.ca

J. Llorin
e-mail: jllorin@appleby.on.ca

© Springer International Publishing Switzerland 2015
T. Hammond et al. (eds.), *The Impact of Pen and Touch Technology on Education,*
Human-Computer Interaction Series, DOI 10.1007/978-3-319-15594-4_24

tablet computers—any kind of content should be able to be created and exchanged seamlessly with others.

We found that Microsoft OneNote 2010 was the first step in providing a solution. OneNote works under a binder metaphor, with each Notebook made up of Sections (or groups of Sections), and each Section made up of any number of pages. Each page can be of any length as each grows to fit the content. The content of the pages can be text, images, embedded files of any type, and links to external materials. Users have the freedom to ink on the page at any point and there are graph paper and lined paper templates on which they can work.

In the past, each user created their own Notebooks for each course on the hard drive of their tablet computer. Content, including outgoing notes or incoming homework, was distributed via a Learning Management System (LMS) or via email. This process consumed considerable time in the classroom when material had to be distributed; there were issues with email size limitations and students efficiently moving files from the LMS to the OneNote Notebook. OneNote's environment doesn't translate well to the idea of "files" since a file could be a Notebook, Section, or Page. For instance, there is no Save button in OneNote since the program saves continually.

During teaching, there was no easy way for teachers to observe or comment on the student's Notebook without taking physical control of the student's tablet; they were limited to classroom time in which to engage with the student's work. While they could email or place the OneNote pages in an LMS-based dropbox folder, that process was cumbersome. Sending files back and forth didn't allow for students to continue to revise work on the page that was being sent to the teacher. When material was returned, filing the sheet in the appropriate place within the student Notebook was equally challenging and as a result often not done, leaving gaps in the student's work history. Emailing allowed for the distribution of OneNote material but it didn't reflect the dynamic nature of the OneNote content since the original page could still be changed while the teacher held a copy. When the material was returned, the flexibility of OneNote allowed for students to edit (or delete) teacher feedback. Teachers often fell back to printing out student work and then assessing and returning it physically.

An attempt was made to use the built-in function of OneNote and have each student create a two-person shared Notebook with their teacher for each of their courses but that required each teacher to have a shared Notebook for each of their students, for each of their classes, plus one for their own teaching content. This was difficult to set up with individual students, who had to create the Notebook and send the link to the teacher. And it was a challenge to manage for the teacher and student on an on-going basis; the sheer number of Notebooks alone overwhelmed OneNote's display. Since the files were stored on the student (and teacher) tablet, the backup of material was inconsistent and student work was often getting lost through misadventure. There were also difficulties with the built-in synchronization feature of OneNote that hindered this kind of implementation. Synchronization between student and teacher laptops was haphazard and subject to the different levels of user ability.

Fig. 24.1 A typical class Notebook made up of a visible-to-all teacher section group and private student section groups

Fig. 24.2 A teacher section group can be made up of any number of sections

24.2 Method Employed

To avoid the challenges of individual Notebook synchronization, the decision was made to store the Notebooks for each class within a Sharepoint database and route the synchronization process through the Sharepoint system. Permissions were then set using the community's already defined Active Directory.

The provision of OneNote Notebooks on a campus-wide basis followed a basic structure: for each class section (say, Grade 11 Math Sect. 2) a single OneNote Notebook was created in which a OneNote Section Group (a collection of Sections) was made for the Teacher and then another for each student in the class, as shown in Fig. 24.1. This formed the "Binder".

Inside the Teacher Section Group (its name prefaced with an underscore to ensure it appeared first in any alphabetical listing) were any number of Sections that corresponded to the units, projects, exam revision, etc. Teachers could create as many Sections as they wanted to in order to organize their coursework (Fig. 24.2).

The permissions were set on the server so that teachers had (near) complete control over their entire Section Group; the students could read all of the content but could make no permanent changes to it; any changes they did make would disappear when OneNote synchronized back with the server's (i.e. the teacher's) copy. Students could copy pages or whole Sections from the Teacher Section Group to their own Section Group as needed. Depending on their approach to classroom planning, some Teachers would publish their entire unit and have the students copy it into their Section Group; other teachers would publish on a page-by-page basis each day.

Teachers were unable to delete individual Sections from their Notebook from within OneNote; they had to go to the server to delete the file that represented the Section. This produced several cases of the never-say-die tab, as teachers would attempt to delete the Section from within OneNote but the server would re-create the Section and send it back to the teacher's OneNote as soon as the next sync cycle began.

Each Student Section Group (Fig. 24.3) was initially provisioned with two sections: Assignments & Assessed: "Assignments" formed the dropbox for student work so that the teacher was not required to look throughout the entire student notebook for submitted material. When work was ready to be submitted the student could drag

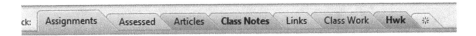

Fig. 24.3 A student section group can have as many Sections as the student wants but the Assignments and Assessed are provisioned by the network

Fig. 24.4 The Teams section, in which predefined groups of students get access to share Section Groups

and drop a copy of the page from wherever they had worked on it into Assignments to be collected by the teacher. The teacher then dragged the page into the Assessed Section. The student only has read privileges in the Assessed Section so they can see the teacher's feedback but not modify it; Assessed becomes a digital portfolio for the course. For convenience, OneNote will **bold** the Notebook, Section and Page names when new information is in a synchronized Notebook that the user hasn't yet seen; a quick glance let the teachers know when things were ready to be assessed.

Parents were given read-only permissions to the Teacher's Section Group as well as their individual student's Section Groups. Parents with OneNote at home could see all content in the same format as their students; parents without OneNote were limited to the web version of the OneNote program which allowed users to see everything except any inking done on the page.

Another Section Group was made called Teams, and within this Section Group, additional Section Groups were nested (Fig. 24.4). Each Section Group was provisioned so that a pre-defined group of students had read/write access to it to allow for collaborative work. As always, the teacher had full control over all content.

The teacher of each individual course was given the ability to attach other teachers to the OneNote Notebook either on a temporary basis (for coverages of absent teachers) or on a permanent basis, in the case of team teaching. This also gave mentors of novice teachers and department heads the ability to observe teacher and student notes for professional development processes.

24.3 Results and Evaluation

The teachers were introduced to the OneNote Binder system a month prior to the start of school through the use of video tutorials. There was immediate and enthusiastic buy-in expressed even before they began the face-to-face introduction to the system; many teachers began the structuring and loading of content from home before beginning planning meetings at the end of the summer. Most rewarding was the interest in using the system that was expressed by departments, such as visual & performing arts and physical education, which were not known to use OneNote or tablets extensively. The sentiment most often expressed was that the new Binder system had produced that largest increase in technology usage in the classroom since the 1:1 laptop program had been put in place 15 years ago. Students expressed an appreciation that the use of OneNote had become universal; some teachers had opted for a paper & pencil in the past.

Feedback from the teachers focused a great deal on the knowledge the synchronized Notebooks provided them about their students. They not only knew immediately which student had done homework, but could also see exactly what the student has struggled with before class starts. Several teachers expressed how this awareness improved the conversation between student, teacher, and parent about responsibility and preparedness.

Because the synchronization occurs whenever the student or teacher is connected to the internet, teachers and students engaged in commenting on each other's work outside of class time, and students often remarked on how teachers' added notes provided support on the work that they were finding challenging. Students also liked the organization the Notebooks provided; middle school Notebooks could be organized by the teacher should the student get overwhelmed without the teacher having to physically access the student computer.

During class, teachers could share individual student work with the class from the projecting teacher laptop by going to that student's Section Group and displaying the Page. It was also easy to add new content to student's Notebooks, either by the teacher adding it themselves or merely posting it within their Teacher Section Group for the students to pick up when they were ready. There has been some negotiation and discussion about the privileges teachers now have with respect to a student's notebook; student concerns about privacy are serious and reasonable and only those designated by the teacher can see student content. Within the classroom situation mentioned earlier, teachers ask for the student's permission before their work is publicly displayed.

One of the immediate clues that the students and teachers engaged quickly with the new format was the massive increase in storage that was required on the network. Since each of the tablets only held a synchronized copy of the notebook, the full notebook rested on the school's storage devices. For the first few weeks of school, data grew by an average 12 Gigabytes each day; over time, this has slowed to an average rate of 5 Gb/day. By the end of the third month, the IT Department ran against a database limit size of 200 Gb per file; they successfully broke the file apart to accommodate any future growth.

The Sharepoint installion has an internal limit of 50 Mb per Section. Fortunately, both text and ink consume very little memory due to rather impressive compression techniques on the part of OneNote. However, since embedded content can be very large (images, files, sound and video) both teachers and students had to be instructed to use a shared network drive location or a cloud based service in which to offload the content (Dropbox.com proved most popular). Users would upload their content to a Dropbox folder, copy the public link and paste it in to their note. For teachers used to posting their Powerpoints or Smartboard files to the LMS, they used this process to avoid distributing these (often quite) large files. If there were no necessary dynamic components to the Powerpoint or Smartboard files, the teacher would "print" the file to the OneNote page, a process which creates a page of screenshots the student can then mark up.

Because OneNote had a native sound recorder and a native video recorder (using the tablet's webcam) there was considerably more use of audio and video content produced by both the student and teacher. It was used not only for the creation of content in the classroom in the form of knowledge work by students but also for feedback. Instead of writing comments on a student's work, teachers would either record or video record themselves, speaking their commentary rather than, or in addition to, writing it. Teachers would also turn their tablet webcam on to a group discussion to capture the conversation for later discussion and analysis.

OneNote synchronizes almost continuously; it only sends and receives any changes that have been made rather than the whole file so it is efficient in terms of network and server usage. Bandwidth has only been an issue after holidays; the network came close to overload after the first 4-day weekend when the entire community returned and began a synchronization. That incident required us to work with faculty and students to proactively encourage synchronizing during the weekend while off campus. OneNote has occasionally had issues with connecting to the Sharepoint server when switching wireless networks and seems to require being closed when wireless networks are changed.

This growth in data obviously caused concern at the network level; not only did all this data need to be stored, it also needed to be backed up. Each night the database was backed up, and these copies were kept for 30 days. That said, this mirroring of data also considerably reduced lost student work; OneNote synchronized at least once every minute so damage or the loss to the student laptop was rendered almost inconsequential, in terms of data. This was a major improvement to the student and teacher experience; far too many students lost their work when their laptop was damaged or lost. This is no longer an issue as students are provided with a replacement laptop and re-connect to their data within minutes.

In the same manner that teachers could observe student work and progress, department heads and curriculum leaders also had the opportunity to see how student and teacher work developed in class. This has improved the conversation for mentoring teachers and encouraged resource sharing amongst teachers in team situations.

Parents were very pleased with the ability to see all of their student's work without necessarily having to be sitting next to the student. Being able to also see the Teacher's notes permitted them to help their child more effectively with homework. The digital portfolio of assessed work provided them with a way of bringing meaning to their student's progress throughout the year.

Teachers were eager to use a similar setup for their extracurricular work such as debating, Model United Nations, or mathematics contests preparation. As extracurriculars do not meet with the same regularity as classes, it allows the discussion and preparation for their meetings to expand into the synchronized environment.

The use of the LMS as an LMS was impacted; students no longer went to Sharepoint for any reason other than their initial connection to the OneNote Notebook. The class calendar was already synchronized with Outlook in a separate process and many teachers used the synchronization available between Outlook and OneNote in terms of tasks and dates. Otherwise, all the other content was organized, stored, distributed, and assessed within the OneNote ecosystem automatically and invisibly. Weblinks to external resources and discussions were incorporated within the OneNote pages.

24.4   Future Work

The present set-up of the OneNote notebooks is based on the course section; it has meant that teachers with several sections of the same course had to copy and paste materials between them. Teachers of the same sections would like an umbrella course so that materials could be created, edited and shared across all the sections of the course, invisible to the students. This would also improve collaborative work amongst the teachers of the same course and an increase in consistency of expectations between sections.

Almost immediately upon implementation, it was realized that there needs to be a temporary section within the student notebook to store assignments that have been submitted but not completely marked. Teachers did not want to place assignments in the Assessed notebook and then mark it; students had the possibility to see the teacher's marking in almost-real-time. By creating a temporary marking area, students couldn't see the material but teachers could take their time to mark it, even over several days, and then drag it in to Assesssed when marking was complete. In the meantime, teachers have created their own Notebook to which they drag the assignment, mark it and then return to the student's notebook. This procedure is dangerous, as teachers can inadvertently drag and drop student work into the wrong Section or Notebook.

24.5   Conclusion

Overall the implementation of the shared & synchronized OneNote Binders has improved the teaching and assessment processes in our classes and expanded the use of OneNote to departments that still relied on paper, PowerPoint, or Smartboard. It has allowed more communication and collaboration between teachers, students, and parents. The availability of assessed work throughout the term has allowed easier articulation of the student's progress and, it is hoped, improved student reflection and preparation for summative exams. While there are additional features that would improve the experience for participants, as a first step this has been an extraordinary improvement on the day-to-day functioning of the relatively mundane task of content creation and organization by both teacher and student.

Chapter 25
Using iPad to Make E-Flashcards and Sharing the E-Cards Through Doceri

Jui-Teng Li and Yi-Nan Fan

Abstract Chinese is logographic and its non-alphabetical nature poses extra difficulties for Chinese language learners to recognize and memorize Chinese characters. To help the learners effectively learn and memorize Chinese words, flashcards serve as an effective strategy for vocabulary development for Chinese language learners. In addition, researchers have found that flashcard drills have positive effects on the accuracy of word reading and the growth of vocabulary size. In this study, however, the main instrument was not traditional flashcards, but e-flashcards. E-flashcards were created to incorporate textual hints, visual aids such as images, and audio recordings. Students rely on visual resources to build word-image association, and video and audio resources to learn Chinese pronunciation. Forty-seven students from fourth and fifth grade in a Basic Chinese Class participated in this study. The participants used Doceri, an interactive whiteboard for iPad, to make e-flashcards. Students were encouraged to find visual resources online, and record their own pronunciation using the microphones on their iPad to add to the flashcards. At the final stage of the e-flashcard activity, students were asked to share their e-flashcards using Doceri. Doceri provided the students and the teacher a stage to share their work by using their own iPads. Over 90 % of students had positive feedback when they were interviewed about their perceptions of the use of e-flashcards and Doceri. According to the results of survey, they suggested that students who found Doceri to be technically easily to use are more likely to have confidence of understanding the instructional contents and a sense of accomplishment, and would like to do this activity again. However, a few students found it frustrating to use Doceri to make e-flashcards, indicating that teachers need to lower the technical threshold before introducing a technology assisted learning strategy.

J.-T. Li (✉) · Y.-N. Fan
Center for Research & Development in Dual Language & Literacy Acquisition,
Texas A&M University, College Station, TX, USA
e-mail: juitengli@tamu.edu

Y.-N. Fan
e-mail: yinanf@tamu.edu

© Springer International Publishing Switzerland 2015   249
T. Hammond et al. (eds.), *The Impact of Pen and Touch Technology on Education*,
Human-Computer Interaction Series, DOI 10.1007/978-3-319-15594-4_25

25.1 Context and Motivation

Reading comprehension is a complex cognitive process that cannot be understood without a clear description of vocabulary. This is because vocabulary development and vocabulary instruction play a key role in the understanding what has been read [13, 17]. The National Reading Panel [11] reported the positive effect of vocabulary knowledge had on the development of reading comprehension skills. This indicates that unless language learners know the meaning of words, they will have difficulty understanding what they read. Indeed, vocabulary plays an important role both in learning to read and in comprehending text [11, 16]. Stahl [16] described that "vocabulary knowledge is knowledge; the knowledge of a word not only implies a definition, but also implies how that word fits into the world" (p. 95).

Vocabulary size, however, matters in successful language learning [1]. A small range of vocabulary will decrease students' opportunities to comprehend content. With a limited number of vocabulary words, language learners often feel overwhelmed and find it hard to understand content concepts without adequate vocabulary support. For this reason, it is very important for language learners to build up the size of their vocabulary. Vocabulary learning strategies contribute to increasing vocabulary size [8, 10]. In addition, according to Mancilla-Martinez [8], to achieve successful language learning, having an understanding of how to use vocabulary learning strategies is a prerequisite. It can be said that the larger the vocabulary size, the faster and more effective language learning will be [1].

Vocabulary learning strategies are basically actions made by the learner in order to help them understand and memorize the meaning of the word, and possibly use it in the future. Training second-language learners to use learning strategies concentrates mainly on learning vocabulary. Vocabulary learning strategies (i.e., flashcards) are used most frequently and are probably the most well known type of language learning strategies. Flashcards are an instructional tool and a vocabulary learning drill on vocabulary teaching and learning. Some researchers have found the positive effects of the flashcards on vocabulary learning and the accuracy of word reading [2, 12]. The flashcards are effective on students' vocabulary learning, for they provide verbal or visual cues for the learners to quickly review and recall the learned words. However, traditional flashcards come up short in providing audio and video support. E-flashcards incorporate multi-media resources and provide comprehensive support in vocabulary building. Generally speaking, e-flashcards indeed compensate for the lack of audio and video cues of traditional flashcards.

The purpose of this study is to have students make e-flashcards through Doceri [14], an open app, on their iPads. In the process of making an e-flashcard, students not only practice Chinese character writing but also get familiar with the meaning of the words and the sound of the words. In addition to the use of Doceri to make e-flashcards, the students use Doceri as a tool to share their e-flashcards with their peers. Doceri is an interactive whiteboard which provides the students and the teacher a stage to share their work by using their own iPads. The desired learning outcomes of the lesson are that students will have an understanding of the vocabulary words for the unit as well as an understanding of a new software program.

25.2   Background and Pre-Existing Work

Chinese is a logographic language [7]. Although Chinese is termed as logography, Chinese characters present both meaning and phonology and accordingly can be said to be morphophonological [6] or "logographic-phonetic" [4] or that a character be termed a "morpheme-syllable" [5]. In comparison to alphabetic orthographies (i.e., English), Chinese is less regular in its sound-print mapping (grapheme-phoneme) [9]. For students whose native language is English employing an alphabetical writing system, word recognition is considered the main challenge in an environment where Chinese is their foreign language [15]. When learning a new Chinese word, students need to memorize the form of the word, the meaning of the word, and the sound of the word. Those are also the three critical vocabulary-learning difficulties the students always confront. Therefore, due to massive combination of complex Chinese words, Chinese language learners whose Chinese language proficiency levels are at the elementary level are often frustrated when learning and memorizing Chinese characters. Through e-flashcards, the students are expected to be motivated to learn and memorize the words. Due to the emphasis of the e-flashcards on visual and audio support, the students are expected to correct their Chinese pronunciation and build word-image association, helping them effectively remember the words.

Forty-seven fourth and fifth grade students participated in this study: 22 fourth graders and 25 fifth graders. They have learned Chinese for at least 4 months in a Chinese enrichment class. Their native languages are Spanish and English. Before they were introduced e-flashcards, the students had experience of doing paper flashcards in the class. For this study, they needed to use iPads provided by the school to make e-flashcards in class when they learned targeted words. The students made e-flashcards to learn new vocabulary words as well as learn how to use new open software, Doceri.

Working on the e-flashcards, students needed to be familiar with new vocabulary. They learned the new words through a visual association method in which a reminding phrase, picture and even video accompanies the word. The students used microphones on their iPad to verbally repeat the word, as the audio input for the flashcard. This repetition is proven to have a positive learning effect on the learner as the words are not only repeated but also are done in other forms [18].

25.3   Results, Instrument, and Discussion

Five items were used from the instructional materials motivation scale survey. There are five answering items (not true; slightly true; moderately true; mostly true; and very true) for students to choose; only one answering item can be chosen.

Q1. Doceri is more difficult to use compared with traditional flashcards.

As shown in Fig. 25.1, 44 % of 4th graders and 59 % of 5th graders did not think Doceri was difficult to use while 28 % of 4th graders and 18 % of 5th graders thought

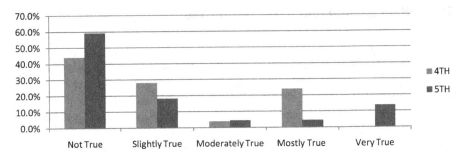

Fig. 25.1 Students' confidence to use Doceri

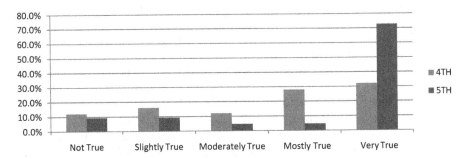

Fig. 25.2 Students' satisfying feeling of accomplishment

Doceri was slight hard to use. Those students were confident to use Doceri to make e-flashcards. The rest of students reported that they found it hard to use Doceri.

Q2. Completing the flashcards gave me a satisfying feeling of accomplishment.

As can be seen from Fig. 25.2, a majority of students were satisfied of using Doceri to make e-flashcards. Only 28 % of 4th graders and 18 % of 5th graders who scaled this item as not true and slightly true were dissatisfied with using Doceri.

Q3. The flashcards are eye-catching.

According to Fig. 25.3, compared with students who answered this item as moderately true, much true and very true, the number of students are three times as many as that of students choosing not true and slightly true on this item.

Q4. When I worked on and look at my flashcards, I was confident that I could learn and understand the contents.

According to Fig. 25.4, few 4th and 5th graders were not confident that they could understand the instructional contents after doing their e-flashcards, 4 % and 9 % respectively. In the vast majority of cases, the students were confident that they could understand the contents when they looked at their flashcards.

Q5. I enjoyed this activity so much that I would like to do this activity again.

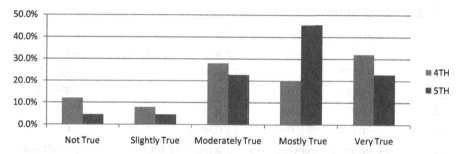

Fig. 25.3 Students' attention on e-flashcards

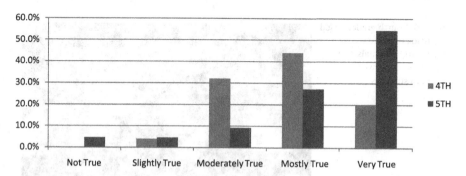

Fig. 25.4 Students' confidence of understanding the contents after doing e-flashcards

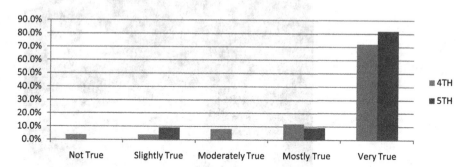

Fig. 25.5 Students' willingness of doing the activity again

From Fig. 25.5, it can be seen that only 8 % of 4th graders marked this item as not true and slightly true while 9 % of 5th graders were not willing to do this activity again. However, most students enjoyed themselves in this activity.

In general, we found that approximately 75 % of students did not find that Doceri was difficult to make e-flashcards. Still, 25 % of students thought Doceri was difficult to use. Based on teachers' and researchers' observations, those students did not look at the manuals. The students also found e-flashcards eye-catching. Most of the students had positive feedback in regard to their confidence and sense of accomplishment. Most importantly, they are strongly willing to do this activity again.

Table 25.1 Correlational relationships between questions

	Q1	Q2	Q3	Q4	Q5
Q1	1	− 0.64*	− 0.13*	− 0.49*	− 0.41*
Q2	− 0.12*	1	0.30*	0.85*	0.37*
Q3	− 0.54*	0.25*	1	0.47*	0.47*
Q4	− 0.07*	0.63*	0.24*	1	0.47*
Q5	− 0.15*	0.42*	0.30*	0.32*	1

The lower half is the value of correlation between questions of 4th graders. The upper half is the value of correlation between questions of 5th graders.
*$p < 0.05$

Fig. 25.6 Fourth graders used their iPads to make e-flashcards. Manuals and teacher's support were offered to students

Correlational relationships of the answers were explored treating the rating scale responses as continuous (see Table 25.1). There was a negative correlation between Question 1 and all the other questions. This suggested that students who found Doceri being technically easily to use are more likely to have confidence of understanding the instructional contents and a sense of accomplishment, and would like to do this activity again. It is comforting to see that the students found that using Doceri

Fig. 25.7 One of the students used Doceri to make an e-flashcard. The student found a picture related to a targeted word on the internet and saved on her iPad. Then, she needed to write the word, the sound of the word, and drew the picture related to the word. After that, she recorded her voice on the iPad

Fig. 25.8 One of the students put the abstract words on the e-flashcards. He took a picture of his classmate and put on his e-flashcard

to make e-flashcards was not difficult, but there were still few students who were frustrated by using Doceri to make e-flashcards. This indicates that teachers need to lower the technical threshold before introducing a technology assisted learning strategy. Positive correlations are found in between all pairs of question 2 to question 5. There is a moderate correlation between 'eye-catching' and students confidence in learning and sense of achievement, suggesting that visual attractiveness is a positive contributor to students' motivation.

25.4 Overview and Impact (Fig. 25.6, 25.7 and 25.8)

Using Doceri to make e-flashcards and share the e-flashcards gets the students to learn new words. We found that Doceri enhances students' learning and motivates the students to learn. Doceri is open software. Open software is the key to global education [3]. If the rest of the world is learning on these collections of open source software, it would only be fitting to attempt to give our students an opportunity to learn some of these tools. Not only will these tools benefit students in the short-term, but students will be motivated to work independently using the tools and more proficient at moving to new software. Also, the students are expected to have some difficulties in using the new software, but they should be encouraged to look up solutions online or use Doceri to share what their difficulties are with their peers and teacher.

References

1. Bromley, K. (2007). Nine things every teacher should know about words and vocabulary instruction. *Journal of Adolescent & Adult Literacy, 50,* 528–536.
2. Browder, D., & Xin, Y. P. (1998). A meta-analysis and review of sight word research and its implications for teaching functional reading to individual moderate to severe disabilities. *Journal of Special Education, 32,* 130–153.
3. Carmichael, P. (2002). Open source as appropriate technology for global education. *International Journal of Educational Development, 22,* 47–53.
4. DeFrancis, J. (1989). *Visible Speech: The diverse oneness of writing systems.* Honolulu: University of Hawaii Press.
5. Hoosain, R. (1991). *Psychological implications for linguistic relativity: A case study of Chinese.* Hillsdale: Erlbaum.
6. Leong, C. K. (1997). Paradigmatic analysis of Chinese word reading: Research findings and classroom practices. In C. K. Leong & R. M. Joshi (Eds.), *Cross language studies of learning to reading and spell: Phonological and orthographic processing* (pp. 379–417). Dordrecht: Kluwer Academic.
7. Liu, Y., Perfetti, C. A., & Wang, M. (2006). Visual analysis and lexical access of Chinese characters by Chinese as second language readers. *Language and Linguistics, 7,* 637–657.
8. Mancilla-Martinez, J. (2010). Word meanings matter: Cultivating English vocabulary knowledge in fifth-grade Spanish-speaking language minority learners. *TESOL Quarterly, 44,* 669–699.
9. McBridge-Chang, C., Chow, B. W. Y., Zhong, Y., Burgess, S., & Hayward, W. G. (2005). Chinese character acquisition and visual skills in two Chinese scripts. *Reading and Writing, 18,* 99–128.
10. Min, H-T. (2008). EFL vocabulary acquisition and retention: Reading plus vocabulary enhancement activities and narrow reading. *Language Learning, 58,* 73–115.
11. National Reading Panel (2000). *Teaching children to read: An evidence-based assessment of the scientific research literature on reading and its implications for reading instruction.* Washington, D.C.: National Institute of Child Health and Human Development.
12. Nist, L., & Joseph, L. M. (2008). Effectiveness and efficiency of flashcard drill instruction methods on urban first-graders' word recognition, acquisition, maintenance and generalization. *School Psychology Review, 37,* 294–308.
13. Pulido, D. (2007). The relationship between text comprehension and second language incidental vocabulary acquisition: A matter of topic familiarity? *Language Learning, 57,* 155–199.
14. Russell, G., & Gilbertson, J. A. (2012). "Doceri: An Interactive White Board for Your iPad" American Association of Law Libraries, Cool Tools Cafe. Boston, MA. Jul. 2012. http://works.bepress.com/jordan_gilbertson/8/.
15. Shen, H. H. (2010). Imagery and verbal coding approaches in Chinese vocabulary instruction. *Language Teaching Research, 14,* 485–499.

16. Stahl, S. A. (2005). Four problems with teaching word meanings and what to do to make vocabulary an integral part of instruction. In E. H. Hiebert & M. L. Kamil (Eds.), *Teaching and learning vocabulary: Bringing research to practice*. Mahwah: Erlbaum.
17. Vidal, K. (2011). A comparison of the effects of reading and listening on incidental vocabulary acquisition. *Language Learning, 61,* 219–258.
18. Webb, S. (2007). The effects of repetition on vocabulary knowledge. *Applied Linquistics, 28,* 46–65.

Chapter 26
Analyzing Trends in Pen Computing among K-2 Students Through Flashcards Application

Radhir Kothuri, Ben Kenawell, Sarah Hertzler, Mark Babatunde, Nicholas Wilke, and Sam Cohen

Abstract The Flashcards application is designed for pen-based computers to create the feel of traditional paper-based flashcards while affording the many benefits of new media. It includes a game-like mode, which allows students to play flashcards, just as one would while using conventional methods. Furthermore, the interface also incorporates pen recognition features that allow for instant gratification of students' work. In addition, teachers are responsible for creating decks consisting of individual cards. Each deck may contain cards that are specifically designed for individual students or for entire content areas. In order to encompass the diversity of decks, cards are marked based on the content area. For K-12 education, standards-based learning has become the indicator of each card's specific content area. Our application is poised to have deep standards integration by making it easier for the teacher to identify problem areas for students based on the current standards set by states and the country. Additionally, teachers can import existing word documents and PowerPoint slides as decks. Pictures can be added to cards for visually inclined students as well. The Flashcard application is being developed using an incremental release approach so that user feedback can be obtained and the product can be adjusted to meet their needs. In this paper, we offer

Completed Under the Supervision of Dr. Ananda Gunawardena, Carnegie Mellon University, School of Computer Science

R. Kothuri (✉) · B. Kenawell · S. Hertzler · M. Babatunde · N. Wilke · S. Cohen
South Fayette High School, McDonald, PA, USA
e-mail: kradhir14@gmail.com

B. Kenawell
e-mail: benkenawell@gmail.com

S. Hertzler
e-mail: sarah.swimchick@yahoo.com

M. Babatunde
e-mail: mbabatunde1519@gmail.com

N. Wilke
e-mail: nick.wilke26@gmail.com

S. Cohen
e-mail: sam1998pa@gmail.com

© Springer International Publishing Switzerland 2015
T. Hammond et al. (eds.), *The Impact of Pen and Touch Technology on Education*,
Human-Computer Interaction Series, DOI 10.1007/978-3-319-15594-4_26

the results from the second iteration of the application, which was designed specifically for grades K-2. The results were gathered from a series of beta tests, which took place in two kindergarten classrooms, one first grade classroom and one second-grade classroom in December of 2013. Based on the data collected, we surmised conclusions that will help foster the development of our application. In addition, we offer possible directions toward which the application could be headed in the future.

26.1 Problem Statement and Context

In recent years, the Common Core standards have been revised to include references to students developing certain technology skills. As explained by Lyndsey Layton in her article "Elementary Students Learn Keyboard Typing ahead of New Common Core Tests," schools are requiring many educators to train their students to be technologically proficient in typing interfaces [2]. As a result, many teachers are becoming increasingly worried, since according to the teachers, the children are "digital natives" and are "comfortable with tablets," but not with keyboards [2]. In our paper, we explore these implications as detailed by Layton. By realigning the Flashcards application for K-2 education primarily, we offer a tool that allows students to learn in a familiar paper-like environment but without the hindrances of learning additional typing skills. As a result, the entire student client for the Flashcards application is pen-based. All workflow and maneuvering of the application is possible through a stylus. Additionally, it is evident that many students in Kindergarten and 1st grade are not able to read just yet. Hence, we have moved away from a text-based design to a more visual one that not only entertains the young students but also becomes more accessible since they only have to rely on pictures to maneuver through the application. Here, we offer results of recent beta tests that were conducted.

26.2 Method

In order to conduct user studies of the Flashcards application, our team observed classes from South Fayette Township Elementary School located in McDonald, Pennsylvania [3]. The Elementary School educates students from Kindergarten to 2nd grade. Individual classes from each grade level were used in the beta tests. One of the key aspects that we wanted to observe was how responsive our new Word and picture import features would be in authoring cards from pre-existing teacher worksheets. For instance, the second grade class was studying an environmental science project and the teacher already had questions for this unit. As a result, the format of this document was simply altered and then it was imported into the Flashcards application (Fig. 26.1).

A similar process was conducted for the 1st grade class currently studying basic addition/subtraction facts. As for the Kindergarten class, we relied on images rather than words to test addition skills, since students are at different developmental stages in their reading and writing abilities (Fig. 26.2).

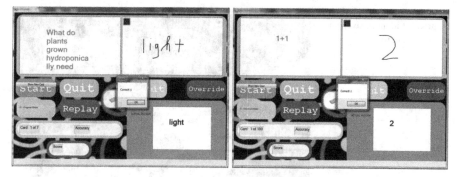

Fig. 26.1 Example of hydroponics and addition cards used for 1st & 2nd grade students

Fig. 26.2 Example of apple addition card used for Kindergarten students

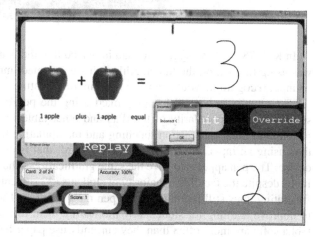

All of these decks were uploaded to a central server that was established so that students could easily access the file from the testing computers. After each respective class completed their assigned deck, each individual student was asked to complete a survey in order to record qualitative data for future development. We present our results in the next section (Fig. 26.3).

26.3   Evaluation and Results

After compiling the results through student feedback, a majority of the responses were largely positive. As an aggregate from the 3 different grade levels, 87 % of the students stated that they enjoyed using the Flashcards application as compared to traditional paper flashcards and 70 % of the students would use the Flashcards application in the future. This was particularly surprising considering the fact that many of the students experienced challenges with the application. Whether it was a recognition error or simply bad workflow, the aggregate data suggests that most students opted for the Flashcards application both now and will in the future.

Fig. 26.3 Picture depicting a
1st grade student answering
an addition card

In K-2, 78 % of the aggregate data indicated that the feature students liked most
was using the pen on the tablet. Although we assumed immediate feedback based
on input recognition would be the most important feature, almost all of the students
(78 %) actually indicated that they liked using the pen on the tablet. This might
suggest that the popularity of the iPad and other tablets results from the fact that
people find great satisfaction touching and manipulating the screen directly rather
than using an input device, such as a keyboard, that is directly removed from the
device. The pen appears to have the same gratification—the sense of touch. Interestingly, despite the fact that a majority of students (42 students) found the recognition
frustrating, they still found using the pen most exciting. Therefore, we may be able
to improve learning for students by motivating them to want to use the pen-based
tablet software more often than they currently use paper-based cards. Students will
have the ability to learn independently rather than asking parents to help deliver
quizzes using paper cards. Therefore through this online platform, we may be able
to increase the frequency of use by allowing students a more independent learning
situation. Combined with the excitement of instant gratification and a pen-enabled
device, students now have a personalized form of education at their fingertips that
requires no outside motivation or intervention (Fig. 26.4).

As for the user interface, only 2.6 % of the Kindergarten class suggested changes.
From the second stage of development, graphical elements suitable for very young
students was of utmost importance to us. As a result, it is rewarding to see that
the younger students seem to favor the new user interface. The other students who
suggested different colors or pictures helped us realize that it is more effective to
make all buttons a picture, instead of text, as these students are still beginning to read
(Fig. 26.5).

In addition to the quantitative data gathered above, many qualitative observations
were taken as well. For example during gameplay, some of the kindergartners wrote
many of their numbers backwards or in different directions. Developmentally, this
illustrates that some Kindergartners are not fully proficient with their numbers yet.

	What do you like more?		What would you use more often?		What do you think about the way the program looks?	
	Paper Flashcards	Computer Flashcards	Paper Flashcards	Computer Flashcards	Looks Good	Needs Different Colors
K Session1	4	19	0	2	13	9
K Session 2	2	15	8	10	9	7
1st Grade Bigley	0	21	5	17	16	8
2nd Grade Colangelo	5	18	6	16	16	5
Totals	11	73	19	45	54	29

	What did you like most about the program?			What was challenging about using the program?		
	Immediate Feedback	Using Pen on Tablet	Seeing My Handwriting	Using the Pen	Didn't Recognize My Handwriting	I Was Confused on How to Use
K Session1	3	19	2	3	5	10
K Session 2	2	15	2	10	5	7
1st Grade Bigley	3	16	2	12	11	6
2nd Grade Colangelo	0	17	5	10	21	3
Totals	8	67	11	35	42	26

Fig. 26.4 Illustration depicting aggregate survey results for all 4 sessions conducted

Fig. 26.5 Student response of a backwards "6" to the question "$1 + 5$"

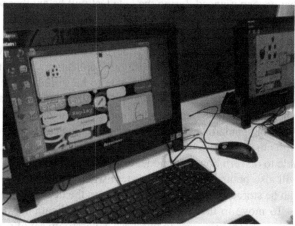

As a result, we could modify the Flashcards application in several ways: (1) develop a better handwriting recognition system to identify an upside down or backwards number, (2) create a button to activate this more specialized handwriting recognition feature to for kindergarten students, and/or (3) create a different type of flashcard that uses images or multiple choice selection rather than handwriting.

Additionally due to their first experience with the digital drawing tablets, the students found it particularly troublesome to coordinate their movements on the tablet to the mouse movement on the computer. In exerting more effort to try to move the mouse, the students accidentally wrote on the answer panel. As a result, these marks were detected during recognition and thus led to a wrong answer. Hence, this illustrates that both our recognition algorithm needs to be improved as well as for the need to investigate tablet PC's. Devices like the Windows Surface Pro allow the user to directly write on the screen, which might be more intuitive for the students rather than writing with digital drawing tablets.

26.4   Future Work

In the future, we plan to improve upon our application through an iterative process. Upon receiving teacher and student feedback, we will use the given suggestions to make our product more user-friendly. We expect to receive continued feedback from a variety of classrooms in order to improve the design so that we know specific areas on which to focus. Areas we plan to improve include the graphical interface so that all the buttons are images, the ability for teachers to import images, and a provision for a detailed student analytics report.

Additionally during the beta test, many of the students left extra marks or their handwriting was simply not able to be recognized by the computer. As a result, developing a more robust recognition algorithm that takes into account all the factors that we experienced during the beta test will be another secondary concentration in improving the user experience and wide scale adoption.

Ultimately, our main developmental goal is to add a complex system of classroom management that extends beyond our district alone. We would like teachers and students to ubiquitously use our application. To do this we must first create a database that allows for student data to be stored and retrieved via the Flashcards application. This added relationship between a database and the application is truly where standards-based learning and personalized education can be implemented. Areas or standards where students are lacking can be recorded to the database along with other statistics like scores and time spent on decks. In doing so, teachers will be able to discern how to remodel each student's education. Additionally, the database will also be used as a cloud system where all decks and cards created by teachers can be stored so that students can access the decks at school or at home.

To move to the next iteration of the application, we must attract funding and the necessary resources to purchase a classroom set of pen-capable tablets. Because many of the young students were simply unable to correctly manipulate the pen on the drawing tablets, we would like to observe our product on a Windows Surface Pro to gauge the results of students writing directly on the screen. Additionally, we are planning to extend the platforms on which the application is available to Android and iOS.

Acknowledgements   The production of this application was not possible without the acknowledgement of several key individuals. Particularly, Dr. Ananda Gunawardena, Associate Professor of Computer Science at Carnegie Mellon University, Ms. Aileen Owens, Director of Technology and Innovation, South Fayette School District, and Mr. Shad Wachter, Instructional Technology Specialist, South Fayette School District were pivotal in aiding us. The expertise and guidance that Dr. Gunawardena provided was very much appreciated by the group. His knowledge and expertise allowed us to go beyond the existing curriculum offered at South Fayette and through his mentorship, we were able to keep the project on task. In addition, Ms. Owens facilitated the connection between Carnegie Mellon and South Fayette that was necessary in order to foster the growth of our application. While Dr. Gunawardena aided us in the technical aspects of the development process, Ms. Owens and Mr. Wachter were instrumental in helping retain the educational component, particularly with the standards-based education information. We are also very thankful to Superintendent Dr. Bille Rondinelli, the South Fayette Board of Education, and the South Fayette Foundation for Excellence, for providing necessary resources and their enthusiastic support for this project over the last 2 years. We are also grateful for the teachers and administration of South Fayette Township Elementary School for being actively involved in beta testing the Flashcards application. We appreciate the time they invested to help us with this project.

References

1. Koedinger, K., & Jeong, Y. (2010). Designing a pen-based flashcard application to support classroom learning environment, In *Proceedings of ACM SIGCHI conference (CHI '10)* (Atlanta, Georgia, April 10–15, 2010). ACM Press, New York, NY, 2010, 978-1-60558-930-5
2. Layton, L. (2013). "Elementary students learn keyboard typing ahead of new common core tests." Washington Post. The Washington Post, 14 Oct. 2013. Web. 15 Dec. 2013.
3. South Fayette Township Elementary School. http://www.southfayette.org/Domain/10. Accessed on 15 December 2013.

Chapter 27
Student Exploration: App(Lying) Technology for Health Education and Promotion

Leigh Szucs, Elisa Beth McNeill, and Kelly Wilson

Abstract Applications (Apps) provide unique opportunities to enhance learning and instruction. In this interactive teaching technique, students build a repository of health-related apps which can be easily integrated into existing health education lessons. *APP(lying) Technology for Health Education and Promotion* uses technology as an effective pedagogical strategy to engage learners in middle school through collegiate classroom settings. The activity is designed to build knowledge and skills for locating useful health-related apps in the Apple/Android market place. National Health Education Standards provide the base of the teaching technique. Although the content area of health will be utilized in this example, the methodology presented could easily be adapted to address multiple content specialties.

27.1 Introduction

Young children grow up today as a "net generation" connected to mobile technologies, the internet and social media [3] all of which impact the way they learn and process information. Finite research is available on the revolution of touch screen interface devices for educational purposes, but predictions of increased interaction, speed, connectivity, and functionality are estimated for student learning [1]. The approach of using unbounded mobility enables students to remain connected and engaged, almost without restriction, to the classroom learning environment and peers. Students' fundamental view of learning, communicating and interacting with peers may vary from the perspective and experience of the educator.

Youth, as mass consumers of health information, require technology as an invaluable vehicle for content mastery and skill acquisition. Recent research using

L. Szucs (✉) · E. B. McNeill · K. Wilson
Department of Health and Kinesiology, Texas A&M University,
College Station, TX, USA
e-mail: leigh.szucs@hlkn.tamu.edu

E. B. McNeill
e-mail: mcneill@hlkn.tamu.edu

K. Wilson
e-mail: kwilson@hlkn.tamu.edu

© Springer International Publishing Switzerland 2015
T. Hammond et al. (eds.), *The Impact of Pen and Touch Technology on Education,*
Human-Computer Interaction Series, DOI 10.1007/978-3-319-15594-4_27

tablet-based instruction in elementary school, yielded results of successful independent student exploration, manipulation of information, and engagement from all learners simultaneously [3].

As youth develop into mature adults, one's health literacy has the potential to impact lifelong health decisions and skills. Health literacy is commonly defined as the ability of individuals to obtain, process, and understand basic health information and services needed to make health-informed decisions [4]. Here, we present a tablet-based lesson plan for engaging students in finding and assessing apps that either help convey or record such information. The technology explored through this activity allows a venue to actively engage the classroom learner by enhancing health literacy skills.

27.2 Lesson Goal

The goal of is teaching technique is to provide students with a methodology for effectively evaluating Apple/Android market place applications (apps). The strategy demonstrated here represents evaluation of health-related content, but could be employed in other diverse content areas.

27.3 Rationale

This teaching technique allows the student to increase their knowledge and skills related to the following indicators aligned with the National Health Education Standards (NHES) [2].

NHES Grades 6 through 8

3.8.1 Analyze the validity of health information, products, and services.
3.8.2 Access valid health information from home, school, and community.
3.8.5 Locate valid and reliable health products and services.

NHES Grades 9 through 12

3.12.1 Evaluate the validity of health information, products, and services.
3.12.3 Determine the accessibility of products and services that enhance health.
3.12.5 Access valid and reliable health products and services.

27.4 Objectives

Learners Who Participate in this Teaching Technique Will

1. Investigate five specific health-related applications (apps) which can be used to promote healthy behaviors.
2. Evaluate the validity and reliability of health information in the five identified apps.

Health Topic:		
App Title	Unique Features	Rating Scale 1(limited benefit) to 5 (extremely beneficial)
	✐	

Fig. 27.1 App analysis chart (1 per group)

27.5   Timing

The length of this lesson is approximately 45 min or one class period.

27.6   Materials

- iPad(1 per group)
- Figure 27.1: *App Analysis Chart* (1 per group)
- Figure 27.2: *App Group Assessment Grading Rubric* (1 per group)
- Figure 27.3: *App Description and Usefulness for Health Education Chart*

27.7   Procedure

Part A: *Small Group App Investigation* **(25 min)**

1. The teacher will assign students to small groups of 2–3 people to work through the teaching technique. Once divided, provide each small group with an ipad and the *App Analysis Chart* (Fig. 27.1).
2. Instruct small groups to select five, free, health-related apps from the Apple/Android marketplace. Health specific app topics or themes might include: nutrition, stress, exercise, general health information, weight management, sex education, first aid, or goal setting. All 5 apps must be representative of the same health-related topic or theme.
3. Using the *App Analysis Chart* (Fig. 27.1) groups will pilot each of their 5 apps and record all unique features and strengths and weaknesses offered by the app. Unique features might include; visual design, user ability, accuracy of information, or interactive mechanisms. Lastly, small groups will rate each app as 1 (limited benefit) to 5 (extremely beneficial) in terms of usefulness to promoting health behaviors on the chart provided.

STUDENT EXPLORATION:		
APP(LYING) TECHNOLOGY FOR HEALTH EDUCATION AND PROMOTION		
Small Group Grading Rubric		
Group Members Names:		
Indicator	**Value**	**Points earned/comments**
Identifies 5 apps (all same topic)	5	
Lists a unique feature for each app (discusses reliability &/or validity aspects)	10	
Rates each app on 1-5 scale	2	
For the highest ranked app chosen by group		
States the pros of the app	2	
States the cons of the app	2	
Tells age group do you believe would find this app most useful and why	2	
Who you recommend this app to a friend or family member? Why or why not?	2	
Based upon the advertisement, did the app meet your expectations, please explain why or why not?	5	
Total	**30**	**Group score:**

Fig. 27.2 App group assessment grading rubric (1 per group)

4. The teacher can scaffold and guide learning by providing example app descriptions by showing students the *App Description and Usefulness for Health Education Chart* (Fig. 27.3).
5. Based on group discussion, students will collectively determine which app provides the most **beneficial** features for promoting healthy behaviors related to the chosen topic. Teacher will instruct small groups to download the app with the highest rating on their provided iPad device.

Part B: *Exploring the Free App (15 min)*

1. Once the highest ranked (5– most beneficial) free application has been downloaded to each iPad, instruct students to investigate and fully use the app. Students may input pseudo data to experience the full potential of the app. Groups must answer the following questions and record answers on the back-side of the *App Analysis Chart* (Fig. 27.1) [5].
   a. What are the pros of the app?
   b. What are the cons of the app?
   c. What age group do you believe would find this app most useful and why?
   d. Would you recommend this app to a friend or family member? Why or why not?
   e. Based upon the advertisement, did the app meet your expectations, explain why or why not?

APP Name	APP Description and Usefulness for Health Education
MyFitnessPal	Food tracker and exercise log for daily intake Calculates: - Calories - Basic nutrients - Fat/sugar/sodium - Exercise duration and intensity (factors exercise contribution to overall caloric balance per day) - Weight management with tracking feature - Hip, neck and weight circumstances (found under the progress tab) Allows user the ability to set goals and weekly targets while communication with Friends via email or other social media sites Under 'More', tutorial videos regarding dairy basics, barcode scanning and recipe ideas
iTriage	Provides a Symptoms-to-Provider Pathway developed by certified physicians - Using male or female anatomical avatar to highlight different areas with common symptoms Vocabulary and definitions with graphics and facility locations for: - Different types of physicians - Health conditions - Procedures - Medications Identifies facilities (emergency, pharmacies, urgent care, home health care, outpatient clinics, community centers) via exact location Personal account will track health information including conditions, medications, and appointments Includes "how to video" (blood under nail) Emergency and National Hotlines Message board with current events, news and research around health topics
VirtualHeart	Allows for exploration of multiple real-time views of the human heart - Electrical Impulses - Anatomy - How Values operate - Interior/Exterior and Anterior/Posterior Views - Adjustment of HR and BPM of the heart
Birdees	Sex Education App for Parents User create a 'Birdee' to navigate throughout activities and tutorials Tree of Knowledge presents information in linear, small pieces to engage adult according to child's specific needs Interactive learning tools (iTools and iBody) throughout content to describe bodily changes, puberty, anatomy, personal boundaries, communication, etc. Provides common 'pitfalls' of parenting and strategies for negotiating effective communication Benefit for parents of younger children to help address information and content that is age and developmentally-appropriate
Solve the Outbreak – Become a Disease Detective	Created by Centers for Disease Control and Prevention Provides user with health scenarios, process through epidemiological data to solve outbreak cases Scenarios provides clued information, dictionary and health prevention techniques Upon solving the epidemic, user is rewarded with points and ability to earn badges CDC24/7 is an outlet on app for further exploration, information about the CDC, videos and blog

Fig. 27.3 APP Description and usefulness for health education

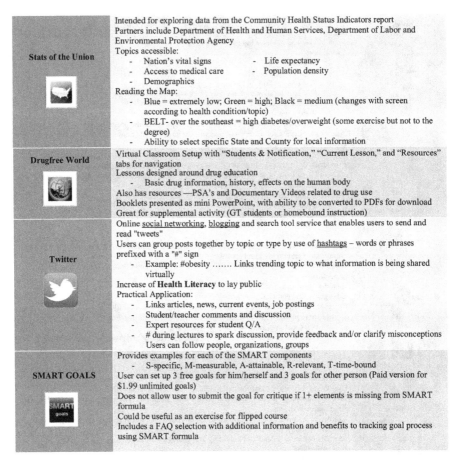

Stats of the Union	Intended for exploring data from the Community Health Status Indicators report Partners include Department of Health and Human Services, Department of Labor and Environmental Protection Agency Topics accessible: - Nation's vital signs - Life expectancy - Access to medical care - Population density - Demographics Reading the Map: - Blue = extremely low; Green = high; Black = medium (changes with screen according to health condition/topic) - BELT- over the southeast = high diabetes/overweight (some exercise but not to the degree) - Ability to select specific State and County for local information
Drugfree World	Virtual Classroom Setup with "Students & Notification," "Current Lesson," and "Resources" tabs for navigation Lessons designed around drug education - Basic drug information, history, effects on the human body Also has resources —PSA's and Documentary Videos related to drug use Booklets presented as mini PowerPoint, with ability to be converted to PDFs for download Great for supplemental activity (GT students or homebound instruction)
Twitter	Online social networking, blogging and search tool service that enables users to send and read "tweets" Users can group posts together by topic or type by use of hashtags – words or phrases prefixed with a "#" sign - Example: #obesity .... Links trending topic to what information is being shared virtually Increase of **Health Literacy** to lay public Practical Application: - Links articles, news, current events, job postings - Student/teacher comments and discussion - Expert resources for student Q/A - # during lectures to spark discussion, provide feedback and/or clarify misconceptions Users can follow people, organizations, groups
SMART GOALS	Provides examples for each of the SMART components - S-specific, M-measurable, A-attainable, R-relevant, T-time-bound User can set up 3 free goals for him/herself and 3 goals for other person (Paid version for $1.99 unlimited goals) Does not allow user to submit the goal for critique if 1+ elements is missing from SMART formula Could be useful as an exercise for flipped course Includes a FAQ selection with additional information and benefits to tracking goal process using SMART formula

Fig. 27.3 (continued)

Part C: *Teacher Debrief* (*5 min*)

1. After all groups finish investigating and answering questions, the teacher will facilitate a large group discussion with all students. Ask each group to share their highest ranked app with the class. The teacher led discussion may include the following prompts and/or questions (student responses will vary depending on the type and selection of health-related apps):

   a. What was the most challenging part of about picking the best app?

   b. Were there members of the group who agreed or disagreed with each other in selecting the highest rank app? How did the group reconcile any differences?

   c. Why is it important to include technology in our classroom?

   d. Will you personally use any of the apps to track your health behaviors? Why or why not?

27.8   Assessment Technique

To assess group achievement of the learning objectives included in this teaching technique, a *App Group Assessment Grading Rubric* (Fig. 27.2) has been provided for the educator.

References

1. Bielec, J. A. (2010). What's in, what's out. *University Business, 12*(8), 22–24.
2. Centers for Disease Control and Prevention. (2013). National health education standards. http://www.cdc.gov/healthyyouth/sher/standards/. Accessed 12 April 2014.
3. Giest, E. (2011). The game changer: Using ipads in college teacher education classes. *College Student Journal, 45*(4), 758–768.
4. Manganello, J. (2007). Health literacy and adolescents: A framework and agenda for future research. *Health Education Research, 23*(5), 840–847.
5. Gilbet, G., Sawyer, R., & McNeill, E. B. (2014). *Health education: Creating strategies for school & community health* (4th ed.). Jones & Bartlett Learning.

Part VI
Technologies in Practice—University Classroom Models

Chapter 28
Tablet Computers in the University Classroom of 2012: Opportunities and Challenges

Carla A. Romney

Abstract Educational institutions face pressure to incorporate the latest technologies into their offerings. Many U.S. K-12 school districts have embraced SMART boards, tablet computers, and "bring your own device" (BYOD) implementations so precollege students can become accustomed to technology-rich learning. U.S. higher education, in general, has been slower to adopt computers use as part of the in-class learning experience. Anecdotally, it appears that technology has taken hold in project-focused or problem-solving-oriented small classes rather than in large lecture classes. To better understand the use of tablet devices in a large urban research institution, classes that used tablet devices at Boston University were observed and faculty members who taught the classes were interviewed. Tablets were used in a number of small engineering, medicine, business, fine arts, and hospitality classes. Faculty members reported that maintaining students' focus on the course material was a challenge. They also bore the costs of teaching with technology- whether it was in the time to teach themselves the technology and evaluate alternatives, the need to arrive early or stay late in order to set up and put away the technology, or the negative comments about technological failures that surfaced on course evaluations. These findings may be generalizable to other higher education settings.

28.1 Problem Statement and Context

Today's undergraduate students in the U.S. are likely to have had extensive exposure to pen-enabled teaching and learning prior to matriculation. For example, SMART claims that more than 2 million SMART Board interactive whiteboards have been installed globally in "K–12 classrooms, reaching more than 40 million students and their teachers" [1]. Slate tablets are also prevalent in the K-12 setting today. In July 2012, Apple reported that 1 million iPads had been sold to schools in the last quarter, including iPad 2s with a slightly reduced price after the launch of the iPad 3 [2].

C. A. Romney (✉)
Boston University, Boston, MA, USA
e-mail: romney@bu.edu

© Springer International Publishing Switzerland 2015
T. Hammond et al. (eds.), *The Impact of Pen and Touch Technology on Education*,
Human-Computer Interaction Series, DOI 10.1007/978-3-319-15594-4_28

This announcement was made prior to the launch of the iPad Mini, an even more affordable iPad option that has garnered the attention of many K-12 institutions since its launch in October 2012 [3]. Further, the Apple devices are only part of the K-12 tablet market; niche tablets such as the Kuno and Kineo use the Android platform and address the needs of students at a lower cost per device. In fact, an Android-based tablet computer, the Aakash 2 by Datawind, is now available in India for under $50 and it should become available elsewhere for a comparable price [4]. As such, an ever-increasing number of undergraduate students have experience with tablets before entering higher education.

While the K-12 world has embraced educational technology such as tablets quite readily, U.S. colleges and universities have been slower to do so. The 2012 Pearson Foundation Survey on Students and Tablets found that 25 % of current students in an institution of higher education now own at least one tablet device and they see these devices as valuable for educational endeavors [5]. This report also indicates that more than 60 % of college students believe that tablet computers help them to study more efficiently and perform better in their classes [5]. However, college faculty have not incorporated tablets into their teaching repertoires as quickly as might be expected based on their students' rapid uptake of these devices. Typing difficulties or notetaking (inking) challenges may have hindered the acceptance of these devices [6]. Concerns about student inattention and distraction due to competition from online lures such as social media websites, email, and games may also be responsible for the reluctance to use tablets in class [7]. Adopters of tablet devices in the classroom counter these claims by arguing that effective teaching with tablets promotes student engagement and participation [7].

In order to understand the contexts in which tablets are used at a major research institution, an investigation of tablet initiatives at Boston University was undertaken. Boston University, with 16 schools and colleges, total enrollment of more than 33,000 students, and a full-time faculty of more than 4000, is representative of many large urban research institutions with its full complement of undergraduate, graduate, and professional degree programs. The findings from this analysis of tablet use at Boston University may be generalizable to other institutions.

28.2 Method Employed

With support from the Information Technology and Educational Media offices throughout the University, classes which used tablet devices during the Spring semester of 2012 were identified. The instructors of these classes were interviewed prior to observation of a class session in which the tablets were used. Faculty granted permission for photography to document in-class use of tablets.

28.3   Results and Evaluation

The classes that used tablet devices during the spring 2012 semester are listed below. The classes are diverse in terms of their subject matter and the level of the students, but all were small (20–60 students) face-to-face classes that were augmented through posting of course materials and assignments to an online learning management system. The Graduate School of Management and School of Medicine courses were for graduate/professional students; the remaining courses were for undergraduates.

School of Hospitality Administration- SHA HF 370 Revenue Management
School of Management- SMG SM 222 Modeling Business Decisions and Market Outcome
Graduate School of Management- Executive MBA Business Marketing Seminar
College of Engineering- ENG EK 301 Engineering Mechanics I
Metropolitan College- MET MA 123 Calculus I and MET MA 124 Calculus II
School of Medicine- GMS Healthcare Emergency Management and MED Anatomy/Histology
College of Fine Arts- CFA AR 484 Graphic Design

The availability of technical assistance varied from school to school. Some classes had dedicated Information Technology assistance on a day-to-day basis (Graduate School of Management, School of Hospitality Administration), others had assistance from Information Technology on an as-needed basis (Metropolitan College and School of Medicine). Still others had additional faculty or teaching/computer lab assistants present at all times to ensure smooth operation of the technology (School of Management, College of Engineering). Thus, different approaches were used to minimize the likelihood of technological problems during class time.

A number of tablet technologies were used and their ownership also varied. For example, the Graduate School of Management gave each student in the Executive MBA program an iPad upon enrollment and students owned their devices. The School of Hospitality Administration and College of Engineering purchased iPads and made them available to faculty to give to students for use during specific classes via a mobile cart that was brought into and out of the classroom each day. The School of Management used SMART boards and school-provided netbooks that were supplemented by students' own devices. The College of Fine Arts instructor used an iPad to teach, but students used college-owned iPads in an out-of-class lab setting. One application at the School of Medicine used SMART boards, iPads, and iPods along with students' own devices. In the other School of Medicine application, the instructor used a PC with a Wacom external stylus/tablet to annotate anatomical images. The Metropolitan College applications used a college-owned tablet PC classroom laboratory that was dedicated to mathematics classes. Thus, many different paradigms for use and ownership of tablets coexist within the University.

The rationale for using tablet devices in the classroom also varied. Individual faculty members, who envisioned tablets as a way to improve their ability to convey information or engage students in their material, catalyzed several implementations.

Other uses were driven by hardware, software, or financial donations. One implementation was initiated at the behest of a dean who thought that putting tablets into the hands of every faculty member would encourage widespread adoption and classroom utilization of these devices. This implementation has had only modest success, while the faculty-initiated uses have been more favorably received.

Another difference among the tablet implementations was the nature of information flow within the classroom. In most applications, the instructor used a tablet to provide annotated content to students in a unidirectional flow of information. The College of Engineering used a close to real time, bidirectional information flow: students worked in groups to solve problems on their tablets and then uploaded their solutions to a collaborative workspace website so that the instructor could retrieve and display them to the class within a minute or two. The Metropolitan College tablet PC implementation used a real time, synchronous, bidirectional information flow. Students viewed their instructors' annotated slides in real time, solved problems on their own or in small groups, and transmitted their work to the instructor so that s/he could display it.

While various tablet devices were used at Boston University, a few common themes emerged from conversations with faculty members who used tablets in their classrooms. First, faculty members were explicitly concerned about creating an exciting, engaging, and productive learning environment for students. They saw tablets as a "hook" to pique students' curiosity and as a way to bring real world applications into the classroom. Second, all faculty in unidirectional tablet applications, especially the BYOD implementations, noticed that students spent significant amounts of class time on non-academic activities (surfing the web, reading email, online shopping, and posting to social media), but the faculty who used tablets in a bidirectional mode reported little to no distraction from the temptations of the internet. Third, faculty members commented that developing and implementing tablet-based teaching was time-consuming and uncompensated. All faculty members said that teaching with tablets required additional preparation time, but there was no consistency to the amount of time spent. Some people spent 15 min or less on adapting each class session to teaching with tablets while others spent more than 2 h per session to prepare their classes. Other instructors said that the "up front" time spent figuring out which tablet device/software to use was more than 20 h but their preparation time per session was minimal. Most faculty members reported that they needed additional time before and after class to set up/put away the tablet devices. Some faculty members indicated that the extra time (approximately 15 min) was a barrier to regular use of technology in class because back-to-back room scheduling could not accommodate the extra time. Fourth, there has been little or no formal evaluation of the tablet implementations to examine satisfaction and changes in learning outcomes, although there were a few reports that students commented on the use of technology on the course evaluation forms. Fifth, there was no way to share best practices and lessons learned with faculty colleagues within the same school or University-wide. Each implementation operated in isolation and most faculty members were unaware of other tablet applications at the University. Thus, faculty members saw both the opportunities and challenges of teaching with tablets.

28.4 Future Work

An initial barrier to the adoption of tablets in higher education was cost, but this obstacle is now surmountable. Tablet devices seem to be a platform that is here to stay; mobile computing technologies provide constant connections to the world of information. Since current and prospective college students today have experienced tablets during their precollege education, the impetus grows stronger for higher education faculty to imbue their classes with these devices.

Faculty must consider their content and pedagogy to ensure that tablets or other mobile devices are the best way to teach their students. Ongoing implementations of these technologies need to be evaluated in order to identify best practices that can be disseminated to others either via publications and presentations or through University-wide hands-on faculty development workshops. In this way, we can create exemplary teaching and learning environments.

Acknowledgments   I gratefully acknowledge the support of Fabian Torres-Ardila, Juan Pedro Paniagua, and Cathy Lysy in analyzing tablet use throughout Boston University.

References

1. SMART Technologies. (2012). SMART quick facts and stats-SMART Technologies. SMART Technologies.   http://www.smarttech.com/us/About+SMART/About+SMART/Newsroom/ Quick+facts+and+Stats/. Accessed 29 Nov 2012.
2. Macworld Staff. (2012). This is Tim: Cook on Apple's third-quarter earnings. http://www. macworld.com/article/1167864/this_is_tim_cook_on_apples_third_quarter_earnings.html. Accessed 29 Nov 2012.
3. Metz, R. (2012). Tablet Makers Pursue Public Schools. http://www.technologyreview. com/news/506321/tablet-makers-pursue-public-schools/. Accessed 29 Nov 2012.
4. Bhusan, K. (2012). India showcases Aakash 2 tablet PC at United Nation. http://www.thinkdigit. com/Tablets/India-showcases-Aakash-2-tablet-PC-at_11549.html. Accessed 29 Nov 2012.
5. Pearson Foundation. (2012). Survey on Students and Tablets 2012. http://www. pearsonfoundation.org/downloads/PF_Tablet_Survey_Summary_2012.pdf. Accessed 29 Nov 2012.
6. Wieder, B. (2011). iPads could hinder teaching, professors say. *Chronicle of Higher Education.* http://chronicle.com/article/iPads-for-College-Classrooms/126681/. Accessed 29 Nov 2012.
7. Sample, M. (2012). Best practices for laptops in the classroom. *Chronicle of Higher Education.* http://chronicle.com/blogs/profhacker/best-practices-for-laptops-in-the-classroom/39064. Accessed 29 Nov 2012.

Chapter 29
Tablet PCs in a Code Review Class

Sam Kamin and Wade Fagen

Abstract We describe an intervention in a code-review class using Tablet PCs. The class, Programming Studio, is a required class for Computer Science students at the junior level, mainly consisting of weekly small-group meetings—3–6 students, plus a moderator—in which each student presents his or her program for discussion. In the traditional format, each student presented their program by displaying it on the class display. In the Tablet PC format, every student has a copy of the presenter's program on their tablet; students can draw on the program, with all students seeing every student's annotations, and can navigate independently in the program. We discuss how the tablets are used, and present the results of an end-of-semester survey indicating that students who participated using both studio formats found the tablets helpful.

29.1 Problem Statement and Context

Numerous authors have reported on uses of pen-enabled computers in classrooms, both large and small [1, 2, 5]. In this paper, we report on the use of Tablet PCs in a somewhat different educational environment: a code review class. Tablet PCs can enhance code reviews by making it easier to point to locations in the code, draw pictures to represent data structures and algorithms, and sketch out alternative coding methods.

Students in the Computer Science department at the University of Illinois (Urbana-Champaign) take CS 242, Programming Studio, typically in the first semester of the junior year. Its purpose is to build individual programming skills by having students do a lot of programming and, more importantly, present their program publicly for discussion each week. Discussion sections have 3–6 students, plus a moderator; each presenter plugs into the room display and discusses their program for 15–20 min.

S. Kamin (✉) · W. Fagen
Computer Science Department, University of Illinois, Champaign, IL, USA
e-mail: kamin@illinois.edu

W. Fagen
e-mail: waf@illinois.edu

© Springer International Publishing Switzerland 2015
T. Hammond et al. (eds.), *The Impact of Pen and Touch Technology on Education*,
Human-Computer Interaction Series, DOI 10.1007/978-3-319-15594-4_29

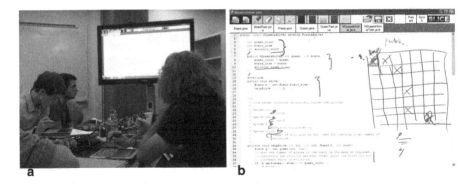

Fig. 29.1 Images from a CS 242 section (**a**) A studio section using Tablet PCs (**b**) Tablet PC screenshot

In describing the Programming Studio in 2007 [7], we noted, "We need to continually work on maintaining the quality of the discussion in the discussion sections." Programs are complicated, and it is hard to have a stimulating discussion on something that only one of the interlocutors understands. In our observations, we often found that only one or two reviewers could completely follow the presentation, while the others got lost at some point and then lost interest. The Tablet PCs were introduced as a way to help the discussions be more engaging and efficient.

Without tablets, the studio set-up is this: The students and moderator sit around a table, with a large monitor at the front, and each student takes a turn presenting their program. With tablets, the physical arrangement is the same, but each student has a Tablet PC (see Fig. 29.1a). Each presenter loads their program (usually in multiple files), and it shows up simultaneously on all the tablets. As the presenter explains the program, everyone can write on it, with all the writing being shared. In other words, the students have a shared whiteboard with the current presenter's program acting as the background image. Furthermore, since each tablet has a separate copy of all the code, each student can explore it independently of the presenter; if the presenter goes too quickly over a portion of the code, a reviewer can remain on that portion while the presenter moves on.

29.2 Method Employed

The system we introduced in the Studio is a straightforward "shared whiteboard" application, developed using the SLICE framework [3, 6]. As each student takes a turn as presenter, he or she loads their program files into the system, where each is represented by a tab. Within each program, the text of the file forms the background of the display; the text cannot be directly edited, but can be annotated upon. All ink strokes entered by any student are immediately shared by all. Figure 29.1b shows the SLICE screen during a studio discussion.

The Tablets provide two capabilities: (1) The ability to write, draw, and point. Drawing is useful to explain the deep structure of a program, data structure, or algorithm; writing makes it easier for reviewers to ask "what if you did it this way?" questions; pointing makes it easier to draw attention to a particular spot in the program. (2) The ability to explore the presented program independently of the presenter. Each student can switch tabs and scroll through the files in the presented programs. This allows a reviewer to spend time understanding a section of code after the presenter has moved on, or simply to explore it in a different order than the presenter uses. (A button on the interface allows a student to sync up with the presenter.) This can allow a reviewer to gain a better understanding of the presented program—or at least of some part of it—and thus make more substantive comments about it.

The screenshot in Fig. 29.1b comes from a Thursday evening section with six students (plus a moderator). The screenshot is taken at the end of the discussion. (Lack of space prevents us from illustrating the sequencing of the annotations.) The assignment was the well-known eight queens problem. This student's program consisted of seven files (represented by the tabs just below the top toolbar), and we are looking at NQueensSolver.java (the green tab). We can see that the presenter drew a chessboard while explaining his program. This image contains ink marks from four of the participants. Timestamps on the ink strokes indicate that this part of the presentation took about 5 min.

This screen shows several features typical of the use of the tablets:

- Drawings are often used to explain programs.
- On the other hand, the majority of pen strokes are used simply to point (underline, circle, etc.). When using tablets, students would refer orally simply to "this line"—indicating the actual line with the pen—whereas without the tablet various locutions were used to identify places in the program. This is one way the tablets made the discussion more efficient.
- The interface allows the students to choose from a (small) palette of colors, but does not assign different colors to them. In practice, the students tended to quickly differentiate themselves by colors. Of the four participants who made annotations on this file, the presenter used red, the moderator green, one other student green, and the fourth used two colors (red and blue).

This figure does not show any examples of participants writing code, which was also common. It also does not show any uses of "laser strokes." The laser stroke is a feature of the interface allowing someone to point to something with a heavy red line which then disappears when anything else is drawn; it is a way to point to items without leaving the screen cluttered.

One observation (for which we have no quantified data) is that students very quickly got into the habit of looking at the code on their own Tablets rather than on the room display. This may be because the tablets were simply easier to read, or because the students were taking advantage of the opportunity to review the presenter's code "out of order." Furthermore, the presenters *always* wrote on the tablets as they presented.

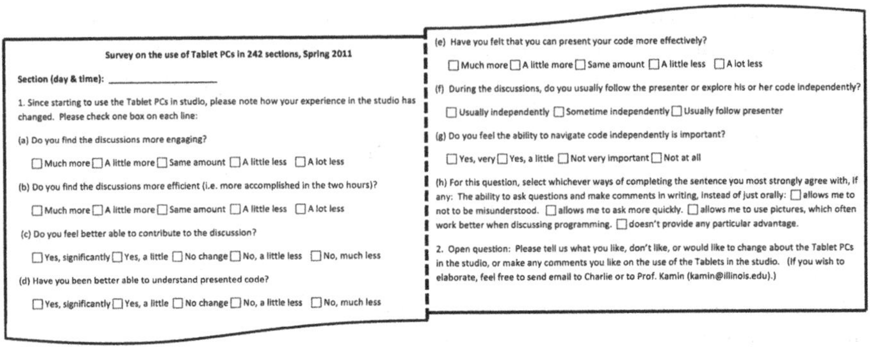

Survey on the use of Tablet PCs in 242 sections, Spring 2011

Section (day & time): ____________

1. Since starting to use the Tablet PCs in studio, please note how your experience in the studio has changed. Please check one box on each line:

(a) Do you find the discussions more engaging?

☐ Much more ☐ A little more ☐ Same amount ☐ A little less ☐ A lot less

(b) Do you find the discussions more efficient (i.e. more accomplished in the two hours)?

☐ Much more ☐ A little more ☐ Same amount ☐ A little less ☐ A lot less

(c) Do you feel better able to contribute to the discussion?

☐ Yes, significantly ☐ Yes, a little ☐ No change ☐ No, a little less ☐ No, much less

(d) Have you been better able to understand presented code?

☐ Yes, significantly ☐ Yes, a little ☐ No change ☐ No, a little less ☐ No, much less

(e) Have you felt that you can present your code more effectively?

☐ Much more ☐ A little more ☐ Same amount ☐ A little less ☐ A lot less

(f) During the discussions, do you usually follow the presenter or explore his or her code independently?

☐ Usually independently ☐ Sometime independently ☐ Usually follow presenter

(g) Do you feel the ability to navigate code independently is important?

☐ Yes, very ☐ Yes, a little ☐ Not very important ☐ Not at all

(h) For this question, select whichever ways of completing the sentence you most strongly agree with, if any: The ability to ask questions and make comments in writing, instead of just orally: ☐ allows me to not to be misunderstood. ☐ allows me to ask more quickly. ☐ allows me to use pictures, which often work better when discussing programming. ☐ doesn't provide any particular advantage.

2. Open question: Please tell us what you like, don't like, or would like to change about the Tablet PCs in the studio, or make any comments you like on the use of the Tablets in the studio. (If you wish to elaborate, feel free to send email to Charlie or to Prof. Kamin (kamin@illinois.edu).)

Fig. 29.2 Survey instrument

To offer just a few summary statistics on this meeting: During the 70 minutes of the meeting, the participants annotated programs with a total of 852 ink strokes. These strokes were not added in uniform numbers by all participants. The most active annotator was the moderator (351 strokes); the most active student added 212 strokes and the least active only 10. Most students wrote most often during their own presentations (though there were exceptions), but varied greatly in the amount of writing they did during other students' presentations; the most active student added 102 strokes during other students' presentations, and the least active just seven.

29.3 Results and Evaluation

To assess the Tablet PC intervention, we did a study in six sections of CS 242 (23 students and 4 moderators). We had students follow the traditional structure for six weeks, then use the tablets for four weeks, and then switch back for three weeks. At the end of the semester (that is, in week 14), we surveyed the 23 students in those sections.

The survey instrument was a single page, with nine questions. The first seven were on a sliding scale, the eighth allowed multiple selections from a list, and the last was an open-ended written response question. Figure 29.2 shows the survey instrument. Figure 29.3 shows the results for all questions except the last; we summarize the results on the latter below.

In retrospect, on some questions we should have offered more responses; for example, on Questions 1(a), 1(b), and 1(e), we should have had an answer in between "somewhat more" and "much more." Nonetheless, what is striking about the responses is their near unanimity:

- Questions 1(a) through 1(e) ask, in various forms, whether the students found the tablets helpful or harmful. On Questions 1(a) and 1(c), not one of the 23 students found them harmful, and on Questions 1(d) and 1(e), only one student found them harmful. With the exception of b, a significant majority found them useful.

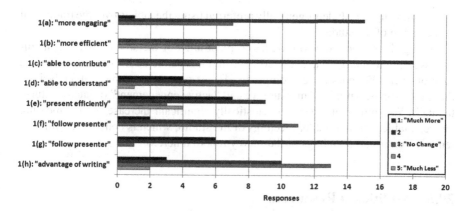

Fig. 29.3 Survey results. (The *inset* gives response choices for **a–e**)

On Question 1(c), all but two students found that the tablets made it easier to contribute to the discussion.

- Responses to Question 1(b) show that students were split on the question of whether the discussions using the tablets were more "efficient." We surmise that technical issues—additional set-up time, and occasional disruptions caused by bugs in the software—detracted from the efficiency of the meetings.
- On Question 1(h), concerning the advantages of writing questions versus speaking them, not one student chose "no advantage." (Note that this question allowed for multiple selections, so the total number of responses is more than 23.)

Question 2 was an open-ended text question requesting feedback on the system. Most of the comments related to shortcomings in the system itself, three in particular: lack of syntax highlighting (mentioned by six students; since added); not being able to present within their normal IDE, or be able to run code (five students); and bugs (two students). There were several positive comments (mainly redundant with questions g and h), and one specific suggestion for a new feature other than syntax highlighting. The answers to this question do demonstrate that students were perfectly willing to make critical comments about the system, suggesting that their responses in Question 1 were honest.

29.4   Future Work

We have presented an application of Tablet PCs in a code review class. The problem we confronted with this class is that reading other people's code is taxing and may be tedious. The Tablet PCs were introduced as a way to ameliorate this problem. In this paper, we have explained the studio set-up both with and without the tablets, discussed how the students used the tablets, and presented the results of a survey showing that students generally preferred using the tablets over the traditional organization of the studio.

During the study, we also took audio recordings of the studio. With each student wearing a microphone and recording into a separate audio stream, we have a total of over 195 hours of recordings. In [4], we present a mechanical analysis of these recordings, defining a measure we call "active engagement" (related to "turn-taking"). We show that there is a statistically significant increase on this measure between tablet and non-tablet meetings of the studio, which is consistent with, and tends to confirm, the findings of the survey reported here.

29.5 Additional Resources

SLICE [3, 6] is a framework for developing tablet applications for education. We have used it to build several in-class applications as well as the code review application described here. Furthermore, it is substantially device-independent, meaning that a single codebase (which is to say, a single set of Javascript functions) can run the same application on Microsoft Tablet PCs and on Android tablets. The SLICE system is freely available at **slice.cs.illinois.edu**.

Acknowledgements We thank Chris Cortez for helping us run this experiment. Studio instructors Mike Woodley and Charlie Meyer were instrumental in getting us access to the class and gaining the cooperation of the studio moderators.

References

1. Anderson, R. J., Anderson, R., Simon, B., Wolfman, S. A., VanDeGrift, T., & Yashuhara, K. (2004). Experiences with a tablet PC based lecture presentation system in computer science courses. Proc. 35th SIGCSE. Norfolk, Va, pp. 56–60.
2. Berque, D. (2006). Pushing forty (courses per semester): Pencomputing and DyKnow tools at DePauw University. in WIPTE '06. Purdue University Press.
3. Fagen, W., & Kamin, S. (July 2012). A cross-platform framework for educational application development on phones, tablets, and tablet PCs. Proc. 2012 Intl. Conf. on Frontiers in Education: Computer Science and Computer Engineering (FECS'12), Las Vegas, NV.
4. Fagen, W., & Kamin, S. (March 2013). Measuring increased engagement using tablet PCs in a code review class. *SIGCSE*, Denver, CO.
5. Kamin, S., & Fagen, W. (July 2012). Supporting active learning in large classrooms using pen-enabled computers. Proc. 2012 Intl. Conf. on Frontiers in Education: Computer Science and Computer Engineering (FECS'12), Las Vegas, NV.
6. Kamin, S., Hines, M., Peiper, C., & Capitanu, B. (March 2008). A system for developing tablet PC applications for education. *SIGCSE*, Portland, OR.
7. Woodley, M., & Kamin, S. (March 2007). Programming studio: A course for improving programming skills in undergraduates. *SIGCSE*, Covington, KY.

Chapter 30
Statistics in the Classroom on Touch-based Smart Phones

Bert Wachsmuth

Abstract Smart phones have become truly ubiquitous and are used by students to communicate and network almost continuously. However, despite their potential, computational power, and ease of use they have not become commonplace in the classroom. The statistical package StatCrunch Mobile (Integrated analytics LLC, http://www.statcrunch.com/mobile), which runs on any touch-enabled smart phone with an HTML5-compatible web browser, was used to support a college-level introductory Statistics class. This paper investigates the advantages and disadvantages of this combination over a more standard setup such as a laptop/tablet with suitable software.

The paper describes the user interface, design principles and usage patterns of *StatCrunch Mobile* and explores the suitability of the touch interface of a smart phone for this application. The reference phone given to all students was a Nokia Lumina 900 with Windows Phone 7, but several students preferred their own iPhones or Android phones. Data was collected from 27 undergraduate students from mixed backgrounds who used their smart phone with the *StatCrunch Mobile* application during most classes and exams. Students were able to quickly and flexibly conduct statistical analysis on the fly, which reinforced statistical concepts learned in class and allowed students to better interpret the output of statistical computations and procedures. Average scores on tests and exams were better than in past, comparable classes and the use of a device that students use on a daily basis reduced the learning curve and increased student satisfaction.

In future work, this project could be expanded to include data collection using the smart phone, which then could be analyzed immediately right from the phone. This would create a more hands-on and real-world approach to statistics than in traditional courses.

B. Wachsmuth (✉)
Mathematics and Computer Science,
Seton Hall University, South Orange, NJ, USA
e-mail: wachsmut@shu.edu

© Springer International Publishing Switzerland 2015
T. Hammond et al. (eds.), *The Impact of Pen and Touch Technology on Education*,
Human-Computer Interaction Series, DOI 10.1007/978-3-319-15594-4_30

30.1   Problem Statement and Context

Statistics courses, especially at an introductory level, provide a great opportunity to see mathematics in daily, real life use. Instead of focusing on abstract textbook examples it is relatively easy to utilize data from every-day life and use concrete examples from real-world problems to illustrate and practice the relevant concepts. However, to utilize real data you need computational tools that are easy to use, readily available, and that do not add yet another barrier between students and subject matter. At Seton Hall University we have used statistical packages such as *SPSS* [7] and the online application *StatCrunch* [8] to help students analyze and understand data and report their findings. However, these tools traditionally require the use of a laptop, which incurs any number of logistical and pedagogical problems [3]. On the other hand, almost all students are using a powerful computational tool on a daily basis, without, however, applying it to course work: their smart phone. Today's smart phone is nearly ubiquitous (one study found that 85 % of college students own a smartphone [2]). Smart phones are as powerful as full-fledged computers were just a few years ago, and students are utterly familiar with its use. Unfortunately, however, smart phones are rarely used for teaching and learning [4].

In this paper, I will show that given the right software, a smart phone can completely replace a laptop even in computationally intensive courses. In addition, because of the familiarity of students with that device and its simple touch interface, it can enhance the learning taking place in class and yield higher student satisfaction, better understanding of the course material, and better test scores.

The statistical software package *StatCrunch* has recently become available as a beta version for mobile devices, so I decided to test this software in an introductory statistics class to determine if it was possible to use a smart phone as the exclusive computational device for such a class while analyzing data from real-life data sets.

30.2   StatCrunch and StatCrunch Mobile

StatCrunch is a web-based statistical package available by subscription to be used in support of statistical courses. It provides easy access to commonly used statistical procedures such as contingency tables, linear regression, one and two sample statistical tests, ANOVA, statistical calculators, etc. It supports several data collection and manipulation tools and includes some limited capabilities to share data sets or results. It can read data in Excel or CSV format via a URL from a web site or from the local computer. Data sets and saved results are stored with the user's *StatCrunch* account and are available the next time the user logs in, even on different devices. The full version of *StatCrunch* is written in Java and runs in any Java-capable web browser (see Fig. 30.1).

StatCrunch presents data in a familiar spreadsheet format with one column per variable. Statistical procedures are accessed via a simple, hierarchical menu structure. Once a procedure is selected, a dialog box lets you choose variable(s) to analyze,

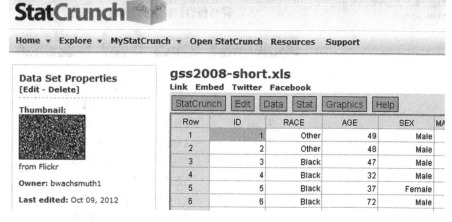

Fig. 30.1 *StatCrunch* main screen

Simple linear regression results:
Dependent Variable: HIGHEST YEAR SCHOOL
Independent Variable: FATHER HIGHEST YEAR SCHOOL
HIGHEST YEAR SCHOOL = 9.8052448 + 0.34786397 FATHER HIGHEST YEAR SCHOOL
Sample size: 1485
R (correlation coefficient) = 0.48137309
R-sq = 0.23172005
Estimate of error standard deviation: 2.661603

Fig. 30.2 Partial output from StatCrunch regression analysis

provide options appropriate to the specific command, and apply some flexible filters to restrict the analysis to only that data you are interested in.

The *StatCrunch* output is particularly geared towards students. It provides easy to understand and clearly labeled results, including graphics, charts, and tables. Instead of creating professional-grade, ready-for-publication output, it focuses on making the output easy to understand and appropriate for a beginning statistician. In Fig. 30.2, for example, the output includes the equation of the least-square regression line using proper variable names.

StatCrunch is also available as a version for mobile devices suitable for most touch-enabled smart phones, called *StatCrunch Mobile* [9]. It is based on HTML5 and runs without major issues on all mobile web browsers (iOS, Android, and Windows Phone). It is currently available as a beta version and can be accessed by anyone with a subscription to the regular version. *StatCrunch Mobile* retains the spreadsheet-like data presentation and manipulation as well as the menu-based access to statistical procedures and provides a fairly comprehensive subset of commands from the full version (see Fig. 30.3). The interface is responsive, clearly designed, and makes

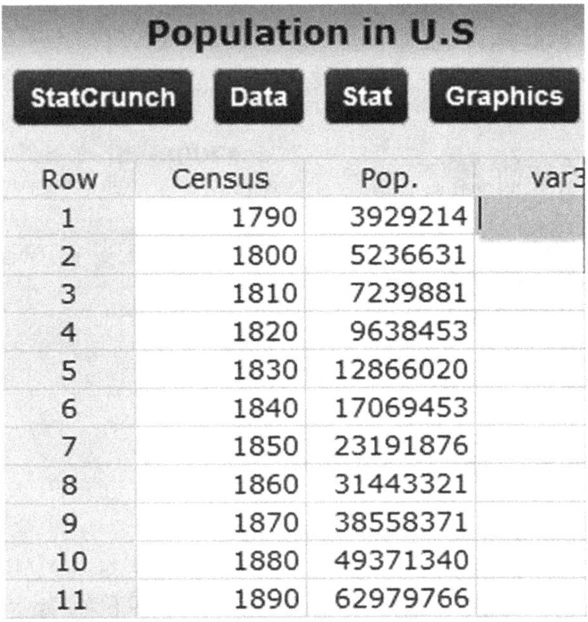
Population in U.S
StatCrunch
Data
Stat
Graphics
Row Census Pop. var3
1 1790 3929214
2 1800 5236631
3 1810 7239881
4 1820 9638453
5 1830 12866020
6 1840 17069453
7 1850 23191876
8 1860 31443321
9 1870 38558371
10 1880 49371340
11 1890 62979766

Fig. 30.3 *StatCrunch Mobile* main screen

good use of standard user interface elements of a smart phone web browser such as lists, selection boxes, etc. You can load data from the web and any data previously loaded into your account is available as well. In addition, you can access shared data sets made available by other users or the instructor.

I found the statistical calculators particularly helpful during class. Instead of resorting to printed tables of values of the standard normal distribution, the Student-t distribution, or a number of other distributions usually located in the appendix of a text book, you can compute probabilities and z-scores on the fly (see Fig. 30.4). This is much more intuitive and allows for experimentation and "what-if" scenarios.

30.3 Method Employed

The results of this paper refer to an introductory statistics course taught at Seton Hall University in the fall 2012 to 27 Undergraduate students with a variety of backgrounds and majors. Seton Hall provided a Nokia Lumina 900 smart phone running Windows Phone 7 with an unlimited data plan to all students in the class to ensure that all participants had comparable hardware. All students had access to the most recent full version of *StatCrunch* as well as *StatCrunch Mobile*. All instructions, demonstrations, and sample computations in class used the Nokia reference phone. A number of real-world data sets were utilized throughout the course, such as the GSS Survey [5] from 2008, some select (anonymous) health care data, and some statistical facts about a number of countries taken from the CIA Factbook [1]. The web site

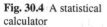
Fig. 30.4 A statistical calculator

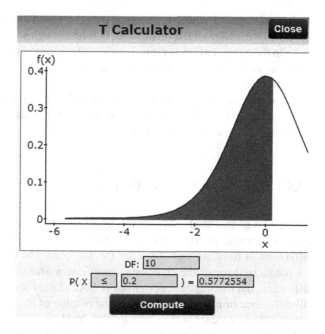

MathCS.org hosts additional data sets suitable for *StatCrunch Mobile*. The control group consisted of 28 students of similar background and experience who took the same course in the previous semester, where we covered the same material using the same book. In the current course we used *StatCrunch Mobile* whenever possible in class and as well as during exams and quizzes, which were otherwise comparable to last semester's course. In the control course we used the regular laptop version of *StatCrunch* for data analysis when feasible.

Seton Hall provided all students with a smart phone for the duration of this study. As it turns out, 92 % of the students already had their own smart phone, all of which would have worked with *StatCrunch Mobile*. Even so, 82 % of the participants chose to use the Nokia phone provided to them for class work.

Some of the typical statistical questions we considered in class were:

- Does attending college pay off? Specifically, is there a relation between the highest degree of education and the income level in the US? (Use the **gss2008-short.xls** data set of [5])
- Is there a relation between "average life expectancy" and "literacy rate" in various countries? If so, could you predict the life expectancy in a country based on its literacy rate? Does that imply that reading more makes you live longer? (Use the **life.xls** data set of [5])
- Conventional wisdom has it that the normal temperature of a person is 98.6 °F. Is that true? Do men and women have different body temperatures? Is there a relation between temperature and heart beat at rest? (Use the **normtemp.xls** data set of [5])

With *StatCrunch*, I would typically assign the actual computations as homework. *StatCrunch Mobile*, on the other hand, is lithe enough so that I could have students perform the computations in class. I could still ask them to prepare a complete written statistical analysis as homework, but students felt more comfortable knowing how to do the calculations.

At the end of the fall course I administered a survey to all 27 students to determine the level of satisfaction with *StatCrunch Mobile* as well as a number of other parameters; 24 students responded.

30.4   Results and Evaluation

The results of this study support the hypothesis that using a smart phone with its easy and familiar interface can be beneficial for this particular type of course. The difference in final averages between the fall class and its control in the spring is 7.4 points in favor of the class using *StatCrunch Mobile*. That is a relatively large difference, but the standard deviations in both classes are large as well. Still, a one-tail difference of means test amounts to a p-value of 0.08 and thus the difference is statistically significant at the alpha $= 10\%$ level.

In addition to an improved class average there is other evidence of improvement:

- 95.6 % of the students found *StatCrunch Mobile* "very easy" or "somewhat easy" to use on their smart phone
- 95.7 % of the students found *StatCrunch Mobile* "helpful for understanding statistical concepts"
- 82.6 % of the students think they "learned more about statistics using *StatCrunch Mobile*"
- 100 % of the students were of the opinion that "*StatCrunch Mobile* made the class easier"
- 87.0 % of the students preferred *StatCrunch Mobile* over the standard version of the software
- 95.5 % of the students prefer a stats class with special software on a mobile device as opposed to using it on a laptop or not using software at all

In fact, this overwhelming support for *StatCrunch Mobile* became clear as the class progressed. Students are so used to carrying a smart phone and using it constantly for other purposes that it quickly became second nature for them to use their phone for statistical analysis as well. There was virtually no learning curve; students were comfortable with the mobile version from day one.

In addition, using the full version of *StatCrunch* on a laptop in the control class came with a number of logistical problems: students frequently ran out of battery power, their laptop was broken, or they felt generally uncomfortable using that device in class because of size or weight issues or for lack of practice. Most of these problems were eliminated by moving to the mobile device: smart phone batteries usually last for the whole day and students are less likely to forget to charge their devices. Also, the touch interface of modern smart phones is easy to use and students have lots of experience with it. Of course not all problems are eliminated completely: one student dropped his smart phone and the glass cover broke, rendering it unusable. But the device was quickly replaced and the student could participate again.

Finally, the mobile nature of the device allowed for quicker and more relevant interaction between instructor and students. I was able, for example, to show a student what would happen if some data values changed by editing the data on her device and letting her recompute the analysis right then and there.

There were a few issues with the mobile version, of course. Most importantly, it was not possible to save the results of a procedure, such as creating a box plot, and inserting that plot in a word processing document. Generally speaking, to take the answers of a statistical procedure out of *StatCrunch Mobile*, you had to copy it manually. But students could use their smart phone to select and optimize an analysis by adjusting parameters quickly, and they could then switch to the full version of *StatCrunch*, using their laptop to copy the results and paste them into, say, a Word document.

It should be noted that in general not all students in a given class might own a smart phone. However, institutions trying to support a smart phone initiative could purchase for example older generation iPods, which do not need an expensive data plan but can run software such as *StatCrunch Mobile* without problems. These devices could be loaned to students without smart phones as a cost-effective solution to providing all students with a computational platform needed in a course.

In summary, the evidence shows that using *StatCrunch Mobile* on a smart phone to accompany an introductory statistics course is an all-around improvement. To quote one of the students: *"I liked everything about StatCrunch Mobile. It was easy to use and helped with the class."*

There are, however, several other factors that could have influenced to the outcome. First, the statistical analysis is based on a rather small sample of $N < 30$ for both control and treatment. Another study with a larger sample size would be helpful to see if our outcomes could be confirmed. Second, the fact that students in the project were given a modern smart phone likely increased their curiosity and motivation to use the device. This could have carried over to a better learning outcome in class. Still, the results of this project were strong enough to be if not convincing then at least to warrant additional studies.

30.5 Future Work

While the data definitely suggests that a smart phone is beneficial for teaching statistics with *StatCrunch Mobile*, a study that directly compares a control group with the group using *StatCrunch Mobile* would be helpful, especially if the sample size is sufficiently large. The project could also be expanded to include data collection using the smart phone, which then could be analyzed immediately right from the phone. This would create a more hands-on and real-world approach to statistics than in traditional courses. Students would exploit the mobile nature of their device during the data collection phase, while using its computational power during the analysis phase.

It would also be interesting to investigate the combination of smart phone and appropriate mobile software for other subjects. As a concrete example: could the *Wolfram Alpha* app running on a smart phone replace the use of computer algebra packages such as *Maple* or *Mathematica*?

Acknowledgements I want to acknowledge the generous support by the Teaching, Learning, and Technology Center at Seton Hall for providing mobile phones to all students in the course and for supporting me in designing and carrying out this study.

References

1. CIA World Factbook. https://www.cia.gov/library/publications/the-world-factbook/index.html.
2. Emanuel, R. C. (2013). The American college student cell phone survey. *College Student Journal, 47*(1), 75–81.
3. Fried, C. B. (2008). In-class laptop use and its effects on student learning. *Computers & Education, 50*(3), 906–914.
4. Garrett, N. (2010). Student mobile technologies: Implications for classroom management policies and procedures. Proceedings of World Conference on Educational Multimedia, Hypermedia and Telecommunications 2010 (pp. 1699–1704). Chesapeake: AACE.
5. General Social Survey (GSS). http://www.norc.org/GSS+Website/.
6. MathCS.org Statistics Data Sets. http://mathcs.org/statistics/datasets/index.html.
7. SPSS. www.ibm.com/software/analytics/spss/.
8. StatCrunch. Integrated analytics LLC. http://www.statcrunch.com/.
9. StatCrunch Mobile. Integrated analytics LLC. http://www.statcrunch.com/mobile.

Chapter 31
Using *InkSurvey* with Pen-Enabled Mobile Devices for Real-Time Formative Assessment: I Applications in Diverse Educational Environments

Frank V. Kowalski, Susan E. Kowalski, Thomas J. Colling, J. V. Gutierrez Cuba, Tracy Q. Gardner, Gus Greivel, Enrique Palou, and Todd Ruskell

Abstract *InkSurvey* is free, web-based software designed to facilitate the collection of real-time formative assessment. Using this tool, the instructor can embed formative assessment in the instruction process by posing an open-format question. Students equipped with pen-enabled mobile devices (tablet PCs, iPads, Android devices including some smartphones) are then actively engaged in their learning as they use digital ink to draw, sketch, or graph their responses. When the instructor receives these responses instantaneously, it provides insights into student thinking and what the students do and do not know. Subsequent instruction can then repair and refine student understanding in a very timely manner.

Although this pedagogical tool is appealing because of its broad theoretical foundations, the cost of pen-enabled mobile technology was until recently a significant barrier to widely implementing this teaching model. However, less expensive tablets, iPads, and Android devices are now filling the market (and student backpacks) and greatly lowering that barrier.

To illustrate the wide applicability of this use of technology, we report a series of seven vignettes featuring instructors of diverse subjects (mathematics, food chemistry, physics, biology, and chemical engineering), with students using diverse pen-enabled mobile devices (tablet PCs, iPads, and Android 4.0 tablets), in diverse educational environments (K-12, community college, publicly-funded engineering

F. V. Kowalski (✉) · S. E. Kowalski · T. Q. Gardner · G. Greivel · T. Ruskell
Department of Physics, Colorado School of Mines, Golden, CO, USA
e-mail: fkowalsk@mines.edu

S. E. Kowalski
Red Rocks Community College, Lakewood, CO, USA
e-mail: kowalsk@mines.edu

T. J. Colling
Rancocas Valley Regional High School, Mt. Holly, NJ, USA

J. V. G. Cuba · E. Palou
Universidad de las Américas at Puebla, Chalula, Puebla, Mexico

© Springer International Publishing Switzerland 2015   297
T. Hammond et al. (eds.), *The Impact of Pen and Touch Technology on Education*,
Human-Computer Interaction Series, DOI 10.1007/978-3-319-15594-4_31

university, private university, graduate school), in two countries (United States and Mexico). In a companion paper, each instructor also shares some data, insights, and/or conclusions from their experiences regarding the effectiveness of this tool.

31.1   Problem Statement and Context

In the National Research Council's seminal summary of current knowledge about how people learn [2], there are compelling and repeated calls to embed formative assessment in the learning process. Based on a broad theoretical foundation, a significant body of research indicates that frequent formative assessment can actively engage learners, effectively inform instruction, and increase student metacognition. However, educators' attempts to gather formative assessment often prove not only cumbersome, but include painful delays until the instructor is able to respond to misconceptions revealed in the formative assessments.

31.2   Method Employed

InkSurvey is web-based software designed to facilitate the collection of real-time formative assessment [3]; it can be used for free (ticc.mines.edu) and is compatible with pen-enabled mobile technology including tablet PCs, iPads, and Android devices (4.0 and higher). Using this tool, the instructor can embed formative assessment in the instruction process by posing open-format questions. By avoiding multiple-choice questions, this affords more insightful probing of student understanding. Students then use digital ink to draw, sketch, write, or graph their responses, which actively engages them in their learning. When the instructor receives these responses instantaneously, it provides insights into student thinking. Both the students and the instructor have a more accurate realization of what the students do and do not know. Subsequent instruction can then repair and refine student understanding in a very timely manner and in a climate where students are receptive to these revisions of their understanding.

To illustrate the wide applicability of this use of technology, the following vignettes describe instructors of diverse subjects, with students using diverse pen-enabled mobile devices, in diverse educational environments, in two countries.

31.3   Results and Evaluation: Seven Vignettes

31.3.1   *University Honors Calculus III*

Greivel recently introduced *InkSurvey* to 87 first-term college students in University Honors Calculus III at the Colorado School of Mines, a publicly funded engineering university. This large, lecture-based course is at times very visual, and *InkSurvey* affords him the opportunity to engage students in active learning and get student feedback in a much more organic form than is possible with multiple choice questions on clickers. This allows students to make common mistakes, understand that their peers are also making these mistakes (they are common for a reason), and actively engage in a discussion of the misconception that led to these mistakes. As a consequence, they are able to learn through this real-time formative assessment and repair misconceptions before they become deep-rooted.

The lecture in this vignette involves the introduction of triple integrals over general regions of three-dimensional space as rectangular or box shaped regions in space. These regions can be defined with inequalities on the coordinate variables (x, y and z) that involve only constant endpoints. For example a $3 \times 3 \times 2$ unit^3 box might be defined by the inequalities $0 \leq x \leq 3$, $0 \leq y \leq 3$, and $0 \leq z \leq 2$. Students are told that in general, regions of integration are bounded by surfaces that may not correspond to constant equations. After a few examples are presented, students are asked to graph and determine the inequalities necessary to define a tetrahedral region bounded by the coordinate planes and the plane $x + y + 2z = 2$.

Sample Student *InkSurvey* Drawing:

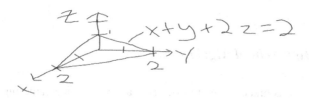

Students are expected to report the inequalities $0 \leq x \leq 2$, $0 \leq y \leq 2 - x$, and $0 \leq z \leq 1 - \frac{x}{2} - \frac{y}{2}$. At this point, many students struggle with the common misconception that all of these inequalities will have constant boundary values, based on the original derivation of the triple integral. This is evidenced by student responses to the following *InkSurvey* question:

Q4: Set up the inequalities to define the first octant region bounded by the coordinate planes and the plane $x + y + 2z = 2$ as a Type I Region.

Sample *InkSurvey* Response (student #84):

$$0 \leq x \leq 2$$
$$0 \leq y \leq 2$$
$$0 \leq z \leq 1$$

As in the sample above, 32 out of 83 student responses showed all constant bounds on these inequalities; four of the students didn't respond at all. Immediately after receiving them, Greivel then projected some of these student responses and discussed in class an appropriate approach to determining these bounds and defining the correct inequalities. After this discussion, the students were asked a slight variation of the question on *InkSurvey*. For this question, the students are expected to report the inequalities $0 \le y \le 2$, $0 \le z \le 2 - \frac{y}{2}$, and $0 \le x \le 2 - y - 2z$.

Q6: Set up the inequalities to define the same region as a Type II Region.

Sample *InkSurvey* Response (student #84):

$$0 \le y \le 2$$
$$0 \le z \le 1 - \frac{1}{2}y$$
$$0 \le x \le 2 - y - 2z$$

Taken together, the sample responses above (from student #84) reveal the real-time progress in a single student's understanding during one class session. When Q6 was posed, all students responded, only 4 still demonstrated the misconception in one dimension, and none of the students provided all constant bounds.

31.3.2 High School Algebra

When Colling was first exposed to *InkSurvey* at a worldwide gathering of educators in New Delhi, he realized it could provide an avenue for using pen-enabled mobile technology to address his public high school's district-wide focus on real-time assessment of standards-based declarative and procedural knowledge of students. He found it particularly appealing since it closely matched his teaching personality and preferred pedagogical methods. Now, his high school Algebra I students use *InkSurvey* to complete problem solving exercises and receive both individual and class-wide feedback on a near-daily basis.

Prior to Colling's implementation of *InkSurvey*, a few selected students in his Algebra classes would show their problem solutions on the board and feedback was given only to those two or three students. Then, due to time constraints, the class would need to move on to another problem. With the use of *InkSurvey*, all of his students now perform their work on Tablet PCs and submit their solutions. Colling quickly reviews all of the answers from the class in order to fix any misconceptions about the lesson prior to students leaving class and practicing the material more on their own at home. He enjoys receiving the instantaneous feedback from all 25 students, so that he can compare and contrast their solutions and fix as many problems as possible. Also, as Colling selected solutions that students have submitted, the class can view alternate options in a constructive and beneficial way, and come to realize that there may be multiple correct mathematical methods that are within the properties and definitions of Algebra I.

31.3.3 University Upper-Level Undergraduate and Graduate Courses in Food Chemistry

In Mexico, the *How People Learn* framework [2, 4] was applied to redesign two courses in Food Chemistry at Universidad de las Américas at Puebla, a prestigious private university. The goal was to improve teaching and learning by creating high-quality learning environments that promote interactive classrooms with formative assessments by means of Tablet PCs and associated technologies [5]. One targeted course is a junior level required course (typically 10–25 students) for food engineering and nutrition BS programs; the other is a first-semester required course (typically 5–10 students) for the Food Science MSc program and also an elective for the PhD in Food Science program. In both courses, a major goal is to help students think the way a food chemist does. Instructors of these courses utilize *InkSurvey* mainly to pose open-ended formative assessment questions to students during class to gauge student learning in real time, provide immediate feedback, and make real-time pedagogical adjustments as needed.

31.3.4 University Introductory Physics (Calculus-Based)

Ruskell is using *InkSurvey* to instruct a freshman calculus-based Physics I course at Colorado School of Mines. This course already employed a variety of techniques to engage students, including teaching in a hybrid studio model [6] and utilizing personal response systems (clickers) to answer multiple-choice questions during lecture. Incorporating *InkSurvey* with Nexus 7 (Android 4.0) tablets allows Ruskell to explore the next level of real-time formative assessment to more deeply probe student understanding.

In many cases, he has recast traditional clicker questions as open-format questions. For example:

Clicker Question A bowling ball and a ping-pong ball both have the same initial momentum. If you exert the same constant force on each, how do their stopping distances compare?

A. distance to stop bowling ball > distance to stop ping-pong ball.
B. distance to stop ping-pong ball > distance to stop bowling ball.
C. It takes the same distance.
D. Not enough information to tell.

InkSurvey Version A bowling ball and a ping-pong ball both have the same initial momentum. If you exert the same constant force on each, how do their stopping distances compare? Why?

With the open-format version, instead of simply sitting back and "thinking about it" (which is often what students do with the clicker version), students need to justify their answers in writing. If equations are involved, as here, students are forced to actually work through the problem, solidifying their understanding, or revealing their difficulties, on the tablets during class. Furthermore, *InkSurvey* responses to the above question revealed to Ruskell that some students arrived at the correct conclusion but with faulty reasoning. Some, for example, displayed thinking in terms of a constant velocity, which is not the case in this situation. This incorrect path to the correct conclusion may not have been apparent without an open-format question. After rapidly scanning *InkSurvey* responses during class, Ruskell was able to immediately address this misconception.

31.3.5 Community College Introductory Biology Class

At Red Rocks Community College, S. Kowalski works with a broad diversity of learners. In the recent past, many students were neither comfortable nor fluent in their use of technology to enhance learning, so she was uncertain if *InkSurvey* would present special obstacles when she implemented its use. Using carts of both HP Tablets and iPads and a portable wireless access point in her classroom, the students needed very little "tech support" as they quickly became proficient at submitting responses.

Since many students struggle to "connect the dots" in the context of the class, she has found it particularly useful to use a sequence of questions to scaffold learning and nurture these skills. For example, the following questions were embedded in a lecture on enzyme activity; they were launched one at a time, with class discussion of the responses interspersed.

1. Review: what does pH measure?
2. A lysosome is a special compartment within a eukaryotic cell, filled with destructive enzymes. The internal pH of the lysosome is 4.5. Thinking about the optimal pH of other enzymes we observed in lab this week, draw a graph predicting the optimal pH of one of these enzymes. (pH on the x-axis and the rate of the reaction on the y-axis)
3. Why does this enzyme become less active at a neutral pH? Sketch the shape of the molecule at each pH to illustrate your understanding.
4. Predict what would happen if destructive enzymes of the lysosome leaked into the cytoplasm.

By completing this series of questions, students were engaged in their learning, motivated to participate in the interspersed discussions, and able to effectively relate previously studied topics (lab observations, pH, weak hydrogen bonds, structure and denaturation of proteins, etc.) to the current topic of enzymes and how they work. This provided practice in "connecting the dots" and served as an opportunity for some self-discovery of important relationships and concepts.

31.3.6 University Upper-Level Undergraduate Chemical Engineering and Physics

Gardner and F. Kowalski couple the use of *InkSurvey* with interactive computer simulations in their advanced undergraduate chemical engineering and physics courses, respectively. Although there is a wealth of simulations ("sims") available online (many free or associated with textbooks) to help students engage with and better visualize difficult concepts, it is challenging to know how to best use these in STEM classrooms. Too little guidance from the instructor, and students may not construct correct understandings; too much, and the "cookbook" atmosphere discourages both self-exploration and engagement in the learning process, and may prevent students from understanding concepts at a level necessary to help remember and apply them in other situations.

Gardner and F. Kowalski typically have their students explore a sim independently, learning all they can on their own. Then, the instructors use a series of *InkSurvey* questions in class to probe student understanding, identify points of difficulty, and then guide students as they return to the sim for further exploration or testing of concepts and subtleties. This guided refinement of understanding during the learning process is seamless, since the same devices are used for exploring the simulations, delivering scaffolding questions to guide explorations, and submitting responses to reveal understanding in real time.

31.3.7 University Upper-Level Creativity in Physics

In a course designed to nurture creativity in undergraduate and graduate level physics students, F. Kowalski successfully utilizes *InkSurvey* in group interactions to generate new ideas. First, a problem is stated to the class; then student responses, anonymous to their peers, are requested and displayed in each of the following steps:

1. Two separate questions, launched simultaneously, solicit individual responses prior to initiation of a class discussion:
   a. ideas (unrestrained ideas, not limited to those that students think are practical).
   b. questions (about constraints, factual information, motivation for studying the problem, etc.)

As the real-time student responses are collected, the facilitator sorts the ideas and questions into categories. The questions are addressed in a class discussion. The categorized ideas are displayed anonymously to the group and discussed by the group as appropriate. The ideation request can then be repeated if appropriate.

2. Next, using the organized list of ideas, two separate questions, launched simultaneously, solicit:
   a. positive critical comments on the ideas, and
   b. negative critical comments on the ideas.

The submitted critical comments are organized by the instructor and then presented to the group and discussed as appropriate. This serves as the foundation for the next step.

3. Students construct and submit a metric to determine the solution based on these positive and negative comments. The final group solution is chosen from these.

This process is then repeated to generate additional new ideas and refine the solution.

Placing all students and ideas on equal footing, *InkSurvey* is used to constructively deal with social issues in the process of generating new ideas. It addresses evaluation apprehension since displayed student responses are blind to the audience (but not the instructor). Since their work contains a student identifier, visible only to the instructor, the student is accountable for their participation, mitigating a group performance degradation issue. The anonymity of the responses also encourages participation of each student in the electronic brainstorming process, regardless of gender, race, etc. The request for questions enhances metacognition by requiring students to write about what they do and do not understand. Step 1 requires independent thinking; captitalize Steps 2 and 3 build on this and force the student to pay careful attention to the ideas of others.

31.4   Conclusion

These seven vignettes demonstrate the wide applicability of this use of technology by instructors of diverse subjects, with students using diverse pen-enabled mobile devices, in diverse educational environments, in two countries. A companion paper [1] addresses indications of the effectiveness of this pedagogical tool.

Acknowledgments   Various facets described here have been supported by: HP Catalyst Program (FK, SK, TC, JC, TG, and EP), NSF grants #1037519 and #1044255 (FK, SK, and TG), the Trefny Endowment (GG, TR), and the National Council for Science and Technology of Mexico (CONACyT) (JC). We appreciate this generous support.

References

1. Kowalski, F.V., Kowalski, S. E., Colling T. J., Cuba, J.V. C., Gardner, T. Q., Greivel, G., Palou, E., & Ruskell, T. (2015). *Using InkSurvey with Pen-Enabled Mobile Devices for Real-Time Formative Assessment II. Indications of Effectiveness in Diverse Educational Environments.*
2. Bransford, J. D., Brown, A. L., & Cocking, R. R. (2000). *How people learn: Brain, mind, experience and school.* Washington DC: National Academy Press.
3. Kowalski, F. V., Kowalski, S. E., & Hoover, E. (2007). Using *InkSurvey*: A free web-based tool for open-ended questioning to promote active learning and real-time formative assessment of tablet PC-equipped engineering students. Proceedings, 2007 ASEE Conference and Exposition, Honolulu, HI, June.
4. Bransford, J. D., Vye, N., & Bateman, H. (2002). Creating high-quality learning environments: Guidelines from research on how people learn. In P. A. Graham, & N. G. Stacey (Eds.), *The*

knowledge economy and postsecondary education: Report of a workshop. Washington DC: National Academy Press.
5. Cuba, J. V. G., López-Malo, A., & Palou, E. (2011). Using Tablet PCs and associated technologies to reveal undergraduate and graduate student thinking. Proceedings of the ASEE Annual Meeting, Vancouver, BC, Canada.
6. Furtak, T. E., & Ohno, T. R. (2001). Installing studio physics. *The Physics Teacher, 39,* 534.

Chapter 32
Using *InkSurvey* with Pen-Enabled Mobile Devices for Real-Time Formative Assessment II. Indications of Effectiveness in Diverse Educational Environments

Frank V. Kowalski, Susan E. Kowalski, Thomas J. Colling, J. V. Gutierrez Cuba, Tracy Q. Gardner, Gus Greivel, Enrique Palou, and Todd Ruskell

Abstract *InkSurvey* is free web-based software designed to facilitate the collection of real-time formative assessment. Using this tool, the instructor can embed formative assessment in the instruction process by posing an open-format question. Students equipped with pen-enabled mobile devices are then actively engaged in their learning as they use digital ink to draw, sketch, or graph their responses. When the instructor receives these responses instantaneously, it provides insights into student thinking and what the students do and do not know. Subsequent instruction can then repair and refine student understanding in a very timely manner.

In a companion paper, we illustrate the wide applicability of this use of technology by reporting a series of seven vignettes featuring instructors of diverse subjects (physics, mathematics, chemical engineering, food science, and biology), with students using diverse pen-enabled mobile devices (tablet PCs, iPads, and Android 4.0 tablets/smartphones), in diverse educational environments (K-12, community college, publicly-funded engineering university, private university, and graduate school), in two countries (United States and Mexico). In this paper, each instructor shares some data, insights, and/or conclusions from their experiences that indicate the effectiveness of this pedagogical model in diverse educational environments.

F. V. Kowalski (✉) · S. E. Kowalski
Department of Physics, Colorado School of Mines, Golden, CO, USA
e-mail: fkowalsk@mines.edu

S. E. Kowalski
Red Rocks Community College, Lakewood, CA, USA

T. J. Colling
Rancocas Valley Regional High School, Mt. Holly, NJ, USA

J. V. G. Cuba · E. Palou
Universidad de las Américas at Puebla, Chalula, Puebla, Mexico

T. Q. Gardner · G. Greivel · T. Ruskell
Colorado School of Mines, Golden, CO, USA

© Springer International Publishing Switzerland 2015
T. Hammond et al. (eds.), *The Impact of Pen and Touch Technology on Education,*
Human-Computer Interaction Series, DOI 10.1007/978-3-319-15594-4_32

307

32.1 Problem Statement and Context

There are broad theoretical foundations for embedding real-time formative assessment in instruction. However, educators need an efficient, robust method for implementing its collection in the classroom and evidence supporting its effectiveness.

32.2 Method Employed

InkSurvey is web-based software designed to facilitate the collection of real-time formative assessment [2]; it is available for free (ticc.mines.edu) and is compatible with pen-enabled mobile technology including tablet PCs, iPads, and Android devices (4.0 and higher). Using this tool, the instructor can embed formative assessment in the instruction process by posing open-format questions. By avoiding multiple-choice questions, this affords more insightful probing of student understanding. Students then use digital ink to draw, sketch, write, or graph their responses, which actively engages them in their learning. When the instructor receives these responses instantaneously, it provides rich insights into student thinking. Both the students and the instructor have a more accurate realization of what the students do and do not know. Subsequent instruction can then repair and refine student understanding in a very timely manner, before misconceptions become deep-rooted, and in a climate where students are receptive to these revisions of their understanding.

32.3 Results and Evaluation

There is a growing body of evidence supporting the use of *InkSurvey* to collect real-time formative assessment.

32.3.1 Evidence of Learning Gains

In the companion paper [1], Greivel describes in a vignette a lesson using *InkSurvey* to reveal and repair a student misconception as they learn about triple integrals over general regions of three-dimensional space. When 87 students were examined in a summative assessment two weeks after the lesson, only one student still displayed this mistake on any of the three exam questions that addressed the concept. By way of comparison, in GG's other large lecture section of Calculus III, in which *InkSurvey* was not being used, this particular misconception was given similar consideration in lecture and 12 out of 103 students made this mistake on the same set of exam questions.

Similarly, TC's high school students, who receive regular and repeated individual and whole-group feedback as part of instruction using *InkSurvey*, have gained traction on mastery of fundamental concepts in Algebra I, as measured by standards-based assessments and in comparison to students who were not exposed to the *InkSurvey* intervention [3]. Interestingly, even though his classes are mixed gender, female students using *InkSurvey* in particular demonstrated much greater learning gains than the control group. Student attitudes toward learning with *InkSurvey* are discussed later in this paper, but it is noteworthy here that when TC's students were surveyed, the females had a much stronger agreement (70 %) *vs.* males (48 %) with the statement: "*InkSurvey* helped me to know what I understood of the topic and where I needed further help." Since these observed differences in both attitude and learning gains in females *vs.* males could have significant implications, particularly in STEM education, further investigation is warranted.

In Food Chemistry courses at Universidad de las Américas Puebla, redesigned to incorporate *InkSurvey* and other research-based pedagogy, EP, JC, and collaborators investigated changes as frequent formative assessment helped make students' thinking visible to themselves, their peers, and their instructor. They documented increased student participation in class discussions and problem-solving activities [4], while instructors utilized the information gained through real-time formative assessment to tailor instruction to meet student needs. Through qualitative and quantitative analysis of the information obtained from six semesters, they report the impact of creating classroom tasks and conditions under which student thinking can be revealed [4–6].

In both undergraduate and graduate courses, formative assessment exercises performed with Tablet PCs and *InkSurvey* had a positive impact on performance on a series of summative quizzes. These summative assessments were compared with performance of students in the same courses 4 years before implementing these revisions, and showed mean improvements of 0.6 (undergraduate course) and 0.5 points (graduate course) out of 10 possible [5]. The frequent formative assessments using *InkSurvey* at UDLAP generated possibilities for self-assessment, allowing students to anonymously analyze their own and classmates' thinking. Other important impacts this team observed include: ability of instructor to identify the most common difficulties and provide immediate feedback; student reflection on their own processes as learners; and improvements in both classroom instruction and student academic success when the instructor has these insights into student thinking [4–6].

At Colorado School of Mines, *InkSurvey* has also been used to strengthen problem-solving skills in an upper-level engineering physics course [7]. As 11 new problems were introduced throughout the course, students, working individually or in groups, provided real-time formative assessment of their problem-solving skills by submitting responses to a standard series of three questions (designed as nearly universally applicable in problem solving). These responses were later analyzed to determine the students' ability to apply the problem-solving strategy; scores were adjusted to reflect the difficulty of the problems. Results show a steady improvement over the semester in problem-solving skills, indicating *InkSurvey* can potentially nurture higher level thinking skills.

When *InkSurvey*'s real-time formative assessment is coupled with interactive computer simulations (sims), strong learning gains are achieved. In two Chemical Engineering courses, TG targeted six concepts for which students in the past have had difficulties visualizing the connections between the calculations and the physical processes [8]. In this study, student understanding was compared at three points in time during the learning process: before a sim was introduced, after the students had played with the sim on their own, and after the instructor used *InkSurvey* to probe student understanding and guide their further explorations of the sim. After playing on their own with the sims, and knowing what question would be asked at the end, students' average level of competence across the six topics in this study increased from ~ 1.8 to ~ 2.3 (on a 4 point scale), indicating students still did not adequately understand the concepts after exploring the simulations in an unguided manner. Without the instructor ever telling students the answers to the questions, but instead posing scaffolded questions based on the students' immediate issues and misconceptions and allowing students to further explore the sims as they answered these questions, students' understanding of these concepts increased to an average of ~ 3.1 on the 4 point scale on these same topics.

Our final evidence in this section addresses the effectiveness of using *InkSurvey* for real-time formative assessment with students of different learning styles. FK and SK hypothesized that perhaps the graphical nature of *InkSurvey* input makes it more appealing or effective for learners with strongly visual or kinesthetic learning styles. However, their data reflects strong learning gains achieved when *InkSurvey* is used for students of all learning styles [9]. This surprising result is particularly encouraging when considering implementation in classes with typical diversity among students.

32.3.2   Student Insights

Student response to the use of *InkSurvey* has in general been very favorable. In the Fall 2012 semester, FK used *InkSurvey* in an Advanced Laboratory class for junior-level undergraduate physics students. In an anonymous survey of 63 students, 54 students (86 %) agreed that their responses with *InkSurvey* gave the instructor a better understanding of what they do and do not understand. Some of their comments include:

- "It gives instant feedback to him so he can see right away if what he just talked about made any sense. If it did, we can move on, if not, he re-explains it in a different way or elaborates on it more which is good."
- "I do think *InkSurvey* has let the professor understand what we know better because it is an efficient way to test us. This quick response lets him see what topics the class is struggling with and what topics we get based on the answers he gets back. If there are a wide variety of responses, we are probably struggling with something. When this happens, we go over the topic slowly so we can understand it better. If there is a common wrong answer, we can go over the mistake made

to get there and prove why it is wrong. If most the class is able to get something correct, we spend very little time discussing what the right answer is because we already get it."

- "Yes, I feel that they give the instructor a better understanding of what I do and do not understand because he is able to look directly at my work and follow my thinking. Every time that I have answered incorrectly or been missing a portion of the question, he has gone over it after he has looked over the *InkSurvey*."
- "I feel that my responses using Ink Survey have given the instructor a better understanding of what I know or don't know. In most classes student understanding is conveyed through homework and quizzes. This is great but by the time quizzes and homeworks are graded the class has moved onto new topics and it is very inconvenient for the class to slow its momentum and revisit old material. *InkSurvey* is a great resource for a teacher because it gives instantaneous feedback to the teacher when a topic is being introduced. Because of this the professor can change his or her teaching style based on the class understanding."

In the same survey, a question was asked to probe the effectiveness of this pedagogical model in increasing student metacognition. Forty-eight students (76 %) found that creating their responses in *InkSurvey* actually helped them better understand what was being covered in class, or helped them realize what they did and did not understand.

- "Having to physically write down my response to all the questions is very helpful and shows me where I am going wrong or what I do not understand so that I may remedy it."
- "Answering questions about what one has just learned often increases, at the very least, your memory of an event. Further, if you didn't understand something, having a fast reiteration of the correct answer is conducive to comprehension. In this regard, *InkSurvey* works well because it is faster than a paper quiz and can have everyone answer independently, unlike an oral exchange."
- "I believe that *InkSurvey* is extremely helpful in the understanding of class topics. This is because it keeps students in the classroom involved and participating in the classroom. Using traditional teaching methods students are not forced to think about what is being taught and often get in a routine of copying notes from the board to paper and then thinking about the topic later when doing homework. *InkSurvey* forces you to stay involved in the classroom because it allows the professor to ask thought provoking questions, making you think about what is being taught at that moment–not later after class when doing homework. Because of this more questions are brought up in class, facilitating the learning environment that *InkSurvey* brings."
- "It sometimes also makes me realize I know something better than I thought I did or I already knew how to do it and that it's not as scary as it may seem when it's presented."
- "I think having to draw out and write the solutions shows me my shortcomings with the material very clearly. You cannot fake knowing an answer when you have to draw things out."

Focus group conversations revealed that sometimes students resent the demand *InkSurvey* places on them to participate in class, rather than passively sitting there. However, in an introductory physics class, TR's students indicate they feel much more engaged with open-format questions than with multiple-choice clicker questions. Because students can't just select an answer, they feel more pressure when writing something because, as one student explained, they "don't want to write something stupid." While they understand that it's acceptable to submit an incorrect response, their self-imposed pressure encourages students' additional engagement with the question. Another physics student at Colorado School of Mines feels that needing to quickly think through a problem and construct a viable solution to submit on *InkSurvey* is providing him/her with excellent preparation for future job interview tasks and on-the-job challenges.

At Universidad de las Américas at Puebla, graduate students using *InkSurvey* felt that this: increased their motivation to participate in class as well as their scores in graded work-products; made the classroom more active and kept them constantly thinking, thus increasing their learning with understanding; enabled the teacher to provide a great deal of real-time feedback to students that made their thinking visible; and gave them chances to revise their understanding [4].

32.3.3 Instructor Insights

Instructors agree that there is an art to effectively using *InkSurvey* for real-time formative assessment, both in construction of appropriate questions and in agilely responding to the student submissions [10]. Two often-opposing needs must be balanced. On one hand, there is a need to take full advantage of the open-format questions and allow students enough room to construct correct understanding and demonstrate higher levels of thinking. On the other hand, if questions are too complex or lengthy, the instructor risks losing the interest of students whose understanding is not yet mature enough to tackle the question. With practice, instructors learn to break questions into appropriate parts.

There is also some skill, which again improves with practice, in knowing how to phrase questions to deeply probe student understanding and yield responses that give clear insights into student thinking. A picture is worth a thousand words, and the power of responses constructed with digital ink is their ability to display a wealth of conceptual understanding in a graph, a sketch, a Venn diagram, the mathematical solution to a problem, or the outline of a proof. These graphical responses can be quickly scanned by the instructor as they are received and can effectively serve as the foundation of subsequent class discussion. In contrast, this is probably not an effective format for soliciting from the students five-paragraph essays defending a particular point of view, or an epic poem in stanzas of iambic pentameter, since real-time formative assessment is neither as useful nor as practical in these cases.

Some instructors implementing the collection of real-time formative assessment use *InkSurvey* in a controlled online environment. However, many others are acutely aware of the temptations to students when they have ready access to the internet during class. One way to address this classroom challenge is to anticipate it and prepare to further engage the faster workers as they wait for their peers to submit their responses. *InkSurvey* allows the instructor to independently launch access to any question at any time. FK sometimes employs this to facilitate differentiated instruction and keep every student on task. He starts the entire class working on a question (or series of questions) on a fundamental concept; as he begins receiving correct responses from students, he then launches another question for them to address. This is often an enrichment question, encouraging deeper student understanding. By the time the majority of students have responded to the original question, a subset of them will have also considered the enrichment question, and some of that group will have submitted responses. Even though not all students will have individually experienced the enrichment question, the responses received can serve as the foundation for class discussion of this after the instructor responds to the real-time formative assessment received from the original question related to the fundamental concept [10].

32.4   Conclusion

A companion paper [1] describes the use of *InkSurvey* for real-time formative assessment to enhance learning; a growing body of data, summarized here, supports the effectiveness of this pedagogical tool. This includes evidence of learning gains, positive student attitude feedback, and instructor insights from a variety of educational environments and using a variety of pen-enabled mobile devices (tablet PCs, iPads, and Android 4.0 tablets).

Acknowledgments   Various facets described here have been supported by: HP Catalyst Program (FK, SK, TC, JC, TG, and EP), NSF grants #1037519 and #1044255 (FK, SK, and TG), the Trefny Endowment (GG, TR), and the National Council for Science and Technology of Mexico (CONACyT) (JC). We appreciate this generous support.

References

1. Kowalski, F.V., Kowalski, S. E., Colling T. J., Cuba, J.V. C., Gardner, T. Q., Greivel, G., Palou, E., & Ruskell, T. (2013). *Using InkSurvey with Pen-Enabled Mobile Devices for Real-Time Formative Assessment I. Application in Diverse Educational Environments.*
2. Kowalski, F. V., Kowalski, S. E., & Hoover, E. (2007). Using *InkSurvey*: A Free Web-Based Tool for Open-Ended Questioning to Promote Active Learning and Real-Time Formative Assessment of Tablet PC-Equipped Engineering Students. Proceedings, 2007 ASEE Conference and Exposition, Honolulu HI, June.
3. Maniglia, R. (2012). Rancocas Valley Regional High School HP Catalyst Final Project Report: Real-Time Assessment of Standards-Based Declarative & Procedural Knowledge of Students. October.

4. Cuba, J. V. G., López-Malo, A., & Palou, E. (2012). Graduate Student Perspectives on Using Tablet PCs and Associated Technologies. Proceedings of the American Society for Engineering Education Annual Meeting, San Antonio TX, June.

5. Cuba, J. V. G., López-Malo, A., & Palou, E. (2011). Using Tablet PCs and Associated Technologies To Reveal Undergraduate and Graduate Student Thinking. Proceedings of the American Society for Engineering Education Annual Meeting, Vancouver, BC, Canada.

6. Palou, E., Gazca, L., Díaz García, J. A., Rojas Lobato, J. A., Guerrero Ojeda, L. G., Tamborero Arnal, J. F., Jiménez Munguía, M. T., López-Malo, A., & Garibay, J. M. (2012). High-quality learning environments for engineering design: using Tablet PCs and guidelines from research on how people learn. *International Journal of Food Studies, 1,* 1–16.

7. Kowalski, F. V., Gok, T., & Kowalski, S. E. (2009). Using Tablet PCs to Strengthen Problem-Solving Skills in an Upper-Level Engineering Physics Course. 39th ASEE/IEEE Frontiers in Education Conference Proceedings, San Antonio TX, Oct.

8. Gardner, T. Q., Kowalski, S. E., & Kowalski, F. V. (2012). Interactive Simulations Coupled with Realtime Formative Assessment to Enhance Student Learning. ASEE 2012 Conference and Exposition Proceedings, San Antonio TX, June.

9. Kowalski, F. V., & Kowalski, S. E. (2012). The Effect of Student Learning Styles on the Learning Gains Achieved When Interactive Simulations Are Coupled with Real-Time Formative Assessment via Pen-Enabled Mobile Technology. ASEE/IEEE Frontiers in Education Conference, Seattle WA, Oct.

10. Kowalski, S. E., Kowalski, F. V., & Gardner, T. Q. (2009). Lessons Learned When Gathering Real-Time Formative Assessment in the University Classroom Using Tablet PCs. 39th ASEE/IEEE Frontiers in Education Conference Proceedings, 18–21 Oct. San Antonio TX.

Chapter 33
An Interactive Learner-Centered Classroom: Successful Use of Tablet Computing and Dyknow Software in Foundational Mathematics

Carol Carruthers

Abstract Community college students in foundational mathematics programs require innovative instruction techniques that resonate with individual learning styles. A synchronous workspace is provided using pen-based tablet PCs and DyKnow collaborative software. Students meet teachers and fellow classmates face to face as well as in a web-enabled environment within the classroom. The interactive features of the software allow for group interaction, self-paced learning, immediate feedback, and sharing of the teaching role to stimulate student engagement. In this active-learning space, weaker students develop the confidence to become part of the learning community due to the anonymizing features of the software. This follow-up project with a larger college class size confirms the initial findings of a pilot study exploring the use of this instructional methodology to improve student success. Grade data suggests that students are more successful at completing this course. Student comments elicited by survey questions give a greater understanding of why participants feel tablet PCs and DyKnow enhances their learning.

33.1 Problem Statement and Context

Pen-based computing provides a unique opportunity for students to take electronic notes when learning mathematics. Writing with a stylus gives students the ability to brainstorm solutions and annotate important concepts with the familiar 'pencil on paper' input. However, simply having advanced technology may not be sufficient to engage students in a subject they may be reluctant to learn. A certain level of mathematical skill and confidence is required to successfully complete college technician/technology programs. Those entering first semester foundational mathematics courses have a wide range of backgrounds and experiences. Re-teaching concepts in a traditional way may have little or no effect on students who believe they 'can't do math'. After several years of observing foundational mathematics students in the

C. Carruthers (✉)
Seneca College of Applied Arts and Technology, Toronto, ON, Canada
e-mail: carol.carruthers@senecacollege.ca

© Springer International Publishing Switzerland 2015
T. Hammond et al. (eds.), *The Impact of Pen and Touch Technology on Education*,
Human-Computer Interaction Series, DOI 10.1007/978-3-319-15594-4_33

classroom, I noted that they demonstrate certain tendencies: an assumption their answer is incorrect, a reluctance to seek help, and a fear that peers or teacher may discover their lack of understanding. An interactive collaborative teaching approach may help students overcome some of these predispositions.

In 2008, Seneca College received an HP Technology for Teaching Grant, which became a catalyst for several projects aimed at evaluating how technology can best be used to increase student learning and engagement. The uniqueness of our project was to go beyond establishing a laptop laboratory (which at that time was not uncommon in higher education institutions): we wanted to develop an online learning community within the classroom. The purchase of DyKnow Vision collaborative software allowed teachers and students to connect in synchronous two-way communication. A pilot study using 20 tablet PCs and DyKnow software provided a convincing argument that this interactive, learner-centered environment resulted in a student perception of increased engagement (supported by increased attendance, persistence in the program, and positive survey answers) and greater success/personal achievement (measured through grades and surveys) [1].

The College Mathematics Project (CMP 2007-12) [2] had found that at least one-third of all students taking first semester mathematics courses were at risk of not completing their chosen program. Since 2007, prospective students take a Canadian Achievement Test (CAT3) and those with a lower score enroll in the Foundations for Technical Mathematics (FTM) course. Those required to take the FTM course may have little confidence in their mathematics abilities, weak language comprehension skills, or a combination of both. Consequently, the goal of this course was to strengthen skill level and enhance students' knowledge to improve success in math-reliant technology courses. As the above-mentioned pilot study had a positive outcome, the next logical progression was to use this instructive methodology for FTM courses. The focus of the current study was to determine the effectiveness of using tablet PCs/DyKnow software for learning mathematics in a more typical college class size (40) and to establish if previous results were reproducible.

33.2 Method Employed

The study was carried out over four semesters from September 2010 to December 2011. The FTM course was offered at two campuses located 17 km (11 miles) apart. Students chose their campus based on career path. One campus was designated as the experimental group, with students in applied science (Biochemistry) disciplines. At the other campus, the control group was made up of students in engineering science (electronics, built environment, advanced technology, fire protection, and aviation). Teachers at both campuses used the same subject outcomes and mark allocation. All students in the FTM course wrote a common final exam. Grading in this non-credit course was calculated as either FAIL ($< 55\%$) or PASS. Final grade data was reviewed only from students that gave consent. Surveys to determine use of technology were administered during week 12 of the 14-week semester. In the experimental groups only, students answered additional questions pertaining to the use of tablets/DyKnow in the classroom. The data collected were of two types: twelve questions with closed Likert responses of strongly disagree, disagree, agree and strongly agree and eight open-ended questions.

Teachers in the control group taught using a tablet PC/electronic podium or whiteboard. Students took notes on pen and paper in the traditional manner, often bringing textbooks to class as required by the instructor.

Students in the experimental group had classroom access to the tablet laboratory and instructors taught at least 90 % of class time using DyKnow in ways similar to the pilot study. Several features of the software promote active learning, which helps students develop their self-confidence. The anonymous poll feature focuses students on the subject matter and initiates discussion. Teachers receive individualized and immediate feedback from students by asking them to send their 'status', 'submit panels', or to 'chat' directly. The status icon lets them send a red ('don't'), yellow ('a little'), green ('well') stoplight to indicate their level of understanding. In practice, it is best to begin by requiring students to respond using the 'request status' feature. Eventually, students will automatically send feedback (e.g. 'red'); they may want additional problems solved without alerting the rest of the class. Teachers ask students to 'submit panels', giving the opportunity of collecting class work electronically. The retrieved panels are added to the class notes, or saved to be returned at a later time. When added to class notes, student solutions are discussed and annotated in real time, providing multiple examples. By viewing other responses, weaker students realize they may not be alone in their misunderstanding. Many use the panel submission without being prompted—they like the immediate feedback without the necessity of identification. Finally, the 'chat' feature gives students the ability to connect with classmates or ask questions directly of the teacher.

For students in the FTM course, this anonymity may enhance their willingness to participate in class. They can be placed in online groups so answers that are difficult to achieve independently are shared and supported by group understanding. The teacher can 'share control' of the classroom screen by designating a willing student to 'ink in' their solution. While sitting at their own tablet, one or several students can demonstrate their approach, providing an answer that may closely resonate with other learners' styles. In this way, students become the 'temporary teacher', which places greater emphasis on being responsible for one's own work. In addition, students determine the pace of their learning. The teacher can make the entire session of panels available and students can scroll back or forward at their will. This is useful in a subject like mathematics where repetition is required to develop competence, but can be 'time wasting' or even 'boring' while all students achieve their understanding. This dynamic classroom complements the learning style of our students by using the collaborative/interactive features of the software. Students save this consolidation of notes that accurately reflect the classroom experience to a server, which they access from any web-enabled computer. Further, once notes are saved, they can activate the 'replay' icon and watch each panel be completed in a stroke-by-stroke fashion. As step-wise problem solutions aid in understanding, this feature is beneficial. It

Table 33.1 Grade data

Grade	Experimental	Control
Pass	79 %	74 %
Fail ($< 55\%$)	21 %	26 %
Total studied (consent)	180	335
Total enrolled	291	583

was assumed the anonymity of response is one of the most desired features of the software—students can participate without feeling centered out until confidence in their abilities is restored or fortified. In this setting, experienced teachers guide students to interact with appropriate digital media and learning activities. This affords students a variety of approaches to become skilled with challenging mathematical concepts and provides opportunities for teachers to identify common errors as well as exemplary approaches.

33.3 Results and Evaluation

33.3.1 Student Success

Data was collected from nine sections of experimental groups and 20 sections of control groups. Out of approximately 900 students, 59% gave consent to use their grade data. As indicated in Table 33.1, an analysis of grades showed that, by comparison, students in the experimental group were more likely to be successful achieving a passing grade (SAT).

33.3.2 Survey Excerpts

Students in both groups were given the same technology survey and 63% of all students responded (57% of the control group and 76% of the experimental). Those in the experimental group were asked additional questions regarding the specific use of this instructive methodology.

Student response of strongly disagree, disagree, agree and strongly agree were aggregated into agree/disagree responses, as illustrated in Table 33.2. At least 60% of students agreed that having the ability to interact with fellow classmates and getting immediate teacher feedback helped them pay more attention, participate in class discussion, increase their understanding, which in their opinion, helped them to improve their performance and grades.

Students in the experimental groups were given the opportunity to express their opinions in response to the following open-ended questions:

Table 33.2 Likert scored answer—survey question 20

Question: The pen based tablet PC and Dyknow software....

Answer options	Agree (%)	Disagree (%)
Was an effective tool for classroom presentation and note taking	74	26
Helped me to be better organized in coursework	58	42
Helped me to pay more attention during classes	65	35
Helped me to participate in class discussion	72	28
Improved my interaction in class by having the ability to "share control" to display my work	71	29
Changed the way I approach learning	65	35
Helped to improve my understanding by being able to submit panels and get instructor feedback	74	26
Helped me to improve my performance/grades in this class	61	39

1. *Please let us know some of the ways that using tablet PCs and DyKnow software helped or made learning more difficult with respect to: notetaking and organizational skills, attention/motivation, participation in class, learning experience, attendance in class and persistence to complete the course.*
2. *Finally, in what ways did the tablet PC/DyKnow change your class experience?*

Analysis of student comments is continuing, however, trends in response can be used in context to gain insight as to how the tablet PC/DyKnow methodology may be effective. Many instructors teach mathematics in the way they were taught—today's students want more flexibility in their learning environment. *"Using the pen on screen was more interesting than making notes with pen and paper."* and *"I started enjoying math lecture just because of such software..."* indicated that they feel they benefited from the use of this technology. Students in the tablet/DyKnow classroom felt that *"Dyknow is the best notebook I can have...",* *"It's easy to take notes...",* *"made me more organized",* and *"There's more time to understand the lecture because I don't have to worry about writing the questions."*

Many commented about the learning experience *"It change my perspective because before I don't wanna go coz its math but now that we don't write lectures it eagers me to go to class[sic]".* They were able to set their own pace for learning as *"If I was ever unclear on an item I can easily go back a few slides and take a glance at it..."* and *"because I had my personal screen I looked at things for as long as I wanted".* This learner-centered environment resulted in student perception of enhanced engagement as *"it grabs my attention",* *"kept us using and paying attention all along. It made math fun"* and *"I pay attention to class more because of how the lessons are displayed".* One student wrote: *"IT MAKES US CONCENTRATE IN ALL ACTIVITIES!"*

Performance increased measurably and comments such as: *"...I was able to get my individual need met",* *"made my self-esteem go high"* and *"participating in class made my mark go up"* indicated this active learning environment encouraged critical thinking skills and improved comprehension. Comments like *"Its makes everyone understand ...and learn from each other"* illustrated the benefits of a personal learning community and its positive impact on confidence. Using the software, the ability to receive immediate feedback helped to build student understanding by having their work regularly reviewed: *"I liked that we can submit work to the instructor to check"* and that it *"helped to include everyone ... instead of a few people doing some examples in front of the class"*. Hesitant students had the opportunity to become contributing members of the class community as they: *"can answer questions without anyone finding out"*, *"it was easy to participate when no one knew who yu were..."*, *"...No one is judging"*, *"...many times students are shy askin or showin their work...using this technology minimises such stress..."*, *"It allows me to participate without being embarrassed giving the wrong answer."*

Finally, comments revealed why student success rate may be higher: *"you dont have to study as much since youre participating so much in class"*, *"made me get higher grade..."* and *"...Dykow make my mind clear what I need to do..."*. This collaborative practice made class time more interesting: *"class is more fun than the traditional math class room, math is usually very boring, students interact more often, there is more teamwork and student involvement in the lesson"*. Of note, several students observed this was active learning, as the technology: *"helped to learn better because we had to do it while we learn"*, *"made it more hands on"*, and *"It enabled me to have a wealth of information at my fingertips..."*. Many students made reference to the fact that *"you can see the lecture close up"* as it was *"right in front of me"*. This comment had not been seen previously in the pilot study, indicating students felt they learned better if the lecture was within their personal space.

Some negative student comments related to poor connectivity issues: *"The constant problems we encountered throughout the semester with connection, saving and other issues dampened the experience"*. At issue was the requirement for 40 simultaneous wireless log-ins maintained for approximately 2 hours at a time. This issue has been addressed as the wireless infrastructure was updated earlier this year at our college. Some mentioned the need to block social media sites *"...because it is a distraction to individual learning"*. Interesting to note that students wanted it blocked from themselves, because *"...the internet is addictive"*. Personally, I do not believe this to be a solution. We prepare students for careers and they will need to learn how to control their personal use of the internet. A final comment: *"I was skeptical about DyKnow at first, I hated[it] to be honest. Over time i learned that it is a great tool to use in the classroom environment. I still refuse to save my notes as i prefer to take down all notes by hand."* Some students enjoyed the interactive workspace, yet still preferred to have their pencil and paper notes.

With this leading technology experience, students are exposed to a learning/teaching environment that encourages the development of the mathematical skills necessary to be successful. Classroom observation demonstrates students are actively involved in problem solving using pens on tablet screen. Due to the anonymity the medium provides, students take risks, engage in discussion with peers, and feel encouraged to participate. As the class works together to take up student solutions, disagreements in process or answer result in lively conversation and sometimes a face-off of differing opinion to find the correct result. Note taking is a collaboration of teacher-provided framework, individual student solution and annotation, and class collaboration to determine correct explanations.

33.4 Future Work

Data analysis from this study continues. This instructional methodology is being tested in other areas of the college, including other subject disciplines. Teaching in some sections of FTM is evolving into hybrid (mixed) mode delivery, based on feedback and lessons learned from this project. Further explorations using pen-based computing include the development of a screencasting library with videos produced by students and teachers. Through multiple external presentations of this work, Seneca is taking the lead to establish a collaborative group between our college and several others in southern Ontario to explore pen and touch technologies.

33.5 Additional Resources

WIPTE contest video http://www.youtube.com/watch?v=il-k65CFqpE
DyKnow contest video http://www.youtube.com/watch?v=Hd7BsEF1x6g

Acknowledgements This work is supported by the Faculty of Applied Science and Engineering Technology, Information Technology Services (ITS), and a grant from the Centre for Academic Excellence at Seneca College.

References

1. Carruthers, C. (2010). Engagement and retention of marginalized college students using Hewlett-Packard PCs and DyKnow software. In R. H. Reed & D. A. Berque (Eds.), *The impact of tablet PCs and pen-based technology on education—going mainstream* (pp. 11–19). West Lafayette: Purdue University Press.
2. Orpwood, G., Schollen, L., Assiri, H., & Marinelli-Henriques, P. (2010). College mathematics project final report 2010. http://collegemathproject.senecac.on.ca. Accessed: 20 Oct 2014.

Chapter 34
Using Biomedical Applications in Touch and Ink Mobile Apps to Engage and Retain Stem Students in Calculus

Roy Pargas, Marilyn Reba, Ellen Breazel, Taufiquar Khan, Irina Viktorova, and John Desjardins

Abstract With support from three Hewlett-Packard Awards and a 4-year NSF-CCLI Grant, the Department of Mathematical Sciences at Clemson partnered with Computer Science to develop and implement pen technology in Engineering Calculus I. Our goals from 2006 to 2011 included personalizing instruction in large active-learning classrooms, reducing the DFW rate through in-class active learning and the analysis of errors in inked submissions. Our current focus, via a 2011NSF-TUES grant, is to motivate interest in calculus by immersing students in bioengineering and biomedical applications, and then converting ideas from these experiences, again with the help of Computer Science, into interactive touch and ink "mobile apps" for both Apple iPad and Android tablets. Beginning in Fall 2011 and continuing into 2013, students with STEM majors can enroll in four (1 credit hour) creative inquiry modules on epidemiology, orthopedics, heat propagation in the human body, or radiology. These modules are taken in parallel with the freshman and sophomore calculus curriculum. Students create presentations on the content in these modules, which include a pedagogical component. We ask them how best to convey the information within a touch and ink environment, so as to engage and clearly convey the connection with calculus. We will present brief descriptions of each module's content, student responses and performance, and how we are developing ink and touch mobile apps with the help of students both in mathematics and computer science.

R. Pargas (✉)
School of Computer Science, Clemson University, Clemson, SC, USA
e-mail: teech@clemson.edu

M. Reba · E. Breazel · T. Khan · I. Viktorova
Department of Mathematical Sciences, Clemson University, Clemson, SC, USA
e-mail: mreba@clemson.edu

J. Desjardins
Bioengineering Department, Clemson University, Clemson, SC, USA

© Springer International Publishing Switzerland 2015
T. Hammond et al. (eds.), *The Impact of Pen and Touch Technology on Education*,
Human-Computer Interaction Series, DOI 10.1007/978-3-319-15594-4_34

34.1   Problem Statement and Context

The NSF has argued that to build a competitive international workforce in STEM fields, colleges and universities must inspire a greater number of students to learn a greater amount of mathematics and statistics [1]. Much research has focused on the importance of success in the first college math course and its correlation with success in engineering, and other STEM fields [2]. Calculus is particularly noted to be a stumbling block [3]. Many incoming freshmen declare a STEM major, but know little about their declared field and know less about the applications of Calculus to any STEM field. Students are insufficiently motivated to work consistently in their Calculus courses in pursuit of vague goals and, consequently, they fail and move out of the School of Science and Engineering. Too often this STEM-attrition scenario disproportionally involves women, under-served minorities, first-generation college students, and community college transfer students [4]. These students may be less knowledgeable about their career options and less prepared for the rigors and pace of college mathematics. The challenge is to catch the attention of these STEM students early and offer applied learning experiences that engage them with the application of mathematics and statistics in professional practice and applied learning applications.

34.2   Method Employed

We have initiated, via an 2011 NSF-TUES grant, an undergraduate applied learning project where students are impacted by the interplay of mathematical and biomedical concepts in the context of interesting applications that may help them formulate career goals while deepening their understanding of mathematics. One benefit of using medical applications is their appeal to a broad range of students. And it is also true that biomedical science and bioengineering, as well as other medical majors, are among the most popular fields for college graduates today.

34.2.1   The Modules

We offer four (1 credit hour) creative inquiry modules and students have the opportunity to enroll in one module per semester (up to four semesters) that is coordinated with their current or previous math course (whether pre-calculus, first semester calculus (calculus of one variable), second semester calculus (calculus of one variable II), or third semester calculus (calculus of several variables):

Module 1 Orthopedics
Module 2 Disease Epidemiology
Module 3 Health Hazards from Arc-flash
Module 4 Mammography and Radiology

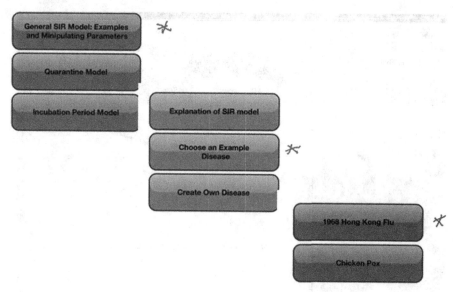

Fig. 34.1 Epidemiology menus

Students create presentations on the content in these modules, which may represent research or an innovative pedagogical approach. In some modules, students are asked to investigate how best to convey the module information within a touch and ink environment, in order to engage users while clearly conveying the calculus connection.

34.2.2 Interactive Mobile Apps

To disseminate the materials and ideas developed in each of these modules, we are developing "mobile apps" for both Apple iPad and Android tablets that use touch and ink. Instructors of the modules from Mathematics and Bioengineering work weekly with Computer Science faculty and computer science students.

Below are some images from the Module 2 App on Epidemiology. Touch enables menu selection (Fig. 34.1), graphing sliders (Fig. 34.2), image movement (Fig. 34.3). Ink will allow the student to try to draw graphs that match specific parameters (Fig. 34.2) and these graphs will be evaluated and replaced with the accurate one if necessary.

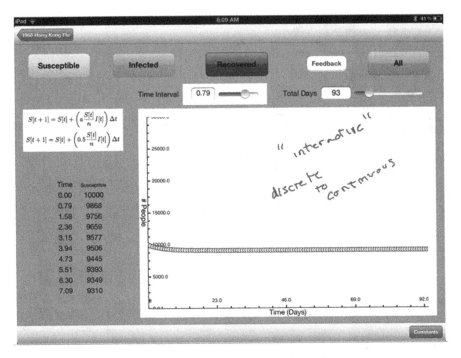

Fig. 34.2 Graphing: Discrete to continuous

34.2.3 Creative Inquiry Course

At Clemson University, certain courses are distinguished as "Creative Inquiry" (CI) courses. These differ from regular courses in that in CI courses students typically work on projects that impact teaching and learning, university life, the environment, cultural activities, international relations, or society in general. The development of this app is the result of such a CI course.

In this course, computer science students who have successfully completed the data structures course work on development of apps. We focus on the iOS platform in fall semesters and on the Android platform in spring semesters.

The structure of the course is identical in both semesters. The first half is spent developing the students' app development skills (Objective-C, the iOS SDK and Xcode in the fall semester; Java, the Android SDK, and Eclipse in the spring semester). Students work on four assignments of increasing difficulty, culminating with an app that works with an internal database using SQLite and an eternal database using MySQL. The apps access the external database using web service scripts written in PHP.

In the second half of the semester, the students work on individual projects many of which are taken from ideas proposed by faculty and staff at the university. In this manner, a small but growing cadre of Clemson students with app development skills become available for continuing the applications started in the class. Or as in the case

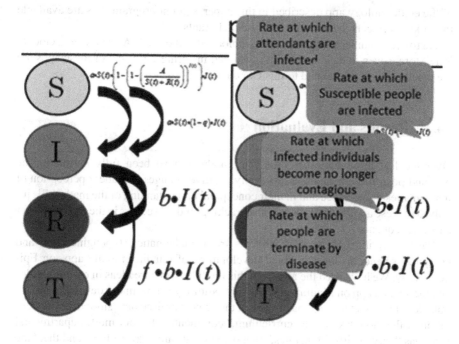

Fig. 34.3 Model explanation

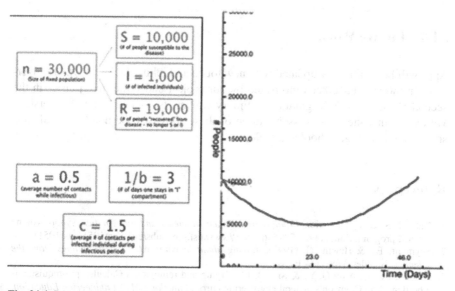

Fig. 34.4 Parameters and graph

of the epidemiology app described in this paper, student programmers are available to work on projects that emerge from funded grants.

A growing number of apps have been uploaded to the Apple App Store and Google Play Store, seven to date, and more scheduled in spring 2015. All of these apps are the result of activities related to this CI course.

34.3 Results and Evaluation

Over the last three semesters, the four modules have been fully enrolled. The pre- and post- module assessments verify positive changes in student perception of mathematics' importance and in their conceptual understanding of the math skills involved in these applications. We are also tracking student success in the four-semester calculus sequence.

We will continue to involve students from mathematics, bioengineering, and computer science in the continued development of our first mobile app, on Epidemiology. We have used the app from this module to inspire ideas in other modules and the second app on Mammography and Radiology is now under development. An outside evaluator in his external review of the project praised our "smooth implementation of the modules into the curriculum," commented that our multi-departmental team has "very positive dynamics," that the students are "having fun," and that "the hands-on activities used in the modules should be widely distributed via the apps."

34.4 Future Work

Apps will be continually updated with new touch and inking features. Other universities in the area have been motivated by our project and some may join us in the second phase of the NSF grant (e.g., Emory University; Georgia State University). We expect that the wider dissemination of these Apps will be helpful to calculus students in both high school and college.

References

1. National Science Foundation. *Proactive recruitment in science and mathematics*. Synopsis of the PRISM program. Solicitation, 09–596. http://www.nsf.gov/pubs/2010/nsf10511/nsf10511.htm
2. Seymour, E., & Hewitt, N. (1997). *Talking about leaving: Why undergraduates leave the sciences*. Boulder: Westview Press.
3. Ohland, M. W., Amy G. Y., & Sill, B. Identifying and removing a Calculus pre-requisite as a bottleneck in Clemson's general engineering curriculum. *Journal of Engineering Education, 93*(3). http://onlinelibrary.wiley.com/doi/10.1002/j.2168-9830.2004.tb00812.x/abstract
4. Schwartz, M., Hazari, Z., & Sadler, P. (2008). Divergent voices: Views from teachers and professors on pre-college factors that influence college science success. *Science Educator, 17*(10), 18–35.

Part VII
Technologies in Practice—Administrator Perspectives

Chapter 35
The Impact of Tablets on School Leadership

Jan P. Hammond

Abstract Over the last decade, accountability demands on school leaders have increased ten-fold. National common core curricula, new state exams for licensing teachers and school leaders, and new assessments for public school students have been driven by public outcries demanding change at the state and national levels, responding to dismal scores of United States students when compared to their global counterparts. As school leaders look for more efficient and more effective ways to collect and record pertinent data that aligns new standards and assessments with new software offerings designed for schools, the latest advances in hardware, such as tablets and smartphones help them meet these challenges. New teacher appraisal systems and student assessments need software to assimilate the vast amounts of data collected in order to operate and evaluate the school environment. This paper studies the daily routine of a high school principal who incorporates a BYOD (Bring Your Own Device) policy and fosters students and staff to use tablets to advance the learning process. A review of governmental laws and regulations that impact this topic ignites further discussion of the hardware and software needed for those who are leading our schools during the next 5 years.

35.1 Overview of the Past Decade and Use of Tablets

Since 2000, educational reform in America has been driven by public outcries demanding change at the state and national levels, responding to dismal scores of United States students when compared to their global counterparts [2]. In a 2007 poll, over 80 % of American voters believed that our students needed to be prepared with the skills needed to succeed in the twenty-first century [4]. Much was written in the education literature on how school leaders could help students succeed through

J. P. Hammond (✉)
Department of Educational Administration,
State University of New York at New Paltz, NY, USA
e-mail: Jan.Hammond@liu.edu

Department of Educational Leadership and Administration,
Long Island University, LIU Post, Brookville, NY, USA

© Springer International Publishing Switzerland 2015
T. Hammond et al. (eds.), *The Impact of Pen and Touch Technology on Education*,
Human-Computer Interaction Series, DOI 10.1007/978-3-319-15594-4_35

the use of technological systems [1]. With a national paradigm shift from paper and pencil to tablets, laptops, and smartphones, it would seem that K-12 educational school leaders would be the first to embrace such innovations.

However, from first-hand experience and observation of over 200 schools while in session, I can tell you that it is not the case. During the first decade in the twenty-first century, most school leaders were reticent to fully embrace the capabilities of technology within the school day. Though many educators and students used technology mainly for their own social needs, such as emails, social media websites, and instant messaging [6], concerns over security as well as their lack of adeptness at using newly developed programs that could easily facilitate their daily routines diminish the desire to incorporate technology.

Despite the passage in most states of the International Society for Technology in Education (ISTE) standards (2001, 2009A) for school leaders (iste.org/standards/standards-for-administrators) which calls for educational administrators to "create, promote and sustain a dynamic, digital age learning culture..." and to "model and promote the effective digital use" in their school life, many school leaders today still grab their yellow pads when observing a teacher, use the loud speaker to call out the daily announcements, and have a secretary write up the formal end of the year teacher evaluation reports.

35.2 National Education Technology Plan

In 2010, the Obama administration's Department of Education led a national study to determine what was needed for our students to have the knowledge and skills needed to compete in the worldwide job market [7]. After meeting with state governors, superintendents of schools, school administrators, and teachers, Secretary Arne Duncan and his administration through the Office Of Educational Technology published *Expanding Evidence Approaches for Learning in a Digital World* (2012) and later and wrote the framework for a National Education Technology Plan (2013).

In the plan, a digital school is one that (a) is engaging and has rigorous programs; (b) uses technology in assessing students and schools to give teachers real time data at the time that they need it, rather than at the end school year; (c) connects teachers and school leaders with peers and experts; (d) builds an infrastructure that can quickly accommodate the demands of advanced technology; and (e) harnesses technology to improve student learning, modeling the "transformative potential" of how schools could reposition themselves to maximize the capacity of technology in a school day. And how is that goal to be accomplished by all schools within the next 5 years? A recent report released in February 2014 [3] from the Government Accountability Office (GAO) which awarded $ 937 million in i3 grants during 2010 through 2012 states that half of the i3 projects (92 in all) use teacher and principal professional development as a key strategy to achieve the goals (http://www.gao.gov/assets/670/660743.pdf).

35.3   A Review of School Leaders' Fears of Embracing Technology

Too Many Changes in Too Short of a Time   Since the turn of the twenty-first century, school leaders have been forced to accept rapid changes affecting academic and technical curricula as well as ways to assess student achievement and teacher performance. States have adopted new state standards, new state assessments, Common Core curricula, and implemented new regulations based on state applications of competitive federal grants such Race to the Top (RTTT) that demand improved data and appraisal systems.

Explosion of Technological Changes   Schools lag behind the technology that students have in their home or backpacks. Many school leaders are scratching their head as to what to do, what policies to adopt, and what hardware and software to purchase.

35.3.1   Fear of Technology Itself from a School Leader's Viewpoint

Students   According to recent data [5], 92 % of the students use tablets or smartphones. Students come to school with tablets, laptops, and smartphones; many bring their devices to school even if the school has a ban on them. School leaders are not in agreement as to what students are allowed to bring in and use during school times. Legal aspects of having technology devices include issues such as cyberbullying, cheating on exams, plagiarizing, noise levels, and who is responsible for loss, breakage, and theft.

Teachers   Teachers come into schools with tablets, laptops, and smartphones. School leaders are not in agreement as to what teachers are allowed to bring in and use during school times. Overseeing that the teacher (a) doesn't view unwanted sites during school, (b) follows the designated curriculum, and (c) focuses on students' needs, rather than reviewing QVC or amazon.com shopping screens takes time from the principal's normal routine.

Parents   Parents come in to schools with tablets, laptops, and smartphones. Parents want to have access to their children 24/7 after tragedies such as Columbine, 9/11, and Newtown's Sandy Hook school. They want their kids to text and tweet them throughout the day. They also have access to legal information such as laws, rules, and regulations, and are quick to inform school leaders if the administrator or teacher infringed on parents' or children's rights. As expected, school leaders are not in agreement as to what devices parents should have in schools.

School Leaders   School leaders themselves are unclear as to what devices they should use in school and where. Some principals are reticent to use devices because if students are not allowed to use tablets in school, should principals model such behavior? They are unclear as to what hardware and software they should invest in, and if they should shift budgetary funds from the constantly used copy machine and the incessant reams of paper to state-of-the-art hardware that could be obsolete in 2 years.

Unions   Union issues are also a concern for school leaders. Are principals allowed to use a tablet in the classroom while observing a teacher? Are they allowed to record the session and take pictures to capture the teaching lesson? Where is the information stored? Is it safe? Who has access to the storage? All these questions and more hamper the ability of principals to use technology within their day-to-day routines.

35.4   Embracing Digital Leadership: One School's Perspective

So, I set out to find a school where school leaders used tablets, smartphones, and pen/touch, similar to Arne Duncan's model. I found one in New Milford, New Jersey. The principal of the high school is Eric Sheninger, author of *Digital Leadership* (2013). How he set out to conquer the fears is a great story to help school leaders transition to using tablets and new technologies. I found Eric very willing to share his experiences during our conversations, by even answering the more challenging questions.

35.4.1   Breaking Through the Fear: BYOD (Bring Your Own Device)

The Beginning   Eric has a BYOD school (personal interview, 2014), which he feels better prepares students for "the real world" where tablets and other devices are essential tools in most professions. First, Eric had to convince his superintendent and school board that having a BYOD culture would improve student achievement. What does a BYOD school look like? Schools that open their schools to accepting BYOD technology often find that they may be the only school in the district that promotes such a culture. So Eric had to state that what he is promoting is just for his school and that there was no need to make it a district-wide policy, allaying the fears of other principals.

Second, students, teachers, administrators, and parents can bring whatever devices they wish to school, as long as the device aligns with the guidelines of the school. That means Eric and his collegial team of teachers, parents, and administrators had to make sure that appropriate guidelines were in place (and added to the list later, when needed). Common policies included no distraction to instruction, no noise to others (use of earphones), no taboo sites, and no use of technology for bullying or harassing others.

Tablets are the technology of preference because of their capabilities, flexibility, and lightness. Students download most all their books and "carry" their many textbooks around with them on their tablets. When I asked Eric how he first knew that it was the right decision to implement a BYOD policy, Principal Eric smiled, "When I saw the effect on the lunchroom. Lunchtime is so much quieter now! No food fights and no bored kids!"

35.4.2 The New Paradigm for School Leaders: A Day in the Life of Principal Eric

Principal Eric's Morning   Eric shares with me (and also writes similar thoughts in his book) that he arrives about 6:30 a.m. at school and greets his assistant principals. He boots up his computer and writes the staff an email message of the day using his Twitter stream and also on his TweetDeck. He browses though tweets from members of Personal Learning Network (PLN) (http://edupln.ning.com) to look for resources to include in faculty email. He finds lists of web-based tools for his staff to integrate in their lessons. He finishes the email and then sends it off. Next, he updates the morning announcements for students on a Google Docs page that they can access on the school website. Once finished, he posts the link on the school's Twitter and Facebook pages and sends it to the official school app that New Milford High School (NMHS) students developed.

By 8:00 a.m., Eric says that he is armed with his smartphone in his pocket and tablet in his hand and heads out of his office to greet students (with much lighter book bags than before BYOD) and staff and meets with parents either in person or through technology. Using his tablet, he begins walking the halls and conducting his morning walk-throughs of classrooms. He observes teachers using the evaluation tools on his tablet, beams observation details to his cloud, and then talks with staff members about their needs. You can easily find him standing in a hallway, chatting with kids while he shares some of the students' work and accomplishments using social media, such as on Twitter, Instagram, and Facebook. Eric shares with me, "Students no longer find administrators confined to offices; we are working toward being entirely paperless."

Principal Eric's Mid-morning   Continuing on his daily routine, Eric captures innovative lessons and projects of the teachers. He shares with me that he sees a teacher using Poll Everywhere (http://www.polleverywhere.com), having students text in their answers to a "do now" question. Students use their own mobile devices to participate. In art class, he observes students using tablets to make a cartoon movie. Later, he heads back to his office to attend to the usual duties that consume school leaders He sees the digital journalism students just posted on The Lance (http://www.theLance.net).

Lunchtime Isn't What It Used to be   Perhaps, says Eric, the most remarkable site is the lunchroom. Students are working on their tablets and phones to get a head start on their homework or are using the social media to converse with one another. Eric reports that he and the other administrators sometimes release teachers from lunch duty so that they can work on their technology skills or other professional development, to incorporate all the changes, thereby, increasing their risk-taking and reducing their fear of failure.

Students may see him standing up along the wall, completing an observation or two, as WiFi is throughout the school. This important infrastructure, according to Eric, means he can work anywhere in the building. "Students chuckle when they see me on my tablet," laughs Eric.

Principal Eric's Afternoon This digital leader ends his day by planning ways that he can strengthen the alignment of the Common Core curriculum. He also shapes out ways to increase his parents' participation and their use of technological skills so they can understand the power of their devices. He invites parents (a) to be part of the strategic planning process, (b) to attend after school workshops, and (c) to be a partner in the BYOB concept by frequently sending them information.

Where He Is Today Eric says that, while he has been working feverishly over the last few years to get the community and the media to support his thinking and philosophy, he still finds that there are still only a handful of schools in New Jersey that support a BYOD strategy. All in all, he reports to me, the students seem much happier, feel empowered, and feel more respected. They feel that it is a privilege to be able to bring their technology to school. Disciplinary issues have diminished significantly. For the most part, union issues have not surfaced because the teachers like the new policies. Now a sought-after national speaker, Eric works to balance his week with the myriad of phone calls from other educators to support them in their transitions to tablets and other devices as well as calls from software and hardware companies who want to better understand the needs of BYOD schools.

35.5 Tablets and Teacher Evaluations

One of the most time consuming parts of a school leader's day is the observation of teachers and collecting appropriate evidence to develop the end of the year evaluations. Federal and state programs such as Race to the Top funded by the American Recovery and Reinvestment Act (2009) have made states comply to the National Common Core standards and curricula and a more rigorous teacher appraisal system that uses student assessment data on state and national exams, student report cards, as well as teacher made exams.

The tablet is the perfect tool to assist this process, according to Richard Voltz (personal interview, 2014), retired superintendent and Executive Director of Illinois Superintendents' Association. Illinois is working to be one of the first states in the U.S. to fully operationalize its school data to improve school performance by having administrators be able to access vast amounts of information with just a tablet in hand.

Software companies are small in number at this time that are helping to align the appraisal system with district data systems, according to Hal Shroats, from Customized Relational Tek (CRT) whom I interviewed a few times (2014). In fact, one company went out of business during the time I was collecting data for this report. These companies focus on having their information run on PCs and Apple computers, assimilating school and district data. Users can also access the database from the local area network by the Internet from a remote location with the ease of a tablet. Those administrators who are using tablets to record information while in the classroom find it less obtrusive to be able to have programs that they can use a keyboard or just use their fingernail if they are drawing out the arrangement of the room. Though it is still in its infancy, the systems available today have made it so much easier to save photos, videos, recordings, and text to each teacher's data.

35.6 Conclusion

As school leaders look for more efficient and more effective ways to collect and record pertinent data that align new standards and assessments with new software offerings designed for schools, tablet usage will continue to assist in the process. Advances in hardware will allow educators to meet accountability demands. Tablets are also positioned to be the device of choice for schools that embrace BYOD policies, in that textbooks can be stored on them with an easy to read screen display.

K-12 teachers and school leaders are slowly adapting to the 24/7 world of the Internet. With tablets and smartphones easily accessible, educators are learning to mass customize students' needs by using assessment data to identify each student's needs. This may lead the way to virtual high schools within or outside of brick and mortar schools, measuring competency rather than seat time. The use of tablets with 24/7 Internet access supporting individualized learning may be just what it takes to have our students rise to the top of the TIMMS report once again and to succeed in college and future careers.

References

1. Fullan, M. (2008). *The six secrets of change.* San Francisco: Jossey-Bass.
2. Martin, M. O., & Mullis, I. V. S. (Eds.). (2012). *Methods and procedures in TIMSS and PIRLS 2011.* Chestnut Hill: TIMSS & PIRLS International Study Center, College.
3. Mueller, P. A., & Oppenheimer, D. M. (2014). The pen is mightier than the keyboard: Advantages of longhand over laptop note taking. *Psychological Science, 25*(6), 1159–1168.
4. Partnership for twenty-first Century Skills. (2007). *Beyond the three Rs: Voter attitudes toward twenty-first century skills.* http://www.p21.org/storage/documents/p21_pollreport_2pg.pdf. Accessed 15 March 2015.
5. Pew Research. (2013). http://www.pewinternet.org/search/tablet/. Accessed 7 March 2014.
6. Suki, N. M. (2013). Students' dependence on smartphones: The influence of social needs, social influences and convenience. *Campus-wide Information Systems, 30*(2), 124–134
7. U.S. Department of Education. (2012). Evidence framework: Expanding evidence approaches for learning in a digital world. http://www.ed.gov/. Accessed 22 March 2013.

Chapter 36
Facilitating Pedagogical Practices Through a Large-Scale Tablet PC Deployment

Joseph G. Tront

Abstract Educational technology has been shown to be an effective mechanism to foster improvements in pedagogical practices in the learning environment. In the fall of 2006, the Virginia Tech College of Engineering became the first and largest public college of engineering to require all 1400 incoming students to own a Tablet PC. The purpose of this requirement program is to better facilitate the pedagogical practice including but not limited to the following mechanisms known to improve learning: highly interactive classroom presentations, student-student and instructor-student collaboration, comprehensive note-taking and review, and a movement of the learning emphasis to more process-oriented lectures and away from simple information broadcasting.

A large deployment effort like the one described here is multi-faceted and requires the enthusiasm and support of a broad number of stakeholders. Decisions on hardware and software choices require input from across the university. Training of faculty and support personnel is central to the success of the initiative. Improvements to infrastructure including network connectivity, additional classroom projection systems and increased availability of power connections are some of the physical plant challenges that require attention. Sound and frequent assessment of the successes and failures of the program, and identification of potentially fruitful avenues to pursue in the future, has been part of the overriding deployment strategy from the beginning. In addition to these infrastructure challenges, the success of this type of program is also dependent on the willingness of the faculty to make changes in the way in which they teach. In this paper we describe our approach to identifying the needs and setting up the infrastructure, and provide information on successes and failures we have had during the first five years of the deployment process. We will also describe the challenges we anticipate as we look to the future of education.

J. G. Tront (✉)
Bradley Department of Electrical & Computer Engineering,
Virginia Polytechnic Institute and State University, Blacksburg, VA, USA
e-mail: jgtront@exchange.vt.edu

© Springer International Publishing Switzerland 2015
T. Hammond et al. (eds.), *The Impact of Pen and Touch Technology on Education*,
Human-Computer Interaction Series, DOI 10.1007/978-3-319-15594-4_36

36.1 Introduction

Undoubtedly, when Socrates met with Plato for their many conversations, they discussed ways to improve student learning. Although they didn't have to ponder the effectiveness of the use of modern computing and communications technology, they must definitely have discussed ways to actively involve students in the learning process. Outstanding teachers of today still rely on Socrates' techniques of drawing the student into the learning process and many of them are turning to technology to help facilitate these active and collaborative exercises. Mobile computing and communication devices like the Tablet PC, along with high bandwidth communication infrastructures, are allowing students and teachers to increase the quantity and quality of teaching/learning interactivity with the expectation of an increase in student learning.

In the fall of 2006, the Virginia Tech College of Engineering became the first and largest public college of engineering to require all 1400 incoming students to own a Tablet PC. The purpose of this requirement program is to better facilitate *pedagogical practices* that are expected to improve learning, but were not readily accomplished in the previous environment. Practices that are projected to be improved include highly interactive classroom presentations, student-student and instructor-student collaboration, comprehensive note-taking and review, and a movement of the learning emphasis to more process-oriented lectures and away from simple information broadcasting.

A large deployment effort like the one described here is multi-faceted and requires the enthusiasm and support of a broad number of stakeholders. Decisions on hardware and software choices require input from across the university. Training of faculty and support personnel is central to the success of the initiative. Improvements to infrastructure including network connectivity, additional classroom projection systems and increased availability of power connections are some of the physical plant challenges that require attention. Sound and frequent assessment of the successes and failures of the program, and identification of potentially fruitful avenues to pursue in the future, has been part of the overriding deployment strategy from the beginning. In this paper we will expound on our approach to each of these task areas, describe how our plan took shape, and provide information on successes and failures we have had during the first year of the deployment process.

36.1.1 Background

Faculty in the College of Engineering at Virginia Tech have a long history of continuously seeking ways to improve the teaching and learning environment in order to effectively provide students with a high quality engineering education. Many teaching innovations have been initiated and implemented with support from the college administration, alumni, and from various research agencies such as the NSF. Innovations include the incorporation of freshman hands-on mechanical dissection labs, integrated subject material courses, and multi-disciplinary projects to name a few. Most notable among the teaching/learning innovations are the College's efforts in the effective use of computing and communication technology in the curriculum.

In 1984, the Virginia Tech College of Engineering was the first public institution to require all entering engineering freshmen to own a personal computer. In the early 90's Virginia Tech participated in the NSF-sponsored engineering education coalition called SUCCEED and assumed the lead role in the association's effort to perform scientific research on the effects of the use of technology on engineering education. By 1996 the computer requirement had been scaled up to the so-called multimedia computer which, at the time, incorporated advanced features including a CD ROM reader, a high resolution graphics system and a sound card—all features we take for granted in today's computers [1]. In 2002, the College moved to a laptop requirement and many of its academic buildings were outfitted with a wireless communication system that allows students to connect to the high-speed Internet from any location on campus. Laptop technology was selected so that students could perform computing and communication operations in a totally mobile environment. Today's ubiquitous use of computers in students' everyday learning practices and lifestyles is the anecdotal evidence that these technology requirement programs have been fruitful. The College once again steps out on the technology forefront by requiring all students to own computationally powerful and well-connected Tablet PCs. In addition, we are making a stronger effort to assess specific effectiveness measures. The goal in the assessment efforts will be to understand if and how important pedagogical and learning practices are improved, and to identify general learning improvements that are improved as a result of these practices.

In 2002, we began pilot projects to explore the use of Tablet PCs in the engineering education environment by seeking ways to take advantage of the electronic ink (e-ink) capabilities of the device. Much like the standard blackboard or whiteboard, this new capability allowed the instructor to make dynamic and adaptive presentations that could be much more responsive to student interaction than a simple PowerPoint presentation. However, PowerPoint presentations do have an important advantage over blackboards in that they are easily organized and are also capable of containing images that help bring real-world situations to the classroom. PowerPoint also allows for broad distribution of classroom notes, which, for engineers and scientists, can contain rather complex drawings that would be near impossible to copy down during a lecture. While searching for Tablet PC presentation tools, we found that free software like Classroom Presenter [2] combines the advantageous capabilities of PowerPoint with the flexibility and spontaneity of traditional blackboard lectures. Using Classroom Presenter, an instructor may prepare drawings and graphics in ready-made form and then annotate important discussion points on these electronic slides during the lecture. Schematic drawings of problems are normally left purposely partially incomplete and are finished during the presentation. This causes students to pay better attention during class rather than having the student occasionally glance up from their stupor as chock full PowerPoint slides glide wistfully by on the screen. Typical student "what-if" questions may be better elicited and answered using the new paradigm that essentially combines PowerPoint and a blackboard. Most importantly, the student may take home a composite of the pre-drawn PowerPoint and the in-class annotations for later review and study. Initial use of this tool produced very positive responses in polls of students taken after Tablet-based classroom presentations. Lecture attendance increased as students found them much more interesting than in the past. Given the early success of using Tablet PCs in simple presentation mode, we began to identify other places where this technology could help to better facilitate pedagogical practices that are known to improve learning.

36.1.2 Targeted Pedagogical Improvements

One of the most important practices known to improve learning is to actively engage the student in the learning process. Classroom activities in which students participate in an active discussion or problem solving session with the instructor and with their peers have been shown to improve learning. In [3, 4], Felder and Prince state "The core elements of active learning are student activity and engagement in the learning process. Active learning is often contrasted to the traditional lecture where students passively receive information from the instructor." Over 6000 students in introductory physics courses were examined using pre and post test data by Hake and in [5] and significantly improved performance was reported for students in classes with substantial use of interactive-engagement methods. The rich communications and multimodal input capabilities of the Tablet PC are believed to provide a facility for classroom interactions which when aptly used can increase the potential for an improved learning interaction.

Collaborative learning consists of one or more students working together to solve a problem or understand a concept as opposed to individual work on a topic [6]. Studies have shown that collaboration improved several desirable key learning outcomes including academic achievement, interpersonal interactivity, self-esteem and retention in academic programs [7–9]. Tablet PCs have the potential for facilitating intense collaborative activities using the built-in capabilities of some of the software either currently available or under development. The differentiating characteristic between notebook and tablet technology is the ability for the user to more naturally jot down ideas and sketch drawings that can be communicated with other collaborators on shared "electronic surfaces". Meaningful tablet-based collaborations have been demonstrated both locally as well as at Internet distances.

Comprehensive, organized, and easy to review note-taking is a skill typically described as an effective learning behavior. When students master effective learning behaviors such as effective note-taking, a demonstratively positive learning outcome is produced with a general increase in subject cognition [10–13]. In [14], Kobayashi researched the impact of note-taking and reviewing on student learning. This work concluded that learning outcomes are substantially positively affected when note-taking is properly performed and that assisting students in improving their note-taking can produce additional positive benefits. It is in this regard that Tablet PCs can improve student learning by increasing the natural manner in which notes are taken, and improving the ability to review notes either through ease of search, or via increased organizational capabilities supported by the Tablet PC.

Achieving the expected outcome of enhanced student learning is based on improving the three key pedagogical practices mentioned above: increased active learning, incorporation of collaborative exercises into the learning process, and improved note-collection and note searching/review. The Tablet PC requirement program is structured to support the improvement of these key practices. In order to do so, the hardware and software selected for student and faculty use must be sufficiently capable, faculty must be trained on the use of the technology as well as on appropriate pedagogical practices, students must be given a baseline understanding of the technology and its expected use, and sufficient infrastructure and support personnel must be in available. The overriding umbrella to all of this effort must be an assessment operation that formatively measures the success of the program and points out the most likely avenues for success as the initiative progresses.

36.2 Computer Specification

Incoming Virginia Tech engineering students purchase their Tablet PCs on the open market based on a set of specifications that the College issues in mid April. The minimum computer specification for students entering in the Fall of 2007, as shown in Table 36.1, is a compromise between price, capability, longevity, and reliability. For example, choosing the minimum Core 2 Duo processor and the associated 2 GB of RAM means that the computers will be capable of running all of the required software at reasonable speeds while at the same time is affordable by the majority of the entering class. Including wireless access cards capable of 802.11a, b, and g formats ensures the best opportunity for non-overlapping broad band communications in the classroom and dormitory wireless infrastructure. While these minimum specifications may seem somewhat high initially, they are also chosen to ensure that the computer will be usable four years after entry when the senior student will likely be performing computational intense calculations and simulations. History has shown that about 40 % of the entering students purchase the minimum hardware package while the remaining 60 % add higher level capabilities to their systems such as an additional flat panel monitor, increased RAM, more disk drive space, or extra video RAM.

One of the less-considered choices that students need to think about is the weight of the tablet they purchase. The student is expected to bring it to class each day, so the system should not be overly cumbersome to carry around. This leads to a conflict between many students' desire to have a large display screen and the additional weight added by upsized screens. Typically, the 12" screen machines weigh about 4.5 pounds which can be considerably less burdensome than the 14" screen which sometimes weigh in at 8.5 pounds. The smaller devices are generally encouraged

Table 36.1 Minimum hardware requirement

Item	Detail
Platform	Tablet PC convertible
OS	Windows XP Pro Tablet Edition
Processor	Pentium Core 2 Duo 1.8 GHz
Memory (RAM)	2 GB
Hard disk	100 GB hard drive; 5400 RPM
Video card	128 MB
Optical drive	DVD/CD +-R writeable DVD
Input/Output	USB 2.0
Wireless	802.11 a/g
NIC/Ethernet	10/100/1000 Ethernet
Warranty	3 Years with accidental damage
External backup	USB external backup drive 160 GB

Table 36.2 Minimum engineering software requirement

Minimum software requirement
Matlab
Autodesk inventor & mechanical desktop
PDF annotator
Labview
Microsoft campus agreement including:
Office professional
OS upgrades
One note
Visual project
Visual studio
Client access licenses

not only because of their lighter weight, but also because of their form factor which lends itself to easier use on typical classroom desktops.

Students are also required to purchase the Engineering Software Bundle, which complements the hardware by providing the computing capability necessary in typical engineering learning environments. The list of software shown in Table 36.2 is similar to what a practicing engineer in industry may have access to in their design environment.

Deliberations on the choice of the hardware and software begin around the first of March and consider both the needs of the educational program as well as the expected offerings by hardware vendors. Discussions take place under the wraps of non-disclosure meetings and with careful consideration of whether or not hardware will truly be delivered in the July through August timeframe. An unfulfilled promise by a vendor can have disastrous results if a student is left without a computer to start the semester. To avoid these difficulties, the College has established working relationships with a set of reputable vendors and publishes pertinent information to support students and their families in making wise vendor-related decisions.

36.3   Classroom Presentations Transformation

To effectively use the facilities provided by the new technology, teachers have been undergoing a transformation in their teaching style and a modification of their teaching materials. Several electronic ink enabled software tools are being used. Classroom Presenter and Dyknow (formally known as Dyknow Vision) are two of the mainstay presentation tools being used to support more dynamic presentations and to increase student interactivity. Using these tools, an instructor generates lecture material by producing a set of PowerPoint base slides that are used as a framework for the lecture. The slides consist of pictures, diagrams, equations, web page clippings, or whatever other electronic materials are deemed important to support the lecture. The instructor then modifies the slides, hiding portions of diagrams or sections of equations that are to be later filled in during the classroom discussion. Hidden portions are visible on the instructor screen, but not on the public view or the student screen. The instructor then fills in the missing material dynamically in the classroom using e-ink. In this way, students are encouraged to reflect on the material throughout the lecture rather than simply listening to a verbal reiteration of what is already shown on the display or in hardcopy pre-printed notes. The power of the e-ink lies in the ability to dynamically show the process of developing a schematic or inking down the terms of an equation just as an engineer does in practice. Showing the personalized process of development is the value-added factor that the instructor brings to the classroom; for without this personalization, the students might as well just read the book and skip the lecture. Students become more engaged in the natural discussions that occur in the classroom because: (1) they now view and participated in the process of design rather than being presented with a design solution and (2) they are not overwhelmed by the perceived need to mechanically copy notes.

Integrating interactivity is a second level effect facilitated by the tools. During the lecture, the instructor poses a somewhat open-ended question and the students are asked to respond with a solution that is typically graphical in nature. Students write-up a solution on their tablets and submit it to the instructor, who may then choose submissions to anonymously display and discuss with the rest of the class. Students become particularly engaged in the class when this technique is used—they look forward to the opportunity to respond and are disappointed if their solution isn't discussed. Figure 36.1 shows an example of an annotated presentation screen in which the instructor spontaneously generates a question and requests the student to respond with individual answers that will be displayed and discussed. The key to success here is e-ink and the high-speed communication that facilitates the interactivity. Using

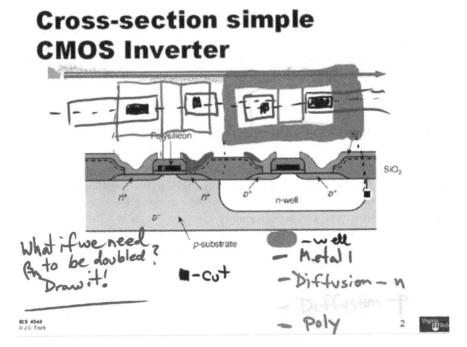

Fig. 36.1 Example presentation screen with annotations and challenge question

this technique accommodates various student personality traits, ranging from those who are outgoing and are the first to volunteer an answer in class to those who are shy and unconfident and rarely proffer a comment. Our observation thus far is a more even distribution of students paying attention in class and much more active discussion both during and after the lecture.

A further advantage to this presentation paradigm is the ability of the students to generate a local personalized electronic version of the class notes. Both Classroom Presenter and DyKnow allow the notes and instructor e-ink to be broadcast in real-time to students in the classroom. The students may then add their own e-ink and save the composite notes on their machine for later review. This is a very powerful mechanism that encourages deep thinking and enables reflections, which are keys to understanding complex concepts.

Engineering and computer science classes typically involve the use of simulators or other visualization tools that are very dynamic in nature. Instructors usually show visual aspects of the simulation in class and ask students to operate the simulator on their own outside of class, leaving students to their own devices to remember what was said or shown during the lecture. A new Tablet-based tool called WriteOn allows the instructor to make notes on top of a dynamically running program and to capture the annotations along with the simulation display as either a set of still images or as a movie of all screen activity [15]. Figure 36.2 contains a screen capture of a logic simulator in which the instructor has made notes about the behavior shown

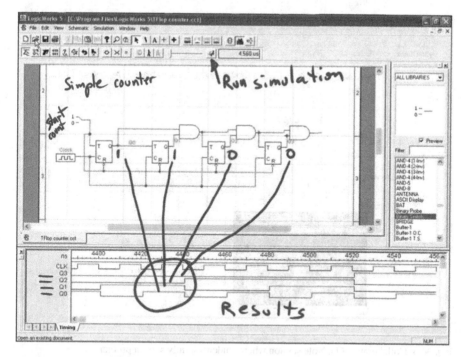

Fig. 36.2 WriteOn is used to annotate directly onto simulator output window

in the waveform generated by the simulator. WriteOn is very effective at allowing an instructor to provide value-added information to what may previously have been presented in a rather dry and difficult to remember demonstration. Several other similar tablet tools are under development or available to support classroom interaction in the Microsoft Education Pack [16].

36.4 Note-Taking & Collaboration

Microsoft OneNote is a tool that is being used for general note taking. The software provides an electronic notebook that mimics a pencil and paper paradigm but has several advanced capabilities. For example, OneNote allows the user to rapidly search over the entire notebook and locate handwritten words that relate to a concept. This is done to a very high level of correctness by the built-in handwriting recognition facility. Students are also using OneNote to record the audio portion of lectures while they take notes for the class. In post-classroom sessions, students may click on the e-ink object contained in OneNote and the audio relevant to that object is played, allowing for very specific review of classroom information.

Collaboration is a very powerful mechanism to reinforce learning and to prepare students for real-world design and development activities. OneNote has a collaboration facility built into it that allows participants to share common sections of

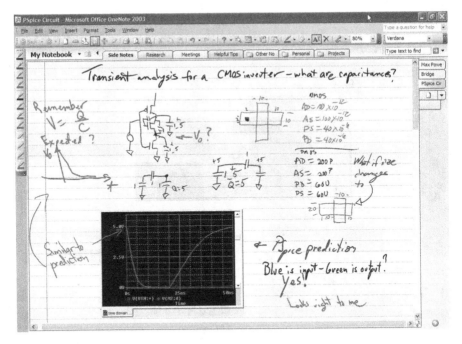

Fig. 36.3 Collaborative OneNote session where students jointly solve a problem

the electronic notebook. Typical exercises being performed involve having several students working together to solve a problem as shown in Fig. 36.3. Students join a Shared Session, and are presented with the e-ink generated by other participants. They may add their own e-ink, typed information, or any other electronic object that can be extracted from the electronic clipboard. Any object on the screen may be erased by any collaborator. Participants can be local or remote; the only restriction is that they have access to the Internet.

Initial classroom experiences in collaboration indicate that most students are willing to participate in this type interaction, but they do not have refined skills for deriving maximum benefit from the exchange of ideas. However, after exposure, the students quickly learn some of the basic requisites for effective electronic collaboration such as: personal identification, appropriate sequencing, and idea formulation.

36.5   Electronic Homework Submission

Electronic homework submission has typically been difficult for engineering students since much of what is submitted consists of not just typed text, but sketches intermingled with text along with the occasional picture. Several Tablet-based tools allow students better flexibility in producing submissions. Word, OneNote, PDF Annotator and Adobe Acrobat all allow e-ink annotations to be applied to typed documents making it much easier for students to produce electronic homework submissions. On the receiving end, electronic homework submissions are generally easier to handle and grade. For example, a faculty member receives a submission file either through email or through a classroom management system, marks it up, and returns it to the student without ever having to take up class time for paper collection or distribution. Student privacy is also more readily preserved. Several faculty members have been using this scheme for a few semesters and are very pleased with the way it has streamlined the process.

36.6   Faculty Training & Support

To take advantage of the new technology, faculty members are encouraged to participate in the Faculty Development Institute, a series of multi-day workshops where faculty are trained on pedagogical practices as well as the details of the operation of the technology. Tablet workshops are taught by early adopters who have learned first-hand of the difficulties and solutions of using the new technology. Five or six times throughout the semester, faculty study groups meet to discuss progress and exchange tips and tricks for success. Additional technical support is provided particularly at semester startup to help faculty get through in-class issues such as projector settings and network connectivity. Thus far, the faculty response has been positive with participants enthusiastically working on developing and modifying materials as they participate in workshop sessions.

36.7   Assessment—Plans and Progress

Assessing the effectiveness of the tablet requirement program is paramount in our efforts to ensure that the schema indeed produces the targeted pedagogical improvements. The assessment process is built around a core set of measures, which are gauged each semester by having students respond to three surveys. A student learning strategies instrument was adapted from the Motivated Strategies for Learning Questionnaire (MSLQ) [17]. The adapted MSLQ is used in a pre/post test design to measure changes in learning strategies using the Tablet from the beginning to the end of each semester. A subset of questions were also added from the national ECAR study to help determine how students' self report on their use of technology as compared to other Engineering students nationally. Mid-semester, a second utilization questionnaire measuring the frequency and nature of technology use is completed. Faculty response to the Tablet PC will be assessed using a survey measure administered longitudinally to a sample of engineering faculty. The survey was developed from extant teaching measures in the literature and addresses not only faculty's use of instructional technology but also their more general teaching practices and pedagogical beliefs. Responses will enable us to determine if the faculty's philosophy and practice change over time and, in particular, if they become more attuned to active learning and the need to promote student engagement and collaboration in their teaching. As the assessment program ramps up, other measures will be made to determine as directly as possible the impact of Tablet PC use on how students, organize and think about course materials, collaborate with other students and participate in class.

Data collected and analyzed so far has focused most heavily on the impact on student note-taking and whether use of Tablet PC encourages metacognitive strategies and critical thinking skills in individual studying and note-taking. Results have confirmed the value of the Tablet PC to collegiate instruction, but have also raised some technical and instructional issues related to its use. Using the MSLQ data we were able to paint a picture of the learning strategies and technology use of an incoming freshman engineering student and assess student changes after a semester in the program. In September, 2006, 61 % of freshman engineering students reported they did not have access to computers in their high school classes; by mid-semester nearly all students reported using their Tablet on a daily basis.

In the preliminary phases of data analysis we see some significant changes in student learning habits as they apply to note-taking and studying and we will continue to measure and analyze changes as students progress though their degree programs. Other results related to the details and the validity of the measurement instruments will be reported on in later as the data is collected and analyzed.

36.8 Summary

The Virginia Tech College of Engineering has begun to explore, on a large scale, the use of Tablet PCs in engineering and computer science courses. Using a multifaceted, collaborative approach we have developed an implementation process that includes computer acquisition, faculty training, infrastructure modifications, and multiple assessments for the purpose of program evaluation. Initial results of this groundbreaking program are positive showing measurable improvements in pedagogical practices that are ultimately expected to lead to learning improvements. Various aspects of the program's processes are scalable and extensible to other institutions and STEM disciplines. As we proceed down this path we imagine back to the types of Tablet PC-based dialogues Socrates and Plato could have had and how useful it would be to have searchable e-ink archives of those conversations.

Acknowledgements The author would like to acknowledge Dr. Glenda Scales, Associate Dean for Engineering Computing for her leadership in this effort and Dr. Deborah Olsen and Ms. Kimberly Filer for their work on the assessment aspects of the program. Thanks also to Microsoft Research and Fujitsu Computers who along with the VT College of Engineering have formed the Premier Alliance which supports the efforts to effectively use Tablet PCs.

References

1. Tront, J. G. (1999). *A personal computer requirement for engineering students.* ICEE '99 Conference at Technical University in Ostrava, Czech Republic; August 10–11, pp. 348–350
2. Anderson, R. UW classroom presenter, http://www.cs.washington.edu/education/dl/presenter/.
3. Prince, M., & Felder, R. (2007). The many faces of inductive teaching & learning. *Journal of College Science Teaching, 36*(5).
4. Prince, M. (2004). Does active learning work? A review of the research. *Journal of Engineering Education, 93*(3), 223–231.
5. Hake, R. (1998). Interactive-engagement vs. traditional methods: A six-thousand-student survey of mechanics test data for introductory physics courses. *American Journal of Physics, 66*(1), 64.
6. Smith, B., & MacGregor, J. (1992). What is collaborative learning? In A. Goodsell, Mahler M., Tinto V., Smith B. L., & J. MacGreger (Eds.), *Collaborative learning: A sourcebook for higher education* (pp. 9–22). National Center on Postsecondary Teaching, Learning and Assessment. PA: State College, Penn State University.
7. Johnson, D., Johnson, R., & Smith, K. (1998). *Active learning: Cooperation in the college classroom* (2nd ed.). Edina: Interaction Book Co.
8. Johnson, D., Johnson, R., & Smith, K. (1998). cooperative learning returns to college: What evidence is there that it works? *Change, 30*(4), 26–35.
9. Springer, L., Stanne, M., & Donovan, S. (1999). Effects of small- group learning on undergraduates in science, mathematics, engineering and technology: A meta-analysis. *Review of Educational Research, 69*(1), 21–52.
10. Ryan, M. P. (2001). Conceptual models of lecture learning guide metaphors and model-appropriate notetaking practices. *Reading Psychology, 22*(4), 289–312.
11. Purdie, N., & Hattie, J. (1999). The relationship between study skills and learning outcomes: A meta-analysis. *Australian Journal of Education, 43.*
12. DiFesta, F. J., & Gray, G. S. (1972). Listening and note taking. *Journal of Educational Psychology, 63*(1), 8–14.
13. Brazeau, G. A. (2006). Handouts in the classroom: Is note taking a lost skill?, *American Journal of Pharmaceutical Education, 70*(2), 38–42.
14. Kobayashi K. (2006). Combined effects of note-taking/-reviewing on learning and the enhancement through interventions: A meta-analytical review. *Educational Psychology, 26,* 459–477.
15. Tront, J. G., & Eligeti, V. (2006). WriteOn: A tool for classroom presentations on tablet PCs. ITiCSE '06, Bologna, Italy, June 26–28.
16. Microsoft Tablet PC Education Pack. http://www.microsoft.com/windowsxp/downloads/tabletpc/educationpack/default.mspx.
17. Duncan T. G., & McKeachie, W. J. (2005). The making of the motivated strategies for learning questionnaire. *Educational Psychologist, v40*(2), 117–128.

Part VIII
Works in Progress

Chapter 37
A Vision for Education: Transforming How Formal Systems are Taught Within Mass Lectures by Using Pen Technology to Create a Personalized Learning Environment

Dwayne Raymond, Jeffrey Liew, and Tracy A. Hammond

Abstract This work-in-progress outlines both a key opportunity to understand the loss of STEM students as well as our vision for a transformative learning tool in development called *Logic Sketch*. *Logic Sketch* will use pen technology to provide a personal learning experience for every student in a mass lecture. It will monitor each student's progress, and offer supplementary instruction and exercises that are specifically tailored to individual needs. By instilling a deeper understanding of how to work with formal systems, we expect to reduce math anxiety. This may aid in overcoming the problem of the underrepresented majority: the demographic that constitutes the majority of university students (females and non-white males) is underrepresented in STEM disciplines. The target demographic is over represented in mass lectures on logic. Thus, we are in a position to better understand a number of ill understood factors such as the extent to which math anxiety inhibits a student's willingness to pursue a STEM degree.

37.1 Problem Statement and Context

The importance of improving the efficacy of large-class-learning for formal systems (mathematics and logic) is highlighted in the 2012 Presidential report on STEM [7]. The ineffectiveness of large-class-learning is part of a much larger problem, the

D. Raymond (✉)
Department of Philosophy, College of Liberal Arts, Texas A&M University, College Station, TX, US
e-mail: raymond@tamu.edu

J. Liew
Department of Educational Psychology, College of Education and Human Development, Texas A&M University, College Station, TX, USA
e-mail: jeffrey.liew@tamu.edu

T. A. Hammond
Sketch Recognition Lab, Department of Computer Science and Engineering, Dwight Look College of Engineering, Texas A&M University, College Station, TX, USA
e-mail: hammond@tamu.edu

© Springer International Publishing Switzerland 2015
T. Hammond et al. (eds.), *The Impact of Pen and Touch Technology on Education*, Human-Computer Interaction Series, DOI 10.1007/978-3-319-15594-4_37

"STEM Exodus Problem," in which students who, upon admission to university, profess a desire to obtain a degree in a STEM subject leave STEM and obtain a degree in a non-STEM subject. According to the Presidential Report, the exodus is of national importance, as the number of STEM graduates is not meeting the demand for STEM graduates. Furthermore, the demographic of graduating STEM students is characterized by the absence of an important group, the underrepresented majority. The group is so-named because this group (females and non-white males), which constitutes the majority in a university, is underrepresented in STEM subjects. According to the report, the number of STEM graduates needs to increase; the greatest potential for growth lies with the underrepresented majority. Realizing this area of growth is problematic; it is widely believed that the underrepresented majority is typically underprepared for STEM subjects. Other factors, such as math anxiety [2, 5], stereotype effects [8], and the current large-class- format are all thought to contribute to the exodus of students from STEM subjects [6].

Indeed, the poor learning environment of a large class, with limited personalized support, does little to help underprepared, but math-capable students obtain a STEM degree. Jungic et al. 2005 [6], for example, point to the lack of resources available to transform "a class from a group of several hundred individuals simply sitting in the same room into a group that is engaged together in learning." Given that limited resources prevent universities from addressing the issue with personalized support for capable-but-underprepared-students, the need to develop transformative tools for large-class-learning looms large.

In this brief discussion, we will reveal a key opportunity to better understand the STEM Exodus Problem, along with a solution that provides a personalized learning environment within large classes.

37.1.1   The Key Opportunity

Teaching one type of formal system—formal logic—to a mass lecture of 300 + students presents both a unique set of challenges and a unique set of opportunities. Both the challenges and the opportunities arise because of the population, and the subject matter being learned. Let us begin with the former: the population. A key opportunity exists because of the university's academic requirements. A class in formal logic fulfills a math requirement. This fact shapes the demographics for formal logic classes. Whereas the student population for math and engineering courses are typically characterized by who is not in the class (namely, the underrepresented majority), the demographic in a formal logic course at Texas A&M University (TAMU), for example, is characterized by an over representation of the underrepresented majority.

Significantly, *a key barrier of under-preparedness does not beset a class in formal logic*. An introductory class in formal logic presupposes no background in content. The entire content is taught to the students. Barriers that result from study habits do, however, exist.

The situation offers a key opportunity to better understand the STEM Exodus Problem. Students taking formal logic comprise the very group that needs to be understood. We need to know, for example, why students who enter university with a professed desire to study a STEM subject, leave for the humanities and social sciences. By studying students in formal logic, we can better understand the level of math anxiety (anxiety can be measured with a standard MARS or AMAS assessment tool), and the level of under preparedness among logic's demographic. Thus, we can either substantiate or draw into question the current wisdom surrounding the reasons behind the exodus from STEM. We can determine, for example, the level of math anxiety, the level of under-preparedness and a link (or lack thereof) between the two: is (some) math anxiety a function of preparation? By improving the efficacy of large-class learning, we can study the extent to which levels of anxiety change in relation to improved comprehension. Our transformative tool is one attempt to provide students with the personalized support believed to be necessary to overcome math anxiety.

37.1.2 The Transformative Solution

We expect that the solution to the STEM Exodus Problem will be multifaceted, we propose to initially limit our attention to one factor: math anxiety.

Studies have suggested that math anxiety impacts learning by influencing attention, memory, motivation and diligence [1]. It is widely held that a student's anxiety can be exacerbated or mitigated by his/her level of understanding. We propose to attempt to minimize anxiety by increasing understanding.

To improve comprehension we will initially focus our efforts on minimizing cognitive impediments such as interference effects. Dehaene et al. [3, 4] argue that interference arises precisely because our ability to perform precise calculations depends on our ability to recruit the linguistic processing areas of the brain. We reason linguistically using a language that is associated with non-mathematical meaning. Thus, the linguistic process of reasoning is disconnected from the desired mathematical concepts. Previous associations (natural language associations) interfere with the new mathematical associations.

The same phenomenon occurs in logic. When students reason through proofs, they draw upon the language processing areas of the brain. The connection between the language with which students reason and the newly associated inference rules required for reasoning through a proof is hampered by both interference effects, and by a poor connection between the language of reasoning and the inference rules. The latter arises from the means by which students memorize inference rules. Students typically memorize the inference rules visually, or in some other way that fails to link the memorized rule with language used to perform the proof. The disconnection (between the language used to reason about the proof and the inference rules used to perform the proof) renders the inference rules functionally unavailable to the student. We hypothesize that the disconnection between memorization and application exacerbates math anxiety.

We propose to have the students memorize the rules in a way that makes them functionally available. This will lay the foundation for improved comprehension and reduced math anxiety. In brief, we begin by introducing the students to a limited set of technical terms that are new to the students (this avoids interference effects). We then teach the students to use these terms in describing formulas and in memorizing inference rules. We then teach the students to describe the givens, and the objectives for a proof. This is part of how we teach the students how to talk through the proof in such a way that a mnemonic link is established between the language used to reason about the problem, and the language used to memorize the inference rules. This simple process improves comprehension. The mnemonic link recalls the rules that may be successful in performing each step of the proof. Thus, the reason for using one rule as opposed to another becomes less mysterious. In this way, comprehension improves.

While the process can and has been successfully implemented in a large-class-learning environment without the aid of pen and touch technology by Raymond, we propose to use a multi-media approach to enhance understanding, and to ensure that students are engaging the material in the desired manner.

In what follows, we begin by outlining an approach that is being employed within 300-student classes to make the learned inference patterns functionally available to students. Next, we will present a scenario that will demonstrate both the functionality of our proposed system, along with the means by which an automated system can enable students to perform proofs.

The Logic Sketch Group at TAMU is developing this novel approach as a novel application of Mayer's (2002) model of multimedia learning. According to Mayer, the highest level of comprehension is obtained when students actively engage the process through multiple modes of learning. In brief, we propose a novel way to use pen and touch technology, within a multimedia environment to enhance each student's ability to learn and employ proof strategies.

37.2   Description of the Activities

37.2.1   Part I: Method for Making Rules Functionally Available

To help students to cultivate a functionally available set of inference rules, Raymond has developed a very simple mnemonic approach. As noted above, students internalize inference patterns in a way that integrates inferential patterns with the language used to perform a proof. The approach builds on Griffin (2002). It provides a platform to associate (i) intuitively understood relations, such as the meaning of the term 'and' as a term that links together two facts about the world, with (ii) a precise set of descriptors with, (iii) its symbolic representation.

Step one capitalizes on the university students' grasp of natural language. Onto their understanding of natural language, a set of descriptors is layered. For example, the term 'and' is called a conjunction. A conjunction is said to conjoin two conjuncts.

Whenever the students see the term 'and', they are asked to verbalize it as "a conjunction that conjoins two conjuncts." The purpose here is twofold: (i) the descriptors provide the set of vocabulary that is free of interference effects; (ii) the student's intuitive understanding of language provides the basis for their understanding the descriptor's meaning.

In step two, the descriptors are linked with symbols: the term 'conjunction', for example, is linked with the symbol '&'. In step three, the rules are made functionally available. The students are taught to perform proofs by verbalizing the givens and the objective using the language of descriptor. We call this the 'descriptor method' of learning proofs.

The steps in the approach lay the foundation for a seamless transition from the students' ability to merely recall a rule, to the students' ability to apply the rule.

The downfall of the approach lies in the fact that some students ignore the descriptor method, learning the patterns visually. Such students typically exhibit difficulties transitioning from the learned visual pattern to performing a proof. To increase the effectiveness of the approach, we need to supplement the approach with a personalized learning environment, one that obligates the use of the descriptor method, along with something that reinforces the learning. To this end, we propose to develop a robust sketch recognition system that enhances the student's comprehension. We call the system *Logic Sketch*. In what follows, we will outline a scenario that illustrates how we envision using pen a touch technology to enhance the students understanding of and ability to perform proofs.

37.2.2 Part II: Enhancing Comprehension Through Multi-Media Learning With Sketch Technology—Learning Proof Strategy

To overcome the problems of large-class-learning the Logic Sketch Group at TAMU proposes to develop an interactive sketch recognition system called *Logic Sketch*. It will ask leading questions designed to scaffold, and take the student through the descriptor method.

The following scenario will illustrate the automated tutoring capability of *Logic Sketch, which is an active learning tool for both the assessment and correction of students, as well as the teaching of new content.* In summary form, *Logic Sketch* is:

1. Innovative Assessment Tool
    a. identify a student's error,
    b. diagnose the error,
    c. supply additional material to aid in correction,
    d. monitor and record progress.
2. Active Learning Tool For New Content
    e. Interactively teaches strategy rather than rote memorization.

Series 1
Teaching a proof strategy

Fig. 37.1 Teaching a proof strategy: Series 1

37.3 Teaching Proof Strategies with an Interactive System: An Imagined Scenario

The following scenario depicts the *Logic Sketch* method of teaching a proof strategy to an imagined student, Victoria. (The following dialogue occurs with reference to Fig. 37.1a, 37.1b.)

We enter the scenario in the middle of a learning session. Victoria is learning how to use various strategies in rendering a proof. We begin with comments by the automated system.

Logic Sketch "We are going to be working with a technique that combines doing the proof from the top-down and the bottom-up. The **bottom-up approach** begins by identifying a specific goal, and it aids in the identification of alternative ways of obtaining that goal. The **top-down approach** increases the number of premises from which we may draw as we endeavor to solve the proof. The two strategies work best in combination. Let us begin with the bottom up. Please write the conclusion at the bottom of the page." Victoria follows the instructions. Logic Sketch recognizes when she has finished.

Logic Sketch "Well done. At this stage in the proof, our goal is 'C'." *Logic Sketch* highlights the 'C' in the workspace.

Logic Sketch "What type of sentence is 'C'? Is it atomic, or is it complex or are you uncertain of the distinction?
    Please circle your reply from the provided list"
    Victoria circles 'atomic', correctly identifying the type of sentence.

Logic Sketch "The sentence is atomic. Given the available rules, we must obtain the 'C' from the premises. Look at the premises. Locate all the occurrences of 'C' by circling them." (Fig. 37.1c)

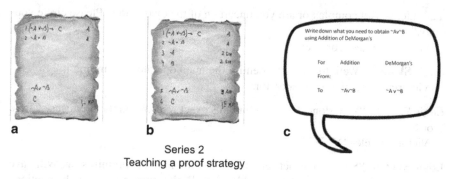

Series 2
Teaching a proof strategy

Fig. 37.2 Teachnig a proof strategy: Series 2

Victoria locates the 'C' and circles it in the first sentence.

Logic Sketch "Well done. Now look at the premise containing the 'C'. Identify the main operator in that sentence by circling it." Victoria locates the main operator, and circles the conditional sign as the main operator.

Logic Sketch "Well done. Write down the name of the sentence and the name of the sentence's component that contains our goal." Victoria writes out the words conditional and consequent, words that she learned with the descriptor method.

Logic Sketch "Well done. The desired sentence is located in the consequent of a conditional. Is there a rule of inference by which we can obtain the consequent of the conditional? If so, write the name of the rule in the justification column beside 'C'." Victoria writes 'MP' in the justification column for C.

The following dialogue occurs with reference to Fig. 37.2a.

Logic Sketch "By doing this you are telling your reader that you hope to obtain 'C' by means of MP. MP requires two conditions. The first is a conditional with 'C' as the consequent. Identify the second condition and write it on the line immediately above 'C'."

Victoria recalls that the MP requires both a conditional and the conditional's antecedent. She looks at the conditional on line 1, identifies its antecedent and writes it above the 'C'.

The following dialogue occurs with reference to Fig. 37.2b, 37.2c.

Logic Sketch "Well done. A fully justified entry requires that reference be made both (1) a rule, and (2) all the required entries that enabled its use. Since the conditional is located on line 1, I'm going to write the one beside the justification of C. Since MP requires two conditions, I will write___ to remind you that information is missing." *Logic Sketch* adds the entries, briefly highlighting each.

Logic Sketch "The sentence '($\sim$A v $\sim$B)' is our new goal. We can ignore the previous goal. I want you to now focus on obtaining '($\sim$A v $\sim$B)'. Let us repeat the same series of questions as before. First, what type of *sentence* is '($\sim$A v $\sim$B)'? Is it atomic, or is it complex or are you uncertain of the distinction? Please circle your reply."

Victoria circles 'complex'.

Logic Sketch "Well done. Now, identify the main operator by circling it."

Victoria circles the main operator.

Logic Sketch "Well done. Can you find this exact *sentence* in the premises? Circle Y or N"

Victoria circles 'N'.

Logic Sketch "Since the exact sentence is not found in the premises, we will have to try and built it. Consider the available rules. Which rules result in a disjunction? Write the names out here _____."

Victoria writes the names of two rules: "Addition, DeMorgan's."

Logic Sketch "Well done. You are probably wondering how to select between the two rules. Let us use trial and error. If one way does not work, we try the other. Our decision is aided by knowing the requirements for each rule and by looking to see if we can obtain any of those requirements from the premises. In the new work window, please write out the requirements to use Addition and DeMorgan's." A window pops up. It lists Victoria's options, the goal and it requires her to indicate the form of sentence from which the goal may be obtained.

Victoria sketches her solution.

Logic Sketch "Well done. If '($\sim$A v $\sim$B)' results from Addition, it must come from one of its disjuncts. If '($\sim$A v $\sim$B)' results from DeMorgan's, we will need a sentence of this form: $\sim$(A&B). Take a look at the premises. Can you obtain either the requirements for addition or the requirements for DeMorgan's? If you are having difficulty, you might try the top-down strategy. The top-down strategy increased the number of premise with which you may work. Take a look at the premises and try to make an inference or two."

Victoria looks at the premises and notices that line 2 can be simplified. She simplifies the conjunction, placing one conjunct on line 3 and one conjunct on line 4. She adds the required line numbers and justifies for each entry.

Logic Sketch "Well done! Recall that we are looking for either $\sim$A, $\sim$B or $\sim$(A&B). Given that you have, $\sim$A within the new list of justified entries, the goal follows via the rule Addition."

Victoria adds the missing line numbers and fills in the miss justifications.

Logic Sketch "Well done! The proof is complete."

37.4 Expected Results

We expect students taking formal logic to score higher on the MARS score, revealing a higher mathematics anxiety as compared to students taking discrete mathematics. It is further expected that the combination of the descriptor method and the personalized learning environment of *Logic Sketch* will enhance student understanding of logic and proof techniques. We expect that by the end of the course students will score significantly lower on the MARS scale. We also hope to identify strong math capable students for the possibility of a mentorship program to reintegrate the capable students back within STEM.

Acknowledgements We thank all the volunteers, and all publications support and staff, who wrote and provided helpful comments on previous versions of this document. Some of the references cited in this paper are included for illustrative purposes only. We thank Texas A&M University, the Dwight Look College of Engineering, the Aggie Challenge program, and the participating students for their efforts to aid in the development of this system.

References

1. Ashcraft, M. H. et al. (2007). Is math anxiety a mathematical learning disability? In D. B. Berch & M. M. Mazzocco (Eds.), *Why is math so hard for some children?: The nature and origins of mathematical learning difficulties and disabilities*. London: Brookes.
2. Betz, N. E. (1978). Prevalence, distribution, and correlations of math anxiety in college students. *Journal of Counseling Psychology, 25,* 441–448.
3. Dehaene, S. (1997). *The number sense: How the mind creates mathematics*. New York: OUP.
4. Dehaene, S. et al. (1999). Sources of mathematical thinking: Behavioral and brain imaging evidence. *Science, 284,* 970–974.
5. Dreger, R. M. et al. (1957). The identification of number anxiety in a college population. *Journal of Educational Psychology, 48,* 344–351.
6. Jungic, V. et al. (2006). Teaching large math classes: Three instructors, example one. *International Electronic Journal of Mathematics Education, 1,* 1–15 (www.lejme.com).
7. President's Council of Advisors on Science and Technology (2012). Report to the President: Engage to Excel: Producing One Million Additional College Graduates with Degrees in Science, Technology, Engineering, and Mathematics. http://www.whitehouse.gov/administration/eop/ostp/pcast/docsreports. Accessed 10 Dec 2012.
8. Spencer, S. J. et al. (1999). Stereotype threat and women's math performance. *Journal of Experimental Social Psychology, 35,* 4–28.

Chapter 38
Pen-Based Problem-Solving Environment for Computational Science

Victor Adamchik

Abstract The paper discusses an introductory computer science course that reflects the current shift in technology toward digital note taking and, in particular, pen-based and touch technology. The concept of digital ink has the potential to dramatically transform and enhance the teaching and learning process by becoming widely used in classrooms—replacing the use of desktops or laptops. One of the potential advantages of the new technology is that it allows the expression and exchange of ideas in an interactive environment using sketch-based interfaces. The cornerstone of the course is the concept of geometrical sketching dynamically combined with an underlying mathematical model with a greater focus on student's ability to produce rigorous and soundproof arguments.

38.1 Introduction

It is pointed out in the ACM report "Computing Curricula 2005", (see [1]), that in the area of Algorithms and Complexity Computer Science professionals ought to have the "performance capability" to "prove theoretical results". However, experience shows that many Computer Science students have great difficulties with the proofs methods encountered in, say, an advanced course on algorithms. Indeed, often the logical foundation of a proof argument seems to escape some of the students. We propose an introductory computer science course that will reflect the current shift in technology toward digital note taking and, in particular, pen-based and touch technology. The concept of digital ink has the potential to dramatically transform and enhance the teaching and learning process by becoming widely used in classrooms—replacing the use of desktops or laptops. One of the potential advantages of the new technology is that it allows the expression and exchange of ideas in an interactive environment using sketch-based interfaces. The cornerstone of the course is the concept of geometrical sketching dynamically combined with

V. Adamchik (✉)
Carnegie Mellon University, Pittsburgh, PA, USA
e-mail: adamchik@cs.cmu.edu

© Springer International Publishing Switzerland 2015
T. Hammond et al. (eds.), *The Impact of Pen and Touch Technology on Education*,
Human-Computer Interaction Series, DOI 10.1007/978-3-319-15594-4_38

an underlying mathematical model. A completely natural way of drawing using a digital pen will generate a system of polynomial equations of several variables. The latter will be fed to a theorem prover that will automatically establish inner properties of the model. Moreover, once a particular mathematical model is created and then checked for accuracy, it will serve as a basis for logical deduction of various geometrical statements that might follow. Lastly, a detailed step-by-step exposition of the proving process will be provided.

The goal of the proposed course is to promote an intuition for problem solving and a way of algorithmic thinking on examples from planar geometry. Choosing the pen-based gesture interface, we will expose students to contemporary software design and development. Integrating elements of formal proofs by definitions and axioms will propel students into a higher level of geometrical thinking. The idea of proofing will be developed and refined as the above cycle progresses (revolves) until students obtain a strong grasp on a logical construction. The new course is built upon existing courses that have been taught at CMU for the last several years—Introduction to Pen-Based Computing, Computational Geometry, Computational Discrete Mathematics, and Modern Computer Algebra. The course is based on utilizing several sophisticated software libraries and packages, such as gesture-understanding interfaces [3, 7, 10], computer algebra system *Mathematica* [12], and a formal theorem-prover Theorema [6].

38.2 Problem-Solving Environment

We are entering a new era of teaching, learning and computing. With an abundance of useful information available on any subject, anywhere, anytime, and on any device, the challenge (faced by all us, educators) is to create a teaching/learning environment that is mobile, smart, easy to use and personable. Next generation's learning tools will require that we receive only the information we need at the right time. Future applications will also require natural interfaces that allow students (as well as instructors) to interact with any computing device with ease. The time for having "problem solving environments" in a classroom has emerged. A problem solving environment (PSE) is an integrated computational system for solving problems in a specific application domain. A PSE, in general, should enable the user to input and work on problems in a manner that is natural to the problem domain. In particular, such environments will integrate symbolic and numeric computing with a natural pen-based interface.

One of the principal aims of the project would be to investigate the suitability of such environments in the classroom setting. As an application domain is limited to a planar geometry. A significant part of the research also includes the development of a prototype PSE for experimentation.

The proposed course is tentatively split into three parts as shown in Fig. 38.1. In the first part "Geometrical sketching" users (students, instructors) will formulate a geometrical problem using a stylus of Tablet PC. Using a library of domain-based gesture recognition tools, the hand drawing will then be recognized. Once the diagram

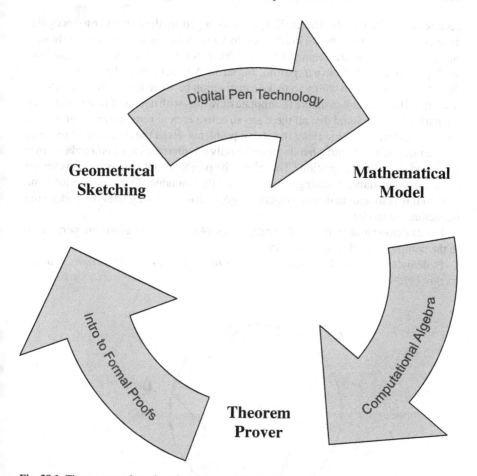

Fig. 38.1 The concept of pen-based problem-solving environment

is understood and interpreted, it will be associated with the underlying "Mathematical Model". It is known that any model in Euclidean geometry is represented by a system of polynomial equations in several variables. Therefore, using the Wu-Ritt method [13] or Gröbner bases theory [4], the system can be solved and therefore, in this way geometrical theorems can be verified by a computer. The automated "Theorem prover" is the last piece of the course. In the next section we elaborate in more details on significant parts of the course.

38.3   Pen-Based Computation

Creating new interfaces is not a simple task; it is a subject of years of intensive research. Our work will be built up upon research projects underway at MIT, Brown and CMU. The primary goal of these projects is to develop a library of domain-based gesture recognition tools. The challenge for us is getting the computer to recognize different types of geometrical drawings—to know which is a circle, a straight line, and a polygon. On more detailed level, the computer must distinguish a circle from an ellipse, a rectangle from a trapezoid, and so on. Another core technique with smart digital ink is to have an ability to make a distinction between handwritten words and drawings That is a human nature to annotate drawings with names of points and lines. We perfectly understand that all these are an active area of research and that there is no yet a perfect tool for solving the above problems. Even the direction of research is under question. Should a handwriting be only an interface or accommodated by a voice and or video recognition? Therefore, the project is not concern in developing these tools but rather utilizing what is currently available. Our contribution (and aim) to this is to automatically associate a geometrical drawing with the underlying mathematical model.

Let us demonstrate a proof-of-concept example; all computations are performed in the computer algebra system *Mathematica*.

Ptolemy's Theorem. *Let a quadrilateral ABCD be inscribed in a circle as in the picture below*

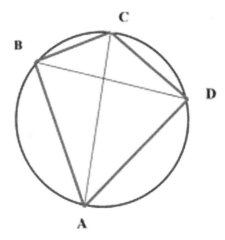

Prove that the sum of the products of the two pairs of opposite sides equals the product of its two diagonals. In other words, prove that $AD \cdot BC + AB \cdot CD = AC \cdot BD$.

The proof starts with the geometric sketching (informal drawing). We assume that using a stylus, students will be able to draw a circle, choose four points on its circumference and connect them by straight lines. This simple drawing is already a challenge for the pen-based libraries. To pattern-match geometric primitives, we must first identify types of vagueness that may occur during sketching. For example, we have to take into consideration the uncertainty of whether the ends of two lines meet at a vertex. The type of shapes are often vague as well—a line segment may be interpreted as a straight line or as an arc. Therefore, we plan to enrich sketch recognition libraries by additional packages intended to refine the original drawings. Now let us concentrate on the main idea. As soon as we recognize a particular geometric primitive, we add a correspondent equation (or a system of equations) to the underlying mathematical model. We start with a circle and its equation:

$$(x - x_c)^2 + (y - y_c)^2 = r^2,$$

where x_c and y_c are the coordinates of the center of the circle, and r is it radius. Next, we pick four arbitrary points on the circle

$$A = (x_1, y_1), B = (x_2, y_2), C = (x_3, y_3), D = (x_4, y_4).$$

Connecting them with the center of the circle, generates the following set of equations

$$(x_1 - x_c)^2 + (y_1 - y_c)^2 = r^2,$$
$$(x_2 - x_c)^2 + (y_2 - y_c)^2 = r^2,$$
$$(x_3 - x_c)^2 + (y_3 - y_c)^2 = r^2,$$
$$(x_4 - x_c)^2 + (y_4 - y_c)^2 = r^2.$$

Finally, we connect those four points by straight lines. This will produce six more equations for the Euclidean distances

$$AC : (x_1 - x_3)^2 + (y_1 - y_3)^2 = d_1^2,$$
$$BD : (x_2 - x_4)^2 + (y_2 - y_4)^2 = d_2^2,$$
$$AB : (x_1 - x_2)^2 + (y_1 - y_2)^2 = s_1^2,$$
$$BC : (x_2 - x_3)^2 + (y_2 - y_3)^2 = s_2^2,$$
$$CD : (x_3 - x_4)^2 + (y_3 - y_4)^2 = s_3^2,$$
$$DA : (x_4 - x_1)^2 + (y_4 - y_1)^2 = s_4^2,$$

where d_1, d_2 denote diagonals and s_1, s_2, s_3, s_4 denote sides of the quadrilateral. The above set of ten equations represents a mathematical system completely describing the original drawing. In the next step we generate a question—what is the product $AC \cdot BD$ or, equivalently, what is the product $d_1 \cdot d_2$? We denote this product by a new variable P and add the associated equation $P = d_1 \cdot d_2$ into the system. Note that due to Euclidean symmetry some of variables (coordinates) can be chosen in a special way. Therefore, without loss of the generality, we can assume that $x_c = 0$, $y_c = 0$ and $x_1 = 0$.

In the next paragraph we demonstrate the result of applying the Gröbner bases approach by providing a screenshot of *Mathematica*'s notebook (Fig. 38.2)

38.4 Mechanical Theorem Proving

Algebraization of geometry in systematic way was originally started by R. Descartes in the early seventeenth century. He proposed to prove theorems of geometry by mere computations in contrast to the proving by purely geometrical reasoning of Euclid.

Fig. 38.2 Screenshot of Mathmatica

It was this framework that inspired C. Gauss for his famous solution to construct a regular 17-gon by ruler and compass. One of the benefits of algebraization is that, having the algebraic structure of the coordinates at hand enables us to manipulate the points and lines of the geometry and study their properties by algebraic means, using the operations of the resulting algebras. Usually geometric constructions can be assembled from a small number of elementary primitives, e.g. drawing a curve through given points, construction of intersection points and curves. In the same way, the coordinate representation of geometric objects can be produced by cascading coordinates of the underlying primitive objects. This means that a geometric proof scheme yields a set of algebraic translations. Then, taking into account the interplay between geometry and algebra, one may develop useful geometric intuition.

In general, mechanical theorem proving deals with the question of developing algorithms which automatically produce proofs for given theorems. This approach for geometric theorem proving by algebraic methods can be described as follows

- Choose a coordinate system
- Translate the geometric objects into algebraic equations
- Carry out algebraic computations
- Convert the algebraic conclusions into geometric statements

The first convincing example of algebraization of geometry is provided by a book of S.C. Chou [8], who proved 512 theorems of geometry with the mechanization approach. The surprising conclusion drawn from Chou's book is that a great number of geometry theorems fall into the class of constructive problems, where the geometric configuration can be constructed step by step in such a way that new coordinates depend rationally on coordinates of constructed objects. Therefore, the geometric conclusion translates into elimination of some coordinate variables. This problem is well understood and admits an efficient solution that is implemented in all major computer algebra systems. There are two well-known approaches to solving a system of algebraic equations. One is based on polynomial ideal theory and generates special bases of polynomial ideals, called Gröbner bases. An algorithm for computing such bases was given by B. Buchberger [4, 5]. The second approach is based on Wu-Ritt's characteristic set construction, motivated by the analysis and decomposition of the zero sets of systems of polynomial equations. This approach has been recently popularized by Wu Wen-tsun [13], who has impressively demonstrated its application to automated geometry theorem proving.

38.5 Computer Algebra Systems

Mechanical Theorem Proving requires combining of both procedural algebraic knowledge and deductive logical reasoning. For example, exploring the theory of Gröbner bases needs set theory, inductive proving, and other proof techniques. The pure theorem prover systems have become surprisingly powerful over the last decade, however they are still too cumbersome to and too limited in their capabilities to have any impact as teaching tools. As a case in point, see the recent study by F. Wiedijk [11], where the major systems available today are challenged to prove that the square-root of 2 is irrational. One way around this problem is to use a hybrid system that combines a pure theorem prover with a computer algebra system: the theorem prover organizes and controls the logical part of the argument whereas the computer algebra system takes care of all algebraic manipulations. In essence, the prover is given access to a new rule "Simplify". Application of this rule shortens some proofs tremendously, and also brings the argument much closer to the form that a human prover would employ. Combining provers and computer algebra systems is rather difficult in general and the subject of considerable research efforts (see [7]). For our purposes, however, a simple pragmatic solution will suffice. To avoid interface issues we chose Theorema [6], a system that is implemented entirely within the computer algebra system *Mathematica*. Sophisticated algorithms such as Gröbner basis and cylindrical algebra decomposition are readily available in this environment, as well as theoretical tools for doing formal mathematics.

38.6   Assessment

Regarding the course evaluation, we will be using CMU's Eberly Center for Teaching Excellence [9] to do a formal evaluation of the project. In the past The Eberly Center has collected data from a pilot group of students who were using tablets and Adaptive Book [2] in an introductory computer science course. We plan to use the same techniques to measure the usability aspect of the tablets and its effectiveness in delivering mathematical content. We also plan that the Eberly Center will be developing specific techniques to follow up with the group of students over a semester period to compare the group's results to another group who has taken a more traditional computer science path.

References

1. ACM Report. (2005). Computing curricula 2005. http://www.acm.org/education.
2. Adamchik, V., & Gunawardena, A. (2005). Adaptive book: Teaching and learning environment for programming education. *Proceedings of the International Conference on Information Technology: Coding and Computing*, ITCC 2005, 04–06 April 2005, Las Vegas, Nevada, IEEE Computer Society, pp. 488–492.
3. Alvarado, C. J. (2000). A natural sketching environment: Bringing the computer into early stages of mechanical design, Master's thesis, Department of Electrical Engineering and Computer Science, MIT.
4. Buchberger, B. (1976). Theoretical basis for the reduction of polynomials to canonical forms. *SIGSAM Bull, 39,* 19–24.
5. Buchberger, B. (1985). Gröbner Bases—an algorithmic method in polynomial ideal theory. Chapter 6 in N.K. Bose 8 ed., *Multidimensional Systems Theory*, D. Reidel Publ pp. 184–232.
6. Buchberger, B. (2001). Theorema: A proving system based on Mathematica. *The Mathematica Journal, 8*(2), 247–252.
7. Caprotti, O., & Sorge, V. (2005). Automated reasoning and computer algebra systems. *Journal of Symbolic Computation, 39*(5), 501–615.
8. Chou, S. C. (1988). *Mechanical geometry theorem proving.* Dodrecht: D. Reidel Publishing Company.
9. CMU's Eberly center for teaching excellence. http://www.cmu.edu/teaching/eberlycenter/.
10. Li, C., Miller, T. S., Zeleznik, R. C., & LaViola J. J. (2008). AlgoSketch: Algorithm sketching and interactive computation in the Proceedings of the Eurographics Workshop on Sketch-Based Interfaces and Modeling, pp. 175–182.
11. Wiedijk, F. T. (2006). The seventeen provers of the world, Lecture Notes in Computer Science 3600, Springer-Verlag.
12. Wolfram Research, Inc. (2012). Mathematica, Version 9.0, Champaign, IL.
13. Wu, W-T. (2000). *Mathematics mechanization.* Beijing: Kluwer Acad. Publ.

Chapter 39
A Ubiquitous, Pen-Based And Touch Classroom Response System Supported By Learning Styles

Ricardo Caceffo, Heloisa Vieira da Rocha, and Rodolfo Azevedo

Abstract The Active Learning Model (ALM) is an educational model which proposes that students should participate, along with the teacher, as direct agents of their learning process. Computer systems created to implement and support the ALM are known as Classroom Response Systems (CRS). The CRS, usually supported by traditional pen-based Tablet PCs, allow the teacher to propose activities and exercises to students, receive back their answers, discuss the results and provide feedback.

However, researchers point several problems regarding the CRS use, as the inadequacy of the traditional pen-based Tablet PCs, which have disadvantages related to their size and weight, hard configuration and usability problems. Another problem is the pedagogical approach applied to build these systems, which don't consider individual student's needs.

Still, we have the ascension of new pen-based and touch mobile devices (e.g., iPad), light and thin enough to support new educational approaches, like the Ubiquitous Learning. This approach proposes the use of context information to measure and customize the applications according to each student's needs, thus supporting the creation of a Ubiquitous CRS (UCRS).

In this way, we propose a UCRS supported by the prediction of student's learning styles. Initially focused on higher education, it supports the automatic identification of the students' learning styles and the submission of activities that best fit each one of the students. We expect it will enhance the students learning experience, thus better supporting the ALM.

R. Caceffo (✉) · H. V. da Rocha · R. Azevedo
Institute of Computing, State University of Campinas (UNICAMP), Campinas, Brasil
e-mail: rec@ic.unicamp.br

H. V. da Rocha
e-mail: heloisa@ic.unicamp.br

R. Azevedo
e-mail: rodolfo@ic.unicamp.br

© Springer International Publishing Switzerland 2015
T. Hammond et al. (eds.), *The Impact of Pen and Touch Technology on Education,*
Human-Computer Interaction Series, DOI 10.1007/978-3-319-15594-4_39

39.1 Problem Statement and Context

39.1.1 The Active Learning Model

Currently, there is a trend to insert technological resources in the classroom, with the use of laptops, tablets, smartphones and similar devices. As mentioned by Cermak-Sassenrath [7], within this new learning context institutional power relationships and individual roles of teacher and learner can be inverted or may become fluid and provocative enough to challenge traditional pedagogical expectations.

In this way, the adoption of these technologies can be used to support and improve the teaching and learning process, like for example supporting the use of specific teaching methodologies, such as the Active Learning Model (ALM) [2, 8]. The ALM is an educational model which proposes that students should participate, along with the teacher, as direct agents of their learning process. Usually, this model is applied to create a collaborative environment where the teacher proposes activities and exercises to students. After students solve the exercises, the teacher can provide feedback to them. Also, the answers can be grouped, analyzed and commented by the teacher and students, allowing everyone to participate together in the knowledge construction process.

39.1.2 Classroom Response Systems (CRS)

In the literature, [1, 6, 14, 15] computer systems created to implement and support the ALM are known as Classroom Response Systems (CRS). The CRS, usually supported by traditional pen-based Tablet PCs, allow the teacher to propose activities and exercises to students, receive back their answers, discuss the results and provide feedback.

However, these systems have drawbacks, like disadvantages related to traditional Tablet PCs size and weight and student's loss of attention and focus [1, 5, 15]. Also, these systems do not consider students' personal characteristics and needs, which compromise the ALM environment.

39.1.3 Ubiquitous Classroom Response System (UCRS)

In earlier work [4, 5], we described the design of a Ubiquitous Classroom Response System (UCRS). The UCRS is a context-aware CRS that allows the creation of a dynamic environment where students can use any available mobile device (e.g. pen-based and touch) to answer activities proposed by the teacher, interact with colleagues and receive feedback.

In order to enhance the collaborative process, based on the Levis et al. [13] approach, we defined context variables, denominated Context Factors [5], which are updated using context information obtained during the UCRS use. These factors measure, for example, how productive was the collaboration among students (e.g. when two students solve together an exercise); how difficult is it for each student to solve determined activity and how educationally relevant was considered an activity proposed by the teacher. However, it is still necessary that UCRS considers individual and unique characteristics of each student, like, for example, their learning styles as described in the following section.

39.1.4 Learning Styles

As explained by Hsieh et al. [11], the learning styles describe the way information is processed by students or the way is better or easier to people to learn. The Felder and Silverman Learning Styles Model [9] describes the teaching and learning styles for engineering students. As Latham et al. [12] explain, this model classifies the learning styles into four distinct dimensions, indicating for each one of them both the nature and the learning preferences.

As proposed by Felder and Silverman [9] and Felder & Soloman [10], and organized by Latham et al. [12], the four learning styles dimensions are:

- **Active and Reflective Learning:** Active learners prefer to manipulate the information directly, interacting with peers through discussions, explanations or group activities. Alternatively, the reflective learners prefer the internal manipulation, thinking and reflecting by themselves about the content.
- **Sensing and Intuitive Learning:** Sensing learners prefer facts, data, and experimentation, for example solving problems through the application of standard and traditional methods. Alternatively, the intuitive learners prefer the related principles and the theoretical basis.
- **Visual and Verbal Learning:** Visual learners prefer the content that is presented and discussed as graphical charts, pictures, diagrams, demonstrations, and time lines. Alternatively, verbal learners prefer written and spoken language.
- **Sequential and Global Learning:** Sequential learners prefer the information described in logical and sequential steps, following a linear and reasoning thinking process. Alternatively, global learners usually make intuitive leaps, learning content without a specific order and then getting out of the blue the big picture about it all.

The learning styles approach is applied successfully in Intelligent Tutoring Systems (ITS). ITS are adaptive systems, which usually do not require a teacher's presence and use intelligent technologies to personalize learning according to individual student characteristics. Some ITS [3, 12] can identify and automatically adapt their behavior accordingly to the students learning styles, thus enhancing the student's learning experience.

Table 39.1 Activities learning styles mapping

Learning style	Activity mapping
Sensing	Activities associated with real-world and practical examples
Intuitive	Abstract and theoretical activities
Visual	Activities with pictures, diagrams, and demonstrations
Verbal	Activities with predominance of written language
Sequential	Activities addressing mainly the current topic, preferably in a logical manner
Global	Activities that address the current topic by relating it to previously topics already seen by the students

A similar approach, as described in the next section, can be used to improve the UCRS system, helping the teacher to propose the most effectively exercises to students, also allowing the students to collaborate with peers in a more effective way.

39.2 Method Employed

39.2.1 Learning Styles Mapping

The first step towards supporting learning styles is the mapping of the activities, categorizing them in each one of their learning style dimensions. In this way, after the teacher creates an activity, he defines and sets its learning style dimension.

For example, if the teacher is creating an activity with a practical example, he sets its "Sensing/Intuitive" learning style dimension to "Sensing". The same procedure happens to the Visual/Verbal and Sequential/Global dimensions. Table 39.1 shows the learning styles dimensions mapping, created from the Felder & Silverman model [9], that can be used by the teacher in the activity creation process.

The "Active/Reflexive" dimension was not mapped because its application is associated with the student's preference to work in groups or alone, and thus cannot be directly associated to the proposed activities. In addition, in order to reach all students, for the same subject the teacher must create distinct activities, each one focused on a specific learning style. This allows the UCRS to submit the activity that best suits each student learning style, thus enhancing the collaborative process and the learning environment.

39.2.2   Students Learning Styles Prediction and Application

The Index of Learning Styles[1] (ILS) is an on-line instrument composed by 44 questions used to assess preferences on the four dimensions of the Felder R. and Silverman (1988) Learning Style Model. However, as Latham A. et al. [12] and Yannibelli et al. [16] explain, this test takes time, and students can consider it long and tiring, which could compromise its accuracy. It also doesn't consider the possible changes in the learning style over time.

In this way, we propose a UCRS that predicts the students learning styles during the collaborative process. In a similar way as proposed and successfully applied by Latham et al. [12] in their ITS research, in order to measure the students learning styles the system can keep, for the extremes of each dimension, a value between 0 and 1. These values together indicate objectively the student×s inclination regarding each learning style. Formula 1, based on the Latham et al. [12] approach, indicates how these values can be obtained for each learning style dimension:

Formula 1[2] $$x = \frac{number\ of\ right\ answers}{total\ activities}$$

For example, in the sensing/intuitive dimension the extremes (sensing and intuitive) can be defined by the proportion of correct answers in the total of the proposed activities of each extreme. If a student answered ten questions defined as "Sensing", and three were correct, his "Sensing Style Value" would be $3/10 = 0.3$. In the same way, if a student answered five questions defined as "Intuitive", and four were correct, his "Intuitive Style Value" would be $4/5 = 0.8$.

Thus, the students' preference for a specific learning style dimension is directly proportional to the result obtained through the Formula 1. In the above example, as the "Intuitive Style Value" is greater than the "Sensing Style Value", an activity eventually defined as "Intuitive" by the teacher would best fit that student learning style than a "Sensing" activity. In the following section is described a use case scenario.

39.2.3   Use Case Scenario

Imagine that in some computer science introductory course, the teacher plans to address the topic "Linked List" (a data structure consisting of a group of nodes that together represent a sequence) in his next class. Figure 39.1 shows a linked list example:

Before the class starts, the teacher inserts into the UCRS two exercises related to the linked list subject:

---

[1] Available at: http://www.engr.ncsu.edu/learningstyles/ilsweb.htmlAccessed: 12/04/2014
[2] Based on the tutorial question style approach from Latham et at. [12], p. 106.

Fig. 39.1 Nodes of a linked list

- **Exercise A:** shows a set of graphics (similar to Fig. 39.1) proposing a linked list problem. To solve the exercise, the student can interact with the graphical elements, for example, moving them to new positions. This process can be done through pen-based or touch interaction, according to the device used by the student. Also, the teacher sets in the system the right answer (in this case, the right sequence) expected from students. The teacher then classifies this exercise as "Visual".
- **Exercise B:** shows a textual alternative question related to linked list, with three possible answers. To solve the exercise, the student must check (using touch or pen-based interaction) the option that he believes is the correct one. The teacher then classifies this exercise as "Verbal".

During class, after explaining the theoretical concept, the teacher activates the UCRS. It automatically submits to students the previously defined exercise, following these steps:

1. The system accesses the students' profile, submitting the "Exercise A" to students who have a visual learning style greater than the verbal learning style. Otherwise, "Exercise B" is submitted.
2. The system identifies the mobile device used by each student, submitting the exercise formatted according to each device features (e.g. support to touch or pen-based and screen size adjustments)

After solving the exercise, the students submit their answers to the teacher. The UCRS automatically corrects the answers, updating the student's learning style profiles through the application of Formula 1. Also, the teacher can review, analyze and organize the answers, providing feedback to students about their performance in the activity.

39.3   Results, Evaluation and Acknowledgements

The UCRS application and evaluation will be done in two steps: (a) validating if the UCRS correctly identifies the students' learning styles, through the comparison of the system results with a test made by the students in the ILS online tool and (b) identifying if the new collaborative process enhances the students learning experience, thus supporting the ALM approach in a better way. Also, we want to adapt the system to support multi-dimensional activities, what we expect will make it more efficient for both students and teacher.

The initial evaluation focuses on undergraduate and graduate courses of Computer Engineering, where students are familiar with the use of computational devices inside the classroom. Even so, in future work we intend to extend the system use to other areas, adjusting if necessary the adopted learning styles model to support other university courses.

The authors are grateful to FAPESP (grants #2009/10586-7 and 2014/07502-4, São Paulo Research Foundation-FAPESP), CAPES, CNPQ, UNICAMP, SAMSUNG, FAPESP-Microsoft Virtual Institute (NavScales project, grant #2011/52070-7) and CNPq (MuZoo project), that supported this research project. In addition, we would like to thank the professors Eduardo Valle, Tania Alencar de Caldas and Rickson C. Mesquita for their important contributions on this research.

References

1. Anderson, R., Anderson, R., Davis, K., Linnell, N., Prince, C., & Razmov, V. (2007). *Supporting active learning and example based instruction with classroom technology.* Proceeding ACM SIGCSE Bulletin, New York, NY, USA, 39(1):69–73 (ACM).
2. Bonwell, C., & Eison, J. (1991). Active learning: Creating excitement in the classroom. *ASHEERIC Higher Education Report Number 1*, Washington DC, USA.
3. Cabada, R., Estrada, M., & García, C. (2011). EDUCA: A web 2.0 authoring tool for developing adaptive and intelligent tutoring systems using a Kohonen network. *Expert Systems with Applications,* 38(8):9522–9529.
4. Caceffo, R. E., & Rocha, H. V. (2011). Ubiquitous classroom response system: An innovative approach to support the active learning model. *In Ubiquitous Learning: An International Journal, 3*(1):41–60 (Common Ground Publishing LLC. Champaign, Illinois, USA).
5. Caceffo, R. E., & Rocha, H. V. (2012). Design and model of a ubiquitous classroom response system through context factors. *Ubiquitous Learning: An International Journal,* 4(3):67–77 (Common Ground Publishing LLC. Champaign, Illinois, USA).
6. Caceffo, R. E., Rocha, H. V., & Azevedo, R. J. (2011). Ferramenta de apoio para o aprendizado ativo usando dispositivos com caneta eletrônica. *Revista Brasileira de Informação na Educação, 19*:25–41.
7. Cermak-Sassenrath, D. (2012). *Beyond arcade machines: students building interactive tangible installations.* In Proceeding The 8th Australasian Conference on Interactive Entertainment: Playing the System, New York, NY, USA. Article No. 16. ACM
8. Ertmer, P., Leftwich, A., Sadik, O., Sendurur, E., & Sendurur, P. (2012). Teacher beliefs and technology integration practices: A critical relationship. *Computers & Education, 59,* 423–435 (Elsevier).
9. Felder, M., & Silverman, K. (1988). Learning and teaching styles in engineering education. *Journal of Engineering Education,* 78(7):674–681.
10. Felder, M., & Soloman, B. (2012). Learning styles and strategies, http://www4.ncsu.edu/unity/lockers/users/f/felder/public/ILSdir/styles.htm Accessed August 20, 2012.
11. Hsieh, S., Jang, Y., Hwang, G., & Chen, N. (2011). Effects of teaching and learning styles on students' reflection levels for ubiquitous learning. *Computers & Education—An International Journal,* 57(1):1194–1201 (Elsevier).
12. Latham, A., Crockett, K., McLean, D., & Edmonds, B. (2012) A conversational intelligent tutoring system to automatically predict learning styles. *Computers & Education—An International Journal,* 59(1):95–109 (Elsevier).
13. Levis, D., et al. (2008). Aperfeiçoamento automático do perfil do aprendiz em ambientes de educação ubíqua. *Em Revista Brasileira de Informática na Educação, 16*(1):29–41. Janeiro a Abril.
14. Vahey, P., Tatar, D., & Roshelle, J. (2007). Using handheld technology to move between private and public interactions in the classroom. In M. Hooft & K. Swan (Eds.), *Ubiquitous computing in education: Invisible technology, visible impact.* (pp. 187–211) Lawrence Erlbaum Associates, Inc., Mahwah, New Jersey.

15. Wolfman, S. (2004). *Understanding and promoting interaction in the classroom through computer-mediated communication in the classroom presenter system.* Ph.D thesis. University of Washington, USA.
16. Yannibelli, V., Godoy, D., & Amandi, A. (2006). A genetic algorithm approach to recognize students' learning styles. *Interactive Learning Environments,* 14(1):55–78 (Routledge Press).

Chapter 40
Feedback from Physiological Sensors in the Classroom

Martha E. Crosby and Curtis S. Ikehara

Abstract The Bill and Melinda Gates Foundation recently announced the development of an "engagement pedometer" that can identify exciting or boring moments to be used in classrooms. Researchers at the University of Hawaii have also developed potential real-time cognitive load indicators that also could be used in the classroom. These real-time cognitive load indicators can be used to optimize the student-computer interaction. Initial research is targeted at extracting real-time cognitive load from a suite of physiological sensors. Physiological sensors we have used collect: eye fixation times, number of fixations, eye saccades, blink rates, pupil dilation, hand/finger pressures on a mouse, relative blood flow, pulse, temperature, general somatic activity and electrodermal activity change. With the advent of tablet technology, our current research is to adapt our pressure mouse technology to finger pressure on a touch screen and add it to our suite of sensors. The goal is to obtain a reliable suite of cognitive load indicators from passive physiological sensors installed in current technology. The development of real-time cognitive load indicators involves different types of cognitive activities, establishing the transform from sensor to cognitive load and controlling the cognitive impact of various multimedia features.

40.1 Introduction

Motivation, aptitude and prior knowledge are unique for each student. A good instructor, knowing the unique characteristics of the student, can judge from the student's body language and responses how to adjust the presentation of the material to be learned to maximize the learning experience. The instructor modifies and changes the material being presented contingent on how the student is approaching the learning goal. When the students are engaged in lessons that require using a computer, a suite of sensors could augment the standard feedback situation.

M. E. Crosby (✉) · C. S. Ikehara
Department of Information and Computer Sciences, University of Hawaii at Manoa,
Honolulu, HIi, USA
e-mail: cikehara%7D@hawaii.edu

© Springer International Publishing Switzerland 2015
T. Hammond et al. (eds.), *The Impact of Pen and Touch Technology on Education*,
Human-Computer Interaction Series, DOI 10.1007/978-3-319-15594-4_40

381

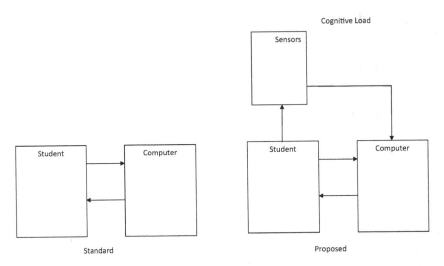

Fig. 40.1 Standard and proposed student–computer interface with real-time cognitive load data

Figure 40.1 illustrates the components of the standard and proposed student-computer interface. Instructional material for the standard system tends towards minimizing cognitive load to improve usability and improve the acquisition of knowledge [1]. Modifications to the instructional presentations are controlled by student-initiated actions (e.g., selecting an option) or computer initiated assessment questions. In effect, the student determines the method of getting through the material by acquiring the minimum knowledge to move to the next step. Knowledge acquisition is important, but two additional goals of improved comprehension and cognitive skill development may be missed with this type of presentation. The proposed use of real-time feedback to the computer of the student's cognitive load can aid in achieving knowledge acquisition, improved comprehension, and help develop cognitive skills.

Humans have a limited amount of cognitive ability. The left side of Fig. 40.2 shows an idealized graph of a student's cognitive load before, during and after the presentation of a new concept. The student's cognitive ability is the dashed line on the top. Cognitive load increases when a new concept is introduced, the load peaks, then, assuming the concept is acquired, the cognitive load drops off. The right side shows the introduction of the first three concepts at ideal locations, but the fourth concept is misplaced and exceeds the student's cognitive ability. Exceeding the student's cognitive ability, as in Fig. 40.2, can be detrimental to learning, but Grace-Martin [1] argues that presenting information that does not challenge the student can lead to shallower processing of the material which is also detrimental to learning.

Figure 40.3 shows the graph of an ideally regulated cognitive load. Initially, each student will need to be tested to determine cognitive ability (i.e., maximum cognitive load) and an optimal range. The optimal range is above zero cognitive load and below the cognitive ability of the subject. A student below the minimum optimal range

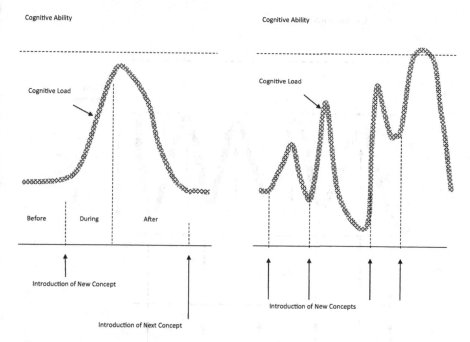

Fig. 40.2 Cognitive load graphs for both single and multiple concepts presentations

may be fatigued or bored, so it would be necessary to increase the cognitive load with short stimulating multimedia presentations so that the student is cognitively ready to receive a new concept. The multimedia presentation is adjusted to prevent the cognitive load from exceeding the optimal range. Using real-time cognitive load information in this way has the potential for enhancing knowledge acquisition, improving comprehension, and helping develop cognitive skills. Knowledge acquisition is enhanced by presenting information when the student is cognitively ready (e.g., not bored or fatigued) and not exceeding the optimal cognitive load. Also, the pattern of normal concept acquisition will verify the acquisition of the concept and the depth of comprehension may be inferred by how close the cognitive load is to the maximum optimal cognitive load. By regulating and monitoring the cognitive load pattern, it may be possible to detect when a student is using new cognitive skills. For example, counting on your hands should have a different cognitive load pattern than counting in your head.

40.2 Classroom Applications

Reuters [2] announced in 2012 that the Bill and Melinda Gates Foundation was supporting the development of an "engagement pedometer" that can identify exciting or boring moments to be used in the classroom. The Gates researchers hope that

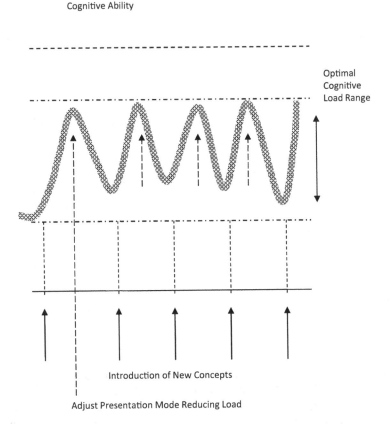

Cognitive Ability

Optimal
Cognitive
Load Range

Introduction of New Concepts

Adjust Presentation Mode Reducing Load

Fig. 40.3 A graph of cognitive load ideally regulated to remain within an optimal range

the devices known as Q sensors can become a classroom tool enabling teachers to gauge students' interest. Goldman-Segall [3] showed the feasibility of this at the MIT Multi Media Laboratory in the middle 1990s. At the University of Hawaii, we have successfully identified cognitive load using a suite of sensors that included the pressure on a computer mouse. This approach works well if students are using a mouse. However, instructional applications are increasingly including touch interfaces. Our current efforts are to adapt our mouse technology to touch interfaces.

While the Q sensor supported by the Bill and Melinda Gates Foundation can give teachers a sense of the classroom excitement, our suite of sensors has the potential to give the teachers information about the students' understanding of the concepts. The suite of sensors is incorporated into the hardware so while the students are busy using tablet applications the teachers will receive real-time feedback on the students' cognitive state. The left side of Fig. 40.4 depicts the setup for students working at their tablets. The teacher can use the cognitive load data to modify the instructional presentation in class for some lessons.

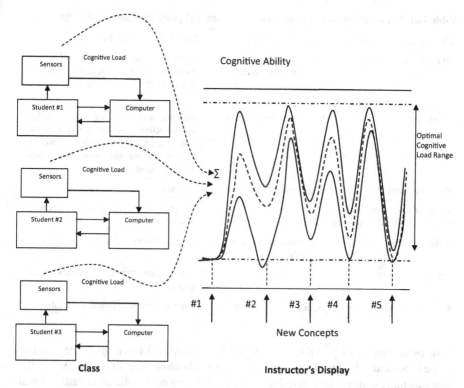

Fig. 40.4 Instructor's display of the aggregate class cognitive load

The following is an example of how the instructor could use the cognitive load information when presenting multiple concepts to a class. Before the first concept is introduced, the instructor gets the attention of the class, which should bring the class near the minimum desirable cognitive load level. The upper and lower solid lines of the graph indicate the range of cognitive load while the dashed line will indicate the optimal cognitive load range. As the students receive concept #1, some students, due to motivation, aptitude or prior knowledge, show a slight increase in cognitive load illustrated by the lower solid line while other students show an increased cognitive load. An example would be when introducing the concept of "fractions" to elementary students as "a part of a whole." Some students may be familiar or disinterested in the topic and show low cognitive load while other students may be confused by the new concept and show a high cognitive load. The cognitive load obtained from the sensors could be used to augment the instructor's information.

As concept #1 is explained, the difference between upper and lower cognitive load range indicates that the class is operating at very different cognitive levels. The instructor changes the multimedia presentation to maintain the optimum cognitive load range for the class so that students are not lost due to boredom or confusion. The experience of the instructor to identify the cognitive load discrepancy and to

Table 40.1 Physiological measures, secondary measures and potential cognitive indicators

Physiological measures	Secondary measures	Potential cognitive indicators
Eye position tracking	Gaze position, fixation number, fixation duration, repeat fixations, search patterns	Difficulty, attention, stress, relaxation problem solving, successful learner, higher level of reading skill
Pupil size	Blink rate, blink duration	Fatigue, difficulty, interest, novelty, mental activity—effort, familiar recall, imagery, abstract vs. concrete words, language, processing, information processing speed
Skin conductivity	Tonic and phasic changes	Arousal
Peripheral temperature (finger, wrist and ambient)		Negative affect (decrease) relaxation (increase)
Relative blood flow	Heart rate and beat to beat heart flow change	Stress, emotion intensity
Pressure sensors		Stress from pressure certainty of response
Pressure position	Speed of mouse motion	Arousal, stress, problem difficulty

draw on a number of possible next steps becomes critical to unifying the mindset of the class and bringing the entire class cognitively closer together as shown in the figure as more concepts are introduced. It should be noted that different instructional situations will have different desirable cognitive load graphs. For example, it may be desirable to present several concepts to generate an above optimal cognitive load before a student group discussion.

40.3 Method

There are several different physiological measures that can indicate different types of cognitive load. The first column of Table 40.1 lists all the different physiological activities currently being measured. The second column shows secondary measures which can be extracted from the physiological measures. Both measures are used to derive potential cognitive and affective states. The third column list several potential cognitive indicators.

A major goal of our research group is to develop a transform from physiological sensors to the different types of cognitive load. To achieve this goal it is necessary to understand how cognitive load is impacted by task factors and individual differences. Experimental tasks that have been used and that have been newly developed require the subject to demonstrate several cognitive abilities including perception, memory, computation, spatial ability, and planning [4–6]. Data from pilot studies have been analyzed using neural networks, autocorrelation, discriminate analysis, and support vector machines. Some of the initial results have shown task difficulty (i.e., cognitive load) correlated with the non-eye-based sensors data (i.e., skin conductivity, peripheral temperature, relative blood flow, pressure sensors and pressure position). A significant amount of pilot testing has been conducted to ascertain the most promising methodological approaches to be used to test the reliability of the transform in a larger study. Once the reliability of the transform has been established, the design, construction and testing of a low cost sensor system will be forthcoming.

40.4   Conclusion

Instruction augmented with real-time cognitive load data can help instructors adapt to the moment-to-moment cognitive changes of their students. This research will help teachers determine students' perceived difficulties with the instructional presentation.

References

1. Grace-Martin, M. (2001). How to design educational multimedia: A "loaded" question. *Journal of Educational Multimedia and Hypermedia, 10*(40), 397–409.
2. Simon, S., Biosensors to Mointor US Students' Attentiveness. reuters.com (June 13, 2012), available at http://www.reuters.com/article/2012/06/13/us-usa-education-gates-idUSBRE85C1-7Z20120613. Accessed 21 Jan 2014.
3. Goldman-Segall, R. (1998). *Points of viewing children's thinking: A digital ethnographers journey.* Mahwah: Lawrence Erlbaum Associates.
4. Crosby, M., Idling, M., & Chin, D. (2001). Visual search and background complexity: Does the forest hide the trees? In M. Bauer, P. J. Gmytrasiewicz, & J. Vassileva (Eds.), *User modeling.* Berlin: Springer-Verlag.
5. Ikehara, C., & Crosby, M. (2003). User identification based on the analysis of the forces applied by a user to a computer mouse. Proceedings of the Hawaii international conference on system sciences, Kona, Hawaii, January.
6. Vick, R., & Ikehara, C. (2003). Methodological issues of real time data Acquisition from multiple sources of physiological data. Proceedings of the Hawaii international conference on system sciences, Kona, Hawaii, January.